THE COMPLETE PUPPY & DOG BOOK

THE COMPLETE PUPPY & DOG BOOK

NORMAN H. JOHNSON, D.V.M.

IN COLLABORATION WITH SAUL GALIN

REVISED, RESET AND UPDATED EDITION

Galahad Books

New York

Published in 1993 by

Galahad Books
A division of Budget Book Service, Inc.
386 Park Avenue South
New York, NY 10016

Galahad Books is a registered trademark of Budget Book Service, Inc.

Published by arrangement with Atheneum Publishers, a division of
Macmillan Publishing Company, Inc.

Library of Congress Catalog Card Number: 77-5685
ISBN: 0-88365-824-0

Printed in the United States of America.

To the Dog Owners of America

Foreword to the First Edition

S OME YEARS ago, a close friend of mine going to Europe with his dog asked me for all the information he would need to take his dog into the countries of his destination. He also wanted to know how he should go about arranging transportation and accommodations, and asked further whether an airplane or ship would be better. I wasn't sure about most of the import regulations, and the laws of countries like Belgium, Spain, and West Germany I didn't know at all. I could give him only the most general information about transportation. Surprisingly, there wasn't even a book to help me. I told my friend that I couldn't be of much assistance to him. "Why not?" he asked me. "You're my veterinarian. You should know these things."

Because his dog was so much a part of his life, my friend wouldn't consider traveling without him, and he had expected me to know a good deal more than a veterinarian is usually responsible for. He wanted knowledge about his dog's whole world, not just his physical well-being. Suddenly there returned the countless questions put to me by dog owners, questions that had very little and often nothing to do with illness or health. Sitting there with my friend, I saw the need to know more than the medical aspect of my work: that services, laws, safety hazards, and innumerable other details were just as important to the average owner.

That was several years ago. I began my research then, and the result is, I hope, a unique book about everything in a dog's life that an owner would want to know. As a special feature, there are histories of the 121 * breeds recognized by the American Kennel Club. But—perhaps of even greater interest—you'll also find the character, temperament, and price range of each of these breeds. Your dog—whether purebred or mongrel— is taken from birth through maturity and old age. I tell you what to expect at every stage of his development, both physical and psychological. You will learn how to train and breed him. I give you specific information about whelping, so that you can help deliver the puppies if your assistance is needed. If your dog gets hurt, you will find virtually every aspect of first aid—from accidents through poisoning and bites. If you worry about feeding him—and many owners understandably do—several diets are listed, all of them nutritious and appetizing. If you need certain services,

* As we go to press, the Bearded Collie brings the number to 122.

vii

an entire chapter provides information on those you have heard about and many you possibly didn't know existed. If you wish to take your dog to Europe, I tell you what to do at every stage of planning, whether you go by airplane or ship. If you are traveling in the United States, there is information on railroads, hotels, and state laws. If your dog falls ill, my chapter on ailments is detailed, complete, and easy to follow. If your dog has behavioral problems—whether slight or deep-rooted—you will find specific directions on how to handle him. If you are anxious about your dog's safety—and I know many of you are—you will find special advice on how to protect him against hazards in his daily life.

In every instance, the information is detailed and in depth. That is, I feel, the least I can provide for every devoted dog owner. Over forty million families and single persons have made dogs a part of their lives, and the number of owners is growing rapidly. These people cherish their dogs and want what is best for them. If you are one of these, this book will give you the kind of information that you need and want.

N.H.J.

Acknowledgments

I want to acknowledge the kind help of the following organizations and individuals who made possible the writing of this book: the American Kennel Club, the dog breeders of America, the Gaines Dog Research Center, the SPCA and other humane societies, the foreign and domestic shipping lines and airlines, the railroads, Railway Express, and the many consulates and tourist offices located in New York City. Above all, I want to acknowledge the help of Mrs. Mary Bloom and Mrs. Enid Rubin, whose knowledge of dogs is exceeded only by their love for them.

Contents

Illustrations

HOUNDS

NONSPORTING DOGS

SPORTING DOGS

TERRIERS

TOYS

WORKING DOGS

THE COMPLETE
PUPPY & DOG BOOK

1

You and Your Dog

Ｆ YOU are thinking of getting a dog, your instincts are right. This genera-
tion is not the first to discover that a dog is a unique animal, and it
will not be the last. The best available historical research now suggests
that our ancestors, either in the Middle East or in southwest Asia, domesticated the dog about fourteen thousand years ago from a race of small
wolves. This makes the dog the earliest of all the animals domesticated
by man. Our ancient ancestors knew him even then for his working
ability and his great loyalty, the protector of human beings, their homes,
flocks, and herds. In all those numberless years, through countless generations, through crossbreeding, inbreeding, linebreeding, through completely indiscriminate breeding, the dog has remained man's favorite pet
and truest friend.

But a dog is more than a highly valued friend, protector, and hunter.
He inhabits a place deep within us; he is a solid fixture in our imagination,
our dreams, and our unconscious. He fulfills some of our strongest psychic
and spiritual needs, and as such links us with the world inside and outside
of man. It is no wonder the dog appears in the mythology of every race.

One of the most famous dogs of the ancient world was the Egyptian
dog-headed god, Anubis, a god of the dead and a conductor of souls
from this world to the next. Anubis also accompanied and guided the
goddess Isis in her search for the body of Osiris. Plutarch tells us that
in ancient times "the Egyptians paid the greatest reverence and honor
to the dog."

The Greeks made room for the dog in their mythology. Artemis,
the daughter of Zeus, proudly bore the title "Leader of Dogs." Asclepius,
son of Apollo and Greek god of medicine, abandoned as an infant by
his mother, was saved and suckled by a bitch. Even Chiron, the wise
old centaur and teacher of the children of the gods and heroes, had a
dog.

The famous story of Romulus and Remus, the founders of Rome, who were saved and suckled by a she-wolf, needs no retelling except to point out that mythological heroes are often saved by helpful animals.

In Hindu mythology, a dog named Sarama is the messenger of the great god Indira; and in Tibet, the god Da, who sits on the shoulders of the devout and helps them to deal with the hardships of life, is always accompanied by a black dog.

The dog has a strong place in Chinese mythology. Here is an astonishing dog-ancestor tale: Once upon a time a great bandit lord called Wu ravaged the land of the emperor, Kao-Hsin (2435–2366 B.C.). The emperor sent out thousands of soldiers to capture him but with no success. In desperation, Kao-Hsin proclaimed one day that he would reward whoever brought him Wu's head with one hundred acres of land, one thousand pieces of gold, and the hand of his youngest daughter in marriage. Pan-Hu, the emperor's favorite dog, listened carefully and then vanished. The next morning he came back with Wu's head. He had killed the bandit lord by gnawing off his head. Pan-Hu and the princess were then married in a great ceremony, and they had twelve children, six sons and six daughters. These children are the ancestors of some of the people of southern China.

Dogs also figure prominently in American Indian mythology. For example, the Chuchacas, Chippewas, and Dogrib Indians believe they originate from the dog. The Dogribs worship the dog as a hero. They believe that long, long ago, a woman driven out by her people married a dog and gave birth to six dogs. One day she surprised them playing in a field without their skins. They were running and laughing as children. She was so overwhelmed and happy that she hid their skins, and the children were forced to grow up as humans. They became the ancestors of the Dogrib Indians.

There are so many other strange and fascinating tales about dogs (the Dalmatian is an old and well-known symbol of the Dominican order, for example, and for Dante the image of the Greyhound had religious and mythic dimensions) that I can't tell them all. But I've thought about these myths a great deal, and, from my own observations and my talks with psychiatrists, psychologists, anthropologists, and specialists in folk lore, I've concluded that the dog has a great symbolic value for men. He is a psychic protector, "a talisman against loneliness and even the fear of death," and, as one psychiatrist has written, "he may serve as a factor in the maintenance of psychological equilibrium."

A dog puts us in touch with reality and, for the most part, keeps us there. He is warm, affectionate, and stable, rather than overwhelmingly complex or fickle. In close to forty years of practice, I've seen dogs help people get over anxiety, depression, grief, terrible loneliness, and other painful feelings.

Because a dog can be an important factor in our psychological health, more and more mental health experts are beginning to recognize his value in therapy. At the Children's Psychiatric Hospital in Ann Arbor, Michigan, Skeezer, a 70-pound dog that is part German Shepherd, part Labrador is a "psychiatric helper," a "resident canine child therapist" that acts as a companion to fifty children, aged six to fourteen, who are undergoing inpatient treatment. A dog can establish a strong and effective substitute parent-child bond when neglect or even tragedy in the home is the cause of the emotional disturbance.

At the Ohio State University Medical School, Dr. Samuel A. Corson used dogs to treat schizophrenic patients. Twenty dogs, chosen for their friendliness and warmth, were utilized to treat patients who did not respond to conventional therapy (drugs and psychotherapy). Dr. Corson found—and this does not surprise me—that all his patients showed improvement, some of it enormous. From Dr. Corson's point of view, "a dog offers the unconditional love we all need," but which the lonely, the disturbed, and the alienated need even more. A dog can be literally a lifesaver to people who, more than anything else, want someone to care about them.

We all like to think of ourselves as psychologically stable, capable of coping with our problems and sound in our relationships with our family, our friends, and our coworkers. And in most cases we are. The vast majority of people do not suffer from schizophrenia or any other serious mental illness. What good, then, will a dog do us? Dr. Corson, a recognized authority in his field, and Konrad Lorenz, a Nobel Prize laureate in behavioral science, both stress the vital role a dog can play in the lives of "normal" people; and this is what I want to talk about.

A dog offers the unconditional love we all need: that is the way Dr. Corson puts it. Konrad Lorenz talks about "inward security" and a sense of identity. Disturbed people may need this more than others; but in a world where far too many people have difficulty finding companionship, we all need these feelings if we are to make the most of our lives.

For the career man or woman living alone, a dog provides warmth, companionship, play, a sense of being needed. The dog also provides protection in the apartment and on the street—certainly an important consideration for those of us who live in large cities. And of course there is the sheer pleasure of going outdoors, playing with him and being played with, enjoying his vitality and naturalness, and having fun because he is having fun.

For the older couple or for older people living alone, a dog is everything that he is for younger people and often much more. For the older couple, he provides freshness and youth and shows that he needs and loves them. For older people living alone, he means a link with life itself. He is an expert in dispelling fear and loneliness. A good protector and an understanding and loving companion, he can relax them, make them laugh, give them a purpose, and so take them out of themselves. All too often older people suffer from a deep sense of loss, from sadness, loneliness, and depression because young people have taken their place at work and in the home. A dog can provide a new interest and help overcome feelings of inadequacy.

The dog supplies companionship, fun, and relaxation for everyone, but most of all for the children. A puppy will grow up with the children and consider himself one of the family. They will come to feel responsible for his welfare. Not only will this build up their confidence, but it will also show them the importance of affection and warmth. The children will see in the dog an example of undying integrity: he will never betray them. And they will have loads of fun with him. A dog is a playmate, someone to run with, wrestle with, tease and be teased by, even talk to. In time, the children can help with the feeding, grooming, and walking. At a certain age they will demand to do so. There is no need for me to tell you how children feel about dogs. Their relationship is something very special. No child should miss it.

Further, as Dr. Harold F. Searles points out in his important book, *The Nonhuman Environment in Normal Development and Schizophrenia,* a dog enables a child to recognize and accept his feelings and understand them. If he is mean to his dog, he will have to acknowledge it. If he is kind and loving, he will know that, too, and acknowledge these positive feelings. By being with a dog a child thus gets closer to reality. In other words, Dr. Searles says, "he can see himself the way he really is to a much greater extent than he can with his parents." We should remember, Dr. Searles reminds us, that the "nonhuman environment (everything in our world with the exception of people) constitutes one of the most important ingredients of human psychological existence, and a dog is part of that environment."

Is it any wonder, then, that over forty million American families and single persons own a dog or dogs? If you own a dog now, you have strong feelings about him and you know what he means to you and what you mean to him. If you don't, the joy of having a dog should be your own discovery. *But before you get one, read the next section and all of Chapter 2, especially Chapter 2.* There, among other things, you will find the temperament and disposition of each of the 121 breeds recognized by the American Kennel Club. I've written these parts to take the care and worry out of choosing a dog and to help you find the greatest pleasure and satisfaction from your choice. No matter what kind of dog you plan to own—mongrel or purebred—these sections will help you understand the new addition to your family.

Simply to want a dog, as I have said, is a good instinct. But before you go ahead and get one, ask yourself some important questions. *Begin with yourself.* What kind of temperament do you have? Do you have children? What is your income? *Now for your place of residence.* In what part of the country do you live? What are the climate and terrain like? Do you live in the city, the suburbs, or the country? On the ground floor or on the top in a walkup? *As for the dog himself,* do you want a bitch or a dog (male)? Do you understand the advantages of each? The drawbacks, few as they are? Do you want more than one dog? A puppy or a fully grown dog? Do you want a purebred, crossbred, or a mongrel?

Some of these considerations may seem unnecessary for choosing a dog. Perhaps no one factor will make or break your relationship with your dog. But there may be a "wrong" dog for you, and you can surely avoid certain discomforts and tensions, and possibly heartaches, especially if there are children in the family, by choosing the "right" one.

Let us say that you are attracted to an English Bull, in itself a fine, rewarding breed, ·but, for reasons of space, the dog must sleep in your room or on the other side of a flimsy partition. If you are a light sleeper or a downright insomniac, don't get yourself an English Bull because he may snore like a buzz saw. And unless you can put a couple of feet of concrete or plaster between his bed and yours, you might very well end up a nervous wreck or giving him away.

Or you might be completely enchanted by a Chihuahua and bring him home to two small children, two and four years old. The children will come to love him, and in their enthusiasm they may be much too rough and boisterous—remember he probably weighs under five pounds and is rather brittle. Chihuahuas are somewhat temperamental and high-strung and may well bite, not out of malice but simply to protect themselves. You will then have to give the dog away, causing heartbreak and sorrow all around. Had you known these things about a Chihuahua, you probably would not have brought him into a house with small children. You can see, then, that asking yourself the proper questions is absolutely necessary if you want to make sure of getting the right dog for your own home environment.

Your Temperament

First, then, who are you? If you are nervous and easily excitable, perhaps a terrier or a toy is not for you, certainly not a Chihuahua. Like dogs of other breeds, terriers and toys differ enormously among themselves, but most of them tend to be more nervous than hounds and bark a lot, although they generally adapt easily to apartment life. There are of course terriers which do not fit this loose generalization. Still, I would think that a hound is better suited for you. Hounds, as well as the sporting and working breeds, are generally of an even and mild disposition. Try an English Springer Spaniel or, if you have the space, a Golden Retriever.

Affection is not here at issue, for terriers and toys are as affectionate as hounds, work dogs, the nonworking and the sporting breeds. The question is whether you want a placid animal or one who will make demands on your nerves.

Children

There are so many breeds that get along famously with children that restrictions in this category are indeed few. Breeds like most Spaniels (especially the Springer), most of the hounds (particularly the Basset and Beagle) and working dogs (Boxer, Bullmastiff, Great Pyrenees, Newfoundland, Collie, Old English Sheepdog, Rottweiler, Samoyed, Schnauzer) as well as sporting dogs (Retrievers, Setters) will take pummeling, pinching, pulling, and pushing without showing any displeasure. Many of them, in fact, will return for more, reveling in the attention even if it does lead to a twinge of pain now and then. Dogs of middle and large size are generally tougher than we realize. Their hair and skin protect them better than our skin protects us, and their bodies are usually covered by a solid layer of muscle.

Only their noses and eyes are vulnerable. Even their ears cannot really be injured unless a child sticks something sharp inside or tries to yank them off. No matter what his size, a dog does not like to have his ears yanked, but the large dog seems to sense that no injury can result from such rough handling. Very often a dog will obtain some of his much-needed exercise from roughhousing with the children, and at the same time the children will enjoy an unforgettable relationship.

Your Dog and Your Income

A large dog obviously eats a great deal. A Great Dane, Mastiff, or Irish Wolfhound, to name three of the largest, may eat up to 4 or 5 pounds of food every day (perhaps even more as a large puppy), costing possibly $15 to $20 a week—depending on how you decide to feed him. A small dog will eat less than a pound a day (the toys considerably less) and cost no more than $3 a week—again depending on the kind of food you choose for him. Canned foods or dry meal bought in large sacks cost much less than fresh meat, with dry meal being by far the cheapest. All are nutritious, but many owners prefer to feed their dogs meat. If you are one of these, your food costs will be a consideration in your choice of a dog.

Food, however, is only one part of the potential expense. After the initial outlay of the purchase price, with the cost of food figured in, the next expense will be for the veterinarian. Your dog will need inoculations and boosters. If he is a puppy, he may have to be wormed—even later, worming may be necessary—often more than once and for a prolonged period of time. And you should be prepared for the small ailments that soon disappear with good professional care.

Dogs are generally hardy animals, although some breeds are more subject to illness and disease than others, and here you may encounter expense. Short-nosed breeds may have trouble in very warm and humid climates and need treatment for upper respiratory troubles. Some Boxers seem more prone to tumors than other breeds. Longhaired dogs unless groomed often may more readily have skin disorders—since their skin is covered by long hair, skin lesions are not easily discovered. On the other hand, some shorthaired dogs are more subject to inherited follicular mange. Floppy-eared dogs are more disposed to ear trouble than straight-eared dogs. Larger breeds like the German Shepherd are somewhat prone to hip dysplasia (abnormal development), as are all dogs in general over 25 pounds, while those under are not. Toys often cannot stand sharp changes in weather and may get sick. Large dogs as a group tend to be shorter-lived than small dogs. The Great Dane, for example, has a life expectancy of only 8 or 9 years, while the smaller terriers might live for 14 or 15 years, or longer. Always remember, however, that members of a breed differ from each other as much as the breeds themselves differ.

If you are away a good deal, then figure in kenneling costs, unless you take your dog with you or can leave him with a neighbor.

If you have a longhaired dog, there may be additional expenses for grooming. Certain breeds, like the Poodle, Bedlington Terrier, Schnauzer (all sizes), Wire Fox Terrier, Scottie, and the Dandie Dinmont, are in a class by themselves: They should be clipped according to patterns or designs determined by current style or tradition.

Climate and Terrain

Climate is another important consideration in your choice of a dog, for certain dogs will thrive in a hot, dry place while others may suffer and not be at their best. Short-nosed breeds (Boston Terrier, Bulldog, English Toy Spaniel, French Bulldog, Brussels Griffon, Pug, Boxer, Pekingese) are generally subject to upper respiratory conditions, and a damp climate is not good for them—although most do adapt.

Dogs bred for work or sport in cold climates may be uncomfortable in great humidity and heat. And toys (Maltese, Pug, Japanese Spaniel, Pekingese, Chihuahua) may not take well to sharp changes in temperature and climate. As a result of having been bred down, the toys are not particularly rugged and are more subject to ailments than are other breeds. In this respect they are like infants.

These considerations aside, most dogs will adapt to any terrain, although certain breeds are obviously better suited to hilly country than others—see the sections in Chapter 2 on the Afghan, Borzoi, and other long-legged breeds. For the brush or wooded areas, a short-legged dog, like the Basset Hound, is best.

Where You Live

Perhaps more important than the climate is whether you live in a city apartment, a suburban house, or a house in the country. The city dog is a special problem, for dogs by instinct are not suited for city life. Every dog, no matter how attached he is to his master, has to make an adjustment to apartment life.

Most apartment owners compromise, as they must. They walk a dog less than he needs, but enough to keep him well and the apartment clean. *The best thing to do is not to select a breed that requires a great deal of exercise, unless you are able to walk him often and extensively.*

Terriers and toys adapt easily to apartment life in that they require little exercise. Working dogs, some sporting dogs, and hounds, on the other hand, even the small, adaptable Beagle, are accustomed to hard exercise and tend to grow fat on a fifteen-minute daily walk. They have big appetites and must work off what they eat. Many apartment dwellers, of course, do satisfactorily keep large dogs. Usually there is no disaster, but the dog is often not at his best physically and psychologically and may become more disposed to minor ailments.

For the suburbanite, the size of the dog is not so much the difficulty as is the problem of controlling his movements. The large dog may jump fences and destroy property, leaving the owner liable to lawsuits. The small dog may run loose and join packs of marauders. Or since he is small and hard to see, he might be struck by a car. *But these are matters of training rather than of size or temperament.*

Similarly, for the country dweller, whether or not he lives on a farm, the breed of dog will be determined by the owner's particular needs as well as by his desire for an affectionate and loving companion. If his property is overrun by rats or other vermin, he will need a terrier, which for centuries has been bred as a ratter. If he wants general protection for his property, then a Bullmastiff is a superb choice. This breed combines the strength of the Mastiff and the aggressiveness and alertness of the Bulldog. A Great Pyrenees makes an excellent sheepdog, the Welsh Springer a fine gun dog. Above all, keep one thing in mind: Don't buy a particular breed simply because you admire your friend's or neighbor's dog. Clearly, each person has his own needs, and a neighbor's pet may suit a completely different temperament and often a completely different environment. A dog that is attractive in one home may be alien and strange in another. There is at least one breed for everyone; there are surely several for you. In every instance, make a choice based on what you know about yourself and your needs.

Dog (Male) or Bitch (Female)

Once you have made your decision about the puppy's breed, the next choice is relatively easy. Should you own a dog or a bitch? Each sex has its virtues, with the bitch *generally* easier to handle and easier to train. The bitch is usually friendlier and more obedient. She is more even-tempered, perhaps because she is untroubled by sexual needs except during her season twice a year. And if you should ever want pups, your bitch can be mated. The male, on the other hand, is almost always sexually ready and therefore may be irritable from time to time. He is more apt to fight with other dogs, and he also tends to attach himself to one person, while the bitch may spread out her affection. The male is less doting, more ruggedly self-dependent. Both male and bitch make equally good pets, provided you know which you want. If you plan to buy a second dog and already have a male, sometimes bringing in another male may lead to fights. If you have a bitch, get another bitch.

Puppy or Grown Dog

When very young children are involved, you should consider whether you want a puppy or an older dog. Here the needs of the children and the wishes of their parents are often in conflict. There is no question that puppy care takes time. The issue is whether the parents, already burdened by the needs of the children, will want to bring in another "baby." On the other hand, a young puppy of a month or two will attach himself more completely to the family than a grown dog.

Many veterinarians claim that the best time to get a puppy is at about 4 to 6 months and usually not much before 3. By the later age, he will have come through his most difficult time. He will have received his inoculations, gone through worming (if necessary), have partially finished with teething, and survived most of the ailments that can attack the young dog. If the breed is an expensive one, you take a smaller chance of losing a considerable investment, not to speak of the personal anguish involved, when you buy a 6-month-old puppy. Also, the older puppy is easier to house-train, and if you buy him from a kennel he may already be trained or well on his way.

The choice, then, is evenly divided between gaining a dog's loyalty from puppyhood on, with the chance for easy adaptation, and, on the other hand, acquiring an older dog who is doubtless easier to handle. If there are small children in the house and their mother or father is already busy, then the family should not get a very young puppy (under 6 months), for he will need more attention than can be given to him.

There is possibly one exception to this. If one of the children is an older child, say ten or more, then getting a young puppy may be a very good idea. The puppy will become the older child's "baby," and the two will develop a wonderful relationship based on need, love, and trust.

Purebred, Crossbred, Mongrel

Whether your choice is an expensive purebred purchased from a kennel or a mongrel adopted at the local SPCA, your selection should not be idle or arbitrary. When you buy a purebred, you know what you are getting; and you know also what you will get should you mate your dog to another purebred. A purebred, incidentally, is a dog whose sire and dam (father and mother) are of the same blood and are of unmixed descent since the breed was recognized (often fifty or sixty years ago).

With a crossbred animal, you know the mixture of blood in the dog. Should you mate him to another crossbred or to a purebred, you will have some idea what the puppies will be like. A crossbred is a dog whose sire and dam are of different recognized breeds. When you acquire a mongrel, all you really know is what the dog looks like—in itself a big factor in most people's choice of a dog. But his other characteristics are a mystery because his parents are of mixed origin. And when you mate him to another dog, whether purebred, crossbred, or mongrel, you will not know what the pups will be like until they are born.

These are of course considerations the owner must himself take into account. The pedigree dog (a purebred whose papers indicate his line of descent)—while excellent for shows—is not necessarily the companionable pet you want. A young mongrel adopted from your local SPCA or from a neighbor may be a much better companion than a high-strung dog whose lineage can be traced back through sire and dam since the acceptance of the breed.

Responsibilities of Owning a Dog

A dog lives with you almost as long as a child does. The child may leave home at seventeen to enter college, get married, or work. A dog lives twelve years, sometimes much longer. Further, a dog is around the house more than the child: The child goes to school, visits friends, plays outdoors. The dog is almost always in the company of his owner or his owner's family, and it is this fact that the owner must keep in mind if he wants his dog to respond in certain predictable ways. You as owner are responsible for your dog in every way. You should be sure when you choose a dog, whether purebred or mongrel, that you are prepared to care for him for the rest of his life. You should remember that the vibrant puppy grows sluggish with old age, that illness and disease are possibilities, that as the dog grows older he demands greater care and more attention. An old dog cannot be tossed aside: He needs comforting and has special needs. It is precisely when your dog is old that he needs your love and devotion most.

A dog gives so much of himself that it is tragic if an owner cannot give of himself when he is needed. It is just this exchange of loyalties that makes owning a dog such a rich experience. If the warmth of feeling is one-sided—that is, on the dog's part only—then the owner demonstrates selfishness and a closed heart.

Your main responsibility is to keep your dog healthy and sound. This seems so obvious that most people take it for granted. For the puppy, it means giving him inoculations against distemper, hepatitis, leptospirosis, and rabies. It may involve worming, extended if necessary. It of course means providing correct nutrition for both the young and the older dog.

The dog is a hardy, healthy animal if his life is not seriously distorted to fit the life of his owner. Nutrition is one of the ways in which you as owner are responsible for fulfilling your dog's needs. In Chapter 3 I offer some typical diets that you might consider for your dog, and in Chapter 4 I discuss some of the theory behind canine nutrition. The diets are by no means the final word on the subject. There are an infinite number of ways to feed a dog well.

In another respect, if you consider how much exercise a dog needs, you can see that he requires more than a turn around the block to approximate his natural life. Terriers and toys, among all the breeds, have perhaps adapted best to little exercise, the customary walk around the block twice a day. But hounds, sporting dogs, and working dogs in particular need a good amount of exercise—a 2- or 3-mile run to keep their bodies trim and their minds alert. Remember that hounds and sporting dogs may do 25 miles a day in the field when they are working, and the large work dogs are accustomed to exercise from dawn to dusk.

It all depends on what you want in your dog. If you want an alert, dynamic animal, then you should fulfill his needs. If you are willing to settle for sluggishness, then you can cut down here and there. The dog will survive, but at less than his full potential.

These warnings are directed not only to the city dweller but also to the suburbanite. In the suburbs, an owner must walk his dog or else build a kennel with a running aea. It is unsafe to let a dog run free unless he has been fully trained. Even then, there is always the danger of automobiles. They rarely strike the city dog, who is securely leashed. It is the suburban dog who stands the greatest danger. A dog like a Dachshund will challenge a car; only here, David will not defeat Goliath.

In the country it is true that a dog can run free, but here he must be trained not to attack livestock. You are liable for damages. You can take out insurance to cover any such property damage, but a situation like this is ugly beyond just the costs involved. An owner must feel responsible for everything his dog does, as if he himself had done it. There is one added danger for the country dog who runs free, slight though it may be: He may be bitten by a rabid fox or bat, or may himself bite a wild animal with rabies.

Other Considerations

There are several other matters that fall under the heading of responsibility, some of them as important as those already mentioned. Beyond a dog's physical needs are certain psychological needs, those things connected with morale. Like a child, he needs more than food and drink. A dog should get a certain amount of play—even to retrieving a stick that is thrown for him. There should be some roughhousing, unless the dog is sick or very fragile. There should be playful cuffs, some scratching of his belly and neck, so that he knows you like his presence. Without such attention he may lose spirit and drive.

Further, the dog should really feel like part of the family. All dogs want to be accepted and loved by everyone in their immediate group. Haven't we all seen a dog come up to a small child and push him until the child pays attention, even though the dog probably senses some stiff ear pulling and nose punching will follow? Often a dog will court a sharp word simply to make his presence known. Nothing destroys a dog's morale as thoroughly as indifference.

The dog owner with children must be prepared for certain incidents. When severely provoked, nearly any dog will snap in self-protection. He has no other way to assert himself. Only the largest of breeds will take rough treatment from children and simply shrug it off. Most of the middle and smaller breeds (not the toys) will take a great deal before asserting themselves. You must allow for scratches and minor bites if you do not teach your children how to treat a dog. You must in any event be prepared for minor accidents. *You should repeatedly warn your children not to corner their pet.* A dog who finds a wall at his back and a taunting child at his face will get upset and begin to fight his way out, as would a person under similar circumstances. Such incidents rarely result in serious injury to the child, but the owner should try to avoid their happening at all. A child who is repeatedly scratched or touched by the dog's teeth may become dog-shy, although it is clearly the fault of the child.

Similarly, a dog who is beaten for doing things that are not his fault will begin to develop strange reactions, become shy of the owner, and refuse to play with the child who has hurt him, simply because he is afraid. Once this happens, you may have a withdrawn, neurotic pet.

What to Look For in a Dog

Now that you know what sort of dog you want, or think you do, there are some things you should look for when you buy a dog. The best procedure is to check off each of the following points against the dog you are considering. If he fails in several major ways, then you are asking for trouble if you buy him. We all know how difficult it is to resist a pair of eyes that have caught our attention, but if the dog whose eyes are so appealing is seriously defective, you will be disappointed in him. Some of the points are obviously more important than others, but all indicate your best buy: a healthy, sound dog who will give you a maximum of pleasure.

1. The dog should be well filled-out, but not potbellied. An enlarged stomach may mean bad nutrition or parasites.

2. Check the dog's eyes for redness or discharge. Such a condition may indicate an infection, either present or incubating. Also, if you are at all interested in showing your dog, be on the lookout for unmatched

eyes. Only in certain breeds, like the Dalmatian, are unmatched eyes—
that is, one blue and one brown eye—considered acceptable. In all cases,
the eyes should be clear, without spots or a bluish cast.

3. The dog's nose should be moist unless the room is very warm
or the dog has been sleeping near a radiator. Then the dryness is only
temporary. Watch out for any discharge from the nose. That may mean
an upper respiratory infection.

4. Check the dog's teeth. If he is a very young puppy—under 3 or
4 weeks—the teeth are not yet in. From that time until he is 5 months
old, he will have his milk teeth (32 in all); after that, these fall out and
he gets his permanent set of 42. The teeth should be free of stains and
discoloration, as well as obvious imperfections. Also, if the owner tells
you that a dog is a certain age, you can sometimes check *generally, but
not accurately,* by the teeth. If he has a full set of canines and molars, he
should be over 6 months old. The teeth should be white, and the gums
pink and firm.

5. Look out for listlessness and general "unthriftiness." Dull eyes
may mean that the dog is not healthy or is infested with parasites. Such
a dog may have already been undermined by disease, and all your good
care will be of no avail.

6. Check the insides of the dog's ears—they should be pink and
free from inflammation.

7. Check also for hernia—small swellings protruding from the navel.

8. Test the dog for deafness, if possible. Make some noise behind
his back to see if he reacts. Make sure he cannot see you. If there is
any suspicion of deafness, the dog should be checked professionally.

9. Have the dog's temperature taken, if possible. Normally a dog's
temperature is about 101.5° F., although it may vary: higher for small
breeds and lower for large. The temperature is a check on possible infections. Some signs of distemper are eye and nose discharge, cough, diarrhea,
general unhealthiness and discomfort, often severe.

10. If you are interested in showing, watch out for a pink nose. A
pink nose or a pink-and-black nose is in no way indicative of bad health,
but it will make him undesirable in the show ring.

11. The dog's skin should be clear, free from parasites.

12. Look for patches on the coat—they mean an unhealthy skin
condition, maybe mange or ringworm.

13. Watch out for fleas, lice, ticks; check the skin on the abdomen
for rash. If the dog is scratching away madly, he may be infested with
parasites that you can see.

14. A shy dog may appeal to you at the moment, but he may be
troublesome later on. His shyness may be permanent and indicate a psychological quirk, the result of rough handling, lack of attention, or
infection.

15. Look for enlarged leg joints, or crooked legs, or any other deform-
ities in the feet or legs.

16. Check the dog's anus. Look for signs of diarrhea (damp or dried feces clinging to the rear end). Diarrhea may indicate parasites or intestinal infection.

17. If you are interested in showing, don't buy the smallest of the litter. The small one may be perfectly lovely, but he may also fail to grow to the requirements set by the American Kennel Club for that breed and therefore be excluded from the exhibition ring. (This rule does not apply, of course, in the case of many of the toy breeds, which have height limits that may not be exceeded. If two Chihuahuas are of equal quality, for example, the smaller one is preferred.)

18. Check on the puppy's diet at the kennel or pet shop so that you can continue it as you gradually change to the diet you are going to feed him.

19. Ask for a certificate of inoculations—what kind and when the dog received them. Make sure you ask whether the dog has been wormed, how many times, for what kind of worms, and when (the last time). If you are in any doubt about the proof shown you, have the dog rechecked for worms. Distemper, hepatitis, and leptospirosis shots are usually given in a combination injection, while rabies vaccination is generally given after the puppy is 6 months old. For details on these diseases and the precautions to take against them, see Chapter 6, Ailments.

20. Try to arrange to buy the puppy on a trial basis to be sure he is healthy and will adjust to your home.

21. If you buy a purebred from a kennel and want to see what he will be like later, spend a few minutes with his dam and sire, if that is at all possible. He will look like them and probably act like them.

22. Since hip dysplasia (abnormal development) is common in some of the larger breeds, if you buy one over 6 months old you should have an agreement that the puppy is free from this condition.

23. If you buy a pedigree dog, arrange for papers testifying to his lineage. His pedigree papers indicate the names of his close ancestors written in chart form. The kennel will of course have this information, and the pet shop owner should also have it. Another form you will need is registration papers—proof that your puppy's dam and sire were registered in one of the several registry organizations that exist around the world. You can obtain such an application from the American Kennel Club and from the kennels. The license is something you obtain from your local SPCA, or, in some cases, from your town hall or the county courthouse in the area where you are going to keep the dog. Procedures vary in each locality. Every dog needs a license.

The Older Dog

If you buy an older dog, there may possibly be special problems. Here are some of the questions you should try to answer. Why is he being sold or given away? Where was he raised and to what environment is he accustomed? Is she possibly pregnant? Is he a biter? Is he untrainable? Has he had any serious diseases? Has he malformations? Does he need medical treatment? An older dog can of course be a source of great pleasure, but he may present certain problems that you should be aware of.

Buying from a Pet Shop

If you buy from a pet shop, you must make a specially careful selection, as you can't always see the parents of the pup. In judging whether or not you want to buy from this source, consider the following points.

1. The pet shop should present a clean appearance, and the animals should look healthy and well-groomed. The shop should smell clean; animal odors do not predominate. On the other hand, too strong an odor of disinfectant may mean that the animals are not themselves clean and their odor is being overwhelmed with the disinfectant. Your eyes and nose should note the condition of the shop.

2. Remember that the dog you are buying has passed through many hands, and he may be somewhat weakened and confused by each transaction, from changes in food and water, environment, and owner. This does not mean that you cannot get a fine dog from a pet shop. It does mean that your dog may need more care as a result of these changes.

3. If you want a purebred (and possibly pedigree) dog, it is best to buy him from a kennel that specializes in that breed—especially if you want to see the parents. If you do purchase from a pet shop, the owner should give you all the necessary information on age, background, stock, and kennel where he was sired. You may wish to check this information with the kennel, and the owner should cooperate. A purebred dog, whether pedigree or not, is an investment, and if you are disappointed you don't want to take it out on the dog.

4. Most shop owners are willing to return payment if something turns out badly. A written agreement indicating terms is of course necessary, and you should read such agreements carefully.

5. If at all possible, take a veterinarian with you to check the dog and the shop. For most people, this is difficult or impossible. Most owners-to-be wait until they have the dog and sometimes until he is sick before they get in touch with a veterinarian. They could save themselves considerable trouble if a veterinarian saw the dog before they made the purchase.

6. Never be taken in by the claims of the shop owner. He is anxious to sell the puppy to make room for another. Check your breeds (Chapter 2); know what to expect. If he has a strangely colored dog, be sure from the description that the coloring is correct for that breed.

7. The pet shop will also have application forms for you to register a purebred with the American Kennel Club.

Buying from a Kennel

If you buy from a kennel approved by the American Kennel Club, then you are reasonably assured of certain guarantees. Kennels themselves, like all enterprises, are uneven. The advantage of buying from a kennel is that the owner is experienced in handling the breed you are interested in. He has specialized in that breed, and the chances are excellent that your dog has received fine care. The kennel's reputation rests on the dogs that it sells.

The kennel itself should have a tidy appearance. The runs and pens should be clean, free of day-old droppings. The dogs should look healthy, well-groomed, well-fed. Check to see if they are active or listless. Are their eyes clear? Do they seem enthusiastic or indifferent?

You will also be able to see the parents of your pup when you buy from a kennel, and this is not always possible when you buy from a pet shop.

One final word: All dogs regardless of where you obtain them—whether from the SPCA or other humane society, pet shop, kennel, or friend—should be thoroughly examined by a veterinarian. This initial expense is the best insurance you have of getting a sound, healthy pup.

The American Kennel Club will give the prospective buyer the names and addresses of breeders. To obtain this information, write to the American Kennel Club, 51 Madison Avenue, New York, New York 10010. Specify the following about the dog you want: breed, age, color preference (individual dogs of a breed may vary), sex, price range, purpose, future environment, disposition preferred.

For many prospective owners, the most common way to obtain a dog is to call the local SPCA or humane society to see what is available. Many put their names on a list for a particular breed of dog and wait. Most people, however, walk through the pens at their local SPCA, humane society, or pound and pick out the dogs that appeal to them, or they get their dogs from friends. Whatever your choice, a fine, healthy pet will more than reward you for your care in making a selection.

THE GUARD DOG

Owning a guard dog has become a fact of life for millions of Americans. And for millions of others it is becoming a serious option.

To the business community, specially trained guard dogs, usually

Dobermans or German Shepherds, have become an extension of corporate activity. We see them in industry, shops, department stores, office buildings. Guard dogs are now a standard feature of business planning.

To individuals, they represent an extension of the police force, guaranteeing safety and security for them, their families, and their property. Correctly trained, a guard dog can protect you from bodily harm in the streets and parks, where you have a right to walk free and unmolested, and he can protect your home from burglars and other undesirable intruders.

But what do we mean when we talk about a guard dog? The vast majority of people, I suspect, don't really know what a guard dog is. The term remains fuzzy, undefined, and usually conjures up images of a large, ferocious dog ready to defend, attack, maim, even kill on command.

There are, roughly, three categories into which the guard dog falls. First, there is *the dog trained to bark;* he sounds an alarm so as to frighten off people who intend to rob your home, mug you, or do you bodily harm. Such dogs are trained to do nothing else but let out a rough, aggressive bark so as to put fear and trembling into a criminal's heart. If you just want a dog to sound the alarm while you are away from home, any size dog will generally do. In fact, size alone is not a real consideration. Some of the toy breeds and all the terriers are more alert than most of the large breeds. A housebreaker needs silence because his success depends on it. The last thing he wants is a persistent barker. Of course, the larger the dog the deeper the bark, and you may want a working breed to discourage an intruder. German Shepherds, Giant Schnauzers, Rottweilers, Siberian Huskies, and Dobermans are all excellent prospects. Remember: The alarm dog will take no protective action. He may do so on his own, but not as part of his training.

Two other considerations: First, a large dog by his very appearance will discourage any aggressors on the street. Your dog may be the gentlest, sweetest creature in the world, but the mugger doesn't know that. Appearance here is the same as reality. Second, to back up this appearance, you want your dog to bark on command and heel with precision instantly. A well-disciplined dog is always taken more seriously than the casual loafer who comes to you when he feels like it. If you can train your dog to do these two things, all well and good; but I would suggest that both of you enroll in a dog training school for one or two weeks, and that you do so when your dog is 6 months old.

In the second category is *the dog who sounds the alarm and takes some kind of protective action*—jumping, snarling, seizing, chasing—should you be attacked. In general, the working dogs, especially the Airedale Terrier, Belgian Sheepdog, Bouvier des Flandres, Rottweiler, Boxer, Briard, Doberman, German Shepherd, Siberian Husky, Giant Schnauzer, and Chow Chow, are excellent for this purpose. I recommend that you do not attempt to train this dog yourself, unless you have worked with trainers or have had a lot of experience with dogs. When he is about 6 months old, enroll him in a dog training school that will teach him the protective measures you want from him, and take the course (usually 2 to 4 weeks) with him. Whether you want an alarm or a protective dog, the school will teach you how to control your pet, discipline him, and make certain he carries out the orders you give. Having a well-trained dog is to your advantage in every way. Not only will he obey your every command, but he will give you that peace of mind you may need in walking your streets and enjoying your home.

The third kind of guard dog is *the all-out attack dog,* expertly trained so as to be agitated to the point, where, if necessary, he can kill. Police, industry, department stores, shipyards, and the Armed Forces use these dogs. They are maimers and potential killers, deadly weapons that only experts can control. Most of them—the Rottweiler and Shepherd are good examples—have great physical power and exceptional biting ability. These dogs should not be owned by the general public. The responsibility is simply too great. The dog may attack and even kill a person who acts in an apparently suspicious way—indeed, he has been trained to do so. Or else, the trainer may have made a small mistake, and the dog will turn on the owner or a member of the family. You could be in for a major law suit because of what the dog might do.

In my opinion, only first-rate dog trainers and experts in handling attack dogs should be permitted to own them. You should not put an instrument of such destruction in the hands of an amateur. The vast majority of people want pets with some protective power, but they are just not capable of fully controlling attack dogs.

Select your dog from the first two categories if you want a guard. I don't think the last kind has any place in your home.

2

The Breeds

IN THIS chapter there are brief histories and descriptions of the 121
breeds currently recognized by the American Kennel Club that can
be registered and shown. (Since 1959, the Manchester Terrier and the
Toy Manchester Terrier have been registered as a single breed.) They
are divided into six groups: hound (page 22), nonsporting (page 45), sporting (page 58), terrier (page 84), toy (page 107), and working (page 127).

In each instance, as a service to the potential owner, I have also
listed a range of prices. These prices are of course dependent upon many
factors: popularity of the breed; age of the dog when purchased; the
quality of the dog, whether for companionship or show purposes; the
breeder himself and his reputation; whether the dog is male or female.
Usually the price listed is for an 8-week-old pup, sometimes for one
slightly older—up to 3 months.

The disparities in price among breeders are great and very often
for good reasons. One breeder who seems expensive is not necessarily
overcharging, although another's prices seem more reasonable—each one
is probably offering a different quality of dog, and you pay accordingly.
Keep this in mind if you see a list price that is different from what
your local breeder asks. Prices vary in different parts of the country,
depending on the popularity and availability of that particular breed in
that section. Sometimes dogs have to be shipped across the country, and
that too adds to the cost. Dogs of show quality will fluctuate tremendously
in price, depending, for example, on pedigree and stud potential. Once
you have decided to buy a purebred, however, then you should be willing
to get the best you can to suit your own individual needs.

In each place where I indicate breed characteristics, please keep in
mind that these are only *general* traits. Obviously, there are numerous
exceptions within each breed.

THE HOUND BREEDS

The hounds are hunters who specialize in animals, not birds. They are generally divided into sight or gaze hounds (the long-legged dogs who are speedy and hunt by sight) and scent hounds (the short-legged and slow dogs who hunt by smell). The 19 hound breeds are:

AFGHAN HOUND	GREYHOUND
BASENJI	HARRIER
BASSET HOUND	IRISH WOLFHOUND
BEAGLE	NORWEGIAN ELKHOUND
BLACK AND TAN COONHOUND	OTTER HOUND
BLOODHOUND	RHODESIAN RIDGEBACK
BORZOI	SALUKI
DACHSHUND	SCOTTISH DEERHOUND
FOXHOUND, AMERICAN	WHIPPET
FOXHOUND, ENGLISH	

AFGHAN HOUND

HISTORY AND ORIGIN: The Afghan Hound goes back in history five or six thousand years, when he was accepted among Egyptian royalty. The modern Afghan dates from the First World War, although for centuries Afghanistan has contributed to the makeup of the breed. Originally the Afghan was developed for hunting in hilly terrain.

CHARACTERISTICS: The Afghan, besides being an excellent hunter, is a fine house pet: gentle, highly intelligent, easily trained, a great clown with the family although reserved with strangers. He rarely barks, is almost never vicious, and makes an excellent companion. He is possessive about his home and the people he lives with; he is an individualist.

His somewhat bizarre appearance is the result of the structure of his hipbones, which are higher than in most dogs. As a consequence, he can hurdle and jump in mountainous terrain and in thickets, where he once hunted leopards as a so-called sight hound (as distinguished from a scent hound).

The Afghan will adapt to any climate change. Afghanistan has very hot summers, very cold winters, and the dog is comfortable there in either season. He is especially good for hilly ground, is very powerful and swift. Even with his exciting background, the Afghan is content to lead a quiet life with long daily walks.

The dog's conspicuous appearance immediately makes him an object of attention.

AFGHAN HOUND

BASENJI

COLOR: All colors are acceptable.
COAT: Thick, silky hair, very fine in texture.
HEIGHT: Dog: 26–28 inches. Bitch: 25–27 inches.
WEIGHT: Dog: 58–64 pounds. Bitch: 48–52 pounds.
PRICE RANGE: $175 and up.

BASENJI

HISTORY AND ORIGIN: The Basenji (known also as Belgian Congo Dog and Congo Bush Dog) has a long background as a dog well known to the pharaohs of Egypt. He is native to the Congo regions of Africa. Originally he was trained as a hunter.

CHARACTERISTICS: The Basenji is highly recommended as a house dog. Even though he almost never barks, he makes an excellent watchdog. He utters his bark (really more like a squeal) only when happy and only with those he loves. He is lovable, gentle with children, tireless in play, anxious to please, and obedient by nature. For the owner careful about his home, the Basenji is perfect. He cleans himself like a cat and rarely needs a bath.

The Basenji, besides being highly prized for his intelligence, adapts easily to hot climates and is not unhappy in the cold.

COLOR: Deep chestnut-red, or pure black, or black-and-tan; feet, chest, and tail tip white.
COAT: Short and silky, skin pliant.
HEIGHT: Dog: 17 inches. Bitch: 16 inches.
WEIGHT: Dog: 24 pounds. Bitch: 22 pounds.
PRICE RANGE: Dog: $175–$225. Bitch: $175–$275.

BASSET HOUND

HISTORY AND ORIGIN: Like so many other hunting dogs, the Basset Hound has a long lineage, going back centuries, chiefly in France and Belgium to the old French Bloodhound and the St. Hubert Hound. There he was raised by royalty to serve as a trailer of deer, hares, and rabbits. In the United States he has been used for hunting foxes, rabbits, grouse, pheasants, and raccoons.

CHARACTERISTICS: The Basset Hound is intelligent, docile, kind, and loyal. When trained and handled by his owner only, he tends to be a one-man dog, but in a household situation he will be ideal with all, especially with children. It is virtually impossible to annoy him, and he is therefore excellent for children of all ages. He makes no enemies and can live with any other kind of pet, even rabbits.

His short legs make the Basset Hound an excellent hunter in dense cover. His sensitive nose and long, flapping ears, which stir up the scent, make him particularly skillful as a trailer and flusher.

BASSET HOUND

BEAGLE

The Basset Hound is good for city or country, takes whatever comes along and enjoys it. He should be walked at least three times a day. If he is let off the leash he will run himself out and return to you. He should get plenty of exercise and air, although when he is not outdoors he will rest contentedly.

Of all the breeds, he has generally the least trouble from nervous stomach or digestive difficulty. He is a very healthy dog, except that the tips of his long, floppy ears tend to get sore.

COLOR: Any hound color, such as black, tan, or white, or any combination.
COAT: Close, hard hound coat.
HEIGHT: Dog: 14–15 inches. Bitch: 12–14 inches.
WEIGHT: Dog: 35–45 pounds. Bitch: 25–35 pounds.
PRICE RANGE: $150–$250.

BEAGLE

HISTORY AND ORIGIN: Although the Beagle was once almost solely a hunting dog, and can still be used as such, he is principally a house pet. Descended, according to legend, from the scent hounds used by King Arthur and his knights, the Beagle was supreme as a rabbit hunter.

CHARACTERISTICS: The Beagle is ideal for every member of the family. Since he is small, he is almost perfect as a city house pet. His short coat needs only occasional care, no clipping, and makes him suitable for apartment life. If a pet is needed for children, the Beagle is highly recommended; he is physically capable of withstanding punishment, is not highstrung, almost never turns vicious. He is a good traveler and is suited for any environment.

In the field the Beagle is loyal, courageous, and obedient. He hardly ever tires even under the toughest of conditions, and he remains steady and patient. Occasionally he may become so interested in following a trail that he disappears. Watch him carefully.

Beagles need a good deal of exercise if they are not to get fat. They are heavy eaters (for their size), and without adequate exercise they tend to have digestive trouble. This is a minor disadvantage, however, because apartment dwellers have generally found Beagles quite adaptable to conditions in which exercise is somewhat limited. One warning: Beagles tend to bay if left alone. To avoid this, they should be trained not to do so while young.

COLOR: Any hound color, such as black, tan, or white, or any combination.
COAT: Close, hard hound coat of medium length.
HEIGHT: Beagles are classed in two sizes, those under 13 inches and those from 13–15 inches and over.

WEIGHT: Under 13 inches, 18 pounds; over 13 inches, 30 pounds.
PRICE RANGE: $60 and up.

BLACK AND TAN COONHOUND

BLACK AND TAN COONHOUND

HISTORY AND ORIGIN: Although the Black and Tan Coonhound was registered by the American Kennel Club as late as 1945, his history goes back to the Talbot Hound known in England in the eleventh century. This Talbot was crossed with the Bloodhound and over the centuries with the English Foxhound. When he came to the United States he was crossed with our Virginia Foxhound, and from this cross came the Black and Tan Coonhound.

CHARACTERISTICS: Powerful, agile, and alert, the Black and Tan Coonhound is a great hunter of opossums and raccoons. He is also a good hunter of bears, deer, and bobcats. Tough-skinned and tough-hearted, he can take any terrain, any weather, any water. He is calm, stable, extremely affectionate and almost never quarrelsome with other dogs. If one wants an even-tempered dog who is very fond of children and will never make his owner nervous, the Black and Tan is the perfect dog. He is best for country life, but will, if necessary, adapt to an apartment.

COLOR: Jet-black with tan markings above eyes, on side of muzzle, chest, and legs.

COAT: Short and dense.

HEIGHT: Dog: 25–27 inches. Bitch: 23–25 inches.
WEIGHT: Dog: 75–85 pounds. Bitch: 70–80 pounds.
PRICE RANGE: $75–$150 and up.

BLOODHOUND

BLOODHOUND

HISTORY AND ORIGIN: Father of all the hounds, the Bloodhound goes back
to Egypt, Greece, and Italy centuries before the birth of Christ. In
the third century A.D., a dog resembling the modern Bloodhound,
especially in scenting ability, was described by Claudius Aelianus
in his famous *History of Animals.* The dog he describes was first brought
to Europe from Constantinople and became very popular with hunters. By the twelfth century, kings and barons and even bishops were
using Bloodhounds in the hunt. They became an important part of
medieval monastery life. The dog was called a Bloodhound because
he was kept by so many of the aristocracy.

CHARACTERISTICS: The Bloodhound is of course famous for his nose, so
famous, in fact, that his accuracy in following a trail is legendary.
His evidence has even been accepted in court. Unlike police-trained
dogs, he does not attack the man or animal he is following. The
result is a mild-mannered, tender dog, one who is fatherly with
children as well as with other animals. He is neither ferocious, dangerous, nor forbidding.

His chief drawback as a pet is his hunting instinct. He needs something to do and requires a great deal of exercise. He is not recommended for apartment life.

COLOR: Black-and-tan, red-and-tan, or tawny.
COAT: Thin to touch and extremely loose.
HEIGHT: Dog: 25–27 inches. Bitch: 23–25 inches.
WEIGHT: Dog: 90–110 pounds. Bitch: 80–100 pounds.
PRICE RANGE: $175–$250 and up.

BORZOI

BORZOI

HISTORY AND ORIGIN: The Borzoi originated in the Russia of the beginning of the eighteenth century. About 1705, a Russian duke imported some Arabian Greyhounds or Gazelle Hounds for hunting. These dogs were too fragile for the Russian winter and died. The duke imported another batch, but this time crossed them with a dog very much like our Collie. The result was a dog with a heavy, wavy coat who could withstand the Russian winter—the Borzoi.

CHARACTERISTICS: As a pet, the Borzoi needs little attention and care, and is therefore recommended for professional people. But he needs companionship; he is not a dog whom you can feed at noon and then forget. He shows great affection for his owner and is generally a docile and gentle pet for women and older children. One warning for small children, however: The Borzoi differs from other dogs in the extraordinary speed of his nervous reactions. When he decides to bite, it is too late for anyone to stop him. Incidentally, the Borzoi develops slowly and needs a lot of sleep during his puppyhood.

The Borzoi is completely at home in cold weather; the colder it gets, the happier he is. In hot weather he is usually lethargic.

In his grace, beauty, symmetry, and general aristocratic manner and appearance, he is one of the most magnificent of all the breeds.

COLOR: Any color, white usually predominating.

COAT: Long, silky, either flat or wavy.

HEIGHT: Dog: 28–31 inches. Bitch: 26–29 inches.

WEIGHT: Dog: 75–105 pounds (generally less than 105). Bitch: 60–90 pounds.

PRICE RANGE: $250–$400.

DACHSHUND

HISTORY AND ORIGIN: Dachshund in German means "badger dog." A dog very much like the smooth and longhaired Dachshund first came to the attention of hunters at the beginning of the seventeenth century. He was a good hunter, and his great specialty was badgers. He was also used against wild boars, foxes, and wounded deer. The Dachshund, then as now, is bred for strength, stamina, and courage.

CHARACTERISTICS: These little badger dogs make wonderful pets. They are very intelligent, playful, highly individualistic, and have a great deal of self-will. They are good for the city or the country; they are exceptionally clean, never shed, and they thrive on every family mood. They are also self-reliant and can accustom themselves to any terrain and any climate.

One word of warning: They are susceptible to spinal disc trouble, and when they do get slipped discs they are partially or completely paralyzed. The female is also susceptible to false pregnancy.

COLOR: Solid red of various shades; black with tan spots and black nose and nails; chocolate with tan spots and brown nose.

COAT: Three coats:

1. Smooth or shorthaired—short and dense, shiny and glossy.
2. Wirehaired, like German Wirehaired Pointer—hard with good undercoat.
3. Longhaired, like Irish Setter—soft and silky.

HEIGHT: Dog: 5–9 inches. Bitch: 5–9 inches.

WEIGHT: Dog: 5–20 pounds. Bitch: 5–20 pounds.

PRICE RANGE: $75 and up.

DACHSHUND, SMOOTH

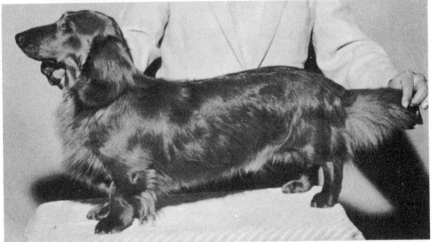

DACHSHUND, LONGHAIRED

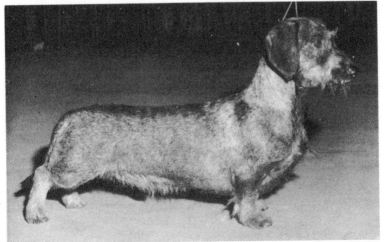

DACHSHUND, WIREHAIRED

FOXHOUND, AMERICAN

FOXHOUND, AMERICAN

HISTORY AND ORIGIN: The first mention of the Foxhound in the United States appears in a diary of one of De Soto's men. Then, we learn, these dogs hunted men, not foxes. Years later, in 1650, a pack of hounds similar to English Foxhounds was brought to this country by one Robert Brooke, and this pack became the stock for many of the Foxhounds we have today.

CHARACTERISTICS: The American Foxhound is loyal, affectionate, and stable, a fine dog for the field and the home. Tremendously versatile, he can be trained to trail any ground game. In stamina, courage, and determination, he is unbeatable. He also has great speed and can manage well in any terrain.

COLOR: Any hound color, usually black-and-tan-and-white.

COAT: Close, hard hound coat.

HEIGHT: Dog: 22–25 inches. Bitch: 21–24 inches.

WEIGHT: Dog: 65–70 pounds. Bitch: 60–65 pounds.

PRICE RANGE: $150–$250, depending on training and quality.

FOXHOUND, ENGLISH

HISTORY AND ORIGIN: Records of English Foxhound breeding have been kept with such care and by such masters that the ancestors of each Fox-

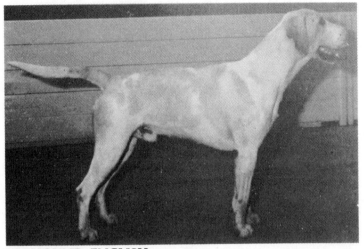

FOXHOUND, ENGLISH

hound can be traced as far as 1800. But the Foxhound goes back to some of the hounds of the fourteenth century. By the eighteenth century, foxhunting had become a favorite sport of the aristocracy and the Foxhound their favorite sporting dog. The pure English Foxhound probably made its first appearance in the United States in 1738. He is somewhat tougher and sturdier than the American Foxhound.

CHARACTERISTICS: The English Foxhound is affectionate and faithful to his owner, but reserved with others. He is versatile in the field and loyal at home.

COLOR: Any hound color, usually black-and-tan-and-white.

COAT: Close, hard hound coat, dense and glossy.

HEIGHT: Dog: 22–25 inches. Bitch: 21–24 inches.

WEIGHT: Dog: 65–70 pounds. Bitch: 60–65 pounds.

PRICE RANGE: $200–$250, or more, depending on training and quality.

GREYHOUND

HISTORY AND ORIGIN: The first written record of the Greyhound in England is Number 31 of the Laws of Canute, enacted in 1016. But the Greyhound existed long before this. Ovid gives the oldest written description of the breed. No one really knows how old the breed is nor where it originated, but we see its type whenever the earliest records

GREYHOUND

of dogs are found, especially on the tombs of Egypt and on Assyrian monuments. The oldest record we have of the Greyhound is in a carving on the tomb of Amten in the Valley of the Nile. This tomb dates back to about 4000 B.C. From this carving we know that the Greyhound has changed less through the centuries than any other breed.

Throughout the ages he has been used to hunt all kinds of small game including deer and foxes, but hares are his natural quarry. In recent years he has become a racing dog.

CHARACTERISTICS: The Greyhound is the fastest dog in the world. He is elegant as well as reserved, cautious, and high-strung. He does not have a good sense of smell and is not suitable for hilly or wooded country. He is extremely nervous. I would not recommend him as a pet for a family with small children. He is best suited for two things: racing and chasing hares.

COLOR: Gray-and-white, or pale fawn-and-white.

COAT: Short, smooth, firm.

HEIGHT: Dog: 26–27 inches. Bitch: 25–26 inches.

WEIGHT: Dog: 65–70 pounds. Bitch: 60–65 pounds.
PRICE RANGE: $200 and up.

HARRIER

HARRIER

HISTORY AND ORIGIN: Authorities do not agree on the origin of the Harrier. The most widely held opinion is that the ancestors of the Harrier were brought to England by the Normans and that they were probably crosses between Beagles and St. Hubert Hounds.

The first pack we know about dates back to the middle of the thirteenth century, when they immediately became a great favorite because they could be followed on foot. From that date until the present, the Harrier has been a favorite of all hunters of small game and takes his name from his ability to hunt hares. The dog as we know him today is a small and exact copy of the English Foxhound.

CHARACTERISTICS: Like the Black and Tan Coonhound and the Beagle, the Harrier as a hunting dog is durable and adaptable to nearly any weather or terrain. He is stable, not at all high-strung, patient. While chiefly a field dog, he makes a good house pet, particularly in the country.

COLOR: Combination of black, tan, and white.
COAT: Short, hard, dense, and glossy.
HEIGHT: Dog: 20–21 inches. Bitch: 19–20 inches.
WEIGHT: Dog: 45–50 pounds. Bitch: 40–45 pounds.
PRICE RANGE: $150 and up.

IRISH WOLFHOUND

IRISH WOLFHOUND

HISTORY AND ORIGIN: The tallest and possibly the most powerful of dogs, the Irish Wolfhound is the great heroic dog of Ireland, constantly associated through stories and paintings with its ancient and glorious history. But this ancient breed existed long before the establishment of Ireland. The first written record we have of it is in the second century A.D., when we are told that the invading Celts brought the dog to Greece in 279 B.C. We next hear of the Wolfhound in 391 A.D., when a Roman consul wrote of their fighting prowess in the circus.

The early literature of Ireland is full of references to the Wolfhounds, especially to their ability to hunt. Often they were presented as gifts to royalty. And so their reputation followed them throughout the centuries; in 1596, Lope de Vega, the great Spanish poet and playwright, wrote a sonnet to the Wolfhound. But by the early nineteenth century, wolves and elks began to disappear and the breed began to dwindle. The danger of extinction was so great that by the middle of the nineteenth century the roaming dogs were collected and carefully cared for. The standard we have for their breed was drawn up in 1885.

CHARACTERISTICS: This is an intelligent, courageous dog who makes a great friend and companion. He is reliable, dependable, a perfect guard. Once established in a home, he does not adjust easily to a new situation. Like most hounds, he expects to stay put.

Although a fierce fighter, the Irish Wolfhound does not seek trouble. He can be trusted with children—he makes an excellent playmate. When walking, he makes a dignified companion. Since he is the tallest of dogs, he fears nothing and has an even, secure temperament.

The Irish Wolfhound makes a striking, commanding appearance and is especially suitable for the aesthetically minded owner. He is better suited to country than apartment life.

COLOR: Best is gray, brindle, red, black, white, or fawn.

COAT: Rough and wiry.

HEIGHT: Dog: 32–33 inches. Bitch: 30–31 inches.

WEIGHT: Dog: 120–140 pounds. Bitch: 105–115 pounds.

PRICE RANGE: $400–$600.

NORWEGIAN ELKHOUND

HISTORY AND ORIGIN: The Norwegian Elkhound goes back about four thousand years to western Norway, where he herded flocks and defended the tribes against wolves and bears. The dog we have today is not a product of crossbreeding. He is the same now as he was thousands of years ago, when his physical characteristics developed out of his needs. He is Norway's great contribution to the canine world.

CHARACTERISTICS: Bold, energetic, with incredible stamina and fierce courage, the Norwegian Elkhound is one of the great hunters of the north. Bears, lynxes, and mountain lions are his natural quarry, but his great specialty is elk hunting. His sense of smell is so highly developed that he can scent an elk two to three miles away.

He is completely devoted to his owner and to the hunt. He is loyal, trustworthy, a quick learner, and a great friend. He can adapt to any circumstances and any conditions. But he is very aggressive and a real barker. He also has a strong will and a mind of his own. The man or woman who wants to own one should have a strong

NORWEGIAN ELKHOUND

will and should know how to train dogs, for the Elkhound requires close supervision.

COLOR: Gray with black tips; chest, stomach, and legs lighter than top of body.

COAT: Thick, dense, hard, and smooth-lying.

HEIGHT: Dog: 19–20½ inches. Bitch: 18–19 inches.

WEIGHT: Dog: 45–50 pounds. Bitch: 40–50 pounds.

PRICE RANGE: $175 and up.

OTTER HOUND

HISTORY AND ORIGIN: There are numerous references to Otter Hounds and otter hunting in the time of King John (1199–1216), but the first description of the Otter Hound comes to us from the reign of King Edward II (1307–1327). The dog then was a combination of hound and terrier. But his origin remains a mystery. Authorities believe that his ancestors were the Southern Hound and the Welsh Harrier. The French opinion is that he is a double for the old Vendée Hound

OTTER HOUND

of France. Whatever his exact origin, he was bred for one thing—
to kill the otters preying on fish in rivers and streams. The great
period of otter hunting in England was in the nineteenth century,
when it became a minor vogue.

CHARACTERISTICS: The Otter Hound is popular neither as a show dog nor
as a pet. He is a scent hound and his one purpose in life is to kill
otters. He is loyal and devoted to his owner and a savage and fearless
fighter. He is a great swimmer and a very good farm dog, for he is
bred purely for work.

COLOR: Grizzle-and-sandy, or black-and-tan, clearly marked.

COAT: Dense, hard and oily, but not curled.

HEIGHT: Dog: 25–26 inches. Bitch: 24–25 inches.

WEIGHT: Dog: 60–65 pounds. Bitch: 55–60 pounds.

PRICE RANGE: $125 and up.

RHODESIAN RIDGEBACK

HISTORY AND ORIGIN: The Rhodesian Ridgeback, often called the African
Lion Hound, is a native of South Africa. The breed goes back about
three hundred years, when the Dutch, Germans, and French

RHODESIAN RIDGEBACK

Huguenots emigrated to South Africa. They brought with them Great Danes, Mastiffs, Greyhounds, Bloodhounds, and Terriers. These dogs mated with a native dog, half wild, with a strange ridge on his back. This crossbreeding established the stock for the modern Ridgeback. The standard for this breed was established in 1922.

CHARACTERISTICS: The Rhodesian Ridgeback is a great friend, loyal and devoted, but he gives his allegiance to his owner only. He is truly a one-man dog. An excellent work dog and hunting dog, he is never outgoing and rarely interested in other dogs. He makes a first-rate guard of property. A good hunter, he can withstand any weather, and can go a day without water. He is also very strong-headed and willful and must therefore be trained early and never permitted to take liberties. He must always know that he has a loving but firm owner. He is not suitable for apartment life.

COLOR: Light wheaten to red wheaten, with a little white in chest and toes.

COAT: Short and dense, sleek and glossy.

HEIGHT: Dog: 25–27 inches. Bitch: 24–26 inches.

WEIGHT: Dog: 70–75 pounds. Bitch: 65–70 pounds.
PRICE RANGE: $200 and up.

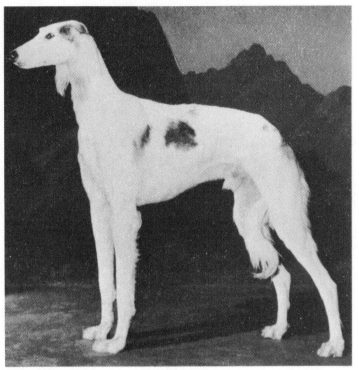

SALUKI

SALUKI

HISTORY AND ORIGIN: Known everywhere as the royal dog of Egypt, the
Saluki, as one authority writes, was a "distinct breed and type as
long ago as 329 B.C. when Alexander the Great invaded India." But
his ancestors go back thousands of years before Alexander, to the
Sumerian period, 5000 B.C. Excavations from this period show us a
dog very much resembling the Saluki. The Saluki was the only dog
held to be sacred and noble by the Moslems, who used him to hunt
gazelle and antelope. The dog was recognized by the American Kennel
Club in 1927.

CHARACTERISTICS: A noble and majestic-looking dog, the Saluki is neither
fragile nor weak. He should never be pampered. He can stand any
climate, and is accustomed to living a hard, rough life. In fact, he
thrives on this kind of life. He is kind, affectionate, and a good
friend, but he is rarely demonstrative. He is an exotic-looking dog,

swift and dignified, but often sensitive and temperamental—therefore not suitable for small children.

COLOR: White, cream, fawn, golden red, or grizzle; or black-and-tan-and-white, or black-and-tan.

COAT: Smooth and silky.

HEIGHT: Dog: 23–28 inches. Bitch: 18–24 inches.

WEIGHT: Dog: 55–60 pounds. Bitch: 45–55 pounds.

PRICE RANGE: Depending on the breeder, roughly $175–$250.

SCOTTISH DEERHOUND

SCOTTISH DEERHOUND

HISTORY AND ORIGIN: The Scottish Deerhound or the "Royal Dog of Scotland" is associated with ancient knights in plumed helmets, with great halls and long banquet tables, with the splendor and the glory of chivalry. The breed goes back to the early sixteenth century, when it was such a favorite with the Scottish chieftains that a brace of the hounds could ransom a nobleman. In the middle of the eighteenth century, with the breakup of the clan system, the breed nearly became extinct. Not until about 1825 was it successfully restored to the position it had previously held.

CHARACTERISTICS: Dignified and gentle, strong and swift, the Scottish Deerhound is one of the kings of the dog world. He is a great hunter—he can bring down a Scottish deer weighing about 250 pounds. He also has a keen scent and is an excellent tracker. But it is not as a hunter alone that he excels. A loving and devoted friend, he will never abandon his owner. His desire for his owner's love and for the love of his family is insatiable. For this reason, Scottish Deerhounds should not be raised in kennels. The dog is also easy to train, tractable, absolutely stable, and therefore wonderful with children.

COLOR: Best is dark blue-gray.

COAT: Harsh and wiry, about 3 or 4 inches long.

HEIGHT: Dog: 30–32 inches. Bitch: 28–31 inches.

WEIGHT: Dog: 85–110 pounds. Bitch: 75–95 pounds.

PRICE RANGE: $350 and up.

WHIPPET

WHIPPET

HISTORY AND ORIGIN: The Whippet—or the miniature English Greyhound, as he is often called—is the fastest dog of his weight in the world, often clocked at 35 miles an hour.

The origin of the dog is uncertain, but his basic stock seems to come from crosses between small English Greyhounds and different terriers. The English gentry needed a new favorite when bull and bear baiting and dog fighting were outlawed; so they developed the

Whippet to hunt rabbits in a small arena. Today the Whippet is still a good rabbit courser, and in Lancashire and Yorkshire, where he is used for racing, he is known as the "poor man's racehorse."

CHARACTERISTICS: Handsome and elegant, the Whippet is an ideal house or apartment dog. He has an amiable disposition, loves his owner completely, doesn't shed, is very easy to housebreak, and is easy to feed and keep clean. He can adjust to any condition and is happiest when he is at home with his owner and family. He should not be allowed to live in a kennel. He must be exercised a good deal.

COLOR: Any color, but usually gray, or tan, or white.

COAT: Close, smooth, and firm.

HEIGHT: Dog: 19–22 inches. Bitch: 18–21 inches.

WEIGHT: Dog: 18–28 pounds. Bitch: 12–20 pounds.

PRICE RANGE: $150 and up.

THE NONSPORTING BREEDS

Many of the dogs in this arbitrarily designated group were once hunters and workers—and some still are—but most are now pets and companions. The 11 nonsporting breeds are:

BICHON FRISE	LHASA APSO
BULLDOG, ENGLISH	POODLE
BULLDOG, FRENCH	SCHIPPERKE
CHOW CHOW	TERRIER, BOSTON
DALMATIAN	TERRIER, TIBETAN
KEESHOND	

BICHON FRISE

BICHON FRISE

HISTORY AND ORIGIN: The Bichon Frise has had a long and interesting background. Related to the Caniche, the Bichon descended from the Barbet (or Water Spaniel), and from that came by the name Barbichon, later shortened to Bichon. In antiquity, it is believed, Spanish seamen introduced the breed to Teneriffe in the Canary Islands, and the Bichon came to be known as the Teneriffe. It was later reintroduced to continental Europe, where the breed became popular in Renaissance courts, especially in France and in Spain. Incidentally, it can be found in many paintings of Velasquez and Goya. After this the dog's popularity fluctuated, until after World War I, when breeders became interested in its development.

CHARACTERISTICS: The Bichon Frise is a lively, but not high-strung dog, of considerable style and intelligence. Since its dense coat is silky and loosely curled (the "Frise" of its name), it does need grooming—scissoring, trimming, and brushing. The dog should have a powderpuff appearance. The Bichon Frise makes a pleasant apartment or house dog for those who like, or do not mind, grooming; and it is suitable for children. It is quite sturdy despite its "lapdog" cuddly appearance.

COLOR: Solid white, or white with cream, apricot, or gray on the ears and body. No black hair.

COAT: Thick, silky and loosely curled, with an undercoat.

HEIGHT: Dog: 8–12 inches. Bitch: 8–12 inches.

WEIGHT: Dog: 10–15 pounds. Bitch: 10–15 pounds.

PRICE RANGE: $200 and up.

BULLDOG, ENGLISH

BULLDOG, ENGLISH

HISTORY AND ORIGIN: The Bulldog originated in Great Britain in the early part of the thirteenth century. He got his name because he was trained to bait bulls, then one of the most popular English sports. Form, beauty, color, grace counted for nothing in this sport. The Bulldog simply had to be savage, absolutely fearless, and insensitive to pain. In 1835, when bull baiting became illegal, the dog no longer had a purpose and was in danger of becoming extinct. But so many breeders loved him that they decided to save the breed. They gradually bred out the savagery, cruelty, and viciousness, until we now have a fine, gentle dog.

CHARACTERISTICS: The Bulldog is affectionate, faithful, companionable, as well as reliable and trustworthy. A good house pet, he is perfectly suited for children, small and otherwise, and even excellent for a baby to grow up with.

He is not a very active dog, despite his origin and history, and can live anywhere, adapting to apartment, suburb, or farm. He is also very good with cats and gentle with kittens. He does not shed and requires little grooming. He is, however, short-lived for his size; his life span with the best of care is about 10–12 years, usually less.

A word of caution. He is subject to heart attacks if exposed to sudden heat. Like most short-nosed breeds, he tends to vomit and snore like a buzz saw.

COLOR: Brindle, white, red, or fawn.

COAT: Straight, short, flat, close, smooth, and glossy.

HEIGHT: Dog: 14½–15 inches. Bitch: 13½–14½ inches.

WEIGHT: Dog: 45–50 pounds. Bitch: 38–42 pounds.

PRICE RANGE: $150 and up.

BULLDOG, FRENCH

HISTORY AND ORIGIN: The proper name for the French Bulldog is Bouledogue français. We don't know his complete history and origin, but we do know that among his ancestors is one of the toy varieties of the English Bulldog. These toy English Bulldogs were never popular with the English, and in about 1860 many of them were shipped to France. French breeders crossed these little Bulls with small native dogs, until what we now call the French Bulldog evolved. In the late nineteenth century these dogs became very popular with fashionable ladies. This is still true today.

BULLDOG, FRENCH

CHARACTERISTICS: Smaller, more refined, and less bowlegged than the English Bull, the French Bulldog makes a perfect apartment dog for single men and women. He is affectionate, exceptionally peaceable, doesn't shed, and doesn't like or need to be exercised. He is not friendly with strangers or children. Like all short-nosed breeds, he does vomit a lot and has a constant quiet wheezing.

COLOR: Brindle, fawn, or white; or brindle-and-white.

COAT: Fine, short, smooth.

HEIGHT: Dog: 11½–12 inches. Bitch: 11–12 inches.

WEIGHT: Dog: 21–28 pounds (23 best). Bitch: 19–22 pounds (21 best).

PRICE RANGE: $125 and up.

CHOW CHOW

HISTORY AND ORIGIN: The national work dog of China, the Chow Chow dates back to the Han Dynasty, about 200 B.C. No one knows his origin, but the general theory is that he did not descend from the ancestors of the Western dog. Some believe that he descended from

CHOW CHOW

the polar bear because he is the only mammal in existence who shares a dark-blue tongue with the polar bear. Others tell us that he is a cross between the old Mastiff of Tibet and the Samoyed. And still others believe that he is the ancestor of the Samoyed, the Husky, the Norwegian Elkhound, the Keeshond, and the Pomeranian. The dog was first imported into England in 1880 and was favored by Queen Victoria.

CHARACTERISTICS: The Chow Chow is a one-man dog, intensely loyal and devoted to his owner. He is reserved, hardly ever expressing joy or delight, shrewd, aggressive, with a strong will of his own. With strangers he is always suspicious or indifferent. He is hardy, healthy, and strong, but not for a family with children. He is not suitable for a hot climate. He also needs a lot of grooming.

COLOR: Red, fawn, black, or blue.

COAT: Abundant, dense, straight, coarse.

HEIGHT: Dog: 19–20 inches. Bitch: 18–19 inches.

WEIGHT: Dog: 55–60 pounds. Bitch: 50–55 pounds.

PRICE RANGE: $175 and up; $400 and up for show quality.

DALMATIAN

DALMATIAN

HISTORY AND ORIGIN: We know very little about the origin of the Dalmatian. But there is no doubt that the ancients knew his ancestors, for a spotted dog similar to the Dalmatian shows up often in the art of ancient Greece and Rome. Since then the Dalmatian has passed through many stages, but we first hear of him as we know him today in the mid-eighteenth century in Dalmatia. From this time on, the activities of the Dalmatian have been more varied than those of almost any other dog. The Dalmatian at one time or another has been a war dog, a sentinel, a draft dog, a shepherd, a ratter, a sports dog, a fine house dog, a stable dog, and a follower of carriages.

CHARACTERISTICS: The Dalmatian is a good all-around pet, best suited for the suburbs or the country. Sturdy, hardy, intelligent, playful, and sweet-tempered, he makes friends easily, loves the family he lives with, and is a good playmate for children. But he is not a friend to all. His true affections belong to his owner and family.

He is not a noisy or quarrelsome dog, but a tough, stable, and even-tempered dog who is happiest when he has freedom, a lot of exercise, and the company of the people he loves. He is also a good guard dog.

He requires very little care and grooming, for he is strong, healthy, neat, and clean.

COLOR: Pure white marked with small, distinct spots of black or dark brown; size of spots should be anywhere from a dime to a half dollar, with spots on the face smaller than those on the body.

COAT: Short, hard, dense, fine, and glossy.

HEIGHT: Dog: 21–23 inches. Bitch: 19–21 inches.

WEIGHT: Dog: 45–50 pounds. Bitch: 35–45 pounds.

PRICE RANGE: $150 and up.

KEESHOND

KEESHOND

HISTORY AND ORIGIN: The national dog of Holland, the Keeshond was named after Kees de Glyselaer, a leader of "The Patriots," a nationalistic political party during the time of internal strife in Holland in the mid-eighteenth century. The ancestors of the Keeshond are the same as the ancestors of the Samoyed, the Norwegian Elkhound, the Finnish Spitz, and the Pomeranian. He seems most closely related to the Pomeranian.

The Keeshond was introduced into England in 1900 as the "Dutch Barge Dog" because he was seen on every barge in Holland.

CHARACTERISTICS: The Keeshond is a tough, very hardy and healthy dog. He can take any cold or heat, any terrain, and any living conditions. A one-man dog, he is devoted to his owner, whom he will defend with his life. With strangers he is polite, but cool and distrustful. One of the best house dogs and guards in the dog world, he must be trained carefully and properly by someone who knows dogs well. For he is high-strung, hypersensitive, and easily spoiled.

COLOR: Mixture of gray and black, outer edge black-tipped, under layer pale gray or cream.

COAT: Long, straight hair, with the hair standing straight out from the undercoat.

HEIGHT: Dog: 18 inches. Bitch: 17 inches.

WEIGHT: Dog: 35–40 pounds. Bitch: 32–36 pounds.

PRICE RANGE: $150 average.

LHASA APSO

LHASA APSO

HISTORY AND ORIGIN: Known in Tibet as "Abso Seng Kye"—Bark Sentinel Lion Dog—the Lhasa Apso has been in existence for well over eight hundred years. From the sixteenth century until as late as 1908, the Dalai Lama of Tibet gave this dog to the imperial families of China and to other important dignitaries from all over the world. The belief is that the Lhasa Apso brings good fortune to his owner.

CHARACTERISTICS: Extremely hardy, watchful, and easily trained, the Lhasa Apso is an excellent one-man dog. He is loyal, affectionate, and very responsive to kindness and love. He is also independent, a bit willful, and will tend to run the house if allowed. Like all the very small dogs, he should not be around young children. He needs a lot of grooming, but only a moderate amount of walking.

COLOR: Gold, black, white, brown, or parti-color; lionlike colors best.

COAT: Heavy, straight, hard, not woolly or silky.

HEIGHT: Dog: 10½–11 inches. Bitch: 10–10½ inches.

WEIGHT: Dog: 14–15 pounds. Bitch: 13–14 pounds.

PRICE RANGE: $150–$400 (the latter figure for show quality).

POODLE

POODLE

HISTORY AND ORIGIN: The name Poodle comes from the German "pudelin," meaning to splash in the water. Although known for years as the national dog of France, the Poodle originated in Germany and was brought into France in the fifteenth century by German mercenary troops. He became popular at once and was used extensively for hunting and retrieving, for which he was perfect because of his very heavy coat. In fact, the custom of clipping came about because part of the heavy coat impeded the dog's progress in water.

There is hardly a dog in existence who appears more often in the art and literature of the Mediterranean peoples. Now he is one of the most favored dogs throughout the world, nowhere more so than in the United States.

CHARACTERISTICS: Possibly the most intelligent of all dogs, the Poodle is even-tempered, affectionate, playful, and very obedient. He is a natural show-off and loves to do tricks. He is perfect for the family, especially if there are children around. A fine companion and friend, he is strong and very healthy. But his coat needs extensive care. It grows faster than that of other breeds, and, if you are going to show him, he must be clipped and trimmed in the standard cut. This is expensive.

Medically, his ears must be watched carefully. The hair there tends to block ventilation and drainage, and the ear passage may become stopped up with wax.

COLOR: Any solid color—black, brown, white, blue, apricot, silver, or café-au-lait.

COAT: Very profuse, harsh, and dense throughout.

HEIGHT AND WEIGHT: *Standard*—Dog and bitch over 15 inches. Dog: 44–55 pounds. Bitch: 40–50 pounds.

Miniature—Dog and bitch 15 inches or under; not under 10 inches. Dog: 15–16 pounds. Bitch: 14–15 pounds.

Toy—Dog and bitch under 10 inches. Dog: 6–7 pounds. Bitch: 5–6 pounds.

PRICE RANGE: $200 and up ($1000 and up for show quality).

SCHIPPERKE

HISTORY AND ORIGIN: The Schipperke or "little captain" goes back to the sixteenth century, to the Flemish provinces of Belgium. Although he resembles the Spitz family, the Schipperke is actually a small version of the old Belgian Sheepdog. This Sheepdog when bred larger gave us the Groenendael, when bred smaller the Schipperke. He became very popular about 1885 when Queen Marie Henriette, wife of Leopold II of Belgium, acquired a Schipperke.

CHARACTERISTICS: The Schipperke is probably the hardiest of all the small dogs. He can adapt to any climate and weather and can sleep anywhere provided he has a draft-free shelter. Combining all the qualities of a ratter, a watchdog, and a pet, he should be worked a lot, not pampered, and never overfed. His life centers around the family and the home. He does need lots of exercise, and he does shed. But he is supreme as a small, sturdy house dog. His appearance is distinctive, resembling no other breed closely.

SCHIPPERKE

COLOR: Solid black.
COAT: Abundant and slightly harsh.
HEIGHT: Dog: 12½–13 inches. Bitch: 12–12½ inches.
WEIGHT: Dog: 16–18 pounds. Bitch: 14–16 pounds.
PRICE RANGE: $125 and up.

TERRIER, BOSTON

HISTORY AND ORIGIN: One of the very few native American dogs, the Boston Terrier is the result of a cross between the English Bulldog and the white English Terrier, followed by constant inbreeding. In 1891 the Boston Terrier Club of America was formed, but the great progress in standardizing the breed rules came from 1900 on.

CHARACTERISTICS: The Boston Terrier is still one of the most popular breeds in the United States. He is a kind, gentle, affectionate, and obedient dog who responds to the slightest moods of his owner. He is also very adaptable and an excellent guard. As an apartment dog he is unbeatable. He has no body odor, does not shed, takes up little space, and is not a barker.

But he does have certain traits that may discourage some people. Like many of the short-nosed breeds, he vomits often, slobbers,

TERRIER, BOSTON

snores, and snorts. People who can't endure to see spots on their upholstered furniture, or are light sleepers, shouldn't get a Boston. This breed also has difficulty during whelping because the puppy has a large head, while the dam has a small pelvis.

COLOR: Brindle or black, with white markings.
COAT: Short, smooth, fine texture.
HEIGHT: Dog: 15–17 inches. Bitch: 14–16 inches.
WEIGHT: Dog: 20–25 pounds. Bitch: 13–19 pounds.
PRICE RANGE: $80–$250, depending on quality (average $175).

TERRIER, TIBETAN

HISTORY AND ORIGIN: The Tibetan Terrier derives, of course, from Tibet, but it is not, strictly speaking, a terrier. According to legend, the Tibetan was bred in monasteries by the lamas almost at the beginning of the Christian era. The dog was considered to bring good luck to owners and was also esteemed as a companion. The breed eventually passed into India, brought there by Dr. A. R. H. Greig, who was given a specimen dog by a patient's husband. When Dr. Greig re-

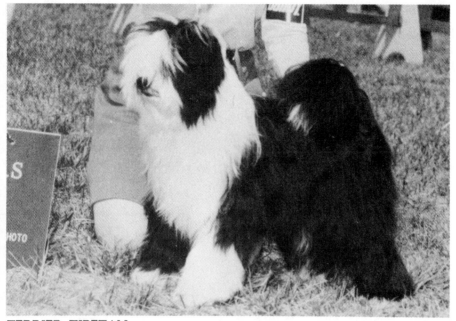

TERRIER, TIBETAN

turned to England, she established the Tibetan.

CHARACTERISTICS: Although called a terrier, the Tibetan is not a digger, nor does he have the yappy terrier disposition; he got the tag because his size was in the terrier classification. In their native land, Tibetans were called "Luck Bringers" or "Holy Dogs." The Tibetan was not raised as a working dog. Although it could take care of flocks, it was a companion rather than a guard or herd dog. And it remains today as a companion pet, sturdy, healthy, adaptable to either the coldest or the hottest weather. The Tibetan's coat will protect it against fierce winter, and yet the dog seems comfortable in extreme heat as well. The breed is recommended for people who want a stable, affectionate, and intelligent pet; it is fully suitable for small children. In appearance, the Tibetan seems like a miniature Old English Sheepdog.

COLOR: Any color, or combination of colors, including white.

COAT: Top coat very dense, fine, neither silky nor woolly; it can be straight or waved. Undercoat of fine wool.

HEIGHT: Dog: 14–16 inches. Bitch: 14–16 inches.

WEIGHT: Dog and bitch: 18–30 pounds, average, 22–23.

PRICE RANGE: $200 and up.

THE SPORTING BREEDS

These dogs hunt, point, and retrieve birds. Depending on the breed, they find and take game birds fallen on land or in the water. The 24 sporting breeds are:

GRIFFON, WIREHAIRED POINTING	SPANIEL, AMERICAN WATER
POINTER	SPANIEL, BRITTANY
POINTER, GERMAN SHORTHAIRED	SPANIEL, CLUMBER
POINTER, GERMAN WIREHAIRED	SPANIEL, COCKER
RETRIEVER, CHESAPEAKE BAY	SPANIEL, ENGLISH COCKER
RETRIEVER, CURLY-COATED	SPANIEL, ENGLISH SPRINGER
RETRIEVER, FLAT-COATED	SPANIEL, FIELD
RETRIEVER, GOLDEN	SPANIEL, IRISH WATER
RETRIEVER, LABRADOR	SPANIEL, SUSSEX
SETTER, ENGLISH	SPANIEL, WELSH SPRINGER
SETTER, GORDON	VIZSLA
SETTER, IRISH	WEIMARANER

GRIFFON, WIREHAIRED POINTING

HISTORY AND ORIGIN: The Wirehaired Pointing Griffon originated in Holland in the last quarter of the nineteenth century. Nevertheless, most breeders think of this breed as French because the dog as we know him today was developed in France. It is not clear precisely what breeds were crossed to make up the Griffon, but we do know that he is partially a mixture of Spaniel, Setter, and Otter Hound, along with traces of the German Shorthaired Pointer. The Griffon is the only pointing breed with a harsh coat recognized by the American Kennel Club.

CHARACTERISTICS: The Wirehaired Pointing Griffon is deliberate and slow in the field, but he has an excellent nose, points well, and performs adequately as a retriever. He is a strong swimmer. His harsh coat makes him suitable for swamp country and serves as a protection against extreme cold.

Calm, reserved, and even-tempered, he is loyal to his owner and good with the family and children. He is not an apartment dog, not a city dog, but a sporting dog who belongs in the country enjoying his natural life.

COLOR: Steel-gray with chestnut splashes, or gray-white with chestnut splashes, or chestnut, or dirty white mixed with chestnut. Avoid black.

GRIFFON, WIREHAIRED POINTING

POINTER

COAT: Hard, dry, stiff. Should never be curly.
HEIGHT: Dog: 21½–23½ inches. Bitch: 19½–21½ inches.
WEIGHT: Dog: 50–60 pounds. Bitch: 45–55 pounds.
PRICE RANGE: $150.

POINTER

HISTORY AND ORIGIN: The exact place of origin of the Pointer is not known, but most authorities agree that he was developed in Spain, France, and Belgium about three hundred and fifty years ago. By the middle of the seventeenth century, he was well known in Spain and France, but it is the English who developed the Pointer we know today; and they did this at the beginning of the eighteenth century. The "Setting Spaniel" is the basic stock of the Pointer, along with a mixture of Foxhound, Greyhound, and Bloodhound.

The first Pointers were used to locate and point hares, after which Greyhounds were brought in for the chase and the kill. At the start of the eighteenth century, wing shooting came into vogue, and from that time the Pointer became the gun dog of England.

CHARACTERISTICS: Generally recognized as the best bird-finding dog in the world, the Pointer is intelligent, affectionate, and loyal to his owner but reserved with strangers. He is large and rangy, needs plenty of room and lots of exercise to insure good health. His coat is short-haired and easy to care for.

The Pointer is not a dog for the city and particularly not for an apartment. Above all, he is a hunting dog and therefore belongs in the country. He is not generally recommended as a family pet, for many Pointers have quick tempers.

COLOR: White with liver markings, or with lemon, orange, or black markings. Head, parts of back, and tail should be colored.
COAT: Short, dense, smooth, with a sheen.
HEIGHT: Dog: 24–25 inches. Bitch: 23–24 inches.
WEIGHT: Dog: 55–60 pounds. Bitch: 50–55 pounds.
PRICE RANGE: $125–$175.

POINTER, GERMAN SHORTHAIRED

HISTORY AND ORIGIN: The German Shorthaired Pointer originated in Germany about three hundred years ago. His ancestors, however, were the Spanish Pointers, which the Germans imported in the seventeenth century. The Bloodhound was then crossed with the Spanish Pointer

POINTER, GERMAN SHORTHAIRED

POINTER, GERMAN WIREHAIRED

to acquire more nose, greater intelligence, and better trailing instinct. The result was also a dog with big bones and much less speed than the original Pointer. The Foxhound was then bred in for speed, but the pointing instinct disappeared. Finally, the English Pointer brought pointing blood, and the Germans had a dog we now recognize as the Shorthaired Pointer.

CHARACTERISTICS: A good all-around hunting dog, the German Shorthaired Pointer has a keen nose, can point well, and has the strength and courage to retrieve from icy waters. He is not a fast dog, but rugged and determined. He should not be used for a long hunt.

He is generally a one-man dog. With his owner he is loyal, affectionate, and playful; with others he is reserved, and he does not make friends quickly. He is hardly ever unpredictable or moody, and almost never mean. He is good with a family and children, but should not be used exclusively as a family pet. He is a hunter and does not belong in the city and certainly not in an apartment. Such a breed needs a lot of room and a good deal of exercise. He is also very easy to groom because his hair is short.

COLOR: Solid liver, or liver-and-white spotted or ticked. Avoid any colors other than liver and white.

COAT: Skin close and tight, the hair short and thick, tough and hard to the touch.

HEIGHT: Dog: 23–25 inches. Bitch: 21–23 inches.

WEIGHT: Dog: 55–70 pounds. Bitch: 45–60 pounds.

PRICE RANGE: $125–$175.

POINTER, GERMAN WIREHAIRED

HISTORY AND ORIGIN: The exact origin of the German Wirehaired Pointer is unknown, but most of the early dogs were a combination of the Griffon, the Pudelpointer (a cross between a Poodle and an English Pointer bitch), and the German Shorthaired Pointer. What breeders wanted was an all-purpose dog to hunt game in any weather in any place. The Wirehaired was developed in Germany in the middle of the nineteenth century.

CHARACTERISTICS: The German Wirehaired Pointer is a tough, rugged, very courageous hunting dog with great stamina. He is highly intelligent, affectionate, kind, but attached only to his owner. With others he is reserved and very cautious. He should not be kept in the city and never in an apartment, for he is a field dog and should be allowed his natural life. He can adapt to any weather and any terrain, is of even temperament, and makes a wonderful companion in the field. His short coat is easy to care for.

COLOR: Liver-and-white, liver-and-white spotted, sometimes solid liver.
COAT: Straight, harsh, wiry, and flat.
HEIGHT: Dog: 24–26 inches. Bitch: 22–24 inches.
WEIGHT: Dog: 60–70 pounds. Bitch: 50–60 pounds.
PRICE RANGE: $150–$250.

RETRIEVER, CHESAPEAKE BAY

HISTORY AND ORIGIN: The origin of the Chesapeake Bay Retriever is uncertain, but we do know that one of his ancestors is the Newfoundland of one hundred and fifty years ago. In about 1807, an English brig went down off the coast of Maryland. Among the rescued were two Newfoundland puppies. They were brought up by a George Law, who crossed them with yellow-and-tan Coonhounds, obtaining the greater nose, strength, and stamina, as well as the "deadgrass" color, yellow eye, and long tail.

CHARACTERISTICS: The Chesapeake is probably superior to any other dog in his ability to withstand icy water. He loves it and leaps in to retrieve fowl. He also has great stamina, along with a remarkable memory. He is a good hunter on land and water, and a marvelous duck retriever.

This is a very rugged and intelligent dog with an intense desire to please. Often he will be a one-man dog, although he is friendly and affectionate with other members of the family. But once trained by one person, he most probably will not allow himself to be retrained by another.

The Chesapeake makes a fine house dog, is trustworthy with children, travels well in cars, and generally takes over the protection of the home and family. Quiet, calm, never high-strung, he is steady, loyal, and devoted.

COLOR: Any solid color from a very dark brown to a faded tan, with or without white spot on breast.
COAT: Thick and short, 1½ inches or under in length, with dense, fine woolly undercoat.
HEIGHT: Dog: 23–26 inches. Bitch: 21–24 inches.
WEIGHT: Dog: 65–75 pounds. Bitch: 55–65 pounds.
PRICE RANGE: $200 and up.

RETRIEVER, CURLY-COATED

HISTORY AND ORIGIN: No one knows the true origin of the Curly-coated Retriever, but most authorities believe that he is descended from

RETRIEVER, CHESAPEAKE BAY

RETRIEVER, CURLY-COATED

RETRIEVER, FLAT-COATED

the sixteenth-century Irish Water Spaniel and the retrieving Setter. The dog as we know him today was described as far back as 1803. To obtain this breed, a small Newfoundland was crossed with either an English or an Irish Water Spaniel or a Poodle. All of these crosses were tried, but no one knows which resulted in the Curly-coated Retriever. The dog was first shown in 1859.

CHARACTERISTICS: The Curly-coated Retriever is tough, eager to go into the water, and possesses incredible stamina. He is also an aggressive dog, smart, and very good in the field. Although naturally cautious with those he doesn't know, he is completely loyal and devoted to his owner and excellent with the family. He is, however, difficult to care for because his curly coat must be brushed often. He is not a dog for the city and never for an apartment. He should be allowed his natural life—permitted to hunt, swim, and run about a good deal. He also needs careful and forceful handling as a puppy, or he may become snappish and mistrustful.

COLOR: Black or liver.

COAT: Crisp curls over the entire body.

HEIGHT: Dog: 23–24 inches. Bitch: 22–23 inches.

WEIGHT: Dog: 65–70 pounds. Bitch: 55–65 pounds.

PRICE RANGE: $200 and up.

RETRIEVER, FLAT-COATED

HISTORY AND ORIGIN: The Flat-coated Retriever originated as a result of a cross between the Lesser Newfoundland and the Labrador Retriever. Gamekeepers then bred this cross with Pointers and Setters, and by 1860 they produced a dog that approximated the Flat-coated Retriever we know today. What they wanted, and obtained, was a great natural water dog and a good retriever.

CHARACTERISTICS: Easygoing and easy to train, with a gentle and serene disposition, the Flat-coated Retriever is one of the best gun dogs around. He is also a natural water dog and can retrieve fowl in any temperature. For someone who enjoys upland hunting and duck shooting and wants a wonderful field companion, this is a fine dog.

No dog is better with children. He has great natural warmth and will endure anything from them, for he never gets excited. With strangers, however, he is cool and reserved, his owner and family being his whole life. He should be exercised about two hours a day.

COLOR: Black or liver.

COAT: Dense, fine texture, as flat as possible.

HEIGHT: Dog: 23 inches. Bitch: 22 inches.

WEIGHT: Dog: 65–70 pounds. Bitch: 60–65 pounds.

PRICE RANGE: $200 and up.

RETRIEVER, GOLDEN

RETRIEVER, LABRADOR

RETRIEVER, GOLDEN

HISTORY AND ORIGIN: There are two legends regarding the origin of the Golden Retriever. The first, colorful and romantic, has it that in 1860 an English nobleman saw a troupe of Russian performing dogs in London and was so impressed with their ability that he bought the whole troupe on the spot. The dogs, called Russian Trackers, were able to withstand the rigors of the worst Russian winters. The Golden Retriever comes from a cross between these Trackers and the Bloodhound.

The second and most recent theory holds that the Golden Retriever originated from a cross between a Gordon Setter and a Lesser Newfoundland. The dogs of this mixture were then crossed with a tough retrieving Spaniel called the Tweed Water Spaniel. The Golden Retriever as we know him is a result of this cross and was recognized in 1913 by the British Kennel Club.

CHARACTERISTICS: One of the greatest of hunting dogs, the Golden Retriever has all the abilities of the Setter and the Retriever on land and on water, along with the scenting power of the Bloodhound. But his greatest ability is in retrieving from water. He has a soft mouth and can withstand the iciest of waters and the coldest of temperatures. Tough, proud, and capable of incredible endurance, he is the perfect companion in the field.

The Golden Retriever is friendly, lovable, and kindly, and therefore an excellent companion to children as well as the whole family. With his owner he is absolutely loyal, cheerful, and trustworthy. In my opinion, the Golden Retriever is one of the best all-around dogs, peerless both as a hunter and as a pet. He is good for the country and the city, but he should be exercised about two hours a day.

COLOR: A rich gold of different shades, without any white spots.

COAT: Texture is not as hard as that of a short-haired dog, yet not as silky as that of a Setter. Coat should be flat against the body, dense, and water-repellent.

HEIGHT: Dog: 23–24 inches. Bitch: 21½–22½ inches.

WEIGHT: Dog: 65–75 pounds. Bitch: 60–70 pounds.

PRICE RANGE: $300 average.

RETRIEVER, LABRADOR

HISTORY AND ORIGIN: Contrary to popular belief, the Labrador Retriever does not come from Labrador but from Newfoundland. The origin of the Labrador, however, remains a mystery. All we know is that his ancestors were brought by fishermen to England in about 1800. Once they reached England, they were crossed with Flat and Curly-Coated Retrievers to give us the Labrador we know today.

CHARACTERISTICS: Large, handsome, and intelligent, the Labrador Retriever is probably the most even-tempered dog extant. He is good for any kind of shooting and is unbeatable as a water retriever. By temperament he is calm, polite, reserved, gentle, and absolutely faithful, but not very affectionate. He is not a fighter, nor is he aggressive. He is responsible and excellent with children. He can adapt to any conditions, which makes him an ideal shooting companion and pet. He needs about two hours of exercise daily, especially if he is kept as an apartment dog. He has one dangerous habit: He loves to swallow rocks. He should, therefore, be watched carefully.

COLOR: Black, or dark chocolate, or yellow from fox-red to light cream.

COAT: Short, very dense, hard to the touch, and without a wave.

HEIGHT: Dog: 22½–24½ inches. Bitch: 21½–23½ inches.

WEIGHT: Dog: 60–75 pounds. Bitch: 55–70 pounds.

PRICE RANGE: $175–$225.

SETTER, ENGLISH

HISTORY AND ORIGIN: The English Setter can trace his ancestors to some of the Land Spaniels that originally came from Spain. In fact, in the sixteenth century he was referred to as a Spaniel (originally the same word as *español,* meaning Spanish), although he did not look like one. His tail, then as now, was not docked, and he resembled the Setter we know today. The Setter was produced from a combination of the Spanish Pointer, the Large Water Spaniel, and the Springer Spaniel, the final development taking place in about 1825 in England.

CHARACTERISTICS: The English Setter is a beautiful, rugged, intelligent dog, with a stable, mild, and sweet disposition. He is a great hunter, as well as a wonderful pet; love and affection are as necessary to him as is food. Also, his hunting ability is not spoiled when he becomes a family pet. Unlike the Labrador, he is openly friendly to everyone.

He reacts extremely well to obedience training. He should, however, receive a good deal of exercise, and therefore I do not recommend him for apartment life unless he can be run at least two hours daily.

COLOR: Black, white, and tan; black and white; blue, lemon, and white; orange and white; liver and white; or solid white.

COAT: Flat, of good length, but without a curl; should not be soft or woolly.

HEIGHT: Dog: 23–25 inches. Bitch: 23–24 inches.

WEIGHT: Dog: 60–70 pounds. Bitch: 50–60 pounds.
PRICE RANGE: $200.

SETTER, GORDON

HISTORY AND ORIGIN: Named after the Duke of Gordon, this handsome Black-and-Tan Setter from Scotland dates back to at least 1620. He became well known to hunters at the end of the eighteenth century, when he acquired a reputation for good staying power and an excellent nose. In the early 1840s, Daniel Webster brought him to America, where he immediately became a great favorite with our hunters.

CHARACTERISTICS: A beautiful and highly intelligent dog, the Gordon Setter is absolutely loyal and devoted to his owner and family, but especially to his owner. He is a perfect one-man shooting dog. His great drawback is that he lacks the speed of the other setters.

He is also excellent with children, for he is good-tempered and not given to jealousy or quarreling with other dogs, except when a strange dog demands the attention of his family. He is much less friendly with strangers than are other setters, probably because of the hound in him, and he is much quieter and more stable than the Irish Setter.

He should not be made to spend days in a kennel and should not be kept with a lot of other dogs. The Gordon needs a good deal of exercise and is therefore better suited for the country than for apartment life.

COLOR: Rich coal-black with tan markings, markings of deep chestnut color on throat, chest, inside of hind legs, and thighs.

COAT: Soft and shining, like silk, slightly waved but not curly.

HEIGHT: Dog: 24–27 inches. Bitch: 23–26 inches.

WEIGHT: Dog 55–75 pounds. Bitch: 45–65 pounds.

PRICE RANGE: $200.

SETTER, IRISH

HISTORY AND ORIGIN: As is true of most breeds, the origin of the Irish Setter is uncertain at best. Some believe that he developed from a cross between an Irish Water Spaniel and an Irish Terrier. The opinion most widely held is that he came from a combination of English Setter, Spaniel, Pointer, and Gordon.

The Irish Setter first came to public attention at the beginning of the eighteenth century, when he was bred to be a gun dog, first and foremost, and it is as a gun dog that he must stand or fall.

SETTER, ENGLISH

SETTER, GORDON

SETTER, IRISH

Then the Setter was red-and-white, and white often prevailed over red. The solid-red Setter we recognize today first appeared in Ireland early in the nineteenth century. He was an instant favorite. By the late 1860s, he was imported to the United States as a bird dog. But his beauty was almost a fatal gift because he was bred mostly for show. Today he is nearly always a pet.

CHARACTERISTICS: The most highly strung and temperamental of the Setters, the Irish Setter is trustworthy and loyal. His ability to search out and find birds, especially in rough country, is probably unsurpassed in the dog world. But he is not an early developer and requires a good deal of training and patient care.

He is happiest when he can be completely devoted to someone. He is boisterous, loves to show off before his owner and family, is a born actor and a real clown. He is extremely possessive and usually wants to run the whole family. He is also independent, a real individual with a mind of his own and a good deal of pride.

A word of warning. Because he has been inbred, the Irish Setter may tend to be nervous and suffer from depression. He may also tend to be headstrong, stubborn, and highly temperamental. The owner must know how to handle him. He is more a country than a city dog.

COLOR: Rich golden-chestnut red or mahogany; no black.
COAT: Moderate length and flat.
HEIGHT: Dog: 24–26 inches. Bitch: 23–25 inches.
WEIGHT: Dog: 55–60 pounds. Bitch: 50–55 pounds.
PRICE RANGE: $175–$250.

SPANIEL, AMERICAN WATER

HISTORY AND ORIGIN: We don't know the origin of the American Water Spaniel, except that he comes from our Middle West, and his color, coat, and body structure suggest that his ancestors were the Irish Water Spaniel and the Curly-Coated Retriever. He was recognized by the American Kennel Club in 1940.

CHARACTERISTICS: The American Water Spaniel is just the dog for the person who loves the outdoors and hunts near water. The dog is a first-rate retriever on land or in the water, with a faultless nose and a curly coat to protect him in any temperature. He is also a great swimmer, and no waterfowl ever escapes him. He also does very well with rabbits, grouse, pheasants, and quail. He is not a pointer—he springs his game.

The disposition of the American Water Spaniel is excellent. Intelligent, alert, always full of vitality, this dog makes you feel like the best hunter alive. Peaceful, stable, and adaptable by temperament, he is fond of people, especially children, and makes a fine family pet. He should, however, be trained carefully, for he is sensitive to praise and blame and will sulk if treated badly. He never seems to forget those who have been unkind to him. He can live in the city as well as the country, but he should get a good deal of exercise.

COLOR: Solid rich liver or dark chocolate, with a little white on toes or chest.

COAT: Closely curled and dense for protection against weather.

HEIGHT: Dog: 16½–18 inches. Bitch: 15–17 inches.

WEIGHT: Dog: 28–45 pounds. Bitch: 20–40 pounds.

PRICE RANGE: $125 and up.

SPANIEL, BRITTANY

HISTORY AND ORIGIN: A French breed familiar to hunters in Europe for hundreds of years, the Brittany Spaniel is much more a Setter than it is a Spaniel. The Brittany's ancestors, like the ancestors of all Spaniels, Pointers, and Setters, came from Spain, the original stock being Spanish Pointer and Spaniel.

The first tailless ancestor of the Britanny we know today was bred about one hundred years ago at Pontou, France. He was a good field dog. The contemporary history of the Brittany begins in the early twentieth century. The breed at that time was almost extinct from excessive inbreeding and had never been shown. The French took an interest in him and by 1907 had completely rehabilitated him.

CHARACTERISTICS: Aggressive, courageous, loyal, but not elegant or handsome, the Brittany is one of the best retrievers and gun dogs. He can take any water, and he is fearless of thickets. He is a one-man dog, deeply devoted to his owner, but ugly and mean with strangers. He is a perfect watchdog, guarding his owner's property even at the cost of his life. He may be kept as a pet, but is best as a working and a sporting dog.

COLOR: Dark orange-and-white or liver-and-white; some ticking is good. Avoid black.

COAT: Dense, flat or wavy; should never be curly or silky; coat not as fine as that of other spaniels.

HEIGHT: Dog: 18½–20½ inches. Bitch: 17½–19½ inches.

WEIGHT: Dog: 35–40 pounds. Bitch: 30–35 pounds.

PRICE RANGE: $100 and up.

SPANIEL, AMERICAN WATER

SPANIEL, BRITTANY

SPANIEL, CLUMBER

SPANIEL, CLUMBER

HISTORY AND ORIGIN: Because the Clumber is so different from the other Spaniels, we cannot be sure what his origin is. The color, coat, and body of the Clumber today do suggest, however, that his long, low body comes from the Basset Hound and the heavy head from the early Alpine Spaniel.

The Clumber got his name from Clumber Park, the home of the Duke of Newcastle in Nottingham. The Duke favored the breed and was responsible for making him popular in England in the mid-nineteenth century.

CHARACTERISTICS: The Clumber is a very serious, cautious, responsible, and faithful dog. A slow worker and a splendid retriever, he has great strength and durability. But he has a sullen disposition, almost always preferring one owner to many.

In appearance, he is a long, low, heavy-looking dog with a large, massive head, overhanging lip of the upper jaw, large, soft, deep-set eyes. He has pear-shaped ears, and his face resembles that of a St. Bernard.

COLOR: Lemon-and-white or orange-and-white; the fewer the markings on the body, the better.

COAT: Dense, silky, and straight, not very long.

HEIGHT: Dog: 16–18 inches. Bitch: 14–16 inches.

WEIGHT: Dog: 55–65 pounds. Bitch: 35–50 pounds.

PRICE RANGE: $125 average.

SPANIEL, COCKER

HISTORY AND ORIGIN: One of the oldest of the land Spaniels, the Cocker goes back as far as the fourteenth century. In fact, the dog is mentioned by the English poet Chaucer in his *Canterbury Tales:* "for as a Spaynel she would on him lepe." Frequent references to Spaniels are made in household records of Henry VIII and throughout the seventeenth, eighteenth, and nineteenth centuries. The dog got the name "Cocker" because he was an excellent hunter of woodcock. When carefully trained, he is still a good hunting dog and will also retrieve. In 1892 he was recognized as a breed by the British Kennel Club. In this century, the English and American varieties have been distinguished from each other chiefly in size and temperament.

CHARACTERISTICS: The Cocker is intelligent, extremely loving and affectionate, and easily trained. But he is prone to illness, especially indiges-

SPANIEL, COCKER

SPANIEL, ENGLISH COCKER

SPANIEL, ENGLISH SPRINGER

tion, for he swallows everything in sight. He has a tendency to discharge from the eyes and to develop ear trouble. He also is subject to cataracts and rheumatism-like ailments.

Although small, he sheds a lot and should have a good deal of exercise. The dog as he is today does not always fit well into family life in an apartment, for he is somewhat temperamental. There are, of course, many individual exceptions.

COLOR: Black, white, and tan or liver. Black is good, but should be coalblack; white in chest and throat only.

COAT: Flat or slightly wavy, silky and of medium length; never curly.

HEIGHT: Dog: 15 inches. Bitch: 14 inches.

WEIGHT: Dog: 24–28 pounds. Bitch: 22–26 pounds.

PRICE RANGE: $125 average.

SPANIEL, ENGLISH COCKER

HISTORY AND ORIGIN: The English Cocker has the same history and origin as the Cocker Spaniel, going back to the fourteenth century. When the Cocker breed was first recognized in 1892, it was in fact the larger-sized English Cocker. The American Cocker (or Cocker Spaniel) is a smaller dog resulting from other Spaniel combinations, and the two kinds of Cockers have gradually been separated for show purposes.

CHARACTERISTICS: The English Cocker's characteristics are generally the same as those for the Cocker Spaniel, except that the English Cocker makes a better house pet on some counts. He is more settled, less temperamental, and less liable to snappishness.

COLOR: Various colors, although no one color should predominate.

COAT: Flat or somewhat wavy and silky on the body, short on the head.

HEIGHT: Dog: 16–17 inches. Bitch: 15–16 inches.

WEIGHT: Dog: 28–34 pounds. Bitch: 26–32 pounds.

PRICE RANGE: $125 and up ($250 and up for show quality).

SPANIEL, ENGLISH SPRINGER

HISTORY AND ORIGIN: We cannot trace the Springer's origin, but most authorities feel sure that the Springer descended from the original Spaniel, and some suspect that this original goes back thousands of years. In the Metropolitan Museum of Art in New York, there is a figure of a dog dating from 3000 B.C. with all the Spaniel characteristics. We cannot be sure, however, if these dogs were the Spaniels as we know them today. But in 1387, Gaston de Foix, a French nobleman, wrote about the Spaniel we now know in one of the most famous hunting books of all time, the *Déduits de la Chasse*.

CHARACTERISTICS: Trained as a field dog and particularly as a duck retriever, the Springer has adapted himself to domesticity. He loves people and life, is completely ingratiating. With children he will endure ear pulling, roughhousing of any kind, and come back for more. His affection embraces the entire family, although he may be cool with strangers.

The Springer makes an excellent watchdog—he will bark fiercely at the approach of strangers. He loves to go out in the woods, but is also a good car traveler. His rugged coat allows him to stand all degrees of cold weather. He adapts well to apartment life provided he receives sufficient exercise. The long coat, however, does need attention, although not as much as the silky-haired coats. The Springer tends to suffer in excessively warm weather. He sheds regularly, is a moderate eater, and seems to exist to please his owners.

COLOR: Black or liver with white markings; liver-and-white or black-and-white with tan markings; blue or liver roan; predominantly white with tan, black, or liver markings.

COAT: Flat or wavy, of medium length.

HEIGHT: Dog: 18–20 inches. Bitch: 17–19 inches.

WEIGHT: Dog: 47–55 pounds. Bitch: 35–45 pounds.

PRICE RANGE: $125 and up.

SPANIEL, FIELD

HISTORY AND ORIGIN: The Field Spaniel was established by repeated crosses of Welsh Cocker with Sussex Spaniel.

CHARACTERISTICS: The Field Spaniel is not very good as a field dog, for he is slow and does not retrieve well. He is best as a companion in the field and as a family pet, for he is calm, emotionally well balanced, loving, and intelligent. He also makes a good house dog because he doesn't have that "doggy" smell many people object to.

COLOR: Black, liver, golden liver, or mahogany red.

COAT: Flat or slightly waved but never curled; dense and silky.

HEIGHT: Dog: 18 inches. Bitch: 17 inches.

WEIGHT: Dog: 45–50 pounds. Bitch: 35–45 pounds.

PRICE RANGE: $125 average.

SPANIEL, IRISH WATER

HISTORY AND ORIGIN: The ancestors of the Irish Water Spaniel may go back as far as 4000 B.C., for there is mention of a dog very much like

SPANIEL, FIELD

SPANIEL, IRISH WATER

SPANIEL, SUSSEX

him in Persian manuscripts of that time. Next we hear of him in about 15 A.D. in certain Irish laws. No one knows how he got there, but current belief is that he was brought through Spain from beyond the Caucasus by the earliest inhabitants of Ireland. From the time he arrived in Ireland, he was a great favorite, and Shakespeare in *The Two Gentlemen of Verona* pays him a high compliment indeed. He has Launce tell us that the girl he loves ". . . hath more qualities than a water-spaniel—which is much in a bare Christian." The breed as we know it today goes back about one hundred years.

CHARACTERISTICS: Known to all as the clown of the Spaniels, yet bearing almost no resemblance to any other Spaniel we know, the Irish is one of the greatest of water dogs. He loves water and can withstand any temperature. Because of his thick coat with its dense crisp ringlets, he is also well adapted to work in bogs and marshes. He has great stamina and speed, as well as a very fine nose, which he uses to full advantage in frosty weather, when scenting conditions are poor.

He loves his owner, and is absolutely loyal and faithful to him or her and the family. He is cool and very reserved with strangers, and in general is not sociable with other dogs.

COLOR: Solid liver.

COAT: Dense, with thick, crisp ringlets; should not look woolly.

HEIGHT: Dog: 22–24 inches. Bitch: 21–23 inches.

WEIGHT: Dog: 55–65 pounds. Bitch: 45–55 pounds.

PRICE RANGE: $150–$250.

SPANIEL, SUSSEX

HISTORY AND ORIGIN: One of the oldest of the Spaniel family, the Sussex as we know him today goes back to the middle of the nineteenth century to the English County of Sussex, from which he gets his name. In those days he was used for rough shooting, when game was in great abundance and when hunting on foot was the custom, for he is slow and determined, and a hunter needs a lot of patience with him. For that reason he has not caught on as a hunting dog in this country.

CHARACTERISTICS: The Sussex Spaniel is a country dog, companionable, massive, and sturdy. He is steady, courageous, determined, as well as calm and serene—the perfect combination for the owner who does not want a fidgety pet. He has no "doggy" odor, and this adds to his attractiveness as a house pet.

COLOR: Rich golden liver is best, a sign of pure breeding.

COAT: Dense, flat or slightly waved, but never curled.

HEIGHT: Dog: 15–16 inches. Bitch: 14–15 inches.

WEIGHT: Dog: 40–45 pounds. Bitch: 35–40 pounds.
PRICE RANGE: $125 average.

SPANIEL, WELSH SPRINGER

SPANIEL, WELSH SPRINGER

HISTORY AND ORIGIN: From a study of old prints, pictures, and manuscripts, we know that the Welsh Springer Spaniel goes back about four hundred years to Wales. The Welsh Springer is still principally a Welsh dog, but many of his brothers are now all over the English-speaking world because of their ability to withstand extreme heat and cold.

CHARACTERISTICS: If well trained, the Welsh Springer makes an excellent hunter, for he is indefatigable, but if he is not well trained he will go off by himself. He is also a good water dog (he has a soft undercoat as well as a flat topcoat) and a superb gun dog. In fact, his normal life is as a gun dog. As a household pet he has a good, even disposition, is merry and devoted.

He will adapt to any extremes of heat and cold as well as to any kind of terrain. He is unequaled for zeal, toughness, and staying power. I recommend him for children and for apartment life, provided he can get the exercise his entire breed demands to stay in good shape.

COLOR: Rich dark-red-and-white.

COAT: Straight or flat, thick and silky, never wiry or wavy, and never curly.

HEIGHT: Dog: 16–17 inches. Bitch: 15½–16½ inches.

WEIGHT: Dog: 35–40 pounds. Bitch: 32–37 pounds.
PRICE RANGE: $125 average.

VIZSLA

VIZSLA

HISTORY AND ORIGIN: The Vizsla, or the Hungarian Pointer, goes back well over one thousand years to the Magyar invasions of Europe. He was then a great favorite with the barons and the lords, and a dog closely resembling the modern Vizsla is mentioned in Hungarian literature of the fourteenth century. He was also used in falconry in the Middle Ages. The Vizsla has remained a favorite hunting dog of the Hungarians to this day.

CHARACTERISTICS: Aristocratic in bearing, the Vizsla is a one-man dog, slavishly devoted and loyal to his owner but at times reserved and aloof with all others, except the immediate family. He is a fine hunter in flat country, swift, cautious, and highly intelligent. He never alerts his quarry, and he is superb as both a pointer and a retriever. He also works well on upland game, especially on rabbits.

COLOR: Solid rusty-gold or dark sandy-yellow; dark brown and pale yellow not desirable.

COAT: Short, smooth, dense.

HEIGHT: Dog: 22–24 inches. Bitch: 21–23 inches.

WEIGHT: Dog 45–60 pounds. Bitch: 40–55 pounds.

PRICE RANGE: $175–$250 and up for show quality.

WEIMARANER

WEIMARANER

HISTORY AND ORIGIN: The Weimaraner dates back to the first years of the nineteenth century, and we are almost certain that one of his ancestors was the Bloodhound.

The dog we see today is the result of very careful crossbreeding, after generations of linebreeding to fix a certain type and temperament. The Weimaraner used to be trained to hunt wildcats, deer, and even mountain lions and bears. When these animals disappeared in Germany, he was trained as a bird dog and retriever. Now he is used more and more as a hunting companion. The Weimaraner became known here in 1929.

CHARACTERISTICS: The Weimaraner respects authority, needs it, and thrives on it. He is also highly individualistic and shows it, but his owner must not let him get away with anything or the dog will lose respect for him.

He is very active and must keep busy. If the owner does not give him things to do, he will invent things. He likes to be a show-off, if permitted. The Weimaraner is adaptable to any climate and any living conditions.

The breed still possesses a remarkable nose and tracking ability and is fearless, extremely courageous, obedient, and eager to please. If trained very young, he will make a good shooting dog. Also, he is more of a watchdog than other hunting dogs are, being very forceful and aggressive. He is good with his family and gentle with children.

COLOR: Shades varying from mouse-gray to silver-gray.

COAT: Short, smooth, sleek.

HEIGHT: Dog: 25–27 inches. Bitch: 23–25 inches.

WEIGHT: Dog: 70–85 pounds. Bitch: 55–70 pounds.

PRICE RANGE: $175 and up.

THE TERRIER BREEDS

The terriers are named after the Latin word for earth, *terra,* where they ferret out rats and other rodents. They were developed to work on farms and estates, although at present they are almost exclusively pets. The 22 terrier breeds are:

AIREDALE TERRIER

AMERICAN STAFFORDSHIRE TERRIER

AUSTRALIAN TERRIER

BEDLINGTON TERRIER

BORDER TERRIER

BULL TERRIER

CAIRN TERRIER

DANDIE DINMONT TERRIER

FOX TERRIER: SMOOTH

WIRE

IRISH TERRIER

KERRY BLUE TERRIER

LAKELAND TERRIER

MANCHESTER TERRIER

NORWICH TERRIER

SCHNAUZER, MINIATURE

SCOTTISH TERRIER ("SCOTTIE")

SEALYHAM TERRIER

SKYE TERRIER

SOFT-COATED WHEATEN TERRIER

STAFFORDSHIRE BULL TERRIER

WELSH TERRIER

WEST HIGHLAND WHITE TERRIER

AIREDALE TERRIER

AIREDALE TERRIER

HISTORY AND ORIGIN: We know nothing precise about the Airedale prior to 1850, but we do know that he goes back centuries to the Broken-haired or Old English Terrier. Early in the nineteenth century, this terrier was crossed with the rough-coated Otter Hound to add nose and swimming prowess to an already alert, agile, and friendly dog. The name of the breed originated in a strange way. In 1879, at an agricultural show at Bingley, Yorkshire, a large group of "Waterside Terriers" so impressed the judges that they named the breed after the show, which was called the Airedale show.

CHARACTERISTICS: Often called the "king of the terriers," the Airedale is the largest of the Terrier family. He is bold, courageous, and, like all terriers, aggressive, but since he has been bred as a working dog he is not high-strung and never hysterical. He is a marvelous hunter—he is one of the few dogs who will go after grizzly bears—and a good retriever of big ducks. Easy to train, generally mild in disposition, and gay and friendly, he is also perhaps the best ratter in the dog world. He is loyal, faithful, and devoted, and good with children who like a spirited, energetic dog. Since the Airedale needs a good deal of exercise to work off his energy, he is best suited for country or suburban life, although many apartment owners have found him satisfactory. He needs little grooming.

COLOR: Rich tan with black or grizzle markings.

COAT: Hard, dense, wiry, lying straight and close.

HEIGHT: Dog: 23 inches. Bitch: 22 inches.

WEIGHT: Dog: 45–50 pounds. Bitch: 40–45 pounds.

PRICE RANGE: $125–$175 (up to $400 for show quality).

AMERICAN STAFFORDSHIRE TERRIER
(formerly STAFFORDSHIRE TERRIER)

HISTORY AND ORIGIN: From about 1800 to 1815, the English Bulldog was crossed with the Old English Terrier to produce a dog who could bait bulls in the pit. To survive, the dog had to be a killer, with the spirit, agility, and courage of the Terrier and the tenacity of a Bulldog. Later on, in the nineteenth century, to perfect the Staffordshire Terrier, breeders crossed him with White English Terriers and Black-and-Tan Terriers.

CHARACTERISTICS: The American Staffordshire Terrier has a Jekyll-and-Hyde personality. With those he loves, he is docile, gentle, and obedient.

AMERICAN STAFFORDSHIRE TERRIER

But when aroused, baited, or confronted by enemies, he is a tiger, fighting on to the death once he has tasted blood. Some of these dogs are naturally boisterous, rough, and pugnacious, while others are gentle, kind, and even meek. No one but a great Terrier lover, and especially one who has seen and fallen in love with a Staffordshire, should buy him. For he must be carefully and patiently trained.

COLOR: Any color, either solid, patched, or in parts; avoid all white or about 80 percent white.

COAT: Short, close, stiff to the touch and glossy.

HEIGHT: Dog: 18–19 inches. Bitch: 17–18 inches.

WEIGHT: Dog: 40–50 pounds. Bitch: 35–45 pounds.

PRICE RANGE: $125 and up, $300 for show quality.

AUSTRALIAN TERRIER

HISTORY AND ORIGIN: The Australian Terrier is a relative newcomer to the dog world, dating back to 1885, when he was first shown in Melbourne. In the early nineteenth century, there was a dog called the

AUSTRALIAN TERRIER

Broken-haired or the Rough-coated Terrier who resembled the old Scottish Terrier, but could not compete in shows with the fashionable "Scottie." This native terrier was then crossed with the "Scottie" to produce the main stock for the modern Australian Terrier. Other Terriers who contributed to his making are the Cairn, the Dandie Dinmont, the Irish, and the Yorkshire. The American Kennel Club recognized the Australian in 1960.

CHARACTERISTICS: The Australian Terrier is one of the smallest of the Terriers, but one of the hardiest and most courageous. He is loyal, affectionate, and full of spirit all day long. He can withstand any weather and any hardship. Since he doesn't shed profusely and doesn't need to be walked for long periods of time, he makes a good apartment dog. He is best for a single person or a couple who want a small, energetic, high-spirited dog.

COLOR: Blue-black or silver-black, with tan markings on head and legs.

COAT: Harsh and straight, about 2½ inches all over the body.

HEIGHT: Dog: 10 inches. Bitch: 9–10 inches.

WEIGHT: Dog: 13–14 pounds. Bitch: 12–13 pounds.

PRICE RANGE: $175–$225, and up for show quality.

BEDLINGTON TERRIER

BEDLINGTON TERRIER

HISTORY AND ORIGIN: Named after the urban district of Bedlingtonshire in Northumberland, England, the Bedlington has been so called for about one hundred and forty years. Before that he was known as the Northumberland Fox Terrier. Originally, the Bedlington came from the eastern end of the border districts in England, where his ancestors were the old border Sleuthhound and the Rough-haired Terrier of the border dales. Both the Bedlington and the Dandie Dinmont have common ancestors, for both have long ears and top-knots (tufts on the head), characteristics not found in the other Terriers.

CHARACTERISTICS: Of all the Terriers, the Bedlington is perhaps the most belligerent. He is very jealous of other dogs in the house and will fight on the smallest provocation. On the other hand, he is affectionate and loyal to his owner, extremely courteous and intelligent, easy to train. However, his lamblike appearance is deceptive, and he is best as the sole pet in the house.

The Bedlington is very hardy, tough, and high-spirited, adapts to nearly any climate, to wetness or dryness, and will eat almost anything. He is a very active breed, should be walked early in the day and also allowed to run free when laws and circumstances permit. He can be kept in the city, suburb, or country, and as a rule is kind to children.

COLOR: Blue, blue-and-tan, liver, liver-and-tan, sandy, or sandy-and-tan.
COAT: Thick and linty, not more than 1 inch long.
HEIGHT: Dog: 16 inches. Bitch: 15 inches.
WEIGHT: Dog: 23–24 pounds. Bitch: 22–23 pounds.
PRICE RANGE: $150 and up.

BORDER TERRIER

BORDER TERRIER

HISTORY AND ORIGIN: One of the rarest of the Terriers, the Border Terrier goes back to the early seventeenth century, when he was used to kill large hill foxes. The dog has been popular in the Scottish borderland right up to this day because he is a magnificent worker and a first-rate killer of foxes, badgers, and vermin. He comes from the same family as the Lakeland, the Bedlington, and the Dandie Dinmont.

CHARACTERISTICS: Exceptionally brave, fearless, and energetic, the Border Terrier is a great favorite with farmers and shepherds. He will promptly get rid of any foxes, badgers, or vermin on the property. He needs little grooming or handling, for he can take care of himself in any weather and in any place. He is trustworthy, loyal, and wants nothing better than to love his owner and work hard all day. Under no conditions should he be pampered; he should be given a hard, tough life. He is primarily a working dog, not a pet.

COLOR: Red, grizzle, and tan; or blue-and-tan; or wheaten with some white on chest. Avoid white on feet.

COAT: Very wiry and somewhat broken, not curly or wavy.

HEIGHT: Dog: 12–13 inches. Bitch: 11–12 inches.

WEIGHT: Dog: 13–15½ pounds. Bitch: 11½–14 pounds.

PRICE RANGE: $150–$225.

BULL TERRIER

BULL TERRIER

HISTORY AND ORIGIN: The Bull Terrier was developed in the 1830s when the English Bulldog was crossed with the now extinct White English Terrier. He was created specifically for fighting, ratting, and bull baiting. In about 1860, the white Bull Terrier as we know him today was developed in England. He immediately became a great favorite with the "gentlemen" of the time and was given the name of the "white cavalier," a name he retains to this day.

CHARACTERISTICS: The Bull Terrier is excellent as a guard and companion, qualities which endeared him to the English Civil Service in India. He should not be kept in the city unless the owner is prepared to walk him a great deal, or can hire a walking service. The Bull Terrier is a big eater, requiring extra rations for a dog his size, and consequently he has 3 or 4 bowel movements a day.

He has fantastic energy and is very powerful. He will not fight unless provoked, but when he does he will kill dogs much larger than himself with a throat hold. Only people accustomed to dogs should purchase him because he must be carefully trained. For such people the Bull can be a good pet.

The female is often preferable to the male because she is gentler and easier to house-train. A very hardy breed with excellent digestion, the Bull Terrier will usually take punishment and roughhousing without loss of balance. Also, he is affectionate, intelligent, and has a sense of humor.

COLOR: White or other solid color with or without white markings.

COAT: Short, flat, harsh to the touch, with a fine gloss.

HEIGHT: Dog: 21–22 inches. Bitch: 19–21 inches.

WEIGHT: Dog: 45–60 pounds. Bitch: 30–50 pounds.

PRICE RANGE: $200 average.

CAIRN TERRIER

HISTORY AND ORIGIN: One of the oldest of the British Terriers, the Cairn originated on the Isle of Skye, and references to his ancestors go back as far as the mid-sixteenth century. He has always been and still is a great favorite with the Scottish lairds, who use him to rout foxes, badgers, vermin, and otters. The smallest of the working Terriers, the Cairn is the ancestor of several Terriers: the Scottish ("Scottie"), the West Highland, and the White and Long-haired Skye.

CHARACTERISTICS: A tough, hardy, and cautious dog, the Cairn has many qualities that make him a wonderful house pet. He is a one-man dog, doesn't require lots of exercise, doesn't shed much, is absolutely loyal, devoted, and high-spirited. He can adapt easily to any surroundings and to any climate. He is best for a single person or a couple who want a small, cheerful, devoted companion.

COLOR: Any color except white; usually wheaten, tan, or grizzle.

COAT: Hard and weather-resistant.

HEIGHT: Dog: 10 inches. Bitch: 9–10 inches.

WEIGHT: Dog: 14 pounds. Bitch: 13–14 pounds.
PRICE RANGE: $175 and up.

CAIRN TERRIER

DANDIE DINMONT TERRIER

HISTORY AND ORIGIN: The origin of the Dandie Dinmont is somewhat obscure, the most widely held theory being that he was bred from selected pups of the Rough-coated Terrier found in the Scottish border country. The dog as we know him today goes back to 1704. In a portrait of the third Duke of Buccleuch, painted by Gainsborough in 1770, we see the Dandie Dinmont.

The dog owes it name to a character in Sir Walter Scott's novel *Guy Mannering*. It is the only breed named after a literary character.

CHARACTERISTICS: Hardy, courageous, and plucky, but extremely affectionate and friendly, the Dandie Dinmont makes an excellent house dog and pet. He is absolutely devoted and loyal, but almost always to one person, although he is courteous and friendly with others in the family. He is long-lived, easily trained, very healthy, and can

DANDIE DINMONT TERRIER

FOX TERRIER, SMOOTH

FOX TERRIER, WIRE

IRISH TERRIER

KERRY BLUE TERRIER

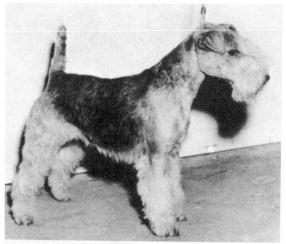

LAKELAND TERRIER

live anywhere. He does, however, need to be combed and trimmed often. He should not be kept in a warm room.

He should be trained early; otherwise he cannot be controlled well. If trained young, he is good with children and with the whole family.

Like many other rough-coated Terriers, he is subject to skin ailments, summer itch, and nonspecific dermatitis.

COLOR: Pepper from blue-black to silver-gray, or mustard from reddish brown to pale fawn.

COAT: Crisp but not wiry, about 2 inches long.

HEIGHT: Dog: 10–11 inches. Bitch: 8–10 inches.

WEIGHT: Dog: 21–24 pounds. Bitch: 18–22 pounds.

PRICE RANGE: $150 and up.

FOX TERRIER

HISTORY AND ORIGIN:

SMOOTH FOX TERRIER: The first record of the Smooth Fox Terrier close to our own time was in 1790, but the one we know today developed in the mid-nineteenth century. He is one of the best-known English dogs, and he can be found all over the world. The important ancestors of the Smooth Fox are the Beagle, the Greyhound, and the Smooth-coated Black-and-Tan Terrier.

WIRE FOX TERRIER: The Wire Fox Terrier is of an older variety than the Smooth, although the Smooth was the first to be known in the show ring. The Wire goes back to the mid-eighteenth century, when he was used to root foxes out of their holes. The ancestor of the Wire is the old rough-coated black-and-tan working terrier of Wales, Derbyshire, and Durham.

CHARACTERISTICS: These Terriers are still used in England to drive foxes out of holes or drains, but their chief use now is as house pets. They are strong, courageous, nervy, suited to live anywhere. They will take on all comers in a fight, and they have so much energy and desire to use it that they must be constantly restrained. They are affectionate, usually one-man dogs, and bark at any noise. Their barking must be controlled when they are young.

They are clowns. A person should consider well before he buys one whether or not he wants to spend years with a high-spirited court jester. Every movement the owner makes is interpreted as an invitation to play.

COLOR: Mostly white, with markings of black or black and tan.

COAT: *Smooth*—smooth, flat, hard, dense, abundant.

Wire—hard, wiry, the harder and more wiry the better.

HEIGHT: Dog: 15½ inches. Bitch: 14½ inches.

WEIGHT: Dog: 16–19 pounds (18 best). Bitch: 15–18 pounds.

PRICE RANGE: $125–$200.

IRISH TERRIER

HISTORY AND ORIGIN: Although he entered the show ring as late as 1879, the Irish Terrier is one of the oldest of the Terrier breeds. In many ways, physical and otherwise, he is similar to the Irish Wolfhound, but on a smaller scale. Developed as a hunter, he is excellent with rabbits and other small game, is a superb ratter and a fine retriever. During World War I, he made a distinguished record as a messenger and a general utility dog.

CHARACTERISTICS: The Irish Terrier is full of high spirits and fire. If the owner wants these qualities, the Irish will make him an incomparable friend and companion. He is adaptable to city, country, and suburb, as well as to cold and heat. Once established in a family, he becomes greatly attached, although he will be independent and aloof with strangers. Even though affectionate, this is no fawning dog.

The Irish Terrier is without fear, never timid or nervous. He has reckless courage and can be belligerent, but with people he knows he is devoted and loyal. He is fine with owner's children if they don't mind some roughness. He might have to be watched when he is with people outside the family.

COLOR: Solid bright-red, red-wheaten, or golden-red with no white except possibly a small patch on the chest.

COAT: So dense and wiry that when hair is parted with finger, the skin doesn't show.

HEIGHT: Dog: 17–18 inches. Bitch: 16½–17½ inches.

WEIGHT: Dog: 27 pounds. Bitch: 25 pounds.

PRICE RANGE: $175.

KERRY BLUE TERRIER

HISTORY AND ORIGIN: Originating in Ireland, the Kerry Blue is an all-around dog, good as a hunter of small game, as a retriever on land and water, as a general utility farm dog, and as a shepherd. He first became known in the rugged mountain regions of County Kerry, from which he gets his name. He has been purebred for about one hundred thirty-five years, from about the late 1820s on. From the evidence we have, the Kerry seems to be related to the old Irish Wolfhound.

CHARACTERISTICS: The Kerry Blue is an outgoing dog who demonstrates his feelings. He has humor, wit, and a blazing temper, with great energy and endurance to match his temperament. Adapting easily to any climate, he is hardy, healthy, long-lived. His long coat makes him particularly suitable for cold weather. He retains his liveliness at an age when most other dogs have slowed down.

The Kerry is not particularly friendly, has a fickle temperament, and is apt to bite at times. He tends to be bullheaded and stubborn. Like most Terriers, he suffers from eczema during the summer.

COLOR: Deep slate to light blue-gray.
COAT: Soft, dense, wavy (avoid harsh or wiry coat).
HEIGHT: Dog: 18–19½ inches (ideal 18½). Bitch: 17½–19 inches.
WEIGHT: Dog: 33–40 pounds. Bitch: 29–34 pounds.
PRICE RANGE: $150 and up.

LAKELAND TERRIER

HISTORY AND ORIGIN: One of the oldest of the working Terriers in Britain, the Lakeland was named for the Lake District of England, where the dog was used to prevent raids by foxes and otters. The dog was bred for toughness and courage. The Lakeland comes from the same family as the Bedlington and the Dandie Dinmont.

CHARACTERISTICS: The Lakeland Terrier was bred for a hard life, and it is best that he continue to live this life. He is incredibly strong for his size, has great endurance and determination, and utterly disregards danger when he is battling with a fox or an otter. He can live in any weather and in any terrain. He is a working dog, and it is best that he remain that way—he needs a lot of exercise.

He is also highly intelligent and good with family and children, but he is essentially devoted to his owner. For a Terrier, he is not unduly boisterous and as a rule is good-tempered.

COLOR: Blue-and-tan, blue, black, black-and-tan, red, mustard, wheaten grizzle (pale yellow and gray).
COAT: Hard, dense, wiry.
HEIGHT: Dog: 14 inches. Bitch: 13–13½ inches.
WEIGHT: Dog: 16–17 pounds. Bitch: 15–16 pounds.
PRICE RANGE: $150 and up.

MANCHESTER TERRIER

HISTORY AND ORIGIN: The Manchester Terrier goes back to the Black-and-Tan Terrier, a dog that was famed long ago for its ability as a ratter. Since the Manchester district of England was well known for the sport of rat killing, the dog we now recognize as the Manchester Terrier was developed there, the result of a cross between a Whippet bitch and a ratter. The breed was designated as such in 1860, but

MANCHESTER TERRIER

NORWICH TERRIER

SCHNAUZER, MINIATURE

SCOTTISH TERRIER

SEALYHAM TERRIER

SKYE TERRIER

it was often called the Black-and-Tan until 1923.

CHARACTERISTICS: The Manchester has remained a fine ratter, but is now more popular as a house pet. His short coat, intelligence, alert and quick manner all make him an excellent house dog. He hardly sheds, has no body odor, and requires little outdoor exercise. Like the toy variety, however, he is a barker, very sensitive to all sounds, and must here be controlled.

COLOR: Black-and-tan (jet-black and rich tan).

COAT: Smooth, dense, close, and glossy.

HEIGHT: Dog: 16 inches. Bitch: 14–15 inches.

WEIGHT: Dog: 16–22 pounds. Bitch: 12–16 pounds.

PRICE RANGE: $125 and up.

NORWICH TERRIER

HISTORY AND ORIGIN: All that we know about the Norwich Terrier is that he is a relatively new breed, first developed in England about 1880. His ancestors seem to be the Irish Terrier, the English Terrier, and the old Border Terrier. Shortly after he was developed, the Norwich became the rage with Cambridge undergraduates.

CHARACTERISTICS: Like all Terriers, the Norwich is strong, aggressive, hard-working, and high-spirited. He is happiest in the field chasing foxes, badgers, and rabbits. He can adapt to any weather, any terrain. He is best suited for ranch or farm life, where he can work continuously. The Norwich is loyal and devoted, generally a one-man dog, and an excellent watchdog.

COLOR: Red and red-wheaten, black-and-tan, or grizzle.

COAT: Hardy and wiry, absolutely straight.

HEIGHT: Dog: 10–11 inches (ideal is 10). Bitch: 9–10 inches.

WEIGHT: Dog: 10–14 pounds (ideal is 11). Bitch: 10–12 pounds.

PRICE RANGE: $150–$200 and up, depending on quality.

MINIATURE SCHNAUZER

HISTORY AND ORIGIN: See Schnauzer's history and origin in section on working dogs. The Miniature comes from selected small Standard Schnauzers crossed with Affenpinschers. The Miniature was first shown as a distinct breed in 1899.

CHARACTERISTICS: Although a good ratter, the Miniature Schnauzer has been used in the United States chiefly as a pet and house dog. He is completely distinct from English Terriers, is not so quarrelsome, and is fine for children. He is easily trained, hardy, sturdy, long-lived.

Eager to please, active and alert, the Miniature Schnauzer makes a good watchdog. He is fine for apartment life and requires little grooming.

COLOR: Salt-and-pepper, black-and-silver, or solid black. Typical is salt-and-pepper with shades of gray, with light gray or silver-white around eyebrows, whiskers, cheeks, under throat.

COAT: Hard and wiry.

HEIGHT: Dog: 13–14 inches. Bitch: 12–14 inches.

WEIGHT: Dog: 14–15 pounds. Bitch: 13–14 pounds.

PRICE RANGE: $225.

SCOTTISH TERRIER ("SCOTTIE")

HISTORY AND ORIGIN: We have no recorded history of the Scottish Terrier prior to 1879, when he was first exhibited as a distinct breed. Most authorities agree that he goes back to the old Highland Terrier, but we do not know what specific type produced the Scottie, except that it was probably a native to the Blackmount region of Perthshire, Loch Rannock, and the surrounding country. Most likely, a good deal of crossbreeding went on, so that it was impossible to keep records.

CHARACTERISTICS: The Scottish Terrier is strong, alert, high-strung, with extremely powerful teeth. He does not feel inferior to any other dog, or to any other animal for that matter. A one-man dog, he will never be swayed by favors or flattery. He is very jealous of the friendship of his owner. An ideal apartment dog, he is best for a single person or couple without children; he likes children only if he is brought up with them.

COLOR: Steel-gray, brindle or grizzled, black-wheaten, with no white marks.

COAT: About 2 inches long, intensely hard and wiry.

HEIGHT: Dog: 10 inches. Bitch: 9–10 inches.

WEIGHT: Dog: 19–22 pounds. Bitch: 18–21 pounds.

PRICE RANGE: $200–$375 (the higher figure for show quality).

SEALYHAM TERRIER

HISTORY AND ORIGIN: The Sealyham was named for the estate of its breeder, Sealyham, in the municipal borough of Haverfordwest, Pembrokeshire, Wales, where since 1850 this dog has been used for hunting badgers, otters, and foxes. The stock for the Sealyham includes the Welsh Pembroke Corgi, the Dandie Dinmont, the West Highland White Terrier, and the Bull Terrier.

CHARACTERISTICS: Usually reserved and self-willed, the Sealyham must be trained early and firmly. But he makes a good friend and a wonderful companion, for he is loyal, devoted, energetic, and cheerful. Because he is small, needs little exercise, and does not shed, he is a good apartment dog. Like all Terriers, he barks readily at strangers and whenever there is a disturbance of any kind, and he therefore makes an excellent watchdog. He is fond of children. Physically, he is subject to nonspecific skin ailments. There has been a recent upsurge of interest in the Sealyham.

COLOR: All white, or white with lemon, tan, or badger markings on head and ears.

COAT: Hard and wiry.

HEIGHT: Dog: 10½ inches. Bitch: 10 inches.

WEIGHT: Dog: 21 pounds. Bitch: 20 pounds.

PRICE RANGE: $200 and up.

SKYE TERRIER

HISTORY AND ORIGIN: Most Terriers were bred to look the way they do today within the past hundred years. The modern Skye, however, goes back to the middle of the sixteenth century; he is described exactly in Dr. John Caius' historic volume *English Dogges,* the first book in England devoted completely to dogs.

The Skye Terrier comes from the Island of Skye, but he is also found on other islands in the Hebrides as well as on the mainland of Scotland. The early Skye was a bit smaller than the present one and more adapted to burrowing and to swimming. The breed was always a favorite with nobles, and Queen Victoria was one of its protectors and champions.

CHARACTERISTICS: Shortest of all the Terriers, the Skye is obedient, loyal, a one-man dog, reserved with strangers and somewhat standoffish. In his terrain, among the rocks, burrows, and treacherous waters, the Skye has no equal.

He has a good nose, especially for badgers, and he can follow a scent two hours old. He has unsurpassed sight and hearing and is fierce in battle, yielding to no animal anywhere or anytime.

He is very sensitive to people, especially his owner. And he always wonders if he is liked. Some Skyes tend to become neurotic if they are not sure of their owners' love.

COLOR: Black, dark or light blue, gray, fawn, or cream.

COAT: Hard and straight, 5½ inches long.

HEIGHT: Dog: 9 inches. Bitch: 8½ inches.

WEIGHT: Dog: 24–25 pounds. Bitch: 23–24 pounds.

PRICE RANGE: $250 and up for show.

SOFT-COATED WHEATEN TERRIER

SOFT-COATED WHEATEN TERRIER

HISTORY AND ORIGIN: The Wheaten has a long history in Ireland and is generally believed to be the ancestor of the Kerry Blue, although there is no documentation for this. Nevertheless, for many years the feats of the Wheaten were preserved by legends, some of them going back as far as the Spanish Armada. The dog was bred chiefly for its hunting ability with small game and as a guard dog with stock. In every sense, it was a work dog, often pitted against other animals of much larger size. Coat and configuration were not the most important matters; courage and tenacity were, and the strongest survived and bred.

CHARACTERISTICS: The Wheaten is very much a Terrier in spirit—pugnacious, aggressive and scrappy, suspicious of other dogs, and full of life and stamina. He is for owners who like an aggressive animal with seemingly unending vitality. The Wheaten is a loyal pet, stubborn, and somewhat high-strung, especially around other dogs. Do not expect a puppy to have the characteristic coat; it takes almost two years to evolve. When the dog is mature, the coat is full, wheaten in color, and abundant and soft, but should not exceed five inches in length.

COLOR: Wheaten only.

COAT: Abundant, soft and wavy, or loosely curled; not fluffed out or trimmed.

HEIGHT: Dog: 18–19 inches. Bitch: 15–17 inches.

WEIGHT: Dog: 35–45 pounds. Bitch: 30–40 pounds.

PRICE RANGE: $150 and up.

STAFFORDSHIRE BULL TERRIER

STAFFORDSHIRE BULL TERRIER

HISTORY AND ORIGIN: The Staffordshire Bull Terrier is a mixture of several breeds: first the Bulldog and Mastiff were mated; the dog was then scaled down to a smaller size gradually, through further crossbreeding between Bulldog and Terrier. The size went from an original 100-pounder to a dog of 30 to 40 pounds. The purpose of these various linkages was to produce a scrappy, fighting animal, initially for bull and bear baiting and then for dog fighting itself. The breed was, in fact, once known as the Old Pit Bull Terrier.

CHARACTERISTICS: Because of its background, the Staffordshire Bull is an aggressive animal. Although his reputation as a fighting dog had to be toned down before he could gain acceptance in England and, later, in America, the breed has a dynamic temperament. The Staffordshire

Bull makes a good pet and lively companion, but is spirited and should not be purchased by an owner who wants a quiet or docile pet.

COLOR: Red, fawn, white, blue, or black, or any of these with white; or brindle, with or without white. Liver or black-and-tan disqualified.

COAT: Smooth, short and close.

HEIGHT: Dog: 14–16 inches. Bitch: 14–16 inches.

WEIGHT: Dog: 28–38 pounds. Bitch: 24–34 pounds.

PRICE RANGE: $125 and up.

WELSH TERRIER

WELSH TERRIER

HISTORY AND ORIGIN: From prints and paintings we know the Welsh Terrier goes back hundreds of years to the rough-haired Black-and-Tan Terriers. From the 1850s, the Welsh Terrier has been purebred in Wales and used in hunting foxes, badgers, and otters. The Welsh Terrier first appeared in the United States in 1888.

CHARACTERISTICS: Although still used as a hunting dog, the Welsh is most widely seen now as a pet, especially in a city apartment. Small, long-lived, a non-shedder, he is loyal, affectionate, and excellent with children. He has terrific energy, steady nerves, and is aggressive with other dogs. He is best with young people or with other people who can cope with his aggressiveness, energy, and high spirits.

COLOR: Best in black-and-tan, or black-grizzle-and-tan, without black marks on toes.

COAT: Wiry, hard, close, and abundant.

HEIGHT: Dog: 15 inches. Bitch: 14 inches.
WEIGHT: Dog: 20 pounds. Bitch: 18–19 pounds.
PRICE RANGE: $125 and up.

WEST HIGHLAND WHITE TERRIER

WEST HIGHLAND WHITE TERRIER

HISTORY AND ORIGIN: The West Highland White Terrier has the same ancestors as the Scottie, the Cairn, and the Dandie Dinmont, the native,
rough-haired Terriers of the border country. The dog as we know
him today originated on the estate of the Malcolms of Poltalloch
in Argyllshire, Scotland, in the first quarter of the nineteenth century.
He was once known as the Roseneath Terrier, named after his place
of origin, the Duke of Argyll's estate in Scotland.

CHARACTERISTICS: The West Highland White Terrier is highly individualistic,
charming, playful, with a sense of self-importance and self-love. He
has no fear of animals, people, or the elements. Adaptable to any
temperature and any terrain, he is good as a general pet but not in
an apartment with children. His shedding can be a nuisance; the
white hair is very noticeable on furniture and rugs. He is a one-
man dog and should be trained early.

COLOR: Pure white only.

COAT: Hard hair, 2 inches long, free from any curl.

HEIGHT: Dog: 11 inches. Bitch: 10 inches.

WEIGHT: Dog: 15–19 pounds. Bitch: 13–17 pounds.

PRICE RANGE: $225 and up.

THE TOY BREEDS

The toys were developed for the purposes of pleasure. They are pets and companions, although several make excellent watchdogs. The 17 toy breeds (including the Manchester and Poodle) are:

AFFENPINSCHER

CHIHUAHUA

GRIFFON, BRUSSELS

ITALIAN GREYHOUND

MALTESE

PAPILLON

PEKINGESE

PINSCHER, MINIATURE

POMERANIAN

POODLE, TOY *(also see Poodle, page 53)*

PUG

SHIH TZU

SPANIEL, ENGLISH TOY

SPANIEL, JAPANESE

TERRIER, MANCHESTER TOY
(also see Manchester Terrier, page 97)

TERRIER, SILKY

TERRIER, YORKSHIRE

AFFENPINSCHER

HISTORY AND ORIGIN: The Affenpinscher was known in Europe as far back as the seventeenth century. But most authorities are not at all clear about his origin. He seems to be a close relative of the Miniature Pinscher, and his wiry coat suggests that there is Terrier blood in him. The dog we know today goes back to 1900.

CHARACTERISTICS: The Affenpinscher—or "monkey terrier" as his name translates from the German—is proud, haughty, and very intelligent. He is very demanding and usually gets what he wants, especially if he senses that his master cannot discipline him. Often, if not trained properly, he is a real tyrant in the house. Like most toys, he is delicate, and his health should be watched carefully.

COLOR: Black, tan-and-black, red, or gray.

COAT: Short, dense, hard, wiry; shaggy in parts.

HEIGHT: Dog: 9–10¼ inches. Bitch: 8–9 inches.

WEIGHT: Dog: 8 pounds. Bitch: 7 pounds.

PRICE RANGE: $175 and up, $400 for show quality.

CHIHUAHUA
(Smooth coat and long coat)

HISTORY AND ORIGIN: The Chihuahua is probably the world's smallest dog, some weighing as little as one pound. Contrary to what most people

AFFENPINSCHER

CHIHUAHUA

CHIHUAHUA, LONG-COATED

believe, the Chihuahua wasn't originally a Mexican dog, at least in his present form. The best evidence we have suggests that the dog came from the Orient and was perhaps crossed with a Mexican dog. His name comes from one of the Mexican states, although today most Chihuahuas come from the United States.

CHARACTERISTICS: Delicate, refined, and tender, the Chihuahua is good for city people, especially middle-aged and older people living alone. The Smooth is clean, does not shed, and is loyal and devoted to his master. He needs no exercise outdoors, and he eats very little. This is a dog who can have the full run of the house. He is, however, very oppressive, temperamental, and will usually try to control his owner. Because of his small size and inability to defend himself, he is not good with small children. He is inclined to be clannish and usually will not be sociable with other breeds.

He is susceptible to rheumatism and tends to develop pyorrhea. He should not be taken out in very cold weather.

COLOR: Any color, solid, marked, or splashed.

COAT: Smooth, soft, close, and glossy; or soft and somewhat curly, with feathering.

HEIGHT: Dog: 5 inches. Bitch: 5 inches.

WEIGHT: Dog: 1–6 pounds (2–4 is best). Bitch: 1–6 pounds (2–4 is best).

PRICE RANGE: $150 and up.

GRIFFON, BRUSSELS

HISTORY AND ORIGIN: The Brussels Griffon's ancestors appear as far back as the fifteenth century in a painting by Jan van Eyck called "Giovanni Arnolfini and His Bride." They also show up in a French painting of Henry III of France. The dog we know today comes from a cross between the German Affenpinscher and the Belgian Sheepdog. However, the Pug and the Ruby Spaniel are also important in his development. The breed became popular in 1870 because it was a favorite of the Belgian queen.

CHARACTERISTICS: The only toy that has a Terrier coat, the Brussels Griffon is intelligent, affectionate, and highly independent, saucy, and willful. The puppy must be strictly trained; if not, the dog will become a yelping, defiant bully. He is good for an apartment, for he does not shed and doesn't take up much space. His coat, like all Terrier coats, requires some attention.

COLOR: Reddish brown; black and reddish brown with black mask (dark shadings on the foreface) and whiskers; or black with uniform reddish brown markings.

COAT: For the two varieties of Brussels Griffon:

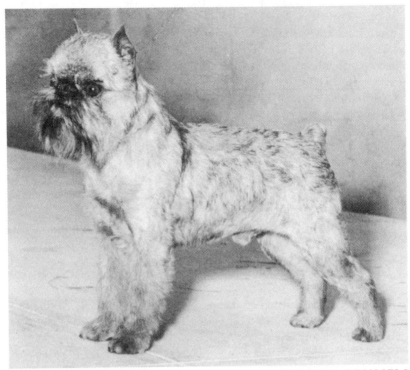

GRIFFON, BRUSSELS

a. Rough coat, wiry, dense—the harder and wirier the better.
b. Smooth coat, similar to that of the Boston Terrier.
HEIGHT: Dog: 7–8 inches. Bitch: 7–8 inches.
WEIGHT: Dog: 10–12 pounds. Bitch: 5–9 pounds.
PRICE RANGE: $300 and up.

ITALIAN GREYHOUND

HISTORY AND ORIGIN: The Italian Greyhound, as his name indicates, comes from Italy, where he is called the Piccolo Levriere Italiano. He is the miniature of the large Greyhound and a rare and ancient breed. From sculpture and paintings, we know that this miniature has existed in his present form for over two thousand years and that he was a great favorite with Egyptian, Greek, and Roman nobility. By the time of the Renaissance, he was very well known in Europe, and by the eighteenth century he was very popular with the ladies on the Continent. He was also a favorite of painters and of royalty,

ITALIAN GREYHOUND

especially Charles I, Frederick the Great, and Queen Victoria. The Italian Greyhound came to England in the early seventeenth century, reaching the peak of his popularity in the late Victorian period. Throughout the centuries, he has never been anything but a pet.

CHARACTERISTICS: One of the most gentle, affectionate, and loving of dogs, the Italian Greyhound is well suited for his native Italy. For he is delicate and susceptible to chills, and therefore needs a warm, sunny climate. Active and highly intelligent, he can be easily trained. Wishing to please and having no temper, he makes an excellent companion. He is a one-man dog.

COLOR: Fawn, red, blue, cream, white, or gray.

COAT: Skin fine and supple; hair thin and glossy like satin.

HEIGHT: Dog: 8–10 inches. Bitch: 6–7 inches.

WEIGHT: Dog: 9–10 pounds. Bitch: 7–9 pounds.

PRICE RANGE: $175 average.

MALTESE

MALTESE

HISTORY AND ORIGIN: Named after the island of Malta, the Maltese has been the aristocrat of the dog world for almost three thousand years. He was the favorite lap dog of noble ladies of Greece and Rome, and statues were erected to him. In Elizabethan times, this dog was such a rage that one sold for the contemporary equivalent of $10,000. The dog we know today first appeared in 1763 in a painting by Sir Joshua Reynolds.

CHARACTERISTICS: The Maltese is one of the most decorative of the toy breeds, especially because of his beautiful coat. He is affectionate and loves human companionship. He must be given much attention.

His physical constitution is rather weak, and he is subject to upper respiratory ailments. He must be fed carefully as well as taken out for plenty of exercise so that his skin remains free of eruptions. He is likely to be snappish, even temperamental. He can be a wonderful pet, but like all toys he needs careful attention, lots of love, and someone to understand his whims. He is very much like a child.

As for his beautiful coat, it must be carefully groomed for hours.

COLOR: Pure white.

COAT: Long, straight, silky, strong.

HEIGHT: Dog: 5 inches. Bitch: 5 inches.

WEIGHT: Dog: 2–7 pounds. Bitch: 2–3 pounds. (The less weight, the better.)

PRICE RANGE: $300–$400 (the latter figure for show quality).

PAPILLON

PAPILLON

HISTORY AND ORIGIN: The Papillon goes back to the sixteenth century; he appears in paintings and tapestries of the period. Rubens and Watteau painted the breed, and the dog became so fashionable that no lady would have her portrait painted unless she could have a Papillon on her lap. For centuries, all royal houses in Europe hailed the Papillon. Madame de Pompadour first made him popular. His name means butterfly in French.

CHARACTERISTICS: The Papillon is exclusively a house dog, especially a city apartment dog. He is not robust, so he must be exercised as well as fed carefully. Bathing should be infrequent, for he is susceptible to cold. He is affectionate, very friendly, has exceptional hearing. Like all toys, he is quick to give an alarm. He is the only sporting toy and, if necessary, will hunt rats or rabbits. He requires a good deal of love, attention, and pampering. His coat needs daily grooming.

COLOR: Either two-colored or tricolored, usually white-and-black, white-and-sable, or white and some shade of red, or white-and-black with tan spots.

COAT: Profuse, shiny, and slightly wavy, never curly.

HEIGHT: Dog: 11 inches. Bitch: 10 inches.

WEIGHT: Dog: 9–11 pounds. Bitch: 5–8 pounds.

PRICE RANGE: $150–$225 and up.

PEKINGESE

PEKINGESE

HISTORY AND ORIGIN: The Pekingese has a great romantic history. The breed goes back two thousand years to ancient China, where they were known as the little lion dogs of Peking. The dogs were cared for by the chief eunuchs of the court and were often nursed by slave girls. They were the sacred dogs of the emperors. In 1860, when the English looted the Imperial Palace at Peking, some of the dogs were taken, then later introduced to the West.

CHARACTERISTICS: Used as an ornamental lap dog and pet, the Pekingese is suited to city life, especially for small apartments. He needs little exercise: a walk around the block once or twice a day. However, he does need careful daily brushing and doesn't like cold, wet, or damp. Overfeeding ruins his health; it tends to cause asthma, as it does with most short-nosed breeds.

The Pekingese is a great individualist, doesn't make friends easily, and barks readily, like all toys. When scolded, he sulks like a child. He is not for children, but for older people who want a companion.

COLOR: Any color—red, fawn, black, black-and-tan, sable, or brindle, with black mask on face.

COAT: Long, straight, flat, and rather coarse, never curly or wavy.

WEIGHT: Dog: 8–9 inches. Bitch: 6–8 inches.

WEIGHT: Dog: 8–10 pounds. Bitch: 6–8 pounds.

PRICE RANGE: $150 and up.

PINSCHER, MINIATURE

PINSCHER, MINIATURE

HISTORY AND ORIGIN: See Doberman Pinscher (page 137) for origin.

CHARACTERISTICS: The Miniature Pinscher is one of the smartest-looking and most stylish of the toy dogs. He is full of life and vigor, always trotting around ready to impress anyone who wishes to be impressed. He is aggressive, cocky, noisy, full of confidence. He is also temperamental, difficult to train, and snappy. Since he is short-coated, there are no grooming problems, but you must be an experienced dog owner with a strong will and mind to own a Miniature Pinscher.

COLOR: Red, rust-red, coal-black, or brown with rust or yellow.

COAT: Smooth, hard, short, with luster.

HEIGHT: Dog: 11–11½ inches. Bitch: 10–10½ inches.

WEIGHT: Dog: 9–10 pounds. Bitch: 8–9 pounds.

PRICE RANGE: $125 and up (higher prices for smaller dogs).

POMERANIAN

POMERANIAN

HISTORY AND ORIGIN: A member of the Spitz group, the Pomeranian claims as his ancestors the sled dogs of Iceland and Lapland. In the early part of the nineteenth century, these dogs weighed as much as 30 pounds. The smallest ones were then bred. Eventually, after generations of breeding, the Pomeranian as we see him was developed. Since much of the breeding took place in Pomerania, that is how the dog received his name. The breed became popular in 1875.

CHARACTERISTICS: The Pomeranian is an excellent dog for small houses and apartments. He is active, intelligent, very obedient, and easier to train than most other dogs. But he is a one-man dog, not at all ideal for very small children. He will not tolerate their maulings. He should be trained early with great care and discipline. If not, he will dominate the house.

COLOR: Black, brown, beaver, red, chocolate, orange, cream, wolf-sable, blue, or white.

COAT: Long, perfectly straight, and glistening.

HEIGHT: Dog: 6–7 inches. Bitch: 5½–6½ inches.

WEIGHT: Dog: 5–7 pounds. Bitch: 3–5 pounds.

PRICE RANGE: $100 and up ($250 and up for show quality).

POODLE, TOY

POODLE, TOY

For history and origin as well as characteristics, see Poodle (page 53). Toys were obtained by breeding the smallest of the Miniatures.

POODLE, MINIATURE

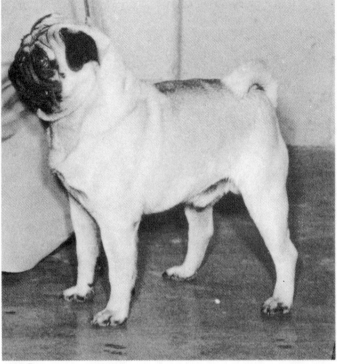

PUG

PUG

HISTORY AND ORIGIN: Like most toys with short noses, large heads, and tails curled over their backs, the Pug originated in China, hundreds of years ago. Dutch traders from the Dutch East India Company brought him from China and introduced him to England, where he immediately became a great favorite with the fashionable ladies and the nobility. He is still a favorite with ladies of fashion throughout the world—the Duchess of Windsor, for example, owns a Pug.

CHARACTERISTICS: The Pug has the appeal of a toy and the stamina and courage of a large dog. He has a placid temperament, isn't finicky or fussy, and is extremely loyal and devoted. He has no "doggy" odor, doesn't shed, doesn't drool as many short-nosed dogs do, doesn't need a lot of grooming. At times he is obstinate, a bit temperamental, and very jealous of other dogs. He is not good with children up to four, but excellent with older children. Since he requires much love, he is not for a cool and indifferent owner. Because his eyes are so exposed, he is susceptible to eye trouble.

COLOR: Black, silver, or apricot-fawn; black face and black markings on tail.

COAT: Fine, smooth, soft, short, glossy.
HEIGHT: Dog: 11 inches. Bitch: 10–11 inches.
WEIGHT: Dog: 16½–18 pounds. Bitch: 14–17 pounds.
PRICE RANGE: $125 and up, $350 and up for show quality.

SHIH TZU

SHIH TZU (pronounced Sheed-zoo)

HISTORY AND ORIGIN: The Shih Tzu (whose name means lion in Chinese) can be traced back as far as 624 A.D., and reappears in the tenth century when the dogs were presented to the court as a tribute. In the seventeenth century, the Shih Tzu was reintroduced into China, and the dog was bred in the Forbidden City of Peking. The dog came by its name because it resembled the lion as depicted in Oriental art. The hair on the Shih Tzu's face appears to grow wildly in all directions, and for that reason it also came to be known as the "chrysanthemum-faced dog." Once the breed as we know it was established, the dog became a house pet and was a favorite of the royal family during the Ming Dynasty. The Shih Tzu became known in England and in Europe in the 1930s when a few were imported through the efforts of Lady Brownrigg, an Englishwoman living in China.
CHARACTERISTICS: The Shih Tzu is a lively companion, very alert and intelli-

gent. He makes an excellent apartment dog, especially for someone living alone or without children. Like many toys, he has a keen sense of himself, is proud, even haughty and arrogant. Because of his long, glossy coat, the Shih Tzu does need to be groomed.

COLOR: All colors are permissible. Black nose and eye rims, but liver markings are acceptable.

COAT: Very luxurious, thick, long, wavy but not curly; the hair on top of the head may be tied. Woolly undercoat.

HEIGHT: Dog: 8–11 inches, with 9–10½ inches ideal. Bitch: 8–11 inches.

WEIGHT: Dog: 12–15 pounds. Bitch: 12–15 pounds. For both, no more than 18 pounds or less than 9 pounds.

PRICE RANGE: $200 and up.

SPANIEL, ENGLISH TOY

SPANIEL, ENGLISH TOY

HISTORY AND ORIGIN: The dog we know today has captivated the royalty of Europe for three centuries. Because the black-and-tan variety of the English Toy Spaniel (King Charles Spaniel) took his name from

Charles II, most people believe that the dog originated at that time. This is false, for the breed is ancient and goes back to the Japan of 2000 B.C. and possibly even earlier to China. How it came to England we do not know, but we do know that it existed in England in the sixteenth century and that one of the dogs was a favorite of Mary Queen of Scots and accompanied her to the scaffold. The breed was also favored by James I, Charles I, Victoria, and the Windsors.

CHARACTERISTICS: The English Toy Spaniel is affectionate, sociable, wonderful with children, and excellent as a house dog. He needs little exercise and has a pleasant, lovable nature. He has a taste for luxury, is a gourmet, and loves to sleep on expensive furniture and rugs.

COLOR: For the four varieties of English Toy Spaniel:

    a. King Charles—black-and-tan.

    c. Prince Charles—white-black-and-tan.

    c. Blenheim—red-and-white.

    d. Ruby—red.

COAT: Long, silk, soft, wavy but not curly.

HEIGHT: Dog: 10 inches. Bitch: 9 inches.

WEIGHT: Dog: 10½–12 pounds. Bitch: 9–11 pounds.

PRICE RANGE: $175–$225.

SPANIEL, JAPANESE

SPANIEL, JAPANESE

HISTORY AND ORIGIN: Belying his name, the Japanese Spaniel had his origin in China, not Japan, about two thousand years ago. The dogs then were brought up by Japanese royalty, raised in Japan, and subsequently given to foreigners who had rendered some outstanding service to Japan. The dog arrived in England when Commodore Perry gave a brace to Queen Victoria. Many were also stolen from Japanese kennels and sold to European nobility.

CHARACTERISTICS: Proud, haughty, highly intelligent, and shrewd, the Japanese Spaniel is the perfect dog for lonely people who need a companion. The Japanese adapts himself to any mood of his owner and wants nothing better than to love him faithfully. He is also gay and vivacious. The Japanese makes an excellent apartment dog if you can put up with the problem you always have with a longhaired dog—shedding. Like other toys, he is fragile and should not be exposed to extreme temperatures.

COLOR: Best is either black-and-white, or red-and-white.

COAT: Profuse, long, straight and silky, no wave or curl.

HEIGHT: Dog: 9 inches. Bitch: 8–9 inches.

WEIGHT: Dog: 7 pounds. Bitch: 6–7 pounds.

PRICE RANGE: $100–$150.

TERRIER, MANCHESTER TOY

TERRIER, MANCHESTER TOY

HISTORY AND ORIGIN: The history and origin are the same as for the Manchester Terrier (page 97). The small pups of each litter were bred to create the toy variety.

CHARACTERISTICS: The Toy Manchester Terrier is very much a Terrier. Hardy, alert, quick, energetic and fearless, he barks at every sound. If the barking is controlled, he is a perfect apartment dog. He doesn't shed, has no body odor, takes up little space, requires little outdoor exercise, and needs a minimum of grooming. He is reserved, often aloof. He is however, adaptable to any conditions and is absolutely devoted to his owner. Physically, he is prone to skin disorders, particularly demodectic mange.

COLOR: Black-and-tan.

COAT: Smooth and glossy.

HEIGHT: Dog: 7 inches. Bitch: 6–7 inches.

WEIGHT: Dog: 9–12 pounds. Bitch: 5–9 pounds.

PRICE RANGE: $150, up to $450 for very small dogs.

TERRIER, SILKY

TERRIER, SILKY

HISTORY AND ORIGIN: A native of Australia, the Silky Terrier comes from a cross between the Australian Terrier and the Yorkshire Terrier.

CHARACTERISTICS: The Silky Terrier is one of the best-loved of Australian dogs. Friendly, energetic, aggressive, this is a toy with all the Terrier characteristics. He is tireless, yappy, and unable to sit still. He usually lives in the suburbs, where he makes a good companion. He is also perfect on a farm, for he is agile and can exterminate snakes and rats. Loyal, devoted, faithful, he can make a wonderful pet, but not for nervous people.

COLOR: Black-and-tan.

COAT: Flat, fine, glossy, silky.

HEIGHT: Dog: 10 inches. Bitch: 9–10 inches.

WEIGHT: Dog: 9–10 pounds. Bitch: 8–9 pounds.

PRICE RANGE: $225 and up, $350 for show quality.

TERRIER, YORKSHIRE

TERRIER, YORKSHIRE

HISTORY AND ORIGIN: The Yorkshire is definitely a man-made breed not much older than one hundred years. His origin is unknown because records were not carefully kept, but he seems to be a descendant of the Skye Terrier crossed with the old Black-and-Tan Terrier. Some believe that the Maltese and the Dandie Dinmont are his direct ancestors. He became fashionable late in the Victorian era, and he is still a very fashionable dog.

CHARACTERISTICS: The Yorkshire Terrier is a small, strong, very lovable and fearless pet. Easy to care for, a slight shedder, and companionable, he is ideal for an apartment. He is sociable with other dogs in the family, an excellent watchdog, friendly, devoted, and loyal. He is very healthy. Since he wants love and attention, he is not a dog for aloof, cool people. His coat demands a lot of grooming—at least a half hour a day.

COLOR: Dark-steel-blue-and-tan. Avoid silver-blue.

COAT: Straight, glossy, with silky texture.
HEIGHT: Dog: 9 inches. Bitch: 8–9 inches.
WEIGHT: Dog: 7–8 pounds. Bitch: 4–6 pounds.
PRICE RANGE: $200 average.

THE WORKING BREEDS

Working dogs have served many useful functions over the years—protecting flocks from wild animals and thieves, drawing sleds, driving cattle to market, acting as guards and watchdogs, helping the police, and rescuing people on land and in water. The 30 working breeds are:

AKITA	MASTIFF
ALASKAN MALAMUTE	NEWFOUNDLAND
BELGIAN MALINOIS	PULI
BELGIAN TERVUREN	ROTTWEILER
BERNESE MOUNTAIN DOG	ST. BERNARD
BOUVIER DES FLANDRES	SAMOYED
BOXER	SCHNAUZER
BRIARD	SCHNAUZER, GIANT
BULLMASTIFF	*(also see Schnauzer, page 151)*
COLLIE	SHEEPDOG, BELGIAN
DOBERMAN PINSCHER	SHEEPDOG, OLD ENGLISH
GERMAN SHEPHERD DOG	SHEEPDOG, SHETLAND *("Sheltie")*
GREAT DANE	SIBERIAN HUSKY
GREAT PYRENEES	WELSH CORGI, CARDIGAN
KOMONDOR	WELSH CORGI, PEMBROKE
KUVASZ	

AKITA

HISTORY AND ORIGIN: Bred in his native Japan as a hunting dog and waterfowl retriever, the Akita is also an affectionate and companionable family pet. The breed is named after the Akita prefecture on Honshu Island and has spiritual as well as purely practical significance for the Japanese. According to tradition, the dog symbolizes good health and general well-being; often, small statues of the Akita are given as gifts to those who are in ill health as a way of wishing them a fast recovery. The breed became popular in the United States when American servicemen returned after World War II with the dogs.

CHARACTERISTICS: The Akita has always been an esteemed hunter in his native land, known best for his ability with bear, deer, and wild boar, and also for his quality as a retriever. Strong, exceptionally sturdy, intelligent, and consistent in the field, the Akita is also a dependable family dog, affectionate and completely trustworthy with small children. Tough in the field, the Akita is gentle in the home.

COLOR: Any color is acceptable: white, brindle, or pinto; undercoat may

AKITA

be a different color from outer coat.

COAT: Outer coat should be harsh and straight, standing clear of the body; undercoat thick, soft, and shorter than outer coat. No ruff or feathering.

HEIGHT: Dog: 26–28 inches. Bitch: 24–26 inches.

WEIGHT: Dog: 85–110 pounds. Bitch: 75–100 pounds.

PRICE RANGE: $150 and up.

ALASKAN MALAMUTE

HISTORY AND ORIGIN: One of the oldest of Arctic sled dogs, the Alaskan Malamute was named for the Eskimo tribe called Malemuit, who bred the dog in the northwestern part of Alaska. No one knows his origin, but most do agree that he is of the Spitz family. He always has been and still is primarily a sled dog and a protector of the people who own him.

CHARACTERISTICS: The Malamute is strong, courageous, with remarkable stamina and absolute loyalty and devotion to his owner. He is friendly

ALASKAN MALAMUTE

with those he knows and even gentle, but since he does have wild traits, he needs careful and intensive training. He must always know that his owner is firm and decisive.

COLOR: Wolf-gray or black-and-white.
COAT: Wolf-gray or black-and-white.
HEIGHT: Dog: 23–25 inches. Bitch: 20–23 inches.
WEIGHT: Dog: 75–85 pounds. Bitch: 50–70 pounds.
PRICE RANGE: $150 and up, $300 for show quality.

BELGIAN MALINOIS

HISTORY AND ORIGIN: The Belgian Malinois is identical in conformation to the Belgian Sheepdog and Tervuren and shares the same breed history as the Sheepdog. The Malinois gained its separate existence just before the turn of the century, in 1898, and its chief distinction from the Sheepdog and Tervuren comes in its coat and color. Its coat is somewhat shorter than theirs, especially on the head and ears, and its color is rich fawn to mahogany. It is a working dog in every

BELGIAN MALINOIS

sense, developed for its adaptability to training as well as for strength and alertness. It was expected to combine stamina as a stock dog with solidity and mental agility.

CHARACTERISTICS: The Malinois has proved to be a good guard dog, elegant in appearance, and intelligent. His characteristics are similar to those of the Belgian Sheepdog (see page 152). He is recommended only for those who have space where he can run.

COLOR: Rich fawn to mahogany, with black overlay, black mask and ears.

COAT: Short and straight, with thick undercoat.

HEIGHT: Dog: 24–26 inches. Bitch: 22–24 inches.

WEIGHT: Dog: 55–60 pounds. Bitch: 50–55 pounds.

PRICE RANGE: $200 and up.

BELGIAN TERVUREN

HISTORY AND ORIGIN: Known and registered in France and Belgium as the Chien de Berger Belge, the Belgian Tervuren, also a shepherd dog, has the same ancestors as the Groenendael (Belgian Sheepdog), the only difference being the color. The Tervuren is colored light fawn until he is 18 months old and then turns mahogany.

CHARACTERISTICS: Same as the Belgian Sheepdog.

COLOR: Rich fawn to russet mahogany with black overlay.

COAT: Strong, straight, dense, not silky or wiry.

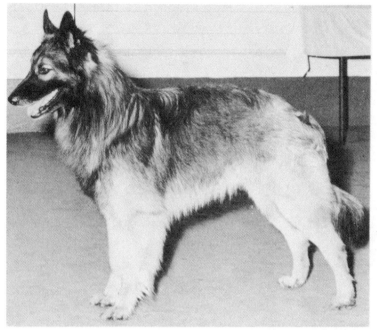

BELGIAN TERVUREN

HEIGHT: Dog: 24–26 inches. Bitch: 22–24 inches.
WEIGHT: Dog: 55–60 pounds. Bitch: 50–55 pounds.
PRICE RANGE: $125, up to $400 for show quality.

BERNESE MOUNTAIN DOG

HISTORY AND ORIGIN: About two thousand years ago, the Roman legions were in Switzerland, and of course they brought their dogs with them. When they departed, many of the soldiers left their dogs behind, and these dogs are the ancestors of the modern Bernese. One of the four kinds of Swiss mountain dog, the Bernese, according to many, is more popular in Switzerland than the St. Bernard. The breed gets its name from the canton of Berne.

CHARACTERISTICS: A tough, hardy dog, the Bernese is extremely faithful and loyal, but he is a one-man dog. He is distant and reserved with strangers, rarely making friends outside the family. He lives in an unheated kennel in any kind of weather. He is not recommended for apartment life, nor for a very warm climate.

COLOR: Jet-black with russet-brown or deep tan markings on all legs.

BERNESE MOUNTAIN DOG

COAT: Soft and silky with a bright, natural sheen, long and slightly wavy, but never curly.
HEIGHT: Dog: 23–27½ inches. Bitch: 21–26 inches.
WEIGHT: Dog: 60–70 pounds. Bitch: 50–65 pounds.
PRICE RANGE: $200 and up.

BOUVIER DES FLANDRES

HISTORY AND ORIGIN: The Bouvier des Flandres is an old breed that has existed for several hundred years in southwest Flanders and in the French northern hills. There these dogs were bred by farmers, butchers, or cattlemen as work dogs and cattle herders. The term "Bouvier" means cowherd or ox driver. The dog first came to the attention of breeding experts in 1910, and in 1912 the standard was adopted.
CHARACTERISTICS: The Bouvier des Flandres is a rugged and powerful dog chiefly owned by farmers and cattle people. He is very sensitive, with a keen intellect, a spirited nature, and rough, boisterous ways. With his owner and family he is warm, tender, absolutely devoted,

BOUVIER DES FLANDRES

BOXER

BRIARD

BULLMASTIFF

COLLIE

COLLIE, SMOOTH-COATED

and loyal. He is good with children, but is not highly recommended for apartment life.

COLOR: Pepper-and-salt, black, gray, or brindle.

COAT: Rough and unkempt.

HEIGHT: Dog: 23½–27½ inches. Bitch: 22¾–27 inches.

WEIGHT: Dog: 65–70 pounds. Bitch: 60–65 pounds.

PRICE RANGE: $250 average.

BOXER

HISTORY AND ORIGIN: As with most breeds, the exact origin of the Boxer is uncertain. The best guess is that he is a cross between a Great Dane and an English Bulldog, and that he was developed to fight wild boars and to bait bulls. The current theory about the origin of his name backs this up. Boxer here is a corruption of the German word *Beisser,* or biter. Thus, a *bullenbeisser* is a bull biter, or bulldog. Another theory has it that he derives his name from his manner of fighting, with his front paws. The first Boxer was registered in 1904.

CHARACTERISTICS: Bred to be both a guard and a playmate, the Boxer has a well-controlled temper that sometimes breaks out. He is renowned for his great love for his owner, as well as for his faithfulness to the entire household. He is alert, fearless, courageous, independent, and modest. As a short-haired dog, he is clean, easy to take care of. He is trustworthy with children—he will take any kind of mauling and roughhousing. He is not difficult to train.

There are, however, some drawbacks. Boxers are subject to tumors of the gum, which start to appear when the dog is about 7. They are not dangerous and can be removed, but if he chews on them they will bleed profusely. Many Boxers are also subject to tantrums all through their lives. He has a habit of salivating a great deal, leaving damp spots on rugs, furniture, and bedding. He is rather awkward, is susceptible to digestive disorders which make him vomit often, and he will snore and snort.

COLOR: Fawn or brindle, usually marked with white.

COAT: Short, shiny, smooth, and tight to the body.

HEIGHT: Dog: 22–24 inches. Bitch: 21–23 inches.

WEIGHT: Dog: 70–75 pounds. Bitch: 60–70 pounds.

PRICE RANGE: $125–$175 and up.

BRIARD

HISTORY AND ORIGIN: The Briard, or Chien Berger de Brie, is the oldest sheepdog of France, going back to the twelfth century. The dog as we know him today appears in many tapestries of the fifteenth and sixteenth centuries. He was then a fearless fighter and defender of his family and the farm animals against wolves and robbers. Today he is a peaceful dog, herding and guarding flocks and acting as protector of farm property. Les Amis du Briard, a society formed in France in about 1900 established the standard for the Briard that we have today.

CHARACTERISTICS: The Briard is a wiry, muscular dog protected by a long, wavy "goat's coat" which enables him to go anywhere and withstand any climate. He is a slow learner, but a very hard and very serious worker. He is a placid dog, but he should not be provoked, for he will fight to the death. He is a one-man dog.

COLOR: Any solid color except white; dark colors best. Usually black, dark or light gray, or tawny.

COAT: Long, slightly wavy, stiff, and strong.

HEIGHT: Dog: 23–27 inches. Bitch: 22–25½ inches.

WEIGHT: Dog: 75–80 pounds. Bitch: 70–75 pounds.

PRICE RANGE: $250 and up.

BULLMASTIFF

HISTORY AND ORIGIN: The Bullmastiff was originally developed as a cross-breed between the Mastiff and the Bulldog, combining the power of the first with the aggressiveness of the second. The result was a dog who reigned supreme as the guardian of estates and grounds.

CHARACTERISTICS: The Bullmastiff is still principally a work dog, used for police work and as a guard for estates and other property. He sees well in the dark and has keen hearing. His immense strength makes him more than a match for any trespasser, whom he will pin to the ground and hold for hours if necessary. Fearless and alert, he is a one-man dog, but he will accept graciously the family of his owner.

COLOR: Any shade of fawn or brindle.

COAT: Short and dense.

HEIGHT: Dog: 25–27 inches. Bitch: 24–26 inches.

WEIGHT: Dog: 110–130 pounds. Bitch: 100–120 pounds.

PRICE RANGE: $300 and up.

COLLIE

HISTORY AND ORIGIN: The Collie goes back hundreds of years to the highlands of Scotland, where he was used for guarding and herding sheep in extremely rugged country. He gets his name from the early Scottish name for sheep. The dog was popular in the late eighteenth century and the early nineteenth. But when Queen Victoria took a liking to him in the 1860s, his popularity and reputation were firmly established.

CHARACTERISTICS: The Smooth-coated Collie is extremely rare, while the rough-coated breed has gained in popularity. The latter's long coat needs grooming, for the Collie is subject to skin disorders, fleas, and ticks, as are all long-haired dogs. Also, this dog is not for the apartment owner who does not want a daily workout. The dog has been bred to remain outdoors for most of the day, especially in a dry, cool place, and both the coat and the dog are not at their best unless these requirements are fulfilled.

The Collie is affectionate, is easily trained, and is excellent with children. Since his guarding instinct is highly developed, he makes a fine watchdog, especially with small children. With those he knows, he is very faithful and loyal, while with strangers he is reserved and distrustful.

One word of warning, however. Many Collies, because of inbreeding, tend to be nervous and therefore a bit unstable. Many of them will shake and bark when a train passes by. Many are also susceptible to detached retinas (you can notice this at 6 months of age) and will eventually go blind. Finally, a Collie's nose is very sensitive to the sun and when exposed will become ulcerated.

COLOR: Sable-and-white, blue merle, white, or black with tan and white.
COAT: Abundant, straight, and harsh.
HEIGHT: Dog: 24–26 inches. Bitch: 22–24 inches.
WEIGHT: Dog: 60–75 pounds. Bitch: 50–65 pounds.
PRICE RANGE: $150 and up.

DOBERMAN PINSCHER

HISTORY AND ORIGIN: The Doberman is a mixture of the Black-and-Tan Terrier, the Rottweiler, and the German Pinscher, a combination that has created an intelligent and able dog. Named after Louis Dobermann, who originated the breed in the town of Apolda, Germany, in 1890, the Doberman is used primarily as a police and hunting dog and as a guard.

CHARACTERISTICS: The Doberman adapts himself to the city, country, or suburbs, but needs a good deal of exercise, as much as one hour a day off the leash. He is easily cared for, his short coat needing little attention except occasional combing and brushing, and he has no odor.

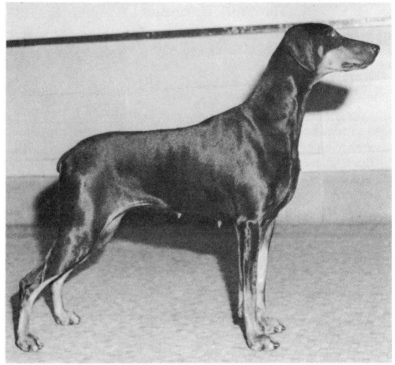

DOBERMAN PINSCHER

GERMAN SHEPHERD DOG

The female is generally easier to train than the male. Both sexes stand the heat well and can be recommended for southern climates. With his high intelligence, the Doberman can be trained for anything.

Best as a personal guard and companion, the Doberman is not recommended for small children. He may have streaks of meanness and viciousness, or he may turn when provoked. The Doberman can be very temperamental, even though he is usually affectionate and companionable.

OLOR: Black or brown.
OAT: Smooth, short, hard, thick, close-lying.
EIGHT: Dog: 26–28 inches. Bitch: 24–26 inches.
VEIGHT: Dog: 65–75 pounds. Bitch: 60–70 pounds.
RICE RANGE: $200 and up.

GERMAN SHEPHERD DOG

HISTORY AND ORIGIN: Primarily a shepherd dog whose ancestors are the old herding and farm dogs of Germany, the German Shepherd has been highly bred into an intelligent and able animal who serves in a variety of ways: as a police dog, Seeing Eye dog, guard, and pet. There has been great interest in the German Shepherd in this century, with speciality clubs honoring the breed springing up all over the world.

CHARACTERISTICS: The German Shepherd can be trained for nearly anything. He is intelligent and discriminating, as well as the possessor of a sensitive nose. He is loyal, courageous, and exceptionally rugged, with a double coat for all-weather protection. He is not pugnacious, but will fight if provoked. Generally he is poised, unexcitable, well controlled. He does not give affection easily, but once his friendship is given, it is for life.

The German Shepherd needs plenty of exercise, and his long coat requires frequent combing and brushing. He is good with children. He is very susceptible to hip dysplasia (hip malformation).

COLOR: Black-and-tan, gray, or black.
COAT: Straight, harsh, close-lying.
EIGHT: Dog: 25 inches. Bitch: 23 inches.
VEIGHT: Dog: 75–85 pounds. Bitch: 60–70 pounds.
RICE RANGE: $200 and up.

GREAT DANE

HISTORY AND ORIGIN: Many authorities believe that the Great Dane is a descendant of the Molossian dog of Greco-Roman times. Others carry

GREAT DANE

him back as far as 2200 B.C., believing the "tiger dog" of Egypt to
be his ancestor. There are paintings, coins, and sculptures to suppor
each theory. The Saxons brought the dog to England, where he wa:
used to hunt boars—which required size, weight, and endurance
The name is a translation of the French *Grand Danois.* The Great Dane
as we now know him owes his development to Germany rather than
to Denmark.

CHARACTERISTICS: The Great Dane needs plenty of room in order to avoic
injuries to his tail, which is particularly sensitive. Generally, he shoulc
not be kept on a chain, but allowed to run free. He craves his owner's
attention and loves children. He is, however, a risky playmate for
young children because of his size—unintentionally, he may knock
a child over.

The Great Dane is somewhat difficult to train unless his owner
is experienced in training a dog of high spirits and keen perception
He is a very quick and alert dog, in this respect like the Terrier
extremely fast and intelligent. His keen sense of smell ranks with
that of the Bloodhound. The Dane has an enormous appetite, obviously, and is not for the city. If he is kept on a farm with other
animals, he may occasionally have a bad temper and kill sheep or
other small stock.

He is subject to heart attacks and kidney ailments, which shorten his life (8–10 years).

COLOR: Brindle, fawn, blue, black, or harlequin.

COAT: Short, thick, glossy.

HEIGHT: Dog: 31–34 inches. Bitch: 28–31 inches.

WEIGHT: Dog: 135–150 pounds. Bitch: 120–135 pounds.

PRICE RANGE: $250–$750 (the latter figure for show quality).

GREAT PYRENEES

GREAT PYRENEES

HISTORY AND ORIGIN: A member of the Mastiff or giant dog family, the Great Pyrenees came originally from Asia Minor and as a breed dates back centuries before the birth of Christ, probably as long ago as 1800 B.C. When these dogs came to Europe, they settled in the Spanish Pyrenees, where they remained until the Middle Ages when they became useful as guardians of châteaus and estates. In 1675, they were adopted by Louis XIV as the royal dog of France. They then became the pets of European royalty, but they were still used mostly by shepherds, who equipped them with spiked collars to frighten off bears and wolves.

CHARACTERISTICS: The Great Pyrenees is a lovable dog in virtually every respect. With children he is gentle, affectionate, and companionable. He gets on well with other animals. With his master he is adoring, loyal, and untemperamental. He is extremely suitable for people living in the country, where the dog has constant access to the outdoors.

He also makes an excellent guard.

His long coat requires no special trimming or plucking, simply a stiff combing and brushing about three times a week. He should never be clipped in the summer, as sunburn may prove disastrous. Despite his large size, he is not an especially heavy eater. He keeps himself clean.

COLOR: All white, or white marked with badger, gray, or tan.

COAT: Long, thick, flat and coarse, straight or slightly waved.

HEIGHT: Dog: 27–32 inches. Bitch: 25–29 inches.

WEIGHT: Dog: 100–125 pounds. Bitch: 90–115 pounds.

PRICE RANGE: $250–$600.

KOMONDOR

KOMONDOR

HISTORY AND ORIGIN: One of the oldest of European dogs, the Komondor originated in Tibet about 2000 B.C. He probably came to Europe with the Magyar invaders. The dog we have now is possibly a descendant of the Aftscharka, a massive, long-haired herdsman's dog found on the steppes of Russia. For the past thousand years, the breed has been kept pure by the Hungarians, who use him to protect the herd from wolves.

CHARACTERISTICS: Powerful, fearless, and looking like a snowy mountain, the Komondor is perhaps the greatest guard of sheep alive. Living in the open most of the year, he protects his herds from dogs, foxes, wolves, and bears. He is also extremely devoted to his owner and family and will attack savagely anyone trying to harm them. He is not demonstrative or playful, but calm, even-tempered, cautious, and deadly serious.

COLOR: White.

COAT: Long, soft, woolly, dense hair, entangled and shaggy; rope-like at maturity.

HEIGHT: Dog: 25½–27 inches. Bitch: 23½–25 inches.

WEIGHT: Dog: 85–90 pounds. Bitch: 75–80 pounds.

PRICE RANGE: $225 and up.

KUVASZ

KUVASZ

HISTORY AND ORIGIN: Another of the old European dogs, the Kuvasz is the best known of the Hungarian dogs. His name, however, is not Hungarian but Turkish, and it means "Guardian of Nobles." The Kuvasz has existed in his present form for over a thousand years. By the fifteenth century, the breed became a favorite with the nobles, who bred the dogs on their estates, and in 1458 King Matthias (1458–1490) made them a favorite at court and personally supervised their breeding.

CHARACTERISTICS: The Kuvasz is an excellent farm dog, intelligent, methodical, and absolutely fearless. He is a one-man dog who selects his friends and never forgets his enemies. He always knows who wishes to hurt his owner or himself and who is a friend. His instinct here is uncanny. Unbeatable as a watchdog and a farm dog, he must be handled properly as a puppy and carefully as an adult.

COLOR: Pure white.

COAT: Long and slightly wavy.

HEIGHT: Dog: 25–26 inches. Bitch: 24–25 inches.

WEIGHT: Dog: 65–70 pounds. Bitch: 60–65 pounds.

PRICE RANGE: $250 and up.

MASTIFF

MASTIFF

HISTORY AND ORIGIN: There are many theories about the Mastiff's origin and a great deal of confusion. One painting of a dog very much like a Mastiff dates from 2200 B.C. Some claim that the dog dates back to the early Assyrian dynasties. Still others claim that the Mastiff originated in Tibet thousands of years ago and then spread to Persia, Egypt, Greece, and finally showed up in England as the Old English Mastiff.

In any event, by 1400 bull and bear baiting were popular in England, and by the time of Henry VIII the sport had obtained the sanction of the king. The dog then became a great favorite with noblemen and was often taken by them to war. The Mastiff fought beside his master at Agincourt and in the War of the Roses. He was prized by royalty from Canute to the present. The name appears to derive from the Latin for "tame, domesticated," and therefore the Mastiff is a "house dog"—that is, guardian of the house.

CHARACTERISTICS: Despite his terrifying appearance, the Mastiff is a gentle, kind, affectionate, and very friendly dog. He is not nervous, not temperamental, has no vicious strain, and is so sure of himself that he can be calm, steady, and absolutely loving. He is great with children. The only drawback here is that he may hurt them by simply leaning on them. He is not for the city, but should live on a farm or an estate.

COLOR: Apricot, silver-fawn, or dark fawn-brindle.

COAT: Short, coarse, lying close.

HEIGHT: Dog: 30–33 inches. Bitch: 27½–31 inches.

WEIGHT: Dog: 175–185 pounds. Bitch: 165–175 pounds.

PRICE RANGE: Dog: $450–$550. Bitch: $350–$450.

NEWFOUNDLAND

NEWFOUNDLAND

HISTORY AND ORIGIN: The Newfoundland is named after the island of that name. The best guess is that he originated in about the seventeenth century when some Great Pyrenees, brought to the island by Basque and French fishermen, were mated with the native dogs or with some wolves or Huskies. Dogs from these crosses were then taken to England where careful breeding gave us the handsome dog we have today.

CHARACTERISTICS: A great swimmer and a natural lifeguard, the Newfoundland is one of the most faithful and the most gentle dogs in the world. If a dog is wanted for companionship and as a protector for the family—and most people want a dog for one purpose or the other—the Newfoundland is the answer. He has a sweet and kind disposition, is even-tempered, completely stable, and slavishly devoted to his master and to the family. He loves children and gets along well with other dogs and even wants their companionship. But he must have a good deal of exercise, about 2 hours a day— therefore, he is not an apartment dog.

COLOR: Dull coal-black.

COAT: Flat and dense, rather coarse, and oily.

HEIGHT: Dog: 27–28 inches. Bitch: 25–26 inches.

WEIGHT: Dog: 140–150 pounds. Bitch: 110–120 pounds.

PRICE RANGE: $200 and up.

PULI

PULI

HISTORY AND ORIGIN: This famous Hungarian Sheepdog of the small variety has been used by Magyar shepherds for about a thousand years. We don't know his origin, but he is similar to the Tibetan Terrier, who may be the ancestor of the Puli. Others think that the Puli comes from Iceland or is a descendant of the wild dogs of Lapland. Like the other Hungarian Sheepdogs, he has a tangled and unkempt coat, which is his natural protection against the elements and wild animals.

CHARACTERISTICS: One of the best and most versatile of the sheepdogs, the Puli very often controls the sheep by jumping over their backs. He also controls wandering sheep by jumping on their backs and riding them. High-strung, with tireless energy, the Puli is kind and loyal, but also somewhat stubborn. He must be handled firmly, but gently. He is, as well, aggressive and not fond of strangers. This strange and bizarre-looking dog is not for children or for apartment life. He should be worked.

COLOR: Black, rusty black, various shades of gray, or white.

COAT: Dense, weather-resistant double coat. It should never be silky, straight, or wavy.

HEIGHT: Dog: 17–19 inches. Bitch: 16–18 inches.

WEIGHT: Dog: 30–35 pounds. Bitch: 25–32 pounds.

PRICE RANGE: $200 average.

ROTTWEILER

ROTTWEILER

HISTORY AND ORIGIN: The history of the Rottweiler goes back to the Roman Empire. Originally, the Rottweiler was a cattle driver for the Roman legions and a guard for their supply dumps. When these legions came to Rottweil in Germany, they brought their dogs with them. When they left, most of their dogs stayed behind, and so it was that the breed took its name from this ancient town. During the Middle Ages and right down to the nineteenth century, merchants took the Rottweiler—with their purses hanging from his neck to protect their money against thieves—with them when they went to town. Now it is a companion, guardian, and police dog.

CHARACTERISTICS: Sturdy, alert, and intelligent, the Rottweiler is a good all-round dog for ranch or farm life. He has a great capacity for outdoor work, and he is a diligent and steady worker. He is tender toward the family he lives with and will guard them with his life. He is rugged, steady, and obedient. He will probably adapt to city or apartment life, but may be unhappy without freedom to roam.

COLOR: Black, with tan and dark-brown markings on cheeks, muzzle, chest, legs and over both eyes.

COAT: Short, coarse, and flat.

HEIGHT: Dog: 23¾–27 inches. Bitch: 21¾–25⅔ inches.

WEIGHT: Dog: 80–90 pounds. Bitch: 75–85 pounds.

PRICE RANGE: $200 and up, depending on quality.

SAINT BERNARD

SAINT BERNARD

HISTORY AND ORIGIN: The Saint Bernard gets his name from the noted monk Bernard de Menthon and from the Hospice of the Saint Bernard

Pass in the Swiss Alps. We have no evidence, however, to show that the dog was used at the time of Saint Bernard. The first reference to him in the hospice records was in 1774. The dog's job was to find the trail and warn people of treacherous footing. The British painter Sir Edwin Landseer is responsible for the popular and romantic conception of the Saint Bernard fighting his way through rain and snow with a small keg of brandy around his neck for the lost traveler. His origin is pure conjecture, running anywhere from his having Tibetan ancestors to his shadowy origin in Central Asia.

HARACTERISTICS: The Saint Bernard demands to be treated with kindness, affection, and respect. If he is treated this way, his owner and family—especially the children—can have no greater friend. He is gentle, warm, placid, with no malice and no vicious streak. He is loyal and devoted.

Outdoors he can withstand any temperature and any storm. His sense of direction is unfailing, and his knowledge of the weather uncanny. He should be kept outdoors and is not an apartment dog.

OLOR: White with red, or red with white, with white chest, feet, and tip of tail.

OAT: Very dense, shorthaired, lying smooth.

EIGHT: Dog: 27–29 inches. Bitch: 25–27 inches.

VEIGHT: 155–170 pounds. Bitch: 140–160 pounds.

RICE RANGE: $175 and up, to $500 for show.

SAMOYED

SAMOYED

HISTORY AND ORIGIN: The Samoyed takes his name from the Samoyeds, a hunting and fishing people who live on the eastern shore of the White Sea in Russia. Of all the dogs known to man, the Samoyed is most like the primitive dog, for he has no wolf or fox in him. And like his people, the Samoyed has remained pure for thousands of years. We can be sure that the dog we have today is the same dog who guarded the reindeer and protected the Samoyed people for thousands of years.

CHARACTERISTICS: One of the most beautiful and impressive dogs in the world, the Samoyed is kind, gentle, highly intelligent, and incredibly faithful. He is also very hardy, healthy, and good-tempered. Perfect with children, he is an excellent house dog. To the Samoyed owner he is the dog of dogs, possessing the best qualities of other breeds. He is happiest in a cold climate.

COLOR: Pure white, or white-and-biscuit, or cream.

COAT: Dense and straight.

HEIGHT: Dog: 21–23½ inches. Bitch: 19–21 inches.

WEIGHT: Dog: 50–65 pounds. Bitch: 35–50 pounds.

PRICE RANGE: $150 and up, to $350 for show.

SCHNAUZER, STANDARD

SCHNAUZER

HISTORY AND ORIGIN: The Schnauzer is an old German breed; there is a statue in Stuttgart dated 1620 of a watchman and a dog identical with the Schnauzer we know today. Originating in Württemberg and in Bavaria, the dog was then primarily a cattle driver and a ratter (part of his terrier background). When cattle driving disappeared, he was taken into the towns by butchers and brewers, where he became very popular and where he remained until he came to the attention of German breeders in about 1900.

CHARACTERISTICS: The Schnauzer is a good-natured, affectionate, high-spirited dog who loves to play, especially at rough sports. He is a one-man dog, highly mistrustful of strangers, but he loves his master's family, especially the children. His terrier ancestry insures his great ratting ability, and his keen intelligence and great sense of responsibility make him an excellent watchdog. He should be trimmed according to standard in spring and autumn and otherwise just brushed every

SCHNAUZER, GIANT

day. He is both a good outdoor and a good apartment dog.

COLOR: Black or pepper-and-salt.

COAT: Close, strong, hard, wiry.

HEIGHT: *Giant*—Dog: 23–25½ inches. Bitch: 21½–24 inches.
  Standard—Dog: 19–20 inches. Bitch: 17–19 inches.
  Miniature—Dog: 13–14 inches. Bitch: 12–14 inches.

WEIGHT: *Giant*—Dog: 73–78 pounds. Bitch: 65–75 pounds.
  Standard—Dog: 32–37 pounds. Bitch: 27–35 pounds.
  Miniature—Dog: 14–15 pounds. Bitch: 13–14 pounds.

PRICE RANGE: $175–$350.

SCHNAUZER, GIANT

For history and origin as well as characteristics, see Schnauzer (above)

SHEEPDOG, BELGIAN

SHEEPDOG, BELGIAN

HISTORY AND ORIGIN: Before 1891, the Belgian Sheepdog was the chief do
used by shepherds in most countries of Europe. He existed in a

sizes, shapes, and colors, and was bred only for his herding ability. In the 1890s, attempts were made to standardize the breed, and at the beginning of the twentieth century agreement was reached in Belgium about hair, color, and type. Black was finally agreed upon, and this black dog became known as the Groenendael, because the dog we know as the Belgian Sheepdog was born and developed in the town of Groenendael.

CHARACTERISTICS: The Belgian Sheepdog is tough and powerful, perfect on the farm for rounding up sheep and cattle. He is considerate and obedient, and he wants the love of his owner. But he is not a dog to trifle with, for he is temperamental and a savage fighter. When still a pup, he must be carefully trained by an experienced owner. He is exceptionally intelligent, adapts to any climate, and makes an excellent watchdog and guardian.

COLOR: Best is black with some white on forechest, between pads of feet, on chin and muzzle.

COAT: Long, straight, and abundant, not silky or wiry.

HEIGHT: Dog: 24–26 inches. Bitch: 22–24 inches.

WEIGHT: Dog: 55–60 pounds. Bitch: 50–55 pounds.

PRICE RANGE: $200.

SHEEPDOG, OLD ENGLISH

SHEEPDOG, OLD ENGLISH

HISTORY AND ORIGIN: The Old English Sheepdog is not very old as histories of breeds go, his going back to 1771, when Gainsborough painted the Duke of Buccleuch with his arms around an Old English Sheepdog. The dog was first developed in the west of England, in Devon, in Somerset and Cornwall. We know little about his stock; some claim that it came from the Scotch bearded Collie, others that it came from a Russian breed.

CHARACTERISTICS: The Old English Sheepdog is a good all-round worker on a ranch or on a farm, especially if there are sheep or cattle for him to tend. He is also faithful, devoted, friendly, and gentle, a perfect companion for children. Further, he is a very clean dog and very adaptable—heat and cold don't bother him. He requires just one good brushing a day. He shouldn't be confined to an apartment or a kennel, but should have freedom to roam. Above all, he must not be chained, for he will become surly and sullen.

COLOR: Gray, grizzle, blue, or blue merle, with or without white. It should not be brown or fawn.

COAT: Profuse and of good, hard texture, shaggy, and curl-free.

HEIGHT: Dog: 23–25 inches. Bitch: 21–24 inches.

WEIGHT: Dog: 60–65 pounds. Bitch: 55–60 pounds.

PRICE RANGE: $200.

SHEEPDOG, SHETLAND

SHEEPDOG, SHETLAND ("SHELTIE")

HISTORY AND ORIGIN: A small version of the Collie, the Shetland Sheepdog came originally from the Shetland Islands, an island group unique for giving the world such small breeds of domestic animals as the Shetland ponies, sheep, and cattle. The Shetland Sheepdog is perfect for his work because the sheep he guards are half the size of mainland sheep.

The earliest record of the "Sheltie" dates back to about 1840, when we hear of him helping to care for sheep in the highland. His ancestors are the old Hill Collie of Scotland and the King Charles Spaniel.

CHARACTERISTICS: The Shetland Sheepdog is one of the great working dogs of the Western world. Farmers swear by his herding instincts for pigs and goats as well as sheep. His small size enables him to walk on ledges, overgrown trails, and mountain paths, where big and clumsy dogs could not possibly go. He is invaluable in deep snow because he does not break through like a big dog, but will run across on the snow's light crust.

He is also a splendid apartment dog, for he takes up little room, makes a great friend, and does not wish to roam. He is excellent in a family and good with children, from whom he will take all sorts of punishment.

Further, he is a fine companion for the handicapped, for he is extremely sensitive to human feelings, gentle, anxious to love and please his owner, and amusing. He does, however, need a lot of grooming.

COLOR: Combination of black, blue merle, and sable from gold to mahogany.

COAT: Long, straight, harsh hair.

HEIGHT: Dog: 14–16 inches. Bitch: 13–15 inches.

WEIGHT: Dog: 15–16 pounds. Bitch: 14–15 pounds.

PRICE RANGE: $175 average.

SIBERIAN HUSKY

HISTORY AND ORIGIN: Often called the Siberian Chuchi, after the Chuchi natives of northeastern Siberia, the Siberian Husky has remained pure for hundreds, perhaps thousands, of years. He is the most valued possession of the Chuchi, for he is a constant companion to their children, a protector of the family, and an invaluable sled dog.

In 1909 he was brought to Alaska, where he established his reputation as sled-dog racer.

CHARACTERISTICS: Hardy, fierce, and highly intelligent, the Siberian Husky, contrary to what most people think, is gentle and friendly. He is completely devoted to his owner and his family. He is alert and graceful, and is generally much friendlier to people than the Alaskan Malamute. He makes a good pet, but he must be trained carefully and thoroughly. He is happiest in the cold weather.

SIBERIAN HUSKY

COLOR: Any color or white, usually shades of gray, tan, or black.
COAT: Soft, smooth, and dense.
HEIGHT: Dog: 21–23½ inches. Bitch: 20–22 inches.
WEIGHT: Dog: 45–60 pounds. Bitch: 35–50 pounds. (Dogs above these weights are probably a crossbreed.)
PRICE RANGE: $175 average.

WELSH CORGI, CARDIGAN

HISTORY AND ORIGIN: The Cardigan Welsh Corgi is one of the most mysterious breeds in its origin. From the little we know, it seems that the dog first was brought to Wales by the Central European Celts about 1200 B.C. He was then used as a cattle dog. Centuries later the Cardigan Corgi was bred with native herding dogs and Dachshunds to produce the cattle-driving dog we know today. The dog gets his first name from the county of Cardiganshire and his last name from the Welsh *cor* (dwarf) and *gi* (meaning dog).

CHARACTERISTICS: One of the very best of the small working dogs, the Cardigan Welsh Corgi is an intelligent, tough, hard-working dog who works well with cattle, horses, and sheep, and destroys all the vermin he can get his paws on. He is long-lived, very healthy, and can withstand any temperature. He is usually a one-man dog on the farm, suspicious of strangers and hostile to stray cats and dogs.

COLOR: Red, brindle, black-and-tan, black-and-white, or blue merle.
COAT: Short, thick, and hard.

WELSH CORGI, CARDIGAN

HEIGHT: Dog: 11½–12 inches. Bitch: 11–11½ inches.
WEIGHT: Dog: 20–25 pounds. Bitch: 15–20 pounds.
PRICE RANGE: $150 average.

WELSH CORGI, PEMBROKE

WELSH CORGI, PEMBROKE

HISTORY AND ORIGIN: Not as ancient a breed as the Cardigan, the Pembroke
goes back to the twelfth century, when his ancestors were brought
across the channel by the Flemish weavers who came to England
at the invitation of Henry I. These weavers eventually went to live

in Wales. The dog they took with them looked very much like the old Schipperke and came from the same family as the Keeshond, the Samoyed, the Pomeranian, the Chow Chow, and the Finnish Spitz. Unlike the Cardigan, the Pembroke has almost none of the Dachshund in him and is in no way related to him. The reason they look so much alike, although their early ancestors were different, is that they were often crossed in the early nineteenth century.

CHARACTERISTICS: Like the Cardigan, the Pembroke is a natural farm dog, alert, very much alive, with an uncanny instinct to take care of and protect animals. He is especially a great help with young and nervous horses, for he is calm, assuring, and steady. He is also a good ratter and a killer of weasels. If trained early enough, the Pembroke makes a good apartment dog as long as he has things to do. He particularly likes guarding children in carriages.

This little dog is tough, very hardy, and may live up to 18 years. He is healthy and almost never suffers from skin ailments. He should be exercised about three times a day.

COLOR: Red, sable, fawn, or black-and-tan, with white markings on legs, chest, and neck.

COAT: Medium length and dense, never wiry.

HEIGHT: Dog: 11–12 inches. Bitch: 10–11 inches.

WEIGHT: Dog: 20–24 pounds. Bitch: 18–22 pounds.

PRICE RANGE: $150 and up.

MISCELLANEOUS CLASS: A NOTE

In addition to the breeds listed in the Stud Book of the American Kennel Club, there are those admitted to the Miscellaneous Class. While in this class, breeds are ineligible for championship points, but they may compete in AKC obedience trials and earn obedience titles. In conformation shows, however, they are limited to the competition in the Miscellaneous Class. Any breed in this class that attracts nationwide interest and serious breeding activity may, when judged ready by the Board of Directors of the AKC, move into the Stud Book. There are, as of 1976, 8 breeds in the Miscellaneous Class:

AUSTRALIAN CATTLE DOGS

AUSTRALIAN KELPIES

BEARDED COLLIES *(As of February, 1977, recognized in the Stud Book)*

BORDER COLLIES

CAVALIER KING CHARLES SPANIELS

IBIZEN HOUNDS

MINIATURE BULL TERRIERS

SPINONI ITALIANI

TIBETAN SPANIEL

Beyond this class, there are literally hundreds of other distinct breeds throughout the world, many of them renowned in their native countries. Some typical ones are: Anatolian Sheepdog (Turkey), Appenzell (Switzerland), Dogue de Bordeaux (France), Bracco Italiano (Italy), Munsterländer (Germany), French Pointer, Portuguese Water Dog, German Spaniel, Austrian Hound, Dunker (Norwegian Hound), Finnish Hound, Finnish Spitz, and Ainu (Japan). Their omission here has nothing to do with their intrinsic worth, but with limitations of space and their relative inaccessibility to American owners.

3
The Puppy

YOU HAVE a puppy, or puppies! That is, you have a dog under 12 months of age. The chances are that he is a few months old. Very seldom does an owner get a puppy at birth. The reasons are obvious: The puppy, like an infant, is kept with his mother until he can be weaned (at about 4 weeks). But suppose you want to raise your own puppies from birth, or someone gives you a puppy whose dam has died. Then you must start from the beginning, right here. If, however, your puppy is older, simply turn to his age group in this chapter and follow him through his first year (which is the end of puppyhood).

The newborn puppy is extremely fragile. It takes him several days to get used to the world in even the simplest way. For the first 10 days, he cannot see; he can barely stand, although he can crawl; he doesn't know where his next meal is coming from, and everything out there is a big buzz of confusion. Not until he is 4 weeks old does he have complete sight and hearing. Frankly, he is worried.

First, make sure that you have picked out a clean spot for him. And *it must be draft-free.* The enemy of all small things is drafts. When you pick a corner for him, test the area well to see that it is draft-free, and then put low sides around his sleeping area just to make sure that no wind is sneaking under the door. The temperature should be kept at about 75° F., even higher at the beginning. If you have several puppies, the area should of course be large enough to accommodate all of them. Also, if you use a carton, allow for some growth—puppies grow at a far greater rate than do infants. A medium-sized dog (50 pounds at a year) may weigh 20 pounds at 2 months.

Since the puppy has little control over his bladder and bowels, you certainly should line the carton with removable material. The best thing is several thicknesses of newspaper, which can be disposed of as soon as they are soiled. In addition, provide something soft like an old blanket, some large, clean rags, even some straw. Many people find that old children's blankets work well for the nest, or torn sheets. This will give the puppy a home, and as he begins to move around he can shape the material to fit his body. Be sure that whatever you use is clean. Puppies are susceptible to all kinds of ailments because their resistance is low. It will be easier for you if you provide washable material that can be reused.

Prepare the shelter before you get your puppy, no matter what his age. If you have a pregnant bitch, you will obviously want to prepare the shelter several days before she whelps. You then need room for the bitch as well as for the entire litter. Remember, you need space. Certain breeds whelp up to 15 puppies. The Foxhound, the St. Bernard, and the Mastiff have been known to produce over 20. This is certainly an embarrassment of riches, but before you lose heart remember that most litters number 6 or 7, with the giant dogs going higher and the toys coming down to 2 or 3. In any event, be prepared.

A puppy bigger than average (over a pound) might do better in a wooden crate. Often, a barrel will do just fine. Prevent it from rolling by propping a couple of chairs against it, or by wedging it in a secure place. If you use wire as a gate, be sure it is heavy-duty wire that the older puppy cannot chew. The edges may otherwise pierce his mouth, and if it is fine-mesh wire he might get his paws caught in it.

The newborn pup won't know what is going on, but the older one will, and it is a good idea to let him hear people moving around. After all, he has been separated from his mother and littermates; he feels a natural loneliness. He is not yet sure where to center his affections. He therefore feels insecure. Studies show that puppies have the same feelings infants have—insecurity, loneliness, and anxiety. The puppy may not feel them in the complex way the infant does, but nevertheless these feelings are present. He needs assurance. And what could be better assurance that all is well than the sound of his master's step, the light from another room, the warmth of the home setting?

All this of course is for those owners who have placed the puppy in a separate room. Many owners prefer to keep the dog in the same room with them. Be sure that the puppy keeps away from any open windows. A direct draft may give you only a stiff neck, but it may make a pup very ill. Don't keep him in a hothouse either; he is not a tomato.

Many owners place their puppies directly outdoors, for if the dog is eventually to live in the open, the sooner he is acclimated the better. In summer, a good-sized pup may live outside at 6 weeks; in winter, at 3 or 4 months. Keep small breeds indoors longer. The toy and other miniature breeds should not be kept outdoors under any conditions since they are by nature delicate.

Whatever outside arrangement you make, pay particular attention to the floor of the kennel. It should be off the ground so that no moisture gets in. Also, it should be covered with soft, warm bedding material. The kennel itself should be protected against the wind by a corner of the house, or some object that will keep any drafts from the young pup. Further, you must situate the kennel within some kind of enclosure: to keep the pup from straying, to protect him against overeager children, and to put a barrier between him and wandering animals that might attack him.

No matter what setup you agree upon for your pup, keep in mind that his reactions at a very young age are similar to an infant's. He is that delicate. Even if you wish to train your dog for the outdoors, do not suddenly put him out in the middle of the winter. Also, do not let him sleep inside one night and outside the next. Once you've established a system, keep to it. Sudden changes in temperature from warmth to cold can give him trouble: upper respiratory ailments and earaches, for example.

Just as you prepared the pup's sleeping quarters before you brought him home, or before your bitch whelped, so you should have on hand several other pieces of equipment, all modest and inexpensive. You need a pan for food, large enough for the dog to get his muzzle into; also a water pan. Both of these should be made of metal that will not rust. An initial investment here lasts for the entire life of the dog. Special pans are made for long-eared dogs, and are excellent, for they taper at the top and the dog's ears do not drag through his food.

You also need a stiff brush, a comb, a collar, a leash or lead, and some toys. Get him a link-chain lead at the start, particularly if he is going to grow large and may break a leather one. All of these are standard equipment, and any pet shop will carry them. A warning: If you buy toys for your dog, remember that a puppy is eager to try his teeth on anything, especially as he teethes, and a soft rubber ball will soon be fragments. There is a danger that he might swallow the pieces, which are indigestible. Get him something hard and tough. A piece of leather or hard rubber is excellent. Some toys may have toxic paint that the puppy will rub off and swallow. A lovely, bright-red toy might well contain a lead paint that can make a pup seriously ill. Buy only those toys made especially for dogs.

If you obtained your puppy from a kennel or from a pet shop, or from a previous owner, continue to feed him what he is accustomed to eating. If you wish to change over to some other recommended foods, do so gradually. This chapter tells you about several systems of feeding, any one of which will enable your puppy to grow to healthy maturity. But remember that a sudden change in food, no matter how nourishing you believe the new one to be, can upset the puppy's delicate system. Keep in mind that may happen to you when you go to a foreign country and change your diet suddenly. And you are fully grown and adaptable.

Before you make any of these preparations it's always a good idea to locate a veterinarian whom you trust and respect. You may have little need for him, but you should know of one in the event that a need arises. One of the best ways is to get information from a friend who owns a dog, much the same way we get a family doctor or a pediatrician. You may ask to meet the veterinarian and inspect his office. Do not necessarily be impressed if he has all the newest equipment, although there is nothing against him if he has. The most important thing to check is cleanliness. Is his office clean? Do his facilities seem to be the ones you want to entrust your dog to? Some of the finest veterinarians have managed with a limited amount of equipment. You can of course get a list of veterinarians from a local veterinary medical society, but usually professional ethics will prevent any qualitative judgments from being made.

Some Pointers on the New Puppy

If you bring home a very young puppy from a kennel or pet shop, do not be surprised if the motion of the car upsets him. Most dogs become good riders in time, but at first the motion brings on car sickness, what many of us feel on board a rolling ship or an airplane. The best precaution to take is to spread a sheet around the area where the puppy is sitting, and perhaps a towel on yourself and under the puppy.

If the pup does vomit, keep a brush and comb handy, a brush with long bristles for a long-haired dog and with short bristles for a short-haired one. Also, some kind of solvent might prove useful; apply some with a rag and wipe off the soiled spot. You cannot bathe the pup for at least 6 months; actually, you shouldn't until puppyhood is over.

The pup is probably upset at what is happening, and this is why he is nauseated. Speak to him soothingly; your tone will indicate you're not angry. Do not yell at the dog to stop—that method has never stopped anyone from vomiting.

Your new puppy may be a great joy and pleasure. The puppy himself, however, doesn't know what an excellent owner you will make. And if he is only a few days or weeks old, he knows nothing. Even if he is a few months old, he needs time to become accustomed to his new surroundings, to new voices, and to what you expect of him. You ought therefore to take some precautions that will insure the safety and happiness of your dog and the fulfillment of your own needs.

1. Try to avoid unnecessary excitement. There is a great tendency to invite everyone to come see the new pup, and young visitors are likely to pile into the house, accompanied by whoops and screams. But the new pup is not ready to receive guests. His delicate nervous system will be affected if his equilibrium is upset before he is prepared. We all know how an infant screams when grandparents and aunts and uncles crowd round to admire him.

2. If there are children in the house, their natural enthusiasm must be held down until the puppy is strong enough to accept it. Once he

attains his size and matures, he will have energy to burn. Then he will try to wear down the children. But until that time, you must keep the children within bounds. You should, of course, encourage them to look and touch. But do not let them lift or poke the puppy, probe into his ears, or try to see what makes him tick.

3. Avoid picking up the young pup too much, and, if you must, pick him up with a secure hold. Some people may tell you to pick up a pup by the skin on the back of his neck, or by the ears. But these are precarious, slippery holds. Even if the dog feels no pain—and he probably does—he must feel somewhat insecure dangling by a lump of flesh or a thread of skin. *It is much better to put one hand firmly under the pup's chest, the other under his hindquarters, and lift him evenly.*

4. Don't take the puppy out in cold weather unless he is being brought up to stand the cold; that is, unless he has been sleeping out. Avoid exposing him to sharp shifts in temperature. Also, do not bathe him until he is 6 months old.

5. Do not give bones to the young puppy. He has only his milk teeth until 5 to 7 months, and at 3 to 4 weeks he has no teeth at all. He will bolt the bones and possibly have trouble digesting them.

6. Be sure to clip the puppy's nails—or have them clipped—when he is a few weeks old. Since you will not be able to take him out, his nails will have no chance to wear down on pavements and roads. Check Chapter 5 for how to clip nails, or have it done for you.

7. If the pup has dewclaws, a kind of thumb part of the way up his leg, then have them removed shortly after birth. Dewclaws serve no use, and if you want eventually to show your dog, remove them early. If you bought the pup from a kennel, the dewclaws are probably already removed. The operation is painless, but must be performed by a veterinarian.

8. Also, if you intend to crop (clip short) the puppy's ears—a procedure usually followed for reasons of style with Great Danes, Boxers, and Dobermans—that too is best done early, at about 6 to 8 weeks. The same is true for the pup's tail, docked at 3 to 5 days, especially with the Miniature Pinscher, Schnauzer, American Staffordshire Terrier, and Boston Terrier. At this early age there is almost no pain, while later on the dog may suffer. If you want your breed to conform to the standard set by show winners, then ear and tail docking may be in order.

If these few precautions and procedures are followed, you are well on your way toward giving your dog a happy life and making him into what you want.

The First Night

On the first night at your house your puppy may cry, and his sobs are as forlorn as those of any helpless creature that has lost its parents and, seemingly, its last friend in the world. There are several things you can do to relieve the pup's loneliness and your own anxiety. Be compassionate, loving, but firm. You cannot run to comfort him each time he whimpers, or else you will spoil the pup. From the beginning, he must be made to realize that you will not come to him every time he sobs. Otherwise you will become a slave to your dog, and he will be spoiled beyond help.

The best thing to do is to calm his fears by diverting them and by soothing him with a kind, patient tone. Something warm—a hot-water bottle, for example—may make him feel that he is back at his mother's side. Or else wrap a towel or blanket in the form of a puppy and place it next to him. The chances are that he'll snuggle up to it. If you provide any electrical appliances for this purpose, make sure he cannot get at the wires. Not only will he chew them, but he may get a serious shock or burn. Some veterinarians suggest placing a clock nearby, so that the ticks will remind the puppy of his mother's heartbeat. Any device is good if it works and it's safe. Your puppy, like millions of puppies before him, must make the break from Mother. Once the start is made, he adapts readily.

THE PUPPY FROM BIRTH TO 4 WEEKS

Let us now return to the newborn puppy or puppies.

If the litter is large—8 or 10—have the dam nurse in shifts of about 3 to 4 hours. This is better for the dam and for the puppies, especially for the smaller and weaker ones who might be shoved away from a nipple. Incidentally, the rear teats are usually the most filled. Try to whisk away half of the litter when the bitch is not looking, or try to distract her from what you are doing. Otherwise she may think she is losing her puppies and resist your helpful efforts. A good method is to take a few away while she is busy feeding the others. Make sure you can distinguish one puppy from another—perhaps put on each a small identification tag so that there is no chance of a mixup. If there is, one of the puppies, or more, may miss a meal. They'll soon let you know how they feel about that. At this tender age, each meal is important.

Each newborn puppy must nurse as soon as possible. The bitch's nipples contain colostrum—milk that provides immunity against disease for the puppy until he can build up his own resistance. Colostrum, which is high in globulin, is nature's way of giving the puppy a chance to survive when he is at his frailest. It is also somewhat laxative. Without this, the puppy is protected against distemper for only about a week, while with it he is generally immune to distemper until his first inoculation at about 4 to 6 weeks. *If you plan to formula-feed from the beginning, the formula should not be used exclusively until after the pup has obtained the colostrum in the first 24 hours.* And if for some reason he fails to get the colostrum, check with your veterinarian about an early distemper injection.

If the litter is more than 6 to 8, the bitch, no matter how diligent she is, may not be able to feed them all. In such an event, supplementary feeding will be necessary. There are several ways of doing this, and I give these methods in the following pages. My suggestions for supplementary feeding can also be followed if the bitch should die or if the puppy is separated from his mother and you have to bottle feed. One can always try to obtain a foster mother from the local SPCA, but there are problems here. The foster mother may resist nursing pups that she does not recognize as her own. You have to trick her by wiping some of her milk on the pups until she thinks they belong to her, and then staying with her while they nurse. Also, you have to be especially careful that she is healthy, and even then there is no guarantee that she can handle the whole litter. Her own milk might be insufficient. Eventually you may have to go back to the bottle feeding.

Bottle Feeding

It is the latter course—bottle feeding—that many owners will follow. A friend's dog whelps, the friend wants to give the pups away, and suddenly you find yourself with a newborn pup. At whatever age you get him—whether at 2 days or 2 weeks—you can feed him correctly by sticking to the following advice.

For the newborn pup you need certain equipment, most of which you will already have if you've had infants in the house. In any event, the equipment is very modest. If you have a baby scale, you will find it useful to check on the pup's weekly gain. But if you have only a regular scale, you can still check by holding the pup in your arms and then subtracting your own weight. Of course, this doesn't work too well if the gain is only in ounces, as it will be for the smaller breeds. Other necessary equipment includes a measuring cup with ounce gradations, spoons, a mixing bowl in which to prepare the formula, a doll's baby bottles and doll's baby nipples. Regular baby-size nipples may be too large. Keep a plastic eye dropper available for an emergency—even the doll's baby nipples may be too large. You should be sure the hole in each nipple is large enough to allow the formula to seep out. If the hole is too small, sterilize a needle over a flame and puncture the nipple until the hole is the size you want. You can see for yourself if the formula feeds out too quickly or too slowly. It should feed steadily, but not in rushes.

The formula itself can take many different forms. There are several preparations that approximate the bitch's milk, just as there are several synthetic milks that contain the ingredients of mother's milk.

1. Use one of the prepared milk powders on the market. You can get them at drugstores, pet shops, and department stores. Bitch's milk,

incidentally, is not the same as cow's milk, nor is it the same as human milk. Most of these commercial formulas simply need the addition of water to make them ready.

2. Another possibility is to take a powdered baby milk and add regular cream, in the proportions of 1 ounce of powdered milk, 1 ounce of cream, and 6 ounces of water.

3. Another formula involves diluting goat's milk with equal amounts of water. You can obtain goat's milk at drug and department stores.

4. Still another formula is a cup of milk with an egg yolk added.

Whatever formula you choose, the pup should be given a vitamin and mineral supplement. Follow directions on the label.

Make sure all equipment is sanitary, as the pup, like a newborn infant, is helpless against common infections. Later on, he can fight them off. Wash your hands before you prepare the formula, making sure the bottles as well as the nipples are thoroughly clean. Wash them with hot water and soap. A bottle brush is a handy utensil for swabbing out the nipples and bottles. Work up a good lather and then rinse thoroughly. Avoid disinfectants, which the dog may lick off. Be sure that no formula remains in the bottle from the previous day. Such a residue can spoil and give your puppy acute diarrhea.

Whatever method of feeding you use, if the bitch's milk is not available be sure to keep the formula refrigerated until just before feeding time. Do not make the formula for more than a day. By trial and error, you can see how much you will need. The amount of course depends on the size of your puppies and on how many you have. For a medium-sized dog (40 to 50 pounds at maturity), the newborn puppy should drink about ¼ ounce of formula the first day *at each feeding*. You should feed him 4 to 6 times a day—you must, however, play it by ear. Some newborn pups take 3 feedings, others up to 8. Thus, each pup at the very beginning receives an ounce or more of formula a day. Each day this amount will increase slightly as the pup grows. His own reactions will tell you if he is getting enough to eat. If he is hungry, he will cry for food. If overfed, he will refuse the food. If you have a litter of 8 pups that when full-grown will be medium-sized dogs, you will need a minimum of 12 ounces of formula at the start—if the pups are older, you will need more. It is best to make extra, especially as the pups grow rapidly and need increasing amounts each day. Stay a few ounces ahead of them. If you have a very large breed, expect very rapid growth.

When you feed the puppy, the bottle should be at about the same temperature as the blood temperature of puppies themselves: figure on 100° F., and do not vary it more than a few degrees either way. The bottle should be warm to the touch, not hot. Sprinkle a drop of milk on your wrist to test it. Make sure the puppy is receiving the formula. If not, follow the directions above for enlarging the nipple hole (do not make more than one hole). And if the hole is too big and the puppy is choking, change the nipple for one with a smaller hole. Generally, both you and the pup can make an adequate adjustment after a very few feedings.

This type of feeding, used when the bitch's milk is not available, must continue for about 3 weeks. The puppy should develop well on daily increased amounts of formula. Check his weight to be sure that he is growing. If you don't have a scale, pick him up. You can usually feel the difference. The larger breeds obviously tend to grow faster.

Always be on the alert for the character of the dog's stool. At this age, his bowel movements are a key to his digestion. If there is diarrhea, regulate the formula so that its water content increases, and then as the diarrhea disappears go back to the original proportions. If diarrhea should continue, be sure to consult your veterinarian. He may prescribe a simple antidiarrhea medication, which is fine if there is nothing seriously wrong with the pup. On the other hand, the pup may have worms from birth, taken in while still an embryo. *Prolonged diarrhea is very dangerous and should never be neglected.* If there are other puppies, keep them away from the droppings, or they too might become infected.

Helping the Puppies

If the puppy or puppies have not been separated from the dam, she will take care of their needs. She stimulates them to make a bowel movement by lapping them, and then cleans up afterward. Without her help, the puppy would simply evacuate wherever he happened to be, on his bedding and pillow as often as not.

In the absence of the dam, you can stimulate the puppy. Massage his abdomen with a piece of cotton, or else gently rub the genitalia until elimination takes place. The best time to do this is shortly (5 to 10 minutes) after a meal. The stimulation also serves to induce a burp, and this too is necessary to remove gas from the stomach. When helping the puppy, hold him over a container. You'll save yourself a lot of washing. After a few days, bowel movements and urination will come almost automatically. Apply mineral or baby oil to his anus after he evacuates, to prevent irritation of the skin.

Keep the puppy clean—wipe him off with a damp cloth or with baby oil so that no feces cling to him. If possible, keep orphaned puppies separate, perhaps in shoe boxes, so that they do not lick and chew each other. This is simply a precaution to prevent one puppy from catching something from the others. If the dam is with the puppies, she will take the necessary measures.

Start Weaning

Most of your work will take place in the first 2 weeks of the puppy's life. The puppy adapts very rapidly. After a couple of weeks of bottle feeding, you can, with a minimum of prodding, begin to move the dog on to dish feeding. He soon gets the idea because his entire life centers on his meals. In fact, by the 4th week or so, it is a good idea to have finished weaning him from the bottle or the teat. Start the weaning by slowly introducing some solid foods into his diet. A mixture of a good high-protein baby cereal and milk, or this cereal and the formula, will usually do the trick. If the dam is taking care of him, she will start him on solid food herself. First she eats some food and then vomits it up, semidigested, for the puppy, in much the same way as the mother bird feeds her young. While this may seem revolting to you, it is nature's way of giving the puppy what he needs. The bitch's responses are probably controlled by some post-whelping instinct, or by hormones, so that her actions fit the puppy's needs. Also, it's her way of informing her young that she is tired of nursing them!

In any case, move the pup on to solids, *gradually*. There are jarred baby meats on the market that you can offer in addition to, or instead of, cereal-and-formula. Or you can warm up some chopped meat and add crumbled cereal and cooked vegetables, mashed all together. The puppy will love it. Even if the dam is still willing to nurse, complete the weaning after 4 weeks. Also, willing or not, she may not have enough milk to keep up with the appetites of the rapidly growing puppies. Keep up this soft diet until the pup is about 6 weeks old. Give him as much as he wants, and continue the vitamin-mineral supplement. See pages 177–179 of this chapter for some sample soft diets.

Your puppies should be thriving long before the end of the first 6-week period. If they are not, or if you notice any abnormalities—persistent vomiting, diarrhea, loss of appetite—do not hesitate to call the veterinarian. Also, a careful reading of Chapter 6, on Ailments, particularly the section on worming, and the section on how to care for the nursing bitch in Chapter 9, should take the worry out of raising your pups.

A Few Warnings

There are certain minor disorders that may cause anxiety, but you can protect yourself against them with a little foresight. The puppy's navel, for instance, is very sensitive to injury and infection. You can try to keep it covered with a gauze pad, but the dam, if she is with her puppies, will probably work off the pad. Even the puppy himself might rub it off. Therefore, your best protection is to keep the sleeping quarters very clean and to make sure that the surface material is soft and not abrasive. If there is a hard or rough surface, the puppy's navel will be irritated, perhaps become infected. If you do suspect infection, call your veterinarian. The infected area will need cleaning with an antiseptic, and perhaps the puppy will have to be treated further. In any event, such a condition will need special attention until the infected area heals.

Although I included a special section on worms and worming in Chapter 6, let me add here that it is a good idea for you to take a sample of each puppy's stools to the veterinarian at about 4 to 6 weeks, even if you suspect none of the symptoms listed in the section on worming. Worms are so common, particularly in puppies, that you might be able to halt a possible infestation long before it becomes serious. The veterinarian can check the stool under the microscope and tell you if the pup has worms. If you have a large litter to take care of, such immediate action will save you a lot of future trouble. One wormy puppy can spread worms throughout the entire litter. Unless you remove the feces right away, the other pups in the area will play with them and perhaps eat them. In this way, worms can easily be spread. If your puppy is alone, the chances of worms are somewhat slighter, but even so there are varieties that can be transmitted before birth. Many pups have worms as a congenital condition.

In any event, do not do anything about worms until you know for sure that the puppy is infested, and with what kind of worms. I warn later on, and I warn you now: *Owners can do severe damage to their young dogs by experimenting with worm medicines.* Your veterinarian is the final authority here. He'll know whether to give medicine, what kind, and under what conditions. If you live far from a veterinarian, then check my section on worming and follow directions carefully.

Some Problems

I mentioned above that some pups like to eat feces. This is a fairly common occurrence. Pups get bored, and the feces become playthings for them. Eventually they may eat them, since they are hungry most of the time. Do not become alarmed. The only sure way to discourage this is to keep the area clean. As soon as a puppy eliminates, remove the droppings. Or else stimulate the bowel movement over a container. Another thing you can do is to give the pups some hard rubber objects to play with. Toys of any kind without sharp edges and free of soft rubber are fine. Old stockings, pieces of leather, a wrapped-up towel—all of these will keep the puppy occupied when he wants to play.

Keep the children away from the dam at this time, and especially when she is nursing. She is very possessive and jealous and may mistake the child's good intentions. She has no way of knowing that he means no harm. All she knows is that she must protect her puppies. At this stage, she should be allowed to direct all her attention and energies toward the care of the pups.

Warn children about the delicacy of the puppy. Like an infant, a puppy has a soft spot on the top of his head that remains until the skull bones grow together, perhaps at 2 or 3 months. On that spot the brain is unprotected except by a thin membrane, which is elastic but easily punctured. If the puppy is accidentally dropped on a sharp object, it can pierce the membrane and kill him. In addition to this weakness, a puppy's bones, tendons, and muscles are all generally delicate and subject to injury. A child's hard shoe, even from an unintentional kick, can hurt the pup, whereas the older dog will take it as part of a game, and even come back playfully for more.

Before the pup is weaned, do not worry about house-training. The puppy is still too unsure of himself to learn anything as complicated as eliminating on a piece of paper. When he is weaned, he starts on the road toward maturity, and at that time you can start making him behave like a gentleman. Do not expect any real results at this still-early date. Anything you try to do before weaning is a waste of time. For house-training, see the section in Chapter 5. If you must start early, the best beginning you can make is to confine the puppy to a small area. Surround his bed with newspapers, so that the only spot not covered by paper is his sleeping quarters. After each meal, put him over the paper and stimulate him. But even this training is premature for the puppy under 6 to 8 weeks.

Do not bathe the pup until he is 6 months old, even if it is summer and the house is very warm, and even if he has had his vaccination. You can keep him clean with a washcloth or with cotton and baby oil. A dog is naturally a clean animal and will help keep himself free from dirt. If the bitch is taking care of the pup, she will do most of the sanitation work. Bathing and puppies do not go together, for no matter how many precautions you take, the pup may suffer a chill and develop an upper respiratory infection.

You may have heard that if a dog's nose is cold and wet, then everything is just fine. Most of the time this is a reliable test, but it is not an infallible one. A warm nose is no sure indication that the dog is ill, so the nose should never be used as a standard of illness or health. If the pup is alert, his eyes clear, his coat healthy, and his tongue pink and wet, then you know everything is fine. His nose, despite his general good condition, may be dry because he is sleeping in a dry room, or near a radiator, or he may have been cradling his nose in his paws while he slept. Any one of these or a dozen other conditions might give him temporarily a dry nose.

If you have any doubt about his health, take his temperature by the rectum. Normal is about 101.5° F.—allow a little variation. Temperatures vary according to dog size: Normal for very large breeds can be as low as 99.5° F. and for very small breeds as high as 102° F. If the temperature is a degree or two over that, call your veterinarian to be sure whether he is ill or not. Certainly if there is diarrhea and vomiting, you know there is trouble. (For a complete discussion of ailments, see Chapter 6.)

With weaning, your puppy is ready to make the giant step toward adulthood. In the next few months he will move on to a steady diet, acquire his permanent teeth, be ready for house-training, learn obedience, pick up any tricks you wish to teach him, and become your close companion for the next dozen years or more.

The following checklist of old and new points might prove useful if you have never owned a puppy before:

1. Make sure that a newborn puppy nurses right away and gets the invaluable colostrum.

2. Keep the puppies in a draft-free place.

3. Make sure that all puppies, particularly a runt (undersized pup), are getting enough to eat.

4. Sanitation is a byword whether you have a single puppy or 12.

5. Feed the formula at body temperature (100° F.) and do not feed too fast. Give a vitamin-mineral supplement to the puppy in the amounts prescribed on the label.

6. Check the puppy's weight to be sure he is growing. Also, watch out for any bad signs—diarrhea, eyes with pus, discharge from the nose, vomiting, blood in the feces or in any other discharge.

7. Keep the dog's feces away from him and from the rest of the litter.

8. At the end of the third week, start weaning the pup.

9. Keep your eye out for minor infections, particularly in a sensitive area like the navel.

10. If there is any reason to suspect worms, take a sample of the stool to your veterinarian for examination. Even if you suspect nothing, it is a good idea to have a microscopic test made when the pup is a few weeks old.

11. Warn your children not to interfere with the nursing bitch or the young pups. Protect the pups against very young children.

12. Be careful in handling a puppy, as his limbs are very fragile and his skull as yet provides inadequate protection for his brain.

13. Do not bathe the pup until he is 6 months old, or until after his permanent inoculations.

14. Forget about house-training until the pup is 6 to 8 weeks old unless you are very ambitious and are not easily disappointed by poor results.

15. Put down fresh water for the puppy after each meal, but do not leave it out—he might bathe himself in it.

THE PUPPY FROM 4 TO 12 WEEKS

Your attention to the puppy at this stage will center around three or four major items: correct feeding and nutrition, inoculations, perhaps house-training, and possibly worming. Also, you can get your pup used to his name at this time. As you follow along in this chapter, I discuss the correct feeding for the puppy until he becomes an adult, at about a year.

For the particulars of house-training, turn to Chapter 5. While house-breaking is not a tremendous problem, it does require a separate section. And do not become nervous—your pup will eventually be trained, just as all children are finally taken out of diapers.

By this time, your puppy has been weaned. If he is part of a large litter, the bitch has by now run out of milk or is unable to sate so many large appetites. She is also beginning to lose interest in nursing her puppies, or has already lost it. In fact, if you prolong the time of weaning, the bitch may become jealous of the pups or come to resent them. More often, she will simply stay out of their way—she may jump up on a couch when they go for a nipple. This is her way of indicating that she is finished. They're on their own. If you have been bottle feeding up to this late date, you have carried your duties further than necessary.

The following directions may ease things for you. Feeding a puppy can be very simple, or it can be complicated. There are several kinds of diet, each one having strong points in its favor. Chiefly, you want to be sure that your pup is getting the essential nutrients for correct and adequate growth. Any diet is good that enables him to grow into a healthy dog. Cost should by no means be the deciding factor. That you spend a good deal on your puppy does not necessarily mean you are giving him a good diet. And if you spend only a little, he may still be getting the nutrition that he needs. The point to remember, then, is correct nutrition.

Some Simple but Basic Nutrition Rules

The growing puppy, as well as the older dog, has certain dietary requirements. Contrary to what most people think, meat is not the only need of the pup. He must have a balanced diet of which protein foods like meat might compose as little as 20 percent. Protein is of course important—it breaks down into several amino acids, all of which are necessary for proper growth, to give heat and energy, and to rebuild systems in the body. But a young dog fed only lean meat would deteriorate because he was not getting proper nutrition.

In addition to protein, a puppy needs fat, in amounts of perhaps up to 10 percent of his diet, while a hard-working dog may need up to 20 percent. Not only does fat give him heat and energy, but it also improves the skin, builds up resistance to disease, tones his nervous system. The chief asset of certain fats is an ingredient called linoleic acid, found in meat fats: pork, lamb, beef. Even lard will supply it in ample quantity. This acid is necessary for adequate growth. Recent experiments in canine nutrition have exploded the ancient myth that a dog needs only lean meat for energy and growth. The dog—and especially the pup—kept on a low fat diet tends to dry out: His skin becomes scaly, his coat dry and coarse. Further, his resistance to disease is lowered.

Fat is also an excellent source of calories for the puppy. A puppy needs many more calories than the grown dog. A rapidly growing large breed may need up to 8,000 calories a day, and fat provides this in abundance. The dog also loves it. If you soak part of his meal in bacon fat, you may consider the mixture unattractive, but not your dog.

Of course, a dog's intake of fat is not the same throughout his life. As you will see when you read Chapter 10 on old age, the older a dog becomes the more careful you must be of his calorie intake. As in a person, the older dog's metabolism slows down, and food is changed into harmful fat. But in the growing puppy the metabolic rate is rapid. The puppy is extremely active, and his developing body is like a furnace that must be stoked. Fat does just this.

For bulk and energy, the pup needs carbohydrates. At one time, people believed that carbohydrates were bad for dogs—one of the old wives' tales about feeding a dog. Carbohydrates are fine—potatoes, rice, macaroni—provided they are cooked. When they are in a raw state, however, a dog has trouble digesting them.

The big three are protein, fats, and carbohydrates, supplemented by multiple minerals and vitamins. Cod-liver oil, incidentally, doesn't supply all the necessary vitamins and minerals. Unlike people, dogs do not need vitamin C, but they do need most of the others if they are to grow properly. Remember, some of the largest breeds may weigh only a pound at birth and gain 100 pounds or more in 10 months. A person weighs 6 to 9 pounds at birth and takes 10 years or more to reach 100 pounds. Clearly, incorrect feeding of your puppy can hold up natural growth at a proportionately greater rate than would the incorrect feeding of a child.

Vitamin A (found in liver, greens, grain, egg yolk) aids the body's growth, is necessary for correct vision and hearing, helps to prevent infection, and gives tone to the skin. Vitamin B (found in meat, fish, vegetables, milk, egg yolk) serves your dog in many important ways, all pointed toward general body health and endurance. It helps the liver, tones the muscles, gives appetite, even (some say) adds to fertility. Vitamin D (found in bone meal; can be gained from the sun) is especially necessary to prevent bone diseases like rickets. Among other things, it gives your dog good muscular coordination. Vitamin E (found in grain products) provides a general body tone. Vitamin F (obtained in normal eating) keeps the skin and coat healthy. Vitamin K (also obtained in normal eating) is a factor in the clotting of blood. Like the vitamins, minerals are also absolutely necessary. Calcium and phosphorus are bone and tooth builders, and work toward giving your dog a healthy heart as well as solid muscles and nerves. Iron is a blood builder, while sodium, chlorine, iodine copper, sulfur, magnesium, and potassium are also important, especially to the growing puppy.

I won't go into the details of nutrition here, but it should be clear to you just how important vitamins and minerals are. All puppies should be given them as supplements to their regular diet. As for the diet itself, there are several possible kinds. If you get a puppy from another owner or from a kennel, continue his current diet for a week or so, gradually leading him into the diet you want him to have. You may keep the old one, of course, provided you are sure it is correct.

Except for kennel owners, I don't think most people keep their dogs on one hard-and-fast diet. There is too much joy in giving the energetic little puppy scraps from the table or tidbits to supplement or replace his diet. There is absolutely nothing the matter with this, but as a rule of thumb do not allow table scraps to make up more than 25 percent of his daily diet.

The four chief diets are:

1. CANNED DOG FOOD: These are commercial preparations with a high moisture content, up to 70 to 75 percent. They are, usually, low in fat content. Since the puppy (especially of a breed that eventually will reach 60 pounds or over) needs bulk and also a fat intake of up to 20 percent or so, you have to choose carefully among the prepared foods. Do not get the idea, however, that you cannot bring up your puppy well on canned dog foods. Many of those on the market meet standards set somewhat above the puppy's daily requirement, and many are fortified with vitamins and minerals. And with a further vitamin and mineral supplement plus milk, the puppy can usually gain well on such prepared foods.

But if you want a diet to take your pup, especially a large breed, right into adulthood, an exclusive canned-food diet can be expensive. You may have to give a 6- or 7-month-old pup 4 or 5 cans of food a day, and some prices run as high as forty cents a can. Cost is less of a problem if you have a small breed.

Another possible drawback to the prepared foods is their high moisture content. A dog eating a few cans a day will take in a lot of water to get enough bulk. He will also drink water after his meals, and therefore have to urinate more frequently. If you are trying to train your puppy, you will have to walk him several times a day, and even after he is grown he may not be able to hold such large amounts of water. These are somewhat minor considerations, but some of them can take away from the pleasure that the dog should give. Also, your dog may be uncomfortable, especially if you are out most of the day and there is no one to walk him. We know that a dog takes pride in his own accomplishments, and if he is constantly uncomfortable with a desire to urinate, he may have to do so indiscriminately and lose a measure of self-respect.

Another point about the prepared foods is that in some cases they do not provide sufficient calories even when eaten in large quantities. The average can gives about 500 calories, while a growing puppy needs several thousand, depending on his size and growth rate. The low fat content of the canned food accounts for the reduction in calories, and necessitates supplementary rations of meat, fat, lard, or butter.

All this should not discourage you from using prepared dog foods. Manufacturers have spent large sums in research on products that can serve your dog well, and there is no question that can feeding is the easiest in point of time. But this is simply one diet among four, and you surely should consider the others before settling for any one.

An alternate feeding method is to give the puppy a formula breakfast followed by prepared dog food. The formula may consist of a high-protein cereal with evaporated milk (or whole milk). Since the puppy at this young age will eat 3 or 4 times a day, it may be a good idea to offer him some kind of variety. Then for his other meals give him canned dog food, perhaps supplemented by fat products.

2. DRY FOODS OR DOG MEAL: These are completely dehydrated products, quite inexpensive to buy, and full of nearly everything your dog needs except sufficient fat. The old-style dry foods contained cereal and animal products in about equal amounts. The newer homogenized product consists of a mixture of nearly everything your dog normally needs: cereals, meat products (scraps, organs), small amounts of fat, as well as vitamins and minerals baked in. These homogenized products are often called complete meals, because, theoretically, all you must do is add water and serve.

As the fat content is usually low, however, you should supplement the dry meal with bacon drippings, oleomargarine, lard, or fat from the butcher. Also, vitamins baked into the meal tend to lose some of their power.

The advantage of the dry meal is that is provides sufficient bulk at a small cost, and with fat mixed in it contains enough calories for the growing puppy. When served, it should be soaked in the fat, softened somewhat for the puppy, although not made soupy. With a vitamin-mineral supplement and perhaps an occasional cooked egg, this food will meet all the puppy's nutritional needs.

3. DOG BISCUITS: These biscuits, made chiefly of flour, may be of several types. Some are whole biscuits; others are in cube form or kibbled (broken into pieces). Another type may be a product made of baked unbleached flour, meat, and fat, somewhat similar to dry meal. Usually biscuits do not provide enough nutrition for the pup, and they serve best as fillers, tasty tidbits when the puppy is hungry between meals. Conceivably, they could fulfill a dog's basic requirements if they were sufficiently supplemented with fat (they are quite low in fat content), vitamins and minerals, and meat scraps. Some of the biscuits on the market now are called complete meals, but many others are simply offered as fillers.

4. PRESCRIPTION DIETS: Such diets, available only from a veterinarian, are complete, supplying everything your puppy needs at each period of growth. Their cost, however, is somewhat higher than a good canned dog food and considerably higher than a diet of meal.

From these four basic methods of feeding a dog, most owners will choose either one or a combination. Scraps, of course, may form part of the dog's diet. With that in mind, I have charted feeding procedures for the puppy from 4 to 12 weeks. I have also offered some home-cooked meals as an alternative to the four fundamental dog foods, as I feel many owners will prefer to diversify their dogs' diet. The amounts obviously will vary according to the individual pup—*I give only average quantities.* Increase the quantities as the puppy grows or seems hungry; decrease them if he is getting fat. Also, don't worry if the puppy doesn't eat everything you offer him. If the dog leaves food, give him that much less at the next feeding.

Some useful measurements: A cup is 8 fluid ounces; a tablespoon is one-half of a fluid ounce; there are 3 teaspoonsfuls in a tablespoon; a standard can of dog food contains 1 pound.

DIETS FOR 4 TO 12 WEEKS
(based on 3 feedings a day at 8 A.M., 12 noon, 6 P.M.)

Toys (3 to 15 pounds as adults)

PREPARED (CANNED) FOOD: 1 ounce (2 tablespoons) per feeding, with some milk on the side.

DRY FEED OR MEAL: Do not give to dog at this age.

BISCUITS OR TABLE SCRAPS: Do not give to dog at this age.

PRESCRIPTION DIET: Follow directions on the label.

HOME COOKING: 1 ounce of chopped meat (raw or cooked lightly) per feeding (mix in the drippings if cooked)
OR 1 ounce of cooked chicken, minced fine, per feeding (mix in some fat).
Mix in some crushed Shredded Wheat and a little milk; give an occasional egg (cooked), some cooked green vegetables, crushed.

GIVE VITAMIN-MINERAL SUPPLEMENT (MIXED WITH FOOD): according to directions on the label.

Small Breeds (15 to 30 pounds as adults)

PREPARED (CANNED) FOOD: 1½ ounces (3 tablespoons) per feeding, with some milk on the side.

DRY FEED OR MEAL: Do not give to dog at this age.

BISCUITS OR TABLE SCRAPS: Do not give to dog at this age.

PRESCRIPTION DIET: Follow directions on the label.

HOME COOKING: 1½ ounces of chopped meat (raw or cooked lightly) per feeding (mix in the drippings if cooked)

OR 1½ ounces of cooked chicken, minced fine, per feeding (mix in some fat).

Mix in some crushed Shredded Wheat and a little milk; give an occasional egg (cooked), some cooked green vegetables, crushed.

GIVE VITAMIN-MINERAL SUPPLEMENT (MIXED WITH FOOD): according to directions on the label.

Medium Breeds (30 to 55 pounds as adults)

PREPARED (CANNED) FOOD: 3 ounces (6 tablespoons) per feeding, with some milk on the side.

DRY FEED OR MEAL: Do not give to dog at this age.

BISCUITS OR TABLE SCRAPS: Do not give to dog at this age.

PRESCRIPTION DIET: Follow directions on the label.

HOME COOKING: 3 ounces of chopped meat (raw or cooked lightly) per feeding (mix in the drippings if cooked)

OR 3 ounces of cooked chicken, minced fine, per feeding (mix in some fat).

Mix in some crushed Shredded Wheat and a little milk; give an occasional egg (cooked), some cooked green vegetables, crushed.

GIVE VITAMIN-MINERAL SUPPLEMENT (MIXED WITH FOOD): according to directions on the label.

Large Breeds (55 to 80 pounds as adults)

PREPARED (CANNED) FOOD: 4–5 ounces (8–10 tablespoons) per feeding, with some milk on the side.

DRY FEED OR MEAL: Do not give to dog at this age.

BISCUITS OR TABLE SCRAPS: Do not give to dog at this age.

PRESCRIPTION DIET: Follow directions on the label.

HOME COOKING: 4–5 ounces of chopped meat (raw or cooked lightly) per feeding (mix in the drippings if cooked)

OR 4–5 ounces of cooked chicken, minced fine, per feeding (mix in some fat).

Mix in some crushed Shredded Wheat and a little milk; give an occasional egg (cooked), some green vegetables, crushed.

GIVE VITAMIN-MINERAL SUPPLEMENT (MIXED WITH FOOD): according to directions on the label.

Very Large Breeds (80 to 185 pounds as adults)

PREPARED (CANNED) FOOD: 5–7 ounces (10–14 tablespoons) per feeding, with some milk on the side.

DRY FEED OR MEAL: Do not give to dog at this age.

BISCUITS OR TABLE SCRAPS: Do not give to dog at this age.

PRESCRIPTION DIET: Follow directions on the label.

HOME COOKING: 5–7 ounces of chopped meat (raw or cooked lightly) per feeding (mix in the drippings if cooked)
OR 5–7 ounces of cooked chicken, minced fine, per feeding (mix in some fat).
Mix in some crushed Shredded Wheat and a little milk; give an occasional egg (cooked), some cooked green vegetables, crushed.

GIVE VITAMIN-MINERAL SUPPLEMENT (MIXED WITH FOOD): according to directions on the label.

A puppy may need from 1 to 4 ounces of food a day per pound of body weight, depending on his breed and his eventual size. If he is very active, he will require more. After he reaches adulthood, at a year, his needs taper off, unless he is a work or sporting dog who requires huge amounts of food. You must estimate with your own dog. Everything about him is unique—his environment, breed, early habits, even his owner. Try giving him as much food as he will take. At the beginning, it is better for him to have too much than too little. If he starts to fatten, there is plenty of time to cut his rations and make him lean and sleek.

Many folk tales about feeding dogs have been making the rounds for hundreds of years. I thought it might be useful to examine them for what they're worth before moving on to tell you more about your own puppy.

1. There are literally hundreds of bizarre stories about the connection between worms and diet. We know now that no food in itself can bring on worms, neither milk nor raw meat nor candy. *Any food, however, that contains worm cyst can produce worms,* but that is because the food is already tainted. If you feed your dog pure, uncontaminated food and he suffers subsequently from worms, the worms have nothing to do with what he is eating. Raw rabbit, however, is best avoided, for it may contain tapeworm cyst. (Avoid raw pork and raw bear meat also; they are relatively indigestible.)

Similarly, certain foods do not get rid of worms. Garlic and onions were once thought to be a cure for worms. There is no evidence that this is so. If your dog likes garlic, and you like him after he eats it, that is fine; it can't hurt him. But if he has worms, do not assume that the garlic will do him any medicinal good.

2. Starch such as that in potatoes and macaroni, does not cause skin diseases and is fine *if cooked.* Dogs usually do not chew their food, and uncooked starch won't be digested readily in the short time that a dog's stomach and intestinal juices can work on it.

3. Do not worry if your dog bolts his food. He has very powerful juices in his stomach that break up his food quickly and efficiently whether he chews or not. Probably a dog's hasty eating is a carry-over from his primitive days when he had to eat and run, or had to eat quickly to get his share. His digestive system, however, has adapted to such conditions.

4. Bones are not at all necessary for a dog. Small bones, particularly chicken bones, may splinter and injure the dog's throat and stomach. In some cases he may choke to death. If you want to give your dog a bone, make it a heavy knuckle or shank beef bone, which he can play with, never soft, brittle bones. The bone may be cooked or uncooked. Bones may cause constipation for some dogs by blocking the intestines. At their best, bones can help clean a dog's teeth of tartar and provide some fun. They can, however, do more harm than good if they are of the wrong kind. Continual gnawing may also wear the enamel off the dog's teeth.

5. Raw meat will not turn your quiet, obedient pet into a wild, raging animal. The smell of fresh blood will not bring back his hunting instinct. Raw meat, in fact, is usually preferable to cooked meat because cooking destroys vitamins. Many dogs, however, have become so domesticated that they prefer their meat warmed up, but there is no reason to make it well done. The dog brought up on raw meat will like it and never know the difference. If he does seem edgy and irritable, look for other reasons than raw meat; he is not waiting to return to the jungle. But do avoid raw rabbit, pork, and bear steak, which are indigestible and may cause tapeworms.

6. You don't have to give your dog a large variety of foods. A dog has certain nutritional needs, and if these can be met, he is perfectly satisfied with nearly the same thing every day. People like variety for taste, not nutrition.

7. Contrary to popular belief, grass is not a tonic for any ailment. Often a dog will bring on vomiting by eating grass, and if he occasionally does so there is no reason for alarm unless the grass has been sprayed with an insecticide.

8. Vegetables are generally good for a dog, particularly for a puppy, but not absolutely necessary if he gets his vitamins and minerals in some other way. Similarly, fruits are not a favorite, although puppies used to receive lime juice in their diets, like British sailors at sea. The mature dog manufactures his own vitamin C and does not need fruit.

9. Do not give highly seasoned food to a dog. It does him no good

and may do him harm by raising his water intake or creating digestion problems. Salt is not necessary (unless the weather is excessively hot), and too much may make him vomit.

10. The widespread belief that a raw egg a day will keep the dog's coat full and glossy is erroneous. The opposite, in fact, is closer to the truth. A whole *raw* egg may harm the dog because the white interferes with the absorption of biotin and the digestion of several minerals. In some cases, it may cause diarrhea. The yolk alone, cooked or not, contains much food value, especially protein, but the cooked white, while not harmful, is of no use to your dog. Neither the cooked white nor the yolk will do anything for the coat except as they contribute to a balanced diet. In that respect, an occasional yolk might be useful.

11. All breeds (mongrels and purebreds) *can* eat the same kinds of food. Only the amount varies, according to the size and needs of the individual dog.

12. Some dogs may not drink water. Do not worry for a moment—the dog is getting enough water from his food. No animal deprives himself of necessary water.

13. Many people worry if their dog skips a meal. *No dog starves himself.* If he occasionally is not hungry, simply pick up his food and make him wait until his next meal. If he shows no appetite for several days, then you have a problem for your veterinarian. The dog is probably sick.

14. Many people believe that sulfur placed in the dog's diet will eliminate worms. There is no truth to this. There is, in fact, no connection between sulfur and worms. Sulfur, also, does not purify the blood, or the water, nor does it act as a tonic.

15. It isn't true that a lot of fat in the dog's diet will make his coat gleam. The average dog needs *at most* 10 percent fat in his diet, a very active dog requiring somewhat more, but an excess will simply make him ill. His basic requirement will keep his coat sleek, but more will do him no good.

Many of these points obviously apply to the older dog as well as to the puppy. In the last fifteen years or so, there has been a great breakthrough in canine nutrition, and several fallacies have been exposed. Modern scientific research has made it possible for your dog to be perfectly nourished, so that he can always be at his best: healthy, loyal, and obedient.

VACCINATIONS
(for the 4- to 12-week-old group)

DISTEMPER

Distemper is a gigantic infection that starts out as a mild infection and then attacks the dog's entire body. It is a virus that weakens the tissues, inflames the mucous membranes, and leaves the dog open to all kinds of secondary infections: pneumonia, tonsillitis, skin diseases. It may even cause brain damage. Its immediate symptoms are diarrhea, dehydration, vomiting, convulsions, twitching. There is no real cure, although some breeds more than others seem to survive it. Certain Terriers—the Bull, for example—tend to pull through while larger breeds like Bloodhounds and Great Danes show high mortality rates. Of course the degree of virulence of the disease is a large factor. Distemper is highly contagious. It can even be passed on by the airborne breath of other dogs, as well as by the stools and urine of an infected dog. The virus develops in the cold and tends to die out in the heat and sunshine. (See Chapter 6 for a full description of the virus.)

If your puppy received colostrum from the immune bitch, he is himself immune to distemper for a couple of weeks, sometimes longer. He is ready at the time of weaning (about 4 weeks) or a little later for his first puppy injections against the dreaded virus. These will immunize him until he is 3 months of age.

If you buy a puppy 12 weeks or older (as is likely) from a pet shop or get one from a friend, be sure to check on the distemper injections. Do the same if you buy a puppy from a breeder, but there you can be reasonably sure everything has been taken care of, especially when he keeps breeding studs.

If you are raising a pup from birth, then you must yourself make all the arrangements with your veterinarian.

CANINE HEPATITIS
(Infectious Hepatitis, Inflammation of the Liver)

This is a virus that was once confused with distemper, but is actually quite different. Some of the symptoms are similar: general dehydration, resulting in the dog's excessive thirst, listlessness, loss of interest in food, diarrhea (often black), vomiting. There is also a high temperature, usually over 104° F. Like human hepatitis, the canine variety results from an inflammation of the liver, a general infection of the gastrointestinal tract. The virus is contagious and is spread through contact with the urine, saliva, or stools of an infected dog. (For further details, see Chapter 6.)

The disease is very serious in puppies, who usually do not recover, and it comes upon them without warning, while they appear to be enjoying excellent health. In addition to the symptoms above, the mucous membranes in the dog's mouth may become blue or bluish. This means that he has an infection in his system. The dog's abdomen may become very tender and sensitive—often you will see him hump his back trying to relieve the pain.

The best treatment is prevention. There is a combination vaccination against both distemper and hepatitis, as well as against leptospirosis and parainfluenza, which I describe below.

LEPTOSPIROSIS

Leptospirosis is a disease caused by infection with spirochetes of the genus Leptospira. It attacks the dog's kidneys and liver. It is transmitted chiefly through the urine of an infected dog and sometimes through rat urine. The dog may sniff and pick up the spirochete on his nose, or lick his coat, which is contaminated.

Some of the signs are a change in the color of the dog's urine to deep yellow or orange, with a strong odor, chronic vomiting of froth and bile, or of recently eaten food, evident discomfort in the abdominal area. The temperature may rise suddenly and sharply (up to 105° F.), followed by a sharp fall to below normal (as low as 97° F.). As the disease advances, the dog will have the symptoms of jaundice: yellowing of the skin and of the eyes, severe dehydration, a bloody, liquid bowel movement.

When you have your dog inoculated against distemper protect him also against leptospirosis (both types).

Incidentally, while canine hepatitis is not transmittable from dogs to humans, leptospirosis may be by direct contamination. Although this rarely happens, protect yourself and your family, as well as your dog, by making sure he gets his vaccination at the right time. This is particularly important if you live in an area infested by rats, or in a city, or if your dog eats dry food, which rats may have contaminated.

PARAINFLUENZA

Parainfluenza, the name given to assorted viruses of the upper respiratory system, can result when dogs gather together, as in a hospital or kennel. Kennel Cough, or Tracheo-Bronchitis, is another condition that can result from dogs congregating in large groups. A vaccination, given with the others, can protect your dog against these ailments.

RABIES

Although rabies is now the least common of all the serious dog diseases in most parts of the United States, it is by far the best known and the most feared. Inoculation against rabies is still the one injection insisted upon by state authorities and by health authorities who control shipments of dogs into foreign countries. It is the one protection dog owners want who do not particularly bother with anything else. It is, in fact, this very care and protection, along with quarantine, that has resulted in the virtual elimination of this dreaded disease in most of the country. Of the more than forty million dogs in the United States, there are fewer than five thousand annual reported cases, or less than one-eighth of 1 percent. Annually, there are fewer than fifteen cases of rabies in human beings as a result of bites from rabid dogs.

Rabies—or, as it was once called, hydrophobia—is a virus transmitted by the saliva (or other excretion) of a rabid dog into the tissue of another dog or a person. The only way a dog can get rabies is through the bite of a rabid dog or other rabid animal. A dog cannot become rabid from the heat during the so-called "dog days" of July and August. And there is no connection between the physical appearance of a dog and his susceptibility or immunity to rabies. It was once believed, for example, that dewclaws on a dog guaranteed immunity. The dewclaws have no more to do with rabies than the dog's tail. .

Rabies is transmitted through a bite (or through contact of the rabid saliva with an open cut or wound) in which the virus in the saliva infects the nerve tissues and there incubates for a period of 10 to 14 days, and occasionally longer. If you or your dog is bitten, the offending dog must be located and quarantined. Then he will be closely watched for signs of rabies, a period of 10 to 14 days. *If you are bitten by a dog (any dog), see your doctor immediately or call the Board of Health. If your dog is bitten, he too must be immediately quarantined.* Call the police, your veterinarian, the local SPCA, or the Board of Health. In all cases, be ready to describe the offending dog so that he can be found. The value of protection is of course obvious.

The signs of rabies are several, depending on whether the dog has the violent or the dumb type. In the violent type, the dog goes wild, nipping and biting everything that moves, either persons or other animals. The dumb type is so called because the dog suffers a kind of paralysis in which he sits around staring with his mouth wide open, his lower jaw hanging useless and uncontrollable. (For further details, see Chapter 6.)

Some symptoms of rabies are general listlessness and loss of appetite, inability to swallow, and foaming at the mouth. The rabid dog becomes excessively thirsty, with an all-consuming thirst, but because of throat paralysis cannot drink. It is for this reason that the word hydrophobia was given to the disease, although the term is misapplied. Hydrophobia means fear of water. Actually the rabid dog wants water, but cannot swallow it. This inability to swallow of course sets many rabid dogs looking frantically for water, and therefore the term "mad dog." Some rabid dogs froth at the mouth or drool, although not all do.

There is no hope for a rabid dog once the nerve symptoms of drooling and shaking start. He generally dies in a short time. Also, the only certain way to discover if a dog is rabid is by means of a laboratory examination of his brain, once the dog has died. And he must be quarantined after the first suspicious symptom.

The best way to prevent rabies is to have your dog vaccinated. Most veterinarians recommend 6 months as the most suitable age. Actually younger puppies can be affected by rabies, and vaccination is often necessary in areas where there are rabies outbreaks. Immunity is never permanent, however. After the vaccination at 6 months, follow with revaccination every year with the killed vaccine or every three years with the attenuated live vaccine. The vaccination certificate will indicate when he received his rabies injection and what type was used, and then if he does bite anyone you will be able to prove he has been vaccinated.

One warning: If you suspect your dog or another dog of having rabies, stay away. If it is your dog, try to isolate him without endangering yourself and then call your veterinarian, the health authorities, or the local police. If you are bitten, wash out the wound immediately with water and strong soap, preferably tincture of green soap, so that it gets well into the flesh. *See your doctor without delay.* Make sure you report the offender so that he can be quarantined and his progress observed. In most cases, there will be no rabies, but the severity of the disease is so intense that no precaution can be too great.

I have provided a chart to indicate when your puppy should receive all his necessary vaccinations. Keep in mind, however, that veterinarians differ widely in their practices; your own will advise you of the proper vaccinations to be given your dog, and of the timing.

SCHEDULE OF VACCINATIONS

CANINE DISTEMPER: The dam's colostrum protects for 4 to 6 weeks. Canine distemper vaccine should be given at 6 to 8 weeks of age and will immunize until 3 months of age.

INFECTIOUS CANINE HEPATITIS: This is given at the same time as the 3-months distemper vaccine.

CANINE PARAINFLUENZA: This is given as a combined vaccine with canine distemper and infectious hepatitis vaccine—that is, at 3 months of age.

CANINE LEPTOSPIROSIS: Both types are given with above vaccines at 3 months of age.

RABIES: Vaccination is necessary at 6 months, followed by a yearly booster of killed vaccine or one of live virus vaccine every three years; dog may be injected earlier if there is a rabies outbreak.

FURTHER DEVELOPMENTS: GENERAL REACTIONS AND TEETHING

Between 4 and 12 weeks, a puppy will begin to repay your time and effort. He has always been cute and affectionate, but now he begins to take on some character of his own.

The pup's physical development is also rapid. Toward the end of the 12-week period, or sometime in the next 4 weeks, he begins to lose his sharp little baby teeth. Some puppies lose them a little earlier, some later. He begins to respond to his environment, especially to sounds and to his name. He may jump at sharp noises he ignored before. He also responds to his littermates with playful tussles. He reacts to you with forays against your legs, nipping at your trousers or dress, gnawing at furniture, chewing on books, rugs, curtains. He is of course still very immature, for his nervous system is not fully developed. You must treat him carefully at this age because his behavior patterns now become somewhat set, as they do with a child of two or three. Do not, however, expect him to be independent as yet. He has had adequate motor skills for only a few weeks, full sight and hearing for an equally short time. Except for your cheerful face, the world is still a buzz of confusion. If he is a one-man dog (see Chapter 2 for those breeds who give their loyalty exclusively to one person), this is the ideal time for you to take over and give your dog direction and focus.

As for the temporary teeth, they simply drop out of their own accord. If the puppy swallows them, don't worry. They will not hurt him. His gums probably will be sore and bloody, and spots of blood may appear on things he touches. If the blood comes from the gums, there is nothing to worry about. Soon, within a few days, the permanent teeth begin to poke through—he gets 42 in all: 3 incisors on each side of the middle of the upper jaw and 3 on each side of the lower; a canine tooth on each side upper and lower; then 4 premolars on each side upper and lower; and finally 2 molars on each side in the upper and 3 molars on each side in the lower.

If your pup is receiving a well-balanced diet, including a mineral supplement, his teeth should grow in straight and strong. Sometimes, however, the permanent teeth begin to come in before the milk teeth have fallen out, and the traffic becomes heavy for the available space. In such cases, the permanent teeth may grow in crooked. If you notice something going wrong with the permanent teeth, get in touch with your veterinarian. He may have to pull the baby teeth to remedy the trouble. It is always a good idea to have a mouth check done on your puppy during teething time, possibly at the same time you bring him in for his distemper vaccination.

If your puppy is listless and unhappy at this time, it does not mean that he is necessarily sick. He is simply uncomfortable. His gums are sore, he has lost some of his ability to chew, and his entire system is concentrating on making those teeth break through. Give him larges doses of sympathy and an occasional baby aspirin if he appears in pain. His appetite may fall off; he may suffer from mild diarrhea; he is generally weakened and open to illness, particularly distemper, unless he has been inoculated at least with serum or gamma globulin. Sometimes you may see a dog with rutted teeth or teeth ringed by dark smudges—these are called distemper teeth, the result of a case of distemper or some other virus while the pup was teething.

By the way, teething may last another 5 or 6 months, although the real difficulty is over long before that. Of course, individual puppies differ, as do babies, and while one may teethe painfully for only a short time, another may spread out the teething process for several months. Still others will get their teeth without any discomfort.

The teething puppy should have something hard to chew on. It is at this time that he will gnaw table and piano legs, in fact anything he can get his teeth on. Furniture damage may be not only expensive for you but damaging to him. The paint may be toxic, and large amounts can do serious harm. A much better idea is to buy him a hunk of leather at a pet shop, or give him a very hard shin or knuckle beef bone on which he can work off his aggressions and pain. Such "toys" may keep him happy for a long time and provide the resistance which his sore gums need. Also, it saves your nerves if you don't have to listen to him grind away. It may also save your slippers, shoes, and clothes. Puppies also like books and magazines.

One warning: Make sure you do not give him a cheap, soft rubber object to chew on. He will bite off pieces, which he cannot digest. They may remain within and obstruct his intestinal tract. The same is true of wooden objects, or any material that can splinter, like chicken bones. Also, do not give him old shoes unless you want him to chew up all shoes he discovers in the house. He does not distinguish between old and new.

Further Advice

The puppy at this age is very curious and mischievous. As yet, he is completely untrained, and if you allow him the run of the house he will deposit little remembrances in corners and doorways. In addition to protecting your own interests, you must take the precautions you would ordinarily take with a baby. Small objects will end up in the puppy's stomach if they are left around. And while a dog's digestion is usually excellent, the system does reject some items: needles, pins, children's tin soldiers, and other such objects. If you do suspect him of having swallowed a foreign object that may do real damage, try to make him vomit it up. (See Chapter 7 for first aid.)

Furthermore, watch out for dangerous areas where the puppy may fall or tumble down. Puppies are the most foolhardy creatures in the world. They do not come any braver. They believe themselves to be indestructible and immortal. Until they grow more mature and, you hope, more cautious, you must protect them from themselves.

Electric Cords

Another thing: Keep your puppy away from electric light cords. Puppies and electricity do not mix. If the cord is plugged in and he chews down through the insulation, he can receive a serious burn and shock.

If this does happen, disengage the cord from the outlet before touching the pup, or else you too will suffer shock and possibly burns. If he needs it, give him first aid for shock, and artificial respiration. (See Chapter 7 on first aid.)

Grooming

Do not bathe your pup yet, even if the weather is warm. Wipe off his face with a damp cloth, or comb and brush his coat clean. Make sure his coat is smooth, or else matted particles may form sharp edges and injure his sensitive skin. Such little injuries can form centers of infection, depending, of course, on the degree of irritation. (For details of grooming, see Chapter 5.)

Keep his toenails trimmed. Once your pup goes outdoors regularly, the friction of nail against sidewalk and pavement or gravel road will wear his nails down to the right length. But while he's a puppy, his nails touch only soft surfaces and continue to grow long. He may repeatedly slip and fall when his nails become too long and sharp. Your veterinarian can show you how to do it. (For further details about nail clipping, see Chapter 5.)

Paper-Training

You can start paper-training your pup at this time. (See Chapter 5 for general procedures and details.)

Puppy and the Family

Do not let children exhaust the pup. There will be plenty of time for that when he is full-grown and can hold his own. Right now he is still fairly delicate and needs frequent naps. Let *him* decide when he wants to play. He is his own best regulator. Also, too much activity right after eating may make him vomit, and too much excitement before dinner can lead him to bolt his meal and then throw it up. While none of this is dangerous, it is annoying.

At this age, you have a growing, alert, learning puppy in your care. He is very impressionable. In his canine fashion, he is going to take after you. If you are nervous, he will tend to become nervous. It doesn't take much to instill your fears in him. After all, he looks to you for everything. You are his model and example, the best and dearest friend he will ever have. He thinks that to copy you is to ingratiate himself still further.

Early Training

If you wish to start training your pup at this age, or at least want to try restraining him, always punish him at the very moment of the crime. Pups and grown dogs have no memory for specifics, and if you punish them later they think it is for what they did at that later time. It can be very confusing for them and very frustrating for you. Suppose your dog is sleeping when you suddenly discover that your favorite tie is now a wet rope. You run toward him, holding the tie like a banner. He'll jump up thinking that you want to play, perhaps that the ropy tie in your hand is a toy. Then you scold him, and he falls back defeated or confused. Do that a couple of times more and he won't know when to play or when to sulk. Too much of this (it takes a lot!) can make your dog neurotic, unable to do what you expect him to.

If you've ever been around a show dog whose show days are now over, you'll readily see what I mean. His entire life has centered around behaving in a certain way. When his show days are over and if he is sold to another owner, he is caught between the habits of his former life and what is expected of him in his new one. The present owner finds that he is often very shy of loud sounds, that the creaking of a newspaper can make him tremble (he expects to be struck with it), and that his behavior is generally neurotic. *This behavior indicates that a dog behaves best when he knows exactly what he is to do.* In this way he is like a young child who wants direction and becomes lost when he doesn't get it. Remember that punishment at the wrong time, or any action on your part which is not perfectly clear to your dog, only confuses him and makes training even more difficult.

One of the fine things about owning a dog is that it usually brings out the best in the owner. The owner finds that he must watch his temper and his moods, that he cannot indulge himself as much as he might like. There is no explaining to your dog that you didn't mean your tone of voice or your hasty anger. You must be consistent and in control of yourself if you want to get the most out of your dog. Clearly, the puppy even at this young age of 3 months or less exerts a good influence on everyone in contact with him.

THE PUPPY FROM 3 TO 5 MONTHS

The person who brings home a pup in this age group should read my previous section on the puppy from 4 to 12 weeks. Many of the points he is interested in are discussed there, particularly inoculations and certain serious puppy ailments; teething, which may continue for several months; the basic elements of correct feeding and nutrition; several misconceptions about a dog's eating habits; procedures on clipping and grooming in general. For certain further precautions about the pup, you should read what I say about the very young puppy (from birth to 4 weeks), specifically how to pick up the young puppy, how to recognize if he is ill, and other points, some of which I repeat here.

For *worming*, turn to Chapter 6, on ailments; for *house-training* (perhaps your chief goal at this stage) and general rules of training (use of collar,. leash, simple commands), turn to Chapter 5.

Your puppy at this age is without question a delightful creature. He is entering a kind of pre-adolescence, is aware of himself and his surroundings, and wishes to share with you the joy of his discoveries. Unless his teeth are bothering him to an extraordinary degree, he is delighted to be alive and to have you for a owner. You should feel the same way or you will let him down.

With Children

At this age, also, the puppy becomes an excellent little friend for your children, provided they learn how to treat him. We have all marveled at the close relationship between dogs and children, and have all felt that such a connection is great for the children and heart-warming for the dog. Such a rich relationship is fully possible, but it must be started correctly when the puppy is about in this age group. Your chief consideration is to be sure that the child is not too rough with the pup. The reverse will rarely be a problem. The youngster must be made aware that the pup has his own private moments, and that he does not belong to the child at all times. If they agree to honor each other, the relationship can be, and usually is, excellent.

In a passage on the much younger pup in this chapter, I discuss how the puppy should be picked up. Let me repeat that the best way is to place your hands under his chest and abdomen. Make sure that he is not hanging loosely, ready to fall, or you will frighten him. When a puppy dangles helplessly, he begins to wiggle, and then there is always the danger he will fall. A puppy should be put down so that his legs touch evenly.

Naming

A fine game that you or your child can play at this time is trying to make the puppy respond to his name—if you haven't started before. Most owners acquire their dogs in this age group, and therefore the naming process usually starts here. Give him a short, clear name, as a long one will escape him and he will probably only catch the first syllable anyway. Also, a small child will have trouble pronouncing it. Through repetition, *especially at mealtimes,* the puppy will come to respond.

Spaying and Castrating (or Neutering)

Many veterinarians recommend spaying the bitch at 6 or 7 months if you intend to have her spayed at all. The pros and cons of spaying have been debated endlessly, and I treat the matter at length in Chapter

8. Here, I simply want to say that if you definitely intend to have your bitch spayed, or altered, this is a good time to do it. The younger the bitch (once the puppy is strong enough, of course), the easier the recovery. Spaying is an operation in which the bitch's ovaries and uterus are removed, so that she will no longer have her seasonal period and no longer attract males. Spaying ends all sexual activity. If she has been temperamental, she may gain a more placid temperament. You can stop her from gaining weight by watching her diet and by giving her enough exercise, things you would do anyway.

Most owners dislike the idea of castrating the male, but some arguments can be offered in its favor. Dogs of certain breeds, or individual dogs which are snappish and fretful, may settle down to become more gentle after castration. Particularly the older male, who might be aggressive and nervous, will perhaps be calmer after castration; there is of course no guarantee. Also, you will have no trouble with the male when a bitch in heat is around. One bitch in heat can draw males from considerable distances and keep them in the area until her season is over. That is why some farm dogs are castrated—to keep them at home.

The chief drawback to having a dog spayed or castrated, other than physical considerations, is that you may regret doing it. As your dog gets older, you may wish to have puppies, and it is of course too late. Or you may find that you are becoming interested in dog shows, but a spayed or castrated dog is ineligible. If, however, your interest in the dog is simply for companionship, then your decision narrows down to that one consideration.

Owners of bitches may be interested in knowing that there is an oral medication that can prevent a bitch from coming into heat for 6 months. See your veterinarian about its properties and use.

Matters of Space

As the pup grows bigger, particularly if he is of a large breed, make sure that his living space is sufficiently roomy. If you live in an apartment, increase his living area, but don't necessarily give him all of the apartment. A good argument for restraining the pup from the whole house is his inability to control his wetting as yet. Until he is fully trained, keep him where damage can be held to a minimum, provided he has stretching and walking room. A carton becomes unrealistic at this time unless the pup is a toy or of another very small breed.

Do not put a dog in a cellar or an attic, or any other out-of-the-way place for a long time. Dogs are social animals, and they like to be around sounds and faces. Cellars are often drafty, and attics either cold or overheated. The pup at this age cannot easily adjust to extremes of cold and heat, and in any event drafts are deadly. Cellars, further, are likely to be damp, and dampness and puppies do not get along well.

Outside

If the weather is mild, there is no reason why the puppy cannot go out—*on a leash,* of course. Under no circumstances allow your pup to run free unless you live deep within the woods where there are no cars. In Chapter 12, I give several ways to protect a dog against cars, his chief killer, but it is never too soon to warn the owner that dogs and moving automobiles should be considered natural enemies. Your young puppy should be leashed whether you live in the city or suburbs.

If the weather is cold and windy, a 3- to 5-month-old puppy is still too young to go outdoors unless he is of a large breed and has a full coat. Most puppies' coats are not yet fully grown and offer only inadequate protection. Also, the pup's skin may be affected by the very hot sun—here too the coat is not yet sufficient protection.

If you do take a young puppy outside, be careful that he doesn't swallow everything in sight. He is not experienced enough to know what he may safely eat and what should only be sniffed and left alone. He is a great experimenter, and he doesn't know that a large stone has trouble making its way down a small throat. Stones, dirt, grass, cigarette butts, candy wrappers, cellophane—all of these may at one time or another find their way into his mouth if you don't take precautions. If you live in the country, the best thing to do is to provide a run for him that you know is clear and harmless.

Car Sickness

At this age, the puppy is a member of the family in several ways. You are house-training him (see Chapter 5); you are training him to accept the collar and walk with you on a leash (see Chapter 5); and you are trying to civilize him. Also, you may want to accustom him to riding in an automobile. Many puppies will vomit on a long journey unless they have been introduced to the experience by easy stages. Their car sickness is understandable, for the motion, the cooped-up quarters, the sense of the unexpected, the lack of water and often of fresh air, their inability to stretch their legs all result in a nervous condition that upsets the digestion. Dogs generally throw up more easily than people, but they can also control throwing up better than people.

If you plan car trips, start by breaking in your puppy for short periods of time. If possible, take the puppy with you to the corner store, take him when you pick up the children, ride him down to get your newspaper. Whatever your situation—single or married, urban or suburban—try to fit the puppy into these short trips. His initial excitement will pass, and with it will pass the anxiety and physical discomfort that make him vomit. At the beginning, keep an old sheet or towel handy in case he vomits, and control his movements so that he doesn't spray the entire car. A damp washcloth is also useful for wiping off his muzzle, and perhaps yourself as well. Most puppies, after a bout or two of car sickness, will accustom themselves to the motion and be fine.

A few might remain chronic cases, just as certain people cannot ride for any length of time in an automobile or bus without getting sick. If his car sickness persists, check with your veterinarian for a prescription to prevent it. Dramamine, tranquilizers, or some other motion-sickness tablet or medicine prescribed by your veterinarian, might do the trick. (Do not use an adult dosage—the pup is probably much smaller than you.) Also, keep the puppy's diet light when he is going to be in the car for some hours, and provide a container of water. Do not feed him for an hour or more before a car trip, and let him empty his bladder or bowels.

When the pup begins to swallow a great deal and starts to lick his lips agitatedly, you know the moment is on him. Stop the car and let him breathe fresh air. That might temporarily clear up the nausea. Even if he doesn't look desperate, give him a breathing spell now and then, as well as a chance to stretch his legs and to relieve himself. Keep him on a restricted supply of water. After a while, most pups come to love a car ride, and you too will enjoy having him in your front or back seat.

Carrying Case

Just as you accustom the puppy to the enclosed confines of an automobile, so you should get him ready for a carrying case. If you ever wish to take him on a bus or railroad, and he is small enough to be portable, you will need to do so in a carrying case. The large dog of course must ride in the baggage car in a crate. When you first put a puppy in a carrying case, keep the top off so that he doesn't get the fully enclosed feeling all at once. Place within the case something he is familiar with, again to lessen the shock of newness. A blanket or sheet or toy will remind him that his world has not fallen apart. At first, leave the case with him in it in one place; then move it a little at a time. Let him come out whenever he wishes, and keep the top open. When he seems used to the new situation, carry him for a little while with the top open, awkward as that may be. Then move him with the top closed, and by this time he should be ready for anything.

DIETS FOR 3 TO 5 MONTHS
(based on 3 feedings a day at 8 A.M., 12 Noon, 6 P.M.)

In the following feeding charts for the 3- to 5-month-old puppy, increase the quantities as the puppy grows or seems hungry; decrease them if he is getting fat. I give only average amounts.

Toys (3 to 15 pounds as adults)

PREPARED (CANNED) FOOD: 1½–2 ounces (3–4 tablespoons) per feeding, with some milk on the side.

DRY FEED OR MEAL: 1½–2 ounces per feeding, with some milk or beef broth mixed in. (Add some fat—bacon, beef, butter, etc.)

BISCUIT OR TABLE SCRAPS: Give only as a snack if you wish.

PRESCRIPTION DIET: Follow directions on the label.

HOME COOKING: 1½–2 ounces of chopped meat (raw or cooked lightly) per feeding (mix in the drippings if cooked).

OR 1½–2 ounces of cooked chicken, minced fine, per feeding (mix in some fat).

Mix in crushed Shredded Wheat and a little milk; give an occasional egg (cooked), some cooked green vegetables.

GIVE VITAMIN-MINERAL SUPPLEMENT (MIXED WITH FOOD): according to directions on the label.

Small Breeds (15 to 30 pounds as adults)

PREPARED (CANNED) FOOD: 2–3½ ounces (4–7 tablespoons) per feeding, with some milk on the side.

DRY FEED OR MEAL: 2–3½ ounces per feeding, with some milk or beef broth mixed in. (Add some fat—bacon, beef, butter, etc.)

BISCUIT OR TABLE SCRAPS: Give only as a snack if you wish.

PRESCRIPTION DIET: Follow directions on the label.

HOME COOKING: 2–3½ ounces of chopped meat (raw or cooked lightly) per feeding (mix in the drippings if cooked)

OR 2–3½ ounces of cooked chicken, minced fine, per feeding (mix in some fat).

Mix in crushed Shredded Wheat and a little milk; give an occasional egg (cooked), some cooked green vegetables.

GIVE VITAMIN-MINERAL SUPPLEMENT (MIXED WITH FOOD): according to directions on the label.

Medium Breeds (30 to 55 pounds as adults)

PREPARED (CANNED) FOOD: 4–6 ounces (8–12 tablespoons) per feeding, with some milk on the side.

DRY FEED OR MEAL: 4–6 ounces per feeding, with some milk or beef broth mixed in. (Add some fat—bacon, beef, butter, etc.)

BISCUIT OR TABLE SCRAPS: Give only as a snack if you wish.

PRESCRIPTION DIET: Follow directions on the label.

HOME COOKING: 5 ounces of chopped meat (raw or cooked lightly) per feeding (mix in the drippings if cooked)

OR 5 ounces of cooked chicken, minced fine, per feeding (mix in some fat).
Mix in crushed Shredded Wheat and a little milk; give an occasional egg (cooked), some cooked green vegetables.
GIVE VITAMIN-MINERAL SUPPLEMENT (MIXED WITH FOOD): according to directions on the label.

Large Breeds (55 to 80 pounds as adults)

PREPARED (CANNED) FOOD: 5–8 ounces (10–16 tablespoons) per feeding, with some milk on the side.
DRY FEED OR MEAL: 5–8 ounces per feeding, with some milk or beef broth mixed in. (Add some fat—bacon, beef, butter, etc.)
BISCUIT OR TABLE SCRAPS: Give only as a snack if you wish.
PRESCRIPTION DIET: Follow directions on the label.
HOME COOKING: 5–8 ounces of chopped meat (raw or cooked lightly) per feeding (mix in the drippings if cooked)
OR 5–8 ounces of cooked chicken, minced fine, per feeding (mix in some fat).
Mix in crushed Shredded Wheat and a little milk; give an occasional egg (cooked), some cooked green vegetables.
GIVE VITAMIN-MINERAL SUPPLEMENT (MIXED WITH FOOD): according to directions on the label.

Very Large Breeds (80 to 185 pounds as adults)

PREPARED (CANNED) FOOD: 9–12 ounces (18–24 tablespoons) per feeding, with some milk on the side.
DRY FEED OR MEAL: 9–12 ounces per feeding, with some milk or beef broth mixed in. (Add some fat—bacon, beef, butter, etc.)
BISCUIT OR TABLE SCRAPS: Give only as a snack if you wish.
PRESCRIPTION DIET: Follow directions on the label.
HOME COOKING: 9–12 ounces of chopped meat (raw or cooked lightly) per feeding (mix in the drippings if cooked)
OR 9–12 ounces of cooked chicken, minced fine, per feeding (mix in some fat).
Mix in crushed Shredded Wheat and a little milk; give an occasional egg (cooked), some cooked green vegetables.
GIVE VITAMIN-MINERAL SUPPLEMENT (MIXED WITH FOOD): according to directions on the label.

THE PUPPY FROM 5 TO 7 MONTHS

The puppy of 6 months is recognized by legal authorities as a dog, and you must obtain a license for him, renewable annually. You can obtain a license from your town clerk, although in large cities the SPCA (or ASPCA) usually handles this function. In some places, the local justice of the peace issues dog licenses in exchange for a fee. (Check Chapter 14 for further information on licensing and what purposes it serves.)

The owner who receives or buys a puppy of from 5 to 7 months old—a good time for acquiring a dog—should read my previous sections on the young puppy from 4 to 12 weeks and from 3 to 5 months for information on inoculations, worming (if necessary), correct nutrition and feeding, teething (continuous until 6 months or more). Also, if your puppy is not house-trained by now, turn to Chapter 5. There you will also find information on certain commands: heeling, sitting, staying, etc. If you have any other questions that are not answered here or in the earlier sections of this chapter, turn to the index.

Your puppy at this age is well on his way toward adulthood. Except for remaining problems in house-training (and they may be over by now) and instruction in simple commands, you can begin to sit back and see what you have. Of course your dog is neither puppy nor adult just yet, but he is taking on characteristics which will remain with him for the rest of his life. His attachment to you and the other members of your family is obvious. He looks to you for both leadership and justice.

You still must take some obvious precautions. Even if your puppy has had his permanent inoculations, you should not unnecessarily expose him to drafts, chilly winds, or cold weather. His full adult coat has not yet grown, and he is sensitive to extremes of cold and heat. If you walk him in poor weather, protect his body with a good sweater or coat. Cover his chest in particular, for this area can be a source of trouble. If it is raining hard and he gets wet, you must dry his coat *and skin* thoroughly to prevent a chill. Make sure you get down under the coat, for it is the wet skin that creates the difficulty, not the coat.

If your dog is longhaired, he may not need a covering, for by this time he is accustomed to the cold. But don't take chances unless you are sure his coat provides sufficient protection. With the smaller breeds and especially with the shorthaired variety, there is no reason to flirt with bronchitis or worse. If your pup is ill and must be walked, of course a good sturdy covering is in order. When buying a coat or sweater, do not be attracted by fancy wear that leaves most of the dog exposed. Get a covering that really covers, and avoid one that is difficult to put on. If you are in a climate that requires the frequent use of a coat, you will be thankful for one that obviates a struggle. Many sweaters come with leg attachments that the puppy as well as the older dog hates. He wants his legs free to fight or run. Going outdoors should be pleasant for all, particularly for the young dog who is still touchy about his training and somewhat unsure of what is expected of him.

Incidentally, it is much easier to keep a dog warm than it is to cool him off. Do not cut his hair short to let his skin breathe. His coat acts as an insulation against the heat and he needs every bit of it. In the summer, you may by daily stripping (with a stripping or saw-toothed comb) remove the under hair which clogs the coat. That hair serves no purpose, and it comes off easily with the proper comb and brush.

In the heat, you can do several things besides brushing to relieve your pup. Keep him out of the sun, hold down his exercise (or let him do it in the cooler parts of the evening and morning), give him plenty of cool, fresh water, try to avoid discomforts such as children's teasing, and give him somewhat less to eat—he needs fewer calories with his exercise cut down. Most pups and dogs come through the heat with a minimum of discomfort if you take these simple precautions. Like many people, they may become irritable, but only if the weather is extremely hot. And don't worry about your pup's developing rabies from the heat. He can't. Heat may cause discomfort, but rabies comes from the bite of a rabid animal.

During these months of your puppy's growth, as in the preceding two months, you will find all kinds of foreign objects in his mouth. Now that his permanent teeth are coming in, he is naturally anxious to try them out. Possibly his gums hurt, and champing on things relieves his pain. In any event, it is up to you to control what he gets hold of: table and chair legs, rugs, shoes, articles of clothing, books, newspapers, even garbage and laundry. He has no discrimination. Everything looks like fun. Keep closet doors closed, keep garbage out of his reach. Keep cellar doors closed.

If he is a large dog, he will surprise you with his jumping ability. Beat him to the punch and place things high. Close off all valuables— vases, lamps, curtains—or keep him closed off. Don't leave expensive jewelry around—good and cheap stuff all taste the same to him.

It's a battle of wits, and remember that the pup has nothing to do all day but sit and figure out ways to outsmart you. Work out a plan of action to protect yourself and then keep to it. The smallest lapse on your part can lead to the loss of a valuable object, or perhaps injury to the puppy (from bones in the garbage or other hard objects he may swallow). Necklaces are particularly enticing—first he can break the string, and then swallow each bead.

It is not vitamin deficiencies or insufficient food that will lead to these antisocial acts of defiance—as you might be inclined to call them— but simply playfulness and high spirits. As yet the puppy has little sense of proportion. Further, he is finding out about the world. The best way to prevent all this is to make him know where he can and where he cannot go. You must be firm at this age or else he might in time become the master whom you must obey. If he destroys something he should not have touched, let him know your displeasure immediately in a firm tone. The repetition of "No!" or "Bad!" will make him understand that his figuring went wrong. Then if he does something that he should be doing, let him know in a pleasant voice that you are pleased. A dog generally responds to your tone rather than to your words. You can get excellent results if you remain consistent in your attitudes. Do not be sarcastic or ironic—the dog will only become confused.

As with a small child, you must make it plain what he can do and cannot do, what he may touch and may not touch. Keep it all simple. Do not try to train him into a social being overnight. Give him a chance to work out the conflicts between your demands and the natural mischievousness of his instincts. Be tolerant. He's young and trying hard. Remember that he wants to please, and your firm tone disturbs his sense of self-importance. That tone is one that he will come to understand and obey. Use it only when necessary, or else he will not think it is something he should pay special attention to. The best way to control the destruction that may be done by a playful puppy is by prevention. Take the same precautions that you would with a young child. Then hope for the best.

If there are small children in the house, do not be surprised if the puppy trails after them from room to room. It may be love, but it is probably also because the puppy hopes to grab a bite of food from a low hand. If the puppy is suddenly getting extraordinarily fat on what you think is a reasonable diet, this may be the cause. Watch to see if your children are secretly feeding him.

It is also at this age that puppies and children become close friends. Take the same precautions that I indicated for the younger puppy in this respect—the pup is still somewhat fragile unless he is of a large breed and already outweighs the child. If you do have a large breed, expect the dog to knock the child over now and then. The damage is usually nothing more than hurt feelings. Great Danes and dogs of other big breeds tend to be awkward at this age—so warn the children. There's nothing wrong with the child's taking the pup into bed with him, provided that the dog's coat is clear of all parasites. Also, be sure the dog is housetrained before you encourage such overnight dates. If there is excessive sneezing and coughing on the child's part, he may be allergic to the dog's coat, and this sleeping arrangement will have to be discontinued.

The puppy, if bored or if incorrectly fed, may eat his own stool. If this does occur, the best preventative is to check his diet to see if there is any deficiency and to watch his living area and keep it absolutely clean. Very often, the puppy will treat the stool as a toy and knock it around. He doesn't know the difference, and he is always ready to eat. Show him your displeasure, but take the actions I mentioned above: Maintain cleanliness and correct diet.

DIETS FOR 5 TO 7 MONTHS
(based on 2 feedings a day at 8 A.M., 6 P.M.)

In the following feeding charts for the 5- to 7-month-old puppy, increase the quantities as the puppy grows or seems hungry; decrease them if he is getting fat. I give only average amounts.

Toys (3 to 15 pounds as adults)

PREPARED (CANNED) FOOD: 2–4 ounces (4–8 tablespoons) per feeding, with some milk on the side.

DRY FEED OR MEAL: 2–3 ounces per feeding, with some milk or beef broth mixed in. (Add some fat—bacon, beef, butter, etc.)

BISCUIT OR TABLE SCRAPS: Give only as a snack if you wish, in the later evening.

PRESCRIPTION DIET: Follow directions on the label.

HOME COOKING: 2–4 ounces of chopped meat (raw or cooked lightly) per feeding (mix in the drippings if cooked)
OR 2–4 ounces of cooked chicken per feeding (mix in some fat).
Mix in crushed Shredded Wheat and a little milk; give an occasional egg (cooked), some cooked green vegetables.

GIVE VITAMIN-MINERAL SUPPLEMENT (MIXED WITH FOOD): according to directions on the label.

Small Breeds (15 to 30 pounds as adults)

PREPARED (CANNED) FOOD: 4–8 ounces (8–16 tablespoons) per feeding, with some milk on the side.

DRY FEED OR MEAL: 4–6 ounces per feeding, with some milk or beef broth mixed in. (Add some fat—bacon, beef, butter, etc.)

BISCUIT OR TABLE SCRAPS: Give only as a snack if you wish, in the later evening.

PRESCRIPTION DIET: Follow directions on the label.

HOME COOKING: 4–8 ounces of chopped meat (raw or cooked lightly) per feeding (mix in the drippings if cooked)
OR 4–8 ounces of cooked chicken per feeding (mix in some fat).
Mix in crushed Shredded Wheat and a little milk; give an occasional egg (cooked), some cooked green vegetables.

GIVE VITAMIN-MINERAL SUPPLEMENT (MIXED WITH FOOD): according to directions on the label.

Medium Breeds (30 to 55 pounds as adults)

PREPARED (CANNED) FOOD: 6–11 ounces (12–22 tablespoons or ¾–1½ cups) per feeding, with some milk on the side.

DRY FEED OR MEAL: 6–9 ounces per feeding, with some milk or beef broth mixed in. (Add some fat—bacon, beef, butter, etc.)

BISCUIT OR TABLE SCRAPS: Give only as a snack if you wish, in the later evening.

PRESCRIPTION DIET: Follow directions on the label.

HOME COOKING: 6–11 ounces of chopped meat (raw or cooked lightly) per feeding (mix in the drippings if cooked)

OR 6–11 ounces of cooked chicken per feeding (mix in some fat).
Mix in crushed Shredded Wheat and a little milk; give an occasional
egg (cooked), some cooked green vegetables.

GIVE VITAMIN-MINERAL SUPPLEMENT (MIXED WITH FOOD): according to directions
on the label.

Large Breeds (55 to 80 pounds as adults)

PREPARED (CANNED) FOOD: 13–16 ounces (26–32 tablespoons or 1½–2 cups)
per feeding, with some milk on the side.

DRY FEED OR MEAL: 12–14 ounces per feeding, with some milk or beef
broth mixed in. (Add some fat—bacon, beef, butter, etc.)

BISCUIT OR TABLE SCRAPS: Give only as a snack if you wish, in the later
evening.

PRESCRIPTION DIET: Follow directions on the label.

HOME COOKING: 13–16 ounces of chopped meat (raw or cooked lightly)
per feeding (mix in the drippings if cooked)
OR 13–16 ounces of cooked chicken per feeding (mix in some fat).
Mix in crushed Shredded Wheat and a little milk; give an occasional
egg (cooked), some cooked green vegetables.

GIVE VITAMIN-MINERAL SUPPLEMENT (MIXED WITH FOOD): according to directions
on the label.

Very Large Breeds (80 to 185 pounds as adults)

PREPARED (CANNED) FOOD: 1⅓ pounds per feeding, with some milk on the
side.

DRY FEED OR MEAL: ¾–1 pound per feeding, with some milk or beef broth
mixed in. (Add some fat—bacon, beef, butter, etc.)

BISCUIT OR TABLE SCRAPS: Give only as a snack if you wish, in the later
evening.

PRESCRIPTION DIET: Follow directions on the label.

HOME COOKING: 1–1½ pounds of chopped meat (raw or cooked lightly)
per feeding (mix in the drippings if cooked)
OR 1–1½ pounds of cooked chicken per feeding (mix in some fat).
Mix in crushed Shredded Wheat and a little milk; give an occasional
egg (cooked), some cooked green vegetables.

GIVE VITAMIN-MINERAL SUPPLEMENT (MIXED WITH FOOD): according to directions
on the label.

THE PUPPY FROM 7 MONTHS TO MATURITY
(10 TO 12 MONTHS)

As your puppy passes through these months, you have a good notion
of what he will be like. He is reaching his full height and full weight.

If he is purebred, you already know what he will look like, and if he is a mongrel you will now possibly be able to determine which, if any, strains are predominant. He will be taking an interest in everything. His puppy curiosity has given way to a more assertive, confident manner, and he feels he has a right to be included in everything. Your dog is becoming a full member of your family, or, if you are single, he is sharing your entire way of life. By now he understands what you expect of him and is most likely house-trained. He is accustomed to the collar and the leash, and if you have been diligent he knows how to come, heel, sit, stay, and turn.

His stomach is now large enough to allow him to eat a day's food at one meal, or two at the most. His permanent teeth are in, and his coat has grown out. His inoculations are things in the past. Worming, if it was necessary, is over. If you intend to have your dog spayed or castrated, the chances are good that you have had it done by now. Also, your dog is set in the kind of life you are going to provide. If he is to be a companion, he is ready for that; if he is to be a show dog, you have already started his training; if he is to work or guard or hunt or retrieve fish and ducks, he is already active in these pursuits, or on his way to doing them. In a few short months he has reached adolescence, what it takes a boy or girl fifteen years to attain. For most breeds, the age of 10 to 12 months means full maturity, although bodily growth may continue for several more months. Bodily growth here does not usually mean greater height, but more filling out, increased muscular development, especially for dogs that are bred for work or for the field.

At the lower end of the age group (7 to 9 months), it may be a good idea to treat your growing dog as a puppy and continue the twice-a-day feeding. As he moves into the 10-to-12-month group, you can switch over to a single feeding. It really makes little difference as long as you are consistent. Feed the dog about the same time every day, whether once or twice, to fulfill his expectations of order and to keep his bowel action regular. Remember: *A dog is a creature of habit.*

Watch the pup's size to see if he has filled out well enough, or too well. He should be suitably plump, not paunchy. If he is putting on too much weight (you can compare his weight with the general expectation for the breed, or simply feel for rolls of fat), cut out all table scraps. Since the dog gets most of his calories from fats, cut them out, and he will live off his own fat. If you feel your judgment needs bolstering, ask your veterinarian. He can tell in a moment if your dog is growing the way he should.

People tend to put a great deal of emphasis on being overweight or underweight, and they should extend the same concern to dogs. As long as a dog takes in what his body needs, a certain leanness will lengthen his life span. As you will read in my chapter on the older dog (Chapter 10), one way in which you can help keep your dog alive longer is to keep his weight down. Since most of us tend to underexercise our dogs—especially the city owner who gives his pet a fast walk around the block twice a day—the diet has to be cut proportionately. I have seen St. Bernards become up to 100 pounds overweight because they cannot possibly receive in city life the kind of exercise the breed is accustomed to.

In these matters it is you who must make the necessary adjustments. As you read through the feeding charts for the dog of 7 to 12 months, you might have to alter the amounts, even whole feedings, to suit your particular pet and his particular needs. Once his young puppy days are over, the quantity, not quality, of his diet must be reduced because he has completed the major part of his growth cycle. The best-looking dog is a lean, hard animal—best as a happy companion and as a healthy, functioning creature.

A good deal depends, incidentally, on the adult size of the dog. Toys and most other smaller breeds develop younger, and their food needs fall off sooner; while the larger breeds are slower in gaining full development (they have further to go), and their food requirements may well remain stable through their 12th month. Once again, these are matters for your own judgment.

Sexual Maturity

Your dog, whether male or bitch, has reached the age, at 6 to 12 months, when he or she becomes sexually mature. The bitch goes into heat at about this time, and the male is about ready to become a sire, although the age varies with certain breeds and individuals. First, the bitch: If you had your bitch spayed or altered before her first heat, then skip this part; it doesn't affect you or your bitch.

The bitch is in heat or has her estrual cycle twice a year, beginning her first heat at 8 to 10 months or sometimes at 12 months (depending on breed and individual). These periods are about 6 months apart, although some bitches have them a month or two sooner or later. The heat lasts 3 weeks, sometimes a day less or more. The bitch is receptive to males during the middle week of this period, that is, when she is ovulating. Incidentally, if you are interested in breeding a bitch who has a history of failing to become pregnant after being bred, your veterinarian by a test can tell the exact day that is best for breeding her with a male or for artificial insemination.

What all this means is this: Your bitch is receptive to the male only during her semi-annual period of heat. At other times, unlike the male, she is uninterested in sex. If you wish to mate her, you must do it during the middle week of her 3-week heat. If you do not want puppies, then you must keep the bitch behind locked doors. Males from far away will catch her scent at this time, and soon every male in the neighborhood will be at your door, barking and scratching to get at her. They will persist, and very often succeed when you are least aware of it. Even on the street a male will attempt to breed with a bitch if she is in heat. The only certain insurance against puppies is to keep the bitch indoors for this period of time.

I mentioned earlier an oral medication given before the onset of heat, or even during it, will halt the period. If you are interested in this kind of control, discuss it with your veterinarian.

For a more detailed description of the bitch during this time, turn to Chapter 9 (Mating, Pregnancy, and Whelping). Here, let me say that you can recognize when the bitch is in heat by the appearance of her vulva or external genital organ. The vulva will appear swollen or inflamed, and the bitch will lick her parts or rub them. Also, her appetite may vary, either increasing or decreasing. This phase lasts 4 or 5 days. Then blood or a bloody discharge begins to drip from the vulva. Some bitches bleed freely, others slightly, some not at all—depending on the individual and the breed. If you have children around, tell them that this is a normal condition and not to be afraid or alarmed.

The bleeding—varying from bright red at the beginning to pink or colorless later—lasts for several days, starting anywhere from the 5th to the 7th or 8th day after the swelling of the genitalia. During this period, the bitch is still not ready for mating, although she is becoming more and more receptive. When the discharge lessens, the bitch is ready for breeding. Her ovulation begins, and she can now be impregnated. This phase lasts for 3 or 4 days, and during the final days of her heat she may repulse any male who approaches her.

During the bleeding period, you should take care that the discharge does not soil rugs or furniture. There are sanitary napkins made especially for dogs, which cover the genitals, and other contraptions which provide similar protection. If you find the napkin unwieldy, the best method is to keep the bitch closed off in a particular area. Don't shut her in a basement or closet, of course, because she is already somewhat unsettled. In fact, reassure her with frequent attention and a warm tone. Try to keep her from those things she can soil without making her feel she is a nuisance, and without making her sense that you would like to banish her for these 3 weeks. If you do feel this way about her season, it is best for you and for her if she is spayed. There are oral contraceptive pills that hold off the heat period, but they are costly and must be used for a long time before ovulation. There is, in addition, a liquid that serves this purpose, but the drawbacks remain the same. The oral medication mentioned earlier (or spaying) before the season is much simpler.

Veterinarians differ on whether a bitch should be mated during her first season or her second; that is, at 8 or 10 months, or 6 months later. Some even suggest the mating of large breeds at their third period when they are about 20 months old. Since the bitch may not be organically ready until she attains full growth, I recommend mating in her second heat period. In this connection, the American Kennel Club will not permit registration of a litter from a dam under 8 months or over 12 years. Most bitches should not be bred after their 8th or 9th year, for the strain, the work, and the general anxiety may be too much for them. There are, of course, many exceptions to this.

If you have a male: The male is sexually ready from the time he is a few months old, although he is not capable of impregnating a bitch until he is 8 or 9 months. Some veterinarians feel that a male under a year has not reached full growth and will produce a weak litter, although here the American Kennel Club sets a lower limit of 7 months (and an upper limit of 12 years). Usually you become aware of your puppy's growing sexual maturity when he rubs his genitals against the furniture or against your ankle and hand. He will also rub against children in the same way. Simply be firm with him and insist that he stop. The action is perfectly natural, not at all a cause for alarm or shame. If it happens with a child, simply tell the child to push the dog away, and if you find the dog trying it again, discourage him with a firm tone.

As for the bitch, cysts may be present, causing her to show signs of heat: discharge, attraction of the male, erratic appetite. If the bitch seems to be in season more than twice a year, or is discharging between seasonal periods, then take her to your veterinarian for a thorough examination.

If the male persists in his behavior and it really bothers you, then you might consider having him castrated. Castration means that you cannot enter him in a show and that you will never have a litter sired by him. Many owners feel that they should not interfere with a dog's natural life even when it involves some personal inconvenience. All medical indications are that castration does not lead to any unpleasant or unhealthy results in the male, just as spaying the bitch has no ill effects. Such decisions, however, are those that every owner must make for himself.

The male who wishes to fulfill his sexual needs will go to nearly any lengths to satisfy himself. He will fight, roam, and chase a receptive bitch anywhere and everywhere. The competition for her is fierce. If there should be a fight, she goes to the victor, and the victor is generally a veteran of such battles. If you wish your dog to remain in one piece and not become a battle-scarred warrior, then keep him out of mischief.

Apartment dogs are usually leashed and therefore controllable, although when they run free in the park they may decide that the reward is worth the fight. Suburban dogs really provide the chief difficulty, for they usually roam the neighborhood looking for an available bitch. Remember that this is probably one of the last remaining instincts left to the domesticated dog, and it is a powerful one. In former times, dogs fought over food, but food is no longer a problem—nearly all pets are well fed, often overfed. Consequently, sex remains the sole area in which they can assert their masculine prowess. The dog, in this respect, is little different from the male of other species.

The male pup discovering his sexuality will often mount a male as well as a bitch, if allowed to roam free. This is perfectly natural because he doesn't really know what he is doing or how to do it. He is simply reacting to an undefined urge. As an owner, do not become upset if your young dog makes passes at males and bitches indiscriminately. Certainly do not rage at him for abnormal behavior. He won't know what you're talking about, and you'll only confuse him. Your best bet is to keep him leashed or on your own grounds, and hope that the other person does the same with his or her dog.

Cryptorchidism and Monorchidism

There are two conditions in a male puppy that you should know about. The first is called cryptorchidism, a condition in which the male's testicles have not descended into the scrotum. Such dogs are usually sterile, unable to breed. The chances are that the undescended testicles have not developed because of some failure in the developmental process. The other condition is monorchidism, in which only one testicle has descended. Such dogs can breed, although they cannot be mated to a purebred bitch—that is, one approved by the American Kennel Club. Some geneticists hold that the trait is hereditary, and therefore this eliminates such a male as a stud and as a show dog.

These problems tend to become magnified as I list them. You should not feel, however, that your dog will give real trouble. Of course, he does have a life of his own, but it is rarely so obtrusive that it upsets the fine relationship between pet and owner. The great majority of owners have come to easy terms with the seasonal cycle of their bitches or with the needs of their males. They have discovered that what the dog offers is much greater than what his momentary troubles involve.

By this age, all dogs conditioned to outdoor kennels can sleep out in all kinds of weather. Make sure that the outdoor house is well insulated from drafts and from damp. The roof should not leak, and the floor should be free from openings through which damp can ooze. The dog should have a comfortable sleeping area—perhaps an old mattress or several thicknesses of canvas. If these are not available, then provide a thick layer of hay or straw. Whatever you use, you must be careful that the dog does not pick up ticks or other parasites from his bedding.

The doghouse should have some hinged part so that you can open it for cleaning and airing. It must be kept clean or the dog will begin to breed all kinds of parasites. Also, be sure you clean away all stool in the dog's run, or they too will breed parasites. Try to build the house itself so that it does not face the north, and if it is portable (as most are) turn the entrance away from the wind as necessary. A sharp wind or draft for the full-grown dog is almost as dangerous as it is for the young puppy. If you can, put in a double protection at the door, perhaps a layer of canvas hung just behind the regular opening. When the dog settles in for the night, he should be dry and cozy.

Controls

There are certain controls necessary for your dog besides those of sitting, staying, coming, heeling, and turning, which I discuss in Chapter 5. You must restrain the full-grown dog, especially if he is particularly demonstrative in his friendliness. Not everyone shares your enthusiasm for a grinning, licking pet that tries to push you over simply out of affection and general well-being. These restraints must really be enforced by the time your dog is a year old, and even earlier. What is cute and ingratiating in the very young puppy becomes, on occasion, annoying in the older dog, especially when he is large and heavy.

The first control concerns the dog's jumping on people. Some dogs are evidently friendlier than others, and it is these you must control. The best way to restrain their overenthusiasm with strangers is to keep them leashed, but if you are in your house when a visitor arrives, obviously the dog will be running free. When he goes to leap, give a sharp "No!" in a firm tone. Clap your hands if necessary, or stamp your foot. If you start this when the habit first appears, you will have it licked before it goes very far. Of course, if a 150-pound dog jumps, warn your visitor to duck. As an owner, you are responsible for your dog's behavior, as much as you are responsible for the behavior of your children. There is no need to discourage affection—it is a marvelous thing that a dog has so much of it to give—but he must come to learn that certain demonstrations are out of bounds.

Just as one dog may be overly friendly, so another may growl and raise his back at certain people. This reaction is virtually impossible to break. Those breeds trained for generations as watchdogs—like Dobermans—are simply reacting instinctively. Also, there may be something about a friend or an acquaintance that the dog does not like. You cannot make him friendly to everyone, and it is doubtful that you would want to. Part of the natural life to which every dog is entitled is the right to like and dislike. As long as his hostile feelings go no further—into biting and nipping—there is little you can or should do to change him.

Another area in which you must control your dog is barking, that is, if you wish to remain on good terms with your neighbors. If your dog barks persistently day and night, do not be surprised if your neighbors knock late one evening and begin to move your belongings out on the street. No matter how much one loves dogs, persistent barking at all hours is deadly. It not only can kill all friendly feeling for the animal; it can also destroy all friendly feeling for its owner.

Certain breeds are more prone to bark than others: Terriers, for example, are nervous, rather high-strung, and full of energy that they rarely use up. They take it out in barking, particularly if they are undere exercised. Good as they are as apartment dogs, they are yappers and should be controlled. If you started in when your dog was a puppy, perhaps you have the problem beaten, or perhaps there is no problem at all. See Chapter 11 for ways in which you can try to control a barker.

A persistent barker may have something the matter with him. If you bought him from a pet shop or even from a kennel, he may have been cooped up for so long that he is cage-crazy. He has been mentally affected, and you may never be able to cure him. Such cases, however, are very rare.

Many dogs spend their time roaming instead of barking, sometimes for days at a time. Even if your dog is correctly tagged (licensed), in many communities he is not supposed to roam the streets. In some localities it is against the law and in many it is frowned upon. After all, your pet, wonderful as he is to you, is a stranger to others. For those who have never owned a dog, a wandering dog is potentially a rabid animal who might bite them and disappear. Also, your roaming dog might himself be bitten by a rabid animal—fox, rabbit, raccoon, rat, or bat. If you own a dog, you are responsible for keeping him close to your house.

If you are in an apartment, there is no problem. If you walk him in the neighborhood park, he is supposed to be leashed, and if not, you surely keep him in sight. In the suburbs, give him a run on a trolley line attached to a couple of trees. Make it long enough so that he has room, but not so long that he gets entwined and can't get free.

A dog will roam for a number of reasons, not one of which means that he doesn't love you and enjoy your company. He smells a bitch in season, and that is enough to make him leave for a few days. Sometimes, even though well fed, he goes off searching for a tidbit in some distant garbage can. Or else he is simply a wanderer who needs an occasional change to keep happy. Give him time and care, keep him occupied with learning some easy tricks, or going through his paces, and you can probably keep the roaming dog at home. If not, attach him to a line that he can't escape from, and then he has no choice.

The full-grown dog should be kept away from moving automobiles. He has little to gain and everything to lose. The car is the worst enemy a dog has, the chief killer of dogs in this country. Car chasing always carries a certain fascination for some dogs, and it is up to you, the owner, to protect yours against something he cannot himself resist. This whole problem is covered in Chapter 11.

In addition to teaching a dog the ordinary elements of restraint, you should train the almost-grown puppy to come when called. If you do let him off the leash, his obedience to your call may well save his life, especially if he runs into the street. In an isolated spot like a hallway or garage, try to make him understand what you mean. In a firm voice, say "Come!" and have someone push him toward you. Repeat this several times a day. If this method doesn't work, attach a long check cord to his collar and repeat firmly the word "Come!" If he fails to respond, pull the cord gently toward you until he is forced to approach. Then start again. Continue for about 10 minutes at a time—the limit of a dog's attention span. When he has mastered the idea in isolation, take him outdoors where there are distractions. He must learn the word and the response in the general situations where his correct reaction may save his life.

At this point, you have a full-grown dog, healthy and happy, trained to do the things required of him for a safe and satisfactory life. For the next 10 or more years (depending on the breed and the individual dog), his life will change little, although at about 6 or 7 his metabolic processes will begin to slow up. He will need, though the middle range of his life, a good deal of exercise, and you must be ready to provide it. Do not make up on weekends what he misses during the week. Like yourself, a dog needs constant and steady exercise, unless the weather is too hot. Like you, he gets tired if you push him past his natural endurance, or if you give him exercise in spurts. See how much he can take. Make it a habit to take your dog with you when you shop, when you go for a newspaper, when you walk to visit a friend. In this way, he gets out of the house often. If you live in the suburbs or the country, you can of course give your dog a concrete or dirt run in your back yard. But even here he needs some sustained exercise—several long walks and some substantial play, like retrieving a ball or a stick. A dog who sleeps all the time because he has nothing else to do will develop an unhealthy personality. In that respect, he is little different from a person who has nothing to do with himself.

DIETS FOR 7 TO 10 MONTHS
(based on 2 feedings a day at 8 A.M. and 6 P.M.)

In the following feeding charts for the 7- to 10-month-old puppy, increase the quantities as the puppy grows or seems hungry; decrease them if he is getting fat. I give only average amounts.

Toys (3 to 15 pounds as adults)

PREPARED (CANNED) FOOD: 3–6 ounces (6–12 tablespoons) per feeding, with some milk on the side.

DRY FEED OR MEAL: 3–4½ ounces per feeding, with some milk or beef broth mixed in. (Add some fat—bacon, beef, butter, etc.)

BISCUIT OR TABLE SCRAPS: Give only as a snack if you wish, in the later evening.

PRESCRIPTION DIET: Follow directions on the label.

HOME COOKING: 3–6 ounces of chopped meat (raw or cooked lightly) per feeding (mix in the drippings if cooked)

or 3–6 ounces of cooked chicken per feeding (mix in some fat).

Mix in crushed Shredded Wheat and a little milk; give an occasional egg (cooked), some cooked green vegetables.

GIVE VITAMIN-MINERAL SUPPLEMENT (MIXED WITH FOOD): according to directions on label.

Small Breeds (15 to 30 pounds as adults)

PREPARED (CANNED) FOOD: 6–12 ounces (12–24 tablespoons or ¾–1½ cups) per feeding, with some milk on the side.

DRY FEED OR MEAL: 6–9 ounces per feeding, with some milk or beef broth mixed in. (Add some fat—bacon, beef, butter, etc.)

BISCUIT OR TABLE SCRAPS: Give only as a snack if you wish, in the later evening.

PRESCRIPTION DIET: Follow directions on the label.

HOME COOKING: 6–12 ounces of chopped meat (raw or cooked lightly) per feeding (mix in the drippings if cooked)

or 6–12 ounces of cooked chicken per feeding (mix in some fat).

Mix in crushed Shredded Wheat and a little milk; give an occasional egg (cooked), some cooked green vegetables.

GIVE VITAMIN-MINERAL SUPPLEMENT (MIXED WITH FOOD): according to directions on the label.

Medium Breeds (30 to 55 pounds as adults)

PREPARED (CANNED) FOOD: 9 ounces–1 pound 1 ounce (18–34 tablespoons or 1–2 cups) per feeding, with some milk on the side.

DRY FEED OR MEAL: 9–14 ounces per feeding, with some milk or beef broth mixed in. (Add some fat—bacon, beef, butter, etc.)

BISCUIT OR TABLE SCRAPS: Give only as a snack if you wish, in the later evening.

PRESCRIPTION DIET: Follow directions on the label.

HOME COOKING: 9 ounces–1 pound 1 ounce of chopped meat (raw or cooked lightly) per feeding (mix in the drippings if cooked)

or 9 ounces–1 pound 1 ounce of cooked chicken per feeding (mix in some fat).

Mix in crushed Shredded Wheat and a little milk; give an occasional egg (cooked), some cooked green vegetables.

GIVE VITAMIN-MINERAL SUPPLEMENT (MIXED WITH FOOD): according to directions on the label.

Large Breeds (55 to 80 pounds as adults)

PREPARED (CANNED) FOOD: 1 pound 4 ounces–1 pound 8 ounces per feeding, with some milk on the side.

DRY FEED OR MEAL: 1 pound 2 ounces–1 pound 5 ounces per feeding, with some milk or beef broth mixed in. (Add some fat—bacon, beef, butter, etc.)

BISCUIT OR TABLE SCRAPS: Give only as a snack if you wish, in the later evening.

PRESCRIPTION DIET: Follow directions on the label.

HOME COOKING: 1 pound 4 ounces–1 pound 8 ounces of chopped meat (raw or cooked lightly) per feeding (mix in the drippings if cooked) OR 1 pound 4 ounces–1 pound 8 ounces of cooked chicken per feeding (mix in some fat).

Mix in crushed Shredded Wheat and a little milk; give an occasional egg (cooked), some cooked green vegetables.

GIVE VITAMIN-MINERAL SUPPLEMENT (MIXED WITH FOOD): according to directions on the label.

Very Large Breeds (80 to 185 pounds as adults)

PREPARED (CANNED) FOOD: 1 pound 8 ounces–2 pounds per feeding, with some milk on the side.

DRY FEED OR MEAL: 1 pound 2 ounces–1 pound 8 ounces per feeding, with some milk or beef broth mixed in. (Add some fat—bacon, beef, butter, etc.)

BISCUIT OR TABLE SCRAPS: Give only as a snack if you wish, in the later evening.

PRESCRIPTION DIET: Follow directions on the label.

HOME COOKING: 1 pound 8 ounces–2 pounds of chopped meat (raw or cooked lightly) per feeding (mix in the drippings if cooked) OR 1 pound 8 ounces–2 pounds of cooked chicken per feeding (mix in some fat).

Mix in crushed Shredded Wheat and a little milk; give an occasional egg (cooked), some cooked green vegetables.

GIVE VITAMIN-MINERAL SUPPLEMENT (MIXED WITH FOOD): according to directions on the label.

DIETS FOR MATURITY
(10 to 12 months for most breeds)

Feed once a day in the morning or evening.

Follow the amounts for the 7- to 10-month-old puppy and scale them up or down as necessary to keep your dog lean and sleek. If you have a toy or a small or medium breed, cut down one-quarter or so of the dog's daily food intake. For the larger breeds, cut down only slightly unless the dog is getting fat—if he is, cut more sharply. For the very large breeds, wait until your dog has reached his full growth (see breed standard in Chapter 2) and then decrease his food slightly.

This has been a long chapter, and there are several important points you may have missed. For this reason, I have made a check list of those things you should be aware of in the first year of your puppy's life:

1. Set up a definite, draft-free spot for the newborn puppy (or puppies) a few days before he is born.

2. Have on hand certain basic equipment. For the new puppy without a dam to nurse it, you will need doll's baby bottles, a plastic eye dropper, doll's baby nipples, a measuring cup with ounce gradations, a mixing bowl, perhaps a baby scale. For the older puppy, a stiff brush, a regular comb, a stripping comb, a collar and leash, some toys of hard rubber or leather, a feeding can big enough for the puppy's muzzle to enter. For long-eared dogs like the Cocker Spaniel and Basset Hound, buy a narrow bowl, so his ears don't go into the food.

3. Keep young children away from newborn and fragile puppies.

4. Clip the puppy's nails when he is a few weeks old. This will prevent him from irritating the bitch's breasts or injuring the eyes of the other puppies in the litter.

5. Do not take a puppy outside before he is 6 weeks old, and then only if the weather is mild. He is subject to upper respiratory infections.

6. Crop the puppy's ears, if you intend to, when he is 8 weeks old; dock his tail and remove dewclaws at 3 to 5 days. Or consult your veterinarian for the best time.

7. Keep all items used by the puppy sanitary.

8. Watch the puppy's stool for any signs of worms or other irregularities—like diarrhea or blood. Call the veterinarian if you see such signs.

9. Begin dish feeding of a nursing puppy in the 3rd week.

10. Start weaning in the 4th week and certainly have the dog weaned by the 6th.

11. Even if you do not suspect worms, take a sample of the puppy's stool to the veterinarian at 4 to 6 weeks, when he is weaned.

12. Never try to worm a dog yourself, unless you know what type of worm he has.

13. Be careful of the soft, flexible spot on the top of the puppy's head.

14. You might try paper-training at about 3 months. Do not expect too much, however, for quite a while.

15. Do not bathe the pup until he is 4 to 6 months old, and not even then unless the weather is warm. Rather, rub him down with a cloth.

16. If you have the slightest doubt about the pup's health, take his temperature rectally. Normal is 101.5° F.

17. Make sure that whatever diet you decide to follow is nutritious and well balanced, containing protein (20 per cent), fat (10–20 per cent, depending on activity), carbohydrates (the rest), plus a vitamin-mineral supplement until the dog is a year old.

18. At the time of weaning (4 to 6 weeks), your puppy is ready for his first protection against distemper. If he received the colostrum from the dam, he has been immune up to now. Canine distemper vaccine should be given at 6 to 8 weeks of age and will immunize until 3 months of age. Rabies vaccination occurs at 6 months.

19. Be sure that your puppy is teething correctly. If his milk teeth do not fall out, check to see if they must be pulled. The period of teething starts at about 3 months and continues for several months.

20. At 3 to 5 months, begin general training: use of collar and leash, simple commands (heel, sit, stay, turn, come). For details, see Chapter 5.

21. Give your dog a name as soon as you acquire him, and repeat it until he responds (after several months).

22. If you intend to have your bitch spayed or male castrated, do it at about 6 months.

23. Expect a certain amount of car sickness in most puppies until they become used to the motion.

24. Accustom the puppy of 5 months or younger to a carrying case—do so gradually.

25. At 6 months or younger—depending on your municipality—your dog requires a license tag, which he must wear at all times. Check with your veterinarian for the requirements in your area.

26. Have a 6-month checkup by the veterinarian.

27. Do not clip a longhaired dog's coat—it keeps him cool in the summer and warm in the winter.

28. Watch your puppy's weight as he grows toward adulthood. If you have been overfeeding, cut down.

29. The bitch will go into her first season at 8 to 10 months, sometimes at 12. See Chapter 9 for details concerning heat, mating, and pregnancy.

30. The male is sexually mature at about the same age as the bitch, although his interest in sex has existed from his early months.

31. Try to control certain behavioral patterns in the mature dog before they get out of hand: jumping on people, excessive barking, roaming, chasing cars.

32. For grooming (combing, brushing, and clipping), see Chapter 5.

4

Nutrition

THE AMOUNT of food your dog needs depends on a great many things. One dog differs from another in his basal metabolism, the amount of energy he uses, the demands of his nervous system, the requirements of growth and general maintenance, and the kind of work he does, if any. In brief, dogs differ in their food needs as much as people do. While one person eats a great deal and remains lean, another may eat far less and become fat. So too with dogs.

The domestication of the dog has meant that, on the average, he does not exercise nearly so much as he did in his primitive state. As a result, one must watch a dog's weight, particularly the weight of a city or apartment dog, or else he will become fat. Too much weight weakens the heart and shortens life. You should feed a dog the minimum that he needs to remain healthy and energetic. If you feed him more than his body requires, you may be satisfying your own needs in some way, but you will not be helping your dog.

The key to correct nutrition is a balanced diet. A dog needs a balance of certain basic nutrients: vitamins, minerals, fats, proteins, and (for bulk) carbohydrates. When he receives these in the right amounts, he will probably also be receiving enough calories, which he can turn into energy. There is no fixed formula—each dog is different. You will have to feel your way, guided by what common sense tells you and what you see with your eyes. If your dog isn't thriving, the cause may be a lack of vitamin and mineral balance, perhaps too few or too many calories, or else insufficient fats and proteins.

In this chapter, I will tell you in untechnical language what diet means for your dog. On the whole a person and a dog need the same foods, although, of course, in different quantities. Usually a person is larger than a dog (the average is terrier size—20 to 30 pounds), and therefore needs much more of everything. Also, the average person is considerably more active than a dog. Even the city dweller burns more energy than the average dog, unless one has in mind a farm dog or an Alaskan Malamute mushing great distances every day through the snow and wind.

In terms of major requirements, a dog and a person differ only in the need for vitamin C and carbohydrates. Mature dogs do not need vitamin C—they seem to manufacture their own. Since our chief source of vitamin C is fruits, you need not worry if your dog rejects them. As for carbohydrates, the dog does not seem to have any nutritional need for them, although in practical terms they may form more than 50 percent of his daily diet.

It may surprise you to learn that the smaller dog needs more calories (or energy) per pound of body weight than the larger dog, provided the activities of both are about the same. Put a different way, the small dog will eat *proportionately* more than the large dog. For example, a small dog of 20 to 30 pounds, fully grown and active, may need 1½ pounds of food daily, while a dog weighing five times as much will not need 7½ pounds of food, but perhaps only 3 to 5 pounds—that is, if both take the same amount of exercise. If the small dog is exceptionally active, he may eat as much as a considerably larger dog who is inactive and placid. Later on in this chapter, I take up estimates of how much food a grown dog should eat.

Puppies need proportionately more food than the fully grown dog, regardless of size and breed. In some cases, the puppy might eat fully twice as much as he should eat when he reaches maturity at 10 to 12 months. In addition, he needs a daily dose of a vitamin-mineral supplement, because his food usually does not provide enough vitamins and minerals. Also, pregnant bitches may need more than their normal amounts of food. In particular their milk intake must increase to provide them with necessary minerals, or else a vitamin-mineral supplement may supply these. The nursing dam (the mother) will usually increase her intake of food, which maintains the flow and richness of her milk. Once her puppies are weaned (at about 4 weeks), the bitch should be returned to her normal feeding schedule; otherwise she may rapidly put on weight. All these shifts to a normal diet—for puppies as they mature, for pregnant and nursing bitches as they return to normal—should be made gradually. Usually you should allow puppies to eat as much as they want, unless they are becoming grossly fat. But don't continue this policy into adulthood, or your animal may become more pig than dog.

Put into figures, what does all this mean? The average mature (fully grown) dog requires about 35 calories per body pound per day. Thus, a reasonably active one-year-old terrier of 20 pounds should consume about 700 calories a day—a little more than a pound of prepared canned food or two thirds of a pound of dry food. For the pregnant bitch or the nursing dam, the calorie intake may double. (For these details, see Chapter 9.) In fact, as her puppies enter the third or fourth week, the mother's calorie intake may increase sharply if she is still nursing.

For the month-to-month diet of the growing puppy, see Chapter 3. The terrier who at maturity will thrive on 700 calories a day requires a good many more as a puppy. On the other hand, your dog may be overweight (not uncommon with city dogs). If this is so, the diet of a 20-pound dog may be cut to half his normal requirement, to 350 to 400 calories. Do it gradually. You need not worry that your dog will starve. As long as he is overweight, he can live off the extra fat. When the fat across his shoulders and around his stomach begins to melt away, then you can start increasing his calorie intake slightly, until you see him getting fat again.

Calories, of course, are only a small part of a dog's needs. As I indicated above, he must also have fats, minerals, vitamins, proteins, and (for bulk) carbohydrates to keep him energetic and healthy. Let us take fats first and see what they do, why the dog needs them, and how much he needs.

Fats

Your dog's daily requirement of fat will depend a great deal on his activity. Since fat provides energy and heat, an active working dog will need a high percentage in his diet, up to 20 percent or so. The lazy city dog who walks or runs a few blocks each day will need far less fat, 5 to 8 percent. With larger amounts of fat, he will grow too heavy.

At one time, people believed that fat was bad for a dog's health. We know better today: Fatty products are essential for good nutrition. Among other things, fats provide energy and help keep the skin healthy. A dog with insufficient fat in his diet will generally develop a dry, scaly skin, and his coat may become coarse and unattractive. A dog on a low-fat diet may become highly nervous and excitable and more subject to ailments.

There are three acids in fats that a dog must have: linoleic, linolenic, and arachidonic. The chief of these is the first, linoleic, and fortunately this one is the easiest to come by. It is found in most meat products, in suet, in corn oil, and in butter. The importance of the other two is less obvious, but they are still necessary. They are found in various oils and in animal fats.

A can of typical dog food will usually contain enough fat for your dog's requirements. Check the amount on the label. However, if you feed dry meal, you might moisten it with as much fat as your particular dog seems to need. The average dog should have 5 to 10 percent fat in his diet, depending on his ability to absorb it. If your dog's skin and coat appear to be healthy, and if he stays lean and energetic, then you have hit upon the right amount. If your dog begins to get pudgy, give him less fat; if his coat looks lifeless, give him more. If you feed your dog a predominantly meat diet, as many owners do, then do not cut away all the fat. Often, the cheaper cuts of meat are preferable, for they have a higher fat content. When you heat a piece of meat, let the fat collect and feed it to the dog with the meat. If you give him table scraps, make sure that some of the scraps include the fat that you cut off from your own meat. The dog loves it, and it's good for him.

Special circumstances may call for a change in diet. The very thin puppy or dog should be given a fat-rich diet—as long as he can absorb it without vomiting or suffering from diarrhea—until his weight and health come up to par. Similarly, the pregnant bitch and the nursing dam will require larger amounts of fat than they do under normal conditions. The very fat dog will need smaller amounts, for he has stored large quantities and can draw upon the reserve. The very active dog—the hunting, retrieving, or working animal—needs larger doses of fat to give him energy. A large active dog (of 100 pounds or more) needs 5,000 calories a day or more if he is to retain his strength, much as a lumberjack or day laborer may need similar amounts to maintain his normal weight. Almost any owner will find that he can make suitable adjustments simply by looking at his dog and taking the necessary step toward raising or lowering the fat intake. By controlling fats, you control calories to a large extent.

Proteins

Most owners are alert to the protein needs of their dogs. In fact, since most owners feed a predominantly meat diet to their pets, they provide their protein needs as a matter of course. The average mature dog needs about 10 to 15 percent of his daily intake in protein. The growing dog will need more—up to double the requirement of the grown animal. Contrary to what many people believe, other products besides meat can provide adequate protein. A diet of dry meal mixed with animal fat will keep your dog healthy and happy. After a few years of such a diet, he may not even want to touch meat.

Specifically, protein helps body growth and repair. Without it, the dog's body gradually declines, and his physical processes slow up. His resistance to infection is lowered. Proteins are themselves compounds made up of various amino acids, about twenty of which have been identified. When your dog eats foods containing proteins, his body breaks them down into component amino acids and then rebuilds them into the right combination of proteins he needs for growth and repair. Those amino acids not used for such protein building are further broken down and transformed into heat or energy.

Some foods are better sources of protein than others. In particular, milk, meat, eggs, and cheese—foods that nearly all dogs eat—are rich in the kind of protein that the body needs. A food like corn, while good for the dog, does not contain all the essential amino acids, and the rare dog fed exclusively on corn may have a dietary deficiency. The same is true of rice and potatoes, wheat flour, peas, and several other foods. A dog whose diet is made up substantially of these items should be given a protein supplement—animal fat, for example.

Carbohydrates

Nutrition experts have not been able to show that a dog needs carbohydrates as an essential part of his diet. But in practice carbohydrates form a good deal of the bulk in a dog's diet and do provide calories. Up to 60 percent of a dog's diet may be carbohydrates. If there is more, other essentials like proteins and fats may be crowded from the diet.

Carbohydrates are found in sugar and starch foods like potatoes, candy, whole grains, milk, cane sugar, and rice. Starches, incidentally, are all right if the food is cooked. Potatoes and rice are fine if your dog likes them and if he isn't becoming fat. However, never give him a raw potato. Uncooked starch is difficult for him to digest, and a diet high in raw starch can cause diarrhea. If a dog is fed raw grains, he will probably pass them whole in his bowel movements, as his digestive system cannot handle them. Prepared dog foods contain cereals already baked or cooked in some other manner. Thus, they can be absorbed.

Vitamins

A vitamin is an organic substance found in very small quantities in natural foods. For many years, vitamins have been recognized as essential to a dog's health, although the precise amounts needed have not been determined. Vitamin deficiencies in your dog can result in a great many health hazards. Everything from his general metabolism to hearing, vision, fertility, muscle control, kidney function, blood clotting, and skin health is dependent upon a sufficient quantity of various vitamins.

If your grown dog eats a well-known brand of dog food, he is receiving all the vitamins that he needs. Manufacturers of the major brands have been careful to include essential vitamins. The puppy, however, will need a supplement of vitamins and minerals (there are several brands on the market) because he is developing very rapidly. So too will the old dog, who no longer gains full benefit from his food. Also, the pregnant bitch and the nursing dam will obviously need vitamin and mineral supplements, as the drain on their bodies may be faster than nature can replace.

If, however, you feed your dog mostly table scraps, then there is a chance that his diet is haphazard and his vitamin intake will not include all the essentials. Of course, some dogs thrive on strange foods indeed, but you cannot assume your dog will be one of them. Like the dog fed on prepared canned food, a dog fed on a dry meal diet with fat supplement will gain necessary vitamins and minerals, for dry meal is prepared with these supplements included. However, a dog on a straight meat diet may need a vitamin and mineral supplement, for meat lacks minerals like calcium and phosphorus and is deficient in vitamin A. Lean meat lacks essential fat. As you read the analysis below, you can check your dog's diet for the essentials.

VITAMIN A

Vitamin A is necessary for growth, good vision, adequate appetite, nerve health, coat luster, good digestion, prevention of infection, and a variety of other things. It is found in most yellow foods like egg yolks, carrots, butter, and corn, as well as in a meat like liver and many green vegetables and grains. While cod liver oil is the most well-known source of vitamin A, your dog can receive all he needs from a vitamin-mineral supplement made by most drug companies. Directions are on the label.

At one time a dog given large amounts of mineral oil to relieve constipation suffered a loss of vitamin A through absorption. At present, mineral oil is medicated so that such a loss is no longer possible.

VITAMIN B COMPLEX

This group includes B_1 or thiamine, B_2 or riboflavin, B_6 or pyridoxine, and B_{12}. Vitamin B in its various forms is needed for the adequate growth and health of most vital organs. It also promotes appetite, prevents anemia, adds to muscle tone, and aids in regular bowel movements.

Thiamine is found in meat, while milk and yeast are rich in riboflavin. Pyridoxine is in liver, egg yolks, fish, vegetables, and milk; and all foods containing proteins have vitamin B_{12}.

When a dog is not getting the vitamins in this group, he may suffer from a niacin (or nicotinic acid) deficiency. Do not confuse this element with the nicotine of tobacco. The tobacco element is poisonous, while nicotinic acid, or niacin, is necessary for your dog's health. A dog suffering from a thiamine deficiency will have "black tongue" or pellagra. The mucous membranes of his mouth will become very sensitive, and his tongue will take on a purplish-blackish color. The dog will become very thin, almost skin and bone, nervous and extremely irritable. He may die if untreated. Treatment consists of improving the diet, with a stress upon foods that are a good source of vitamin B.

Your mature dog will get his vitamin B from commercial dog foods, although the puppy and pregnant (as well as nursing) bitch will need vitamin-mineral supplements. If you have any doubt, check out dog foods with your veterinarian, and find out what he thinks about the need for vitamin-mineral supplements. A straight meat diet will give sufficient amounts of vitamin B, although it will be inadequate in other respects; so will table scraps. A diet of dry meal mixed with meat fat will provide adequate vitamin B as well as other requirements.

VITAMIN C

We all know that people with a vitamin C deficiency will develop scurvy, but recent research indicates that mature dogs manufacture their own vitamin C. In the rare case of an imbalance that might result in scurvy, the dog will respond rapidly to vitamin C, which is found in abundance in fruits and vegetables.

VITAMIN D

Puppies need vitamin D for strong, sturdy bones. The most common ailment that results from a deficiency in vitamin D and calcium and phosphorus is rickets. Rickets is a condition in which the bones do not calcify correctly and as a result become bent or bowed. The dog's teeth are also affected by the deficiency, forming irregularly and breaking through the gums later than they normally would. These bone conditions may be caused not only by a vitamin D deficiency, but also by a mineral deficiency.

For the mature dog, commercial foods provide adequate amounts of vitamin D, as do good grades of dry meal, which contain irradiated yeast and bone meal. Either of these foods, together with exposure to the sun, will be sufficient. The pregnant bitch, the nursing dam, and the puppy himself, however, all need extra amounts of the vitamin, and a vitamin-mineral supplement will provide them. Large breeds, with their rapid development and heavy bones, are in particular need of vitamin D with mineral supplement in the crucial stages of puppyhood.

Do not dose your dog with excessive amounts of the vitamin or the results may be undesirable: hardening of the tissues, deformation of the teeth, poor growth, bloody diarrhea, great thirst, and depression or prostration. To be sure, check with your veterinarian about the necessity for a supplement.

VITAMIN E

Although less known than the other vitamins, vitamin E appears to be necessary for normal reproduction and lactation (secretion of the bitch's milk before and during nursing). There also seems to be evidence for its need in muscle tone. Wheat germ found in grain products supplies the dog with the necessary small amounts of this vitamin. All vitamin-mineral supplements also include it.

VITAMIN K AND OTHERS

Research indicates that a dog needs vitamin K to make his blood clot. When the blood fails to clot, severe anemia may follow. In Warfarin poisoning—which leads to such bleeding—vitamin K is injected. Alfalfa meal is rich in vitamin K, as it is in other essential vitamins.

Other elements that may serve some purpose in the dog's diet are panthothenic acid and folic acid. These are not major considerations for the owner, although panthothenic acid seems to be necessary for good growth and a healthy appetite. It is found in liver, yeast, and crude molasses, and a dog seems to get sufficient amounts if the rest of his diet is balanced. The same is true of choline (not to be confused with chlorine), although the amount that a dog needs has not been determined. Folic acid, which some owners may be familiar with, appears to be a necessary ingredient of hemoglobin.

Minerals

For a dog to have a well-balanced diet he needs adequate minerals as well as vitamins. If you feed your dog a commercial food, the chances are that he is getting all the minerals he needs. Also, a good dry meal will have essential minerals added. If in addition you give your dog a vitamin-mineral supplement or powdered milk, you can be sure that you are fulfilling his basic requirements.

Dogs need calcium, phosphorus, iron, copper, potassium, magnesium, sodium, chlorine, iodine, possibly sulfur, manganese, cobalt, and zinc. This reads like an impressive list of needs, but actually most of the requirements are met with a balanced diet. The chief needs are calcium and phosphorus (usually considered together as a unit) and iron.

CALCIUM AND PHOSPHORUS

For rapidly growing puppies, supplementary calcium and phosphorus, along with vitamin D, are necessary for good bone, blood, and tooth health. The same is true for pregnant bitches and nursing dams—their need for these two minerals is far greater than the requirement of the mature dog who is not bearing pups. Milk is rich in calcium, as are bones and bone meal, as well as alfalfa meal. Phosphorus is found in bones, cereals, and milk.

If table scraps form the chief part of your dog's diet, there is some chance that he will not get enough minerals, particularly calcium and phosphorus. Table scraps should not, in most cases, compose more than 25 percent of the daily diet. The exception would be when the scraps are themselves carefully selected for vitamin and mineral content, but it is the rare owner who has the time to do this. Prepared dog foods—both the wet canned variety and the dry kind—contain adequate amounts of calcium and phosphorus, sufficient for the mature dog. Vitamin-mineral supplements are in order for the growing puppy, the pregnant bitch, and the nursing dam.

Iron is needed only in very small amounts, but it is essential for building red blood cells and for keeping the dog healthy and active. It is found in meats, especially in liver and other inner organs, as well as in egg yolks and cereals like bran. Inadequate iron in the dog's diet can lead to anemia. The pregnant bitch—as a precaution against anemia—must be given a supplement. The iron included in vitamin-mineral supplements meets this requirement.

OTHER MINERALS

Several of the other minerals—copper, cobalt, magnesium, and potassium—are also necessary for good blood and bone health, but these are needed in such small amounts that most dogs receive their requirements in their normal diets. Unless your dog is fed a highly unusual diet without any variation, he will pick up these necessary minerals. For example, iodine, sodium, and chlorine are in ordinary table salt, an ingredient of nearly every food preparation. Sulfur is found in meat and egg yolks, and potassium in the blood of meat.

Minerals compose 5 to 6 percent of your dog's body, with calcium and phosphorus forming more than half of this small percentage. The remaining third or so of the 5 to 6 percent is composed of the other minerals mentioned above, with a relatively important one like iron composing only .004 percent of the body's weight.

As an owner there is little you can do about calculating the exact mineral requirements of your dog. If I tell you that your dog needs so many milligrams of copper and niacin per pound of food, you can hardly put these figures to use. Your best bet is to be sure that the prepared food—whether canned or dry—you give your dog is certified by the Department of Agriculture. When you see its name or shield on the product, you know that the ingredients have met certain minimal specifications.

If you have any doubts about the diet you should give your dog, consult with your veterinarian. Under most conditions, a basically healthy dog will respond well to a prepared canned dog food or to dry meal mixed with fat. If you wish to feed the dog fresh food, a diet of meat supplemented by cereal, an occasional egg, occasional milk, perhaps a small extra piece of liver each week for minerals, will keep your pet healthy and energetic. If you wish to give a vitamin-mineral preparation, check with your veterinarian, and follow directions on the label. *Remember you must scale down any dose you do give* if you buy a preparation designed for human consumption. The average dog weighs 20 to 30 pounds, and therefore should receive about one-fifth of the dose recommended for an adult person. Of course a large dog of 100 pounds or more will receive about the same amounts as a person, but you must keep the dog's weight in mind when you give him vitamins and minerals as well as medicines.

Other Considerations

There are no indications that eating habits differ among the various breeds, or that purebred dogs require a different diet from mongrels. All dogs, regardless of background and breeding, have the same food requirements in terms of vitamins, minerals, calories, fats, proteins, and carbohydrates. The internal structure of one dog is the same as the internal structure of all.

Also, a dog will thrive on the same diet repeated every day for the rest of his life, provided that the diet is balanced. There is no reason to believe that a dog likes variety. If your dog does not eat, there is probably something medically or emotionally wrong with him. He won't lose his appetite because he is bored with his food. Of course, many owners get pleasure from varying their dogs' diet and providing little delicacies and surprises. Such attention is understandable and gratifying. But you should recognize that your dog will also thrive on a single diet that meets his essential needs. Excessive variation, in fact, may result in temporary diarrhea or vomiting, for his digestive system has become accustomed to one kind of food and then must readjust to another. Your dog's health is best preserved by a balanced diet that remains unvaried.

HOW MUCH TO FEED

It may be useful to you if I give some rule-of-thumb measurements for feeding your dog. As I indicated before, you must watch your dog's weight and adjust amounts as necessary. These figures are for the grown dog who is not pregnant or nursing. For the puppy in his various stages of development, see Chapter 3; and for the pregnant and nursing bitch, see Chapter 9.

For the moderately active grown dog, you should figure about one pound (or more) of wet meal or canned food per day for each 20 to 30 pounds of dog. With dry meal mixed with fat, you can figure on a somewhat smaller amount. A middle-sized dog of 30 to 55 pounds might normally eat one to two cans daily of prepared food or a smaller amount of dry meal. Larger breeds would need proportionately more.

Keep in mind, however, that very large dogs, once they have reached maturity, will need proportionately less than the small dog. Unless the large dog is working or hunting, he will grow flabby and gross on a heavy diet. This is especially true for large dogs kept in city apartments. Usually they don't exercise enough to work off their fat. Try to see what keeps your large dog happy, but do not overfeed. *If you follow the scale above without making adjustments, you might find yourself giving your large dog 5 or 6 pounds of food a day, while he may need only 3 or 4. Remember that all these considerations apply to the average dog—yours may of course differ.*

The grown dog will probably eat as much as you give him. If he is indoors a good deal and somewhat bored, he may find that eating is a way of relieving monotony, much as it is for many people. The healthiest dog is the one who eats the minimum he needs to remain active and happy. Much as it gratifies you to feed your dog and watch him lick his chops with pleasure, you can harm him by overfeeding him.

Prescription Diets for Ailing or Old Dogs

All the information above applies to the normally healthy dog. For dogs suffering from various ailments or for dogs with special food problems as a result of old age or some other reason, there are prescription diets. Prescription diets are obtainable only from your veterinarian, and each diet is designed to correct a particular ailment or condition. The price is more than most prepared dog foods cost. The one difficulty is that your dog may not enjoy it.

These diets are especially planned for dogs with specific needs. For example, there is a diet called "k/d" for the mature dog suffering from nephritis (inflammation of the kidney); one called "h/d" for dogs with heart disorders. There is another prescription diet, high in protein, called "p/d," for the growing puppy and for bitches during pregnancy to help with the secretion of the milk (before and during nursing). A fourth prescription diet, called "i/d," is bland and therefore useful for dogs before and after surgery, for those with inflammation of the intestine, and for those requiring rehabilitation after severe illness or following an intake of poison. This diet, "i/d," is also prepared for puppies at weaning time (when they are about 4 weeks old). A fifth diet, called "r/d," is suitable for the very fat dog. It provides everything the mature dog needs for nutrition, but it averages about half the total calories that he would otherwise receive in regular food.

There are other prescription diets that start from basic mixtures and can be changed according to your dog's needs. These diets or menus are established for purposes of growth, for reproduction, or for maintenance during certain illnesses. There are high-fat diets, low-fat diets, meat-free diets. There is even a special prescription menu for old dogs.

All these diets have been laboratory-tested and proven. They contain all the nutritional requirements for your dog and average approximately 500 to 600 calories per pound of food—about the same calorie content as a can of prepared dog food. If your dog is of average size—20 to 30 pounds—one pound per day of a prescribed diet will be enough for him until he returns to normal health.

The needs of any dog on a prescription diet vary according to the kind and severity of the ailment, the amount of exercise permitted him, his temperature, the condition of his intestinal tract, his age. These are conditions that your veterinarian must reckon with.

Unless your dog is sick or needs a special diet, there is no reason to bother with prescription diets. I am sure that most owners prefer to feed their dogs in their own way, and as long as the dog stays healthy, that is the right way.

Cost Factors

Since I do not know how much you as an owner wish to spend on feeding your dog, I can only make some general statements that I hope will be useful to you. I will mention some diets that cost a moderate amount, very little, and a great deal.

If you have an average-size pet—20 to 30 pounds—then a moderately priced diet would consist of a major brand of prepared dog food (one certified by the Department of Agriculture). A one-pound can daily, at a cost of about 25 to 35 cents, would be sufficient. If, however, your dog is of a very large breed and needs 4 or more pounds a day, then your costs will soar to almost $10 a week (about $1.00 to $1.50 a day).

A much less expensive way to feed a large dog is to give him dry meal—a specially prepared and baked meal. Some new brands are complete in themselves, while others need to have fat added. The dry meal can be obtained in bulk (50– or 100–pound sacks), and the animal fat as sold by any butcher is quite inexpensive. In this way, a dog of 100 pounds or more can be fed for under 50 cents a day. Such a diet is perfectly sound, having been laboratory-tested and -tried for several years. Make sure that you buy a meal that has several nutritional supplements baked into it. A smaller dog can also be fed in this way, with the daily cost brought down well under 25 cents.

Both diets—the canned food and the dry meal—are fine. If you have any doubts, talk to your veterinarian about their relative merits. If you are concerned solely with cost, however, the dry-meal menu is far less expensive, a consideration that may count when you must feed one or more large dogs, or several small ones.

If you are an owner for whom cost is not a factor, then I recommend meat, cooked eggs (2 or 3 weekly) and a vitamin-mineral supplement. Fresh food is not necessarily better for your dog than the prepared canned foods or dry diets, but many owners feel safer when feeding their pet this way. If you wish to feed fresh food, then you must be sure that your dog receives a balanced diet, of the kind that I discussed at the beginning of this chapter. Fresh ground sirloin is great for your dog if it contains some fat, and if it is supplemented by an occasional egg, some cereal for bulk, some milk or bone meal for calcium, perhaps by some liver once or twice a week for minerals. If you plan to feed your dog this way, you may wish to work out the precise requirements with your veterinarian, or you can check my list of the dog's needs and estimate yourself what he should receive. One of the multivitamin and mineral supplements on the market can satisfy any of your fears about the dog's needs in this area.

One warning: Very lean or muscle meat should not be the sole basis of a fresh diet. The dog needs fat, a point that I have repeated throughout this book. You do him a disservice if you feed him only the fine cuts of meat you like to eat. He needs a good hunk of fat for the calories, especially if he is at all active.

You can make your dog's diet as simple or as complicated as you wish. If you have time, then by all means cook him fresh food every day. Do not, however, vary his diet too much. Your dog manages best on a steady, balanced diet. If it is changed, it should be because of some real need—either illness or a nutritional deficiency. Once your dog hits his stride, his appetite remains constant and there is no need to tempt him further.

5
Training and Showing

HOUSE-TRAINING

I T WOULD be ideal if the very young puppy of a few weeks could be fully house-trained. Since he may urinate many times a day, house-training at this time would be a great help. Forget about it. In fact, do not expect any great results until he is more than 3 months old. You may have some success now and then, but the puppy before that age usually cannot form any habits. He will forget, and you will become angry and displeased for no good reason.

Paper-Training Inside

You may nevertheless try to paper-train the very young puppy as long as you don't expect too much. Learning takes time, especially if you start before the pup has full physical control of his functions, that is, when he is about 6 months old. To paper-train, spread out newspaper in the area where you want the pup to urinate and evacuate. Keep him confined to this spot, but be sure to separate his sleeping quarters from the newspaper. The theory is that he will not want to foul his own nest, and the newspaper offers him an alternative. This is a fairly subtle point, and, as I say, don't expect too much in the early stages.

When you first begin, help the puppy all you can. When he awakes in the morning, put him on the paper. Put him on the paper after every meal (he may eat four or five times a day). At night, before you go to bed, do the same. Every time he uses the newspaper, reward him with a pat and a warm tone in your voice, or, better yet, with a tidbit. Rub his abdominal area, and this may stimulate him into evacuating—particularly effective, by the way, for very young puppies.

In paper-training the puppy, try to catch him before he squats. Or if he should squat, move him right over to the paper. If you see him sniffing and circling, the time is right; get him to the paper, pet and soothe him. Make the act of using the newspaper seem the most natural and important thing in the world.

If there are accidents—and expect them to happen often—never spank your pup or put his nose in the mess. You simply upset him without serving any purpose. Scold him if you must, but do so right after the "accident." If you wait a few moments, the pup will not know what he is being scolded for. After you have shown him the error of his ways, wash up the spot with disinfectant to remove the odor completely. If he smells the spot, he will return to it and repeat his error. Dogs like places where they recognize their own odor.

Be persistent, patient, and firm. But don't expect too much until the pup is 3 months or older. Remember that paper-training works best for small breeds; obviously the larger dog must be taken outdoors, especially as he grows older. *Also remember:* Paper-training is one thing; training for the outside is a completely different project. The first does not lead into the second. If training outside seems easier, it is usually because the dog is older when you housebreak him outdoors and has better control of his functions.

Outdoor Training

If you want to train your pup for the outside from the start, then follow much the same procedure as with paper. Instead of getting him accustomed to the paper, get him used to going outside whenever he has to urinate or move his bowels. This method, incidentally, works no better than paper-training until the pup is 3 or 4 months old. Take him out right after meals and whenever you see him sniffing and circling around. Also, take him out early in the morning and late at night before retiring. If you live in an apartment on a high floor or in a walkup, there may be a problem in getting down fast enough. Expect accidents, and watch your blood pressure.

By the time the pup is 4 months or older, you should be training him with the definite hope of success. If you have trained him partially on newspapers, and now have started to take him out, you may find it useful to bring some newspapers with you. Put a newspaper down on the street and encourage him to squat on that. Since he is already familiar with the paper, he may perform properly. Of course remove any newspaper from the street, whether the pup has soiled it or not. When he seems to connect the trip outside with his elimination needs, gradually make the paper smaller until you can withdraw it altogether. Follow the same procedure with any other artificial device you may be using.

Also, when you are outside, let your pup nose around and pick his spot, as long as he doesn't soil the sidewalk or your neighbor's lawn. If he wants to evacuate on your lawn, that is your decision to make.

By the way, if you have a new dog who is already housebroken, he may temporarily forget his training in his new surroundings. But as soon as you put him on a regular schedule and he becomes familiar with the fresh smells and sounds, he should remember what he has been taught.

The secret of outside training is to take the pup out often enough so that he connects his urgent needs with the outdoors. Whenever he performs successfully, praise him and pat him lovingly. Your pleased tone and favorable reaction will eventually make the necessary connection in his mind. Once he has performed, take him in. If you let him play, he will not focus on the reason for having gone out in the first place.

In time, your dog will wait for the hour you take him out. *Always* keep him on a regular schedule. If he comes to expect a certain time for going out and then you shift it, you destroy many days or weeks of work. Let your dog fall into a pattern, and unless there is a physical problem he should respond correctly. Gradually lengthen the time your dog must wait to go outside—not by several hours, but by several minutes. The mature dog will normally need to go out only two or three times a day. Some breeds, like the Bull Terrier, may need to go out more often, and some individual dogs, as a result of nervousness or heavy eating habits, must be taken outdoors four or five times a day.

Keep in mind that all dogs want to be house-trained once they get the idea. With a little encouragement, there should be no difficulty. A dog dislikes soiling his sleeping area, and he will control his bladder and bowels as long as he can. It is up to you to establish a routine and to keep to it.

It is best if your dog is both paper-trained and housebroken for the outside. In poor weather, if your dog is small he can use paper and dispense with the walk; this is also very helpful if he is sick. Remember that very young puppies should not go out, especially if the weather is bad. Of course, for the big dog there is no alternative. You must walk him.

A Few Words on Sanitation

If before you become an owner you got angry when dogs evacuated all over the sidewalk and lawn, now is the time to take care that your dog doesn't do so. If you are an experienced owner, you already know that a dog left to his own devices will choose any place he wants to. It is because of careless owners and careless dogs that many motels, hotels, and apartment houses will not allow dogs.

While you will not change this policy overnight, it is up to you as an owner to teach your dog polite habits. When you are training your pup, edge him into the street, whether you live in the country or the city. You may think it "cute" if your dog leaves a pile in the middle of the sidewalk, but by encouraging bad habits you will do all dogs and owners a disservice.

Most dogs can wait until they reach the street. Most dogs, if properly trained, will as a matter of habit move off the sidewalk directly into the street. If your dog does mess on the sidewalk or in a park path, it is up to you to clean up after him. Bothersome as this may seem, it is a courtesy you should extend to other people.

If your dog is paper-trained indoors, it is a good idea to keep the soiled newspapers in a special can, or to take them into the street for disposal in a trash can. If the newspapers are put with the regular garbage and then left in the hall (the trash-disposal method for those apartments without incinerators), they will smell foul, especially if the trash is not collected shortly. Often, the garbage sits in the crowded hallway halfway through the night before an early morning pickup. If you are responsible for such smells, your neighbors will hardly favor your dog. If there is an incinerator, then of course dispose of the soiled newspaper right away. That is the best method.

Collar and Leash for the Puppy

Before you take your puppy outside, you must get a collar and leash. Do not try to train him unless you can control him on a leash. Make sure that the collar fits correctly, and is neither too loose nor too tight. A tight one will give him a lifelong fear of collars, and a loose one will let him slip out. Be sure there are no sharp points—bolts, pins, or nails— that will wear away his hair and gouge his skin. Buy an inexpensive one, as your pup will outgrow it.

Like a pony with a bit, a puppy at first is usually not receptive to the collar, and you must accustom him to it. In fact, he may turn over and over, or try to bite and even eat the collar. He might hide or refuse to let you get near him when he sees it in your hand. Don't take him seriously. You are the master, and you will have to teach him that—if you don't want a spoiled youngster. A good idea is to put the collar on him just before his meals. He is so excited about eating that he'll accept the collar as a burden he must bear to get his food. In time, he'll become used to it.

Some people prefer harnesses to collars. A large dog is usually easier to control with a collar. If your dog has been well trained with the harness, however, you should have no trouble controlling him. On the other hand, if you are very small and your dog is very large, then you should use the collar, but that is an individual choice. With a small dog, you can use either one.

Once you have gotten your dog used to the collar, the leash comes next. Let him smell it, touch it, lick it—so that he can see it's harmless and won't bite or scratch him. Let him run around the house dragging the leash from his collar. The leash should be either pliable leather or chain-link.

No matter how well you prepare your pup, assume that he won't like the leash. In the beginning, don't drag him. Coax him along, a few steps at a time. At first, walk him in the house—it may be embarrassing outside and you may be criticized for hurting him. Once he is outside, let him guide you unless he heads toward a moving bus or subway train. Gently tug him toward the street when he seems ready to go. Whenever he fights your lead, pat him and soothe him. In a short time—provided you do not instill fear in him—he'll be anxious to go out and will jump joyously when he hears the jingle of collar and chain.

SIMPLE COMMANDS

The simple commands that every pup should learn are SIT, STAY, COME, HEEL (walk at your heels), TURN, and STAND. Do not train your pup before he is 6 months old, and do not try to keep his attention for more than ten minutes at a time. You can try training him two or three times a day, but don't tire him or you will build up resistance. When he seems to lose interest, give up for that time. Train him before he eats—when his attention is sharper. Like most animals, dogs become sluggish after eating. Make sure he has been walked and is otherwise comfortable. So as to avoid distractions, do not have an audience, certainly not at first. The best spot is a confined place with only you and the dog present.

Your attitude, as when house-training, must be calm, patient, persistent, and firm. If you lose your temper, your puppy will be upset by your tone, and upset puppies, like upset people, never do well. He hardly knows what to expect next. When your pup performs well, give him lavish praise. Make him feel like a king. When he makes an error, reprimand him, but then follow the reprimand with a gentle note in your voice or a kind pat on his head. A dog must keep his confidence. If you can, build up an atmosphere in which he feels he has to justify your faith in his ability, and yet if he doesn't, he still knows that you love and admire him.

Once you establish this atmosphere, your pup will perform at his peak. There will be no need to reward him with candy or some other tidbit. Such rewards, in fact, are not to be encouraged here, for a puppy must learn to perform correctly whether or not he is rewarded. The chances are that he already knows one command, the word "No!" which you have hurled at him from time to time. Way back in his mind, he knows that certain things are expected of him. But do not assume that he will immediately fit himself into your expectations. Each command may take ten days to two weeks to penetrate, and with some pups *much* longer. Even after a basic command has been mastered, expect some confusion and a few slips.

Sit

When giving a command—whether "Sit!" or any other—use only the word. Do not say, "Sit down here, Rosco." Your dog will not understand whole sentences, unless you have a circus performer in the making. The pup understands your tone and your gestures. Keep words themselves to a minimum. There is, in fact, good reason to believe that a dog doesn't even understand the simple word command, but can tell by the sound and by your movement what is expected of him.

In an isolated room, put on his collar and leash. Keep him on your left side, as that is the side he will walk on when in the street (next to the curb). Hold the leash with your right hand so that your left hand is free to push down his hind quarters. Give the command "Sit!" or "Sit, Rosco!" in a firm, steady voice and at the same time push down on his hindquarters. Press gently but steadily, and pull up with the leash so that he cannot lie or flop down. Pressure from above on the leash will keep his head raised. Keep your hand on the dog's rear until he positions it correctly. Do not let go right away or he might jump up and fail to learn the lesson.

Make all your movements steadily, without jerks or sudden stops and starts. Do not move your feet or that may catch the pup's attention and confuse or distract him. Do not expect immediate results. Until your pup perfects the command, keep him on the leash and do not be surprised if he tries to break away during the first few dozen attempts.

When your dog has learned the spoken command and responds fifty or more times in succession, remove the leash. Repeat the command. If your dog has been well trained, he should respond correctly. If not, hold your temper and put the leash back on. Since a dog usually does not like the leash, he will make the connection and eventually obey the command. Be lavish in your praise and warm in your tone whenever your dog performs well.

It may be useful to have your dog also respond to a hand signal as well as to the verbal command. If you plan to work with him in the field, he will see but not hear you from a distance. Or there may be a lot of noise which keeps him from hearing your command when it may be absolutely necessary. After your dog has mastered the command to sit, hold up your hand, or one finger, whenever you give the word "Sit!" Make sure he can see the gesture. After that, always use the command and the gesture together, so that he comes to connect them.

The "sit" command is quite useful and perhaps the easiest of all to teach. Once your dog has learned this, both you and he will have gained confidence, an important step in his development as a dog and in your mastery as an owner. Also, the sitting position will be a way of controlling him when he begins to pull and tug, especially in the street during a wait at a traffic light or when you meet an acquaintance.

Stay

"Stay" for a dog means that he should remain stationary wherever he is. It is a most important command, for on occasion the dog's life might depend on his obeying you. "Stay" follows "Sit" and is usually coupled with it, into the command "Sit-Stay!" In this way, you can stop your dog from moving.

In teaching your dog to "stay," work with the leash attached to his collar. Run through the "sit" procedure, and follow that with the command "Stay!" Raise your hand, palm toward the dog, as you give the command. He will probably look at you in amazement the first few dozen times. Every time he starts to stand up, respond with a sharp "No!"—a word he probably already recognizes.

Do not give him any leash and tighten your hand on his collar. Once he has mastered this movement, then repeat it several times without the leash. If your dog wants to roam around before being released, then start again with the leash. Immediately praise him whenever he follows directions well and reprimand him whenever he fails to do so. Follow each reprimand with a pat or a caress so that he does not lose confidence.

Teaching a dog to "stay" takes longer than to "sit." Once he has recognized the basic pattern, begin to move away without permitting him to come after you. Back away from him, your eyes on his eyes, repeating the word "Stay!" and holding on to the length of leash in one hand while giving the appropriate gesture with your palm. Repeat the word "Stay!" again and again, for the dog is very tempted to follow you. If he stays, praise him warmly.

If you wish to train him by stages, attach a cord to the leash, so that you can retreat farther and farther without losing control. When he allows you to move to the end of the cord, then begin the lesson without the leash. Soon you will be able to leave the room, and your dog will remain stationary until you return. Start by leaving for only a few minutes at a time, and then increase the length of your absence. Do not, of course, torture the dog by making him "stay" for hours at a time. You have made your point if he sits quietly for a few minutes. Whenever you return to the room, praise him. He deserves it.

Come

To make a puppy come to you is the easiest thing in the world. Simply call out his name—he has known it for a few months—and he'll come running, licking, yipping, and grinning. That is, he'll come if he wants to. What if you want him to come and he has something better to do? Your job is to train him to come whether *he* wants to or not.

The lesson on "come" is a natural follow-up on "sit-stay." Start the lesson by running through the previous two commands as a warm-up. Also, a run-though will give the dog confidence in what he knows he can do. Once he has "stayed" for a few moments, call him by name followed by the command—"Rosco, come!" Perhaps some sharp sound as you call him, like clapping your hands together or slapping your knees smartly with your palms.

Give him plenty of chance to connect the word "come" with your physical movement. Praise him warmly whenever he reacts correctly. If he is stubborn, then tie a cord of 15 or 20 feet to his collar and tug on it as you give the command to come. If he fights the cord, pull steadily, repeating the command in a loud, clear tone. Do not show impatience, and do not drag him on his belly. Remember that you spent some time teaching him to "sit-stay," and now you want him to give up that position for something entirely different. Be firm, and if you feel your temper rising, give up for a few hours or call it a day.

A very stubborn dog may have to be hauled in on the cord countless times, but eventually he will respond; most dogs dislike being pulled. If you wish, you might accompany the word command with a hand gesture, such as one you would use with a child or friend, a motion for him to come. But the best method is a word command to which he reacts immediately. Whenever he fails to obey it, put him once again on the cord until he comes around.

Heeling

If your dog learns to heel, he will walk at your left side or heels. In this way, he will not move across your feet, entangle you in the leash, or bump into other people. Although you must start out by teaching your dog to heel on the leash, your aim eventually is to make him walk correctly without the restraint of the leash, provided of course it is safe for him.

To begin, run through what he already knows—especially "sit-stay." Then place him on your left side. With your left hand, grasp the leash about halfway down to his collar, so that you have a firm grip and can guide him. Hold the remainder of the leash looped around your right hand. If your pup is very small, you will have to lean over to control him.

Start walking forward at a brisk pace so that he knows you mean business. As you start, give the command "Heel!" You may follow the command with the dog's name, both words in a clear, sharp tone of voice. He will of course react in any number of curious ways the first few times you call the word. He may run ahead, pull back, try to jump on you, get under your feet, lick your hand, and grin madly. He is having a great time.

If he dashes forward, pull him short and give the command to heel.

If he holds back, pull steadily on the leash without dragging him. Never force him with a command or you build up a poor atmosphere for learning. Try to coax him into moving up to your heel. Continue to give the command while you tug firmly and steadily. If he is really stubborn either in moving forward or staying back, change the command to "sit-stay," simply to break the sequence and allow him to do something he is familiar with. Then start out again. Give praise whenever he responds correctly.

Whatever the reaction of your dog is, control him firmly with your leash hand (the left one). Act immediately to correct his mistakes. Do not let him fall into bad habits. Practice with him for periods of no more than ten minutes perhaps two or three times a day. When he has mastered the idea of heeling, walk with him and then command him to sit. Since you will want to walk and stop with your dog, it is a good idea to train him to heel and then sit. You may have to repeat the commands "Heel" and "Sit" many times, but eventually the pup will learn to follow you without any signal. As the movements become automatic with him, eliminate the verbal command to heel and the hand signal to sit.

When your dog is perfect on the leash and has made no errors for several successive performances, you should have him heel without the leash. Keep it attached to the collar, but exert no pressure with your left hand. Do not guide him in any way, but let him walk alongside you. At the first sign of a mistake, grasp the leash firmly with your left hand, or grip his collar ring, and lead him steadily in the direction you want him to go. Do not drag him at any time. You may find that he is behaving stubbornly, and this particularly angers you because you thought that he had the lesson down pat. Don't show impatience, but be firm and insistent. When he performs correctly again, praise him warmly.

Once your dog is walking correctly without the guidance of the leash, remove it entirely. If he has been adequately trained to heel with the leash held loosely, then he should respond correctly without it at all. If he falls back into an error, then reprimand him with a sharp "No, Rosco!" If necessary, put the leash back on. Once he knows what he is to do, remove it and try again. Remember to give praise whenever it is earned.

Turning

Turning may seem to be a simple thing, but young dogs have a tendency to follow their noses rather than you. Once you have trained your dog to heel, you must still train him to turn, or else he will walk straight ahead while you go right or left. If you turn left, you will probably walk over him.

Turning is really a part of heeling, rather than a separate learning process. Keep your dog leashed until he has learned the technique. At he beginning you must alert him to the fact that you are going to turn. You do this by slowing up or by shortening your steps. Remember your dog is on your left, and you are holding the leash with your left hand, with the loose end in your right. If you wish to turn left, slow up, and then pivot on your left foot as you make the turn. Swing your right foot around as you would naturally do. With this foot or knee, nudge the dog to turn with you—touch him gently but insistently, so that he knows you aren't suddenly playing with him.

If your dog remains somewhat stubborn—as he well might at the beginning—use leash pressure to bring him around. Give him the command "Heel!" once you've turned into the new direction. Praise him warmly when he seems to be learning the move.

If you wish to turn right, you do not have the advantage of the swinging foot or knee with which to nudge your dog. Pivot on your right foot as you ordinarily would do, and exert pressure on the leash to bring him around with you. Swing the left foot around and start out in the new direction, commanding him to heel.

Continue to practice turns, alternating right and left. Keep him leashed until he has perfected the technique. Remember that your signal to the dog is a conscious slowing up or a shortening of your step. Once he understands the signal, he will sense your intention and move along with you. When he reaches this stage, then you can take him off the leash. If he loses control on the turns, practice again with the leash attached.

Standing

There is one other minor command that you might find useful, and it is very easy to teach to the dog: standing. You may for some reason wish to stop in the street, and it is useful if you can make your dog stand still without fighting him. Start with the leash attached to the dog's collar, as you have done with the other commands. While he is heeling, give the command "Stand!" At the same time, hold your right hand lightly on the dog's head so that he understands he should not move ahead. If he does try to move, hold him back gently but firmly, or press against his nose. He should get the idea rapidly. Praise him when he stands, and once he has perfected his response, try the command without the leash.

Practice these moves every day so that the puppy does not forget them. As he grows older, they will become habitual, but at the beginning he may forget or grow indifferent unless he has a daily run-through. These few minutes of practice are well worth the trouble. A dog trained to obey is a joy to own. You should not feel that you are imposing upon his natural instincts in making him learn the commands. This is simply not true. A dog wants to please, and working with you will give him great pleasure as long as you recognize his worth by giving him praise and respect. From your point of view the time you spend with him in this training can be rewarding and fulfilling. If you obtained your dog for companionship, then this training makes both of you work together. There is something in it for each.

OBEDIENCE AND OBEDIENCE SCHOOLS

Obedience schools, their names to the contrary, are not reform schools or remand shelters for dogs. They are, in fact, schools—places where your dog may learn the different activities that will qualify him for dog shows. If you are not interested in the shows themselves—and many owners do not wish to enter their dogs—you can have fun just working with your dog for a few hours a week under the guidance of a trained handler. Also, if you have great difficulty in training your dog to sit, stay, stand, heel, turn, and come, you will find your problems considerably eased by classes at an obedience school.

The schools have become increasingly popular in the last few years. Particularly popular are those classes or schools that are not run for professional purposes. They provide get-togethers for dog owners who have one thing in common: They want to improve the manners and styles of their dogs. Some of these schools charge a negligible fee, and many are run by the local humane society, where classes may be free. If you are interested, write to your local dog club, the humane society, your local SPCA, or the Gaines Dog Research Center (250 Park Avenue, New York, New York 10017); they can provide a free list of schools, some of which may be in your locality.

If there is no school available in your neighborhood or in your city, you might be interested in forming one with other dog owners. Later in this section I will give you a few tips on how to form an obedience class or school. Let me say here that the cost is small, and the pleasure to be derived is great. For the owner who obtained his dog for companionship, such classes can be the start of a close relationship between him and his pet. When the classes are well organized, you can have great fun. Even your dog likes them because you are spending a lot of time with him, and he likes nothing better than attention from his owner.

If you are a family person, you might let one of your older children take the dog to obedience classes. The time spent together will cement a loving relationship between the child and the dog and will instill in the youngster a marvelous sense of values. As he sees the dog trying hard and learning new commands and tricks, the child will gain respect for his pet and for himself. He will feel proud of his role in having taught the dog several things.

Such classes and schools are for the amateur. The kind of training the dog obtains there will probably not be sufficient for him to win at dog shows. If you are interested in showing your dog, there are special obedience schools that give your dog professional training. These clubs or schools are so set up that the entering dog goes through a series of stages: novice, intermediate, and advanced. There are several additional breakdowns within each category. The aim is to train dogs for exhibition at the thousands of shows that take place around the country during the year. The schools are professionally run and the fee may be considerable, depending on how many courses you choose to take and the special problems your dog presents. Mongrels as well as purebreds are eligible for certificates, but mongrels cannot compete in shows or field trials.

But most dogs in this country are not purebred, and professional schools may be somewhat of a luxury for the average owner of a mongrel; if this is your situation, you should investigate your local SPCA and amateur clubs, or else form your own. As I indicated before, such clubs provide a wonderful way for you to spend time with your dog; and for the individual who likes a broad social life, the clubs can be expanded to provide several other activities: films, picnics, regularly scheduled dinners. You will find dog owners a congenial group.

If you know eight or ten other dog owners, you can get together by chipping in a few dollars each to rent a large room or hall a couple of times a week, or as often as you wish to meet. You may not even have to rent a place. If one of you has a large, dry, draft-free basement, that too is fine. Or sometimes a local school, church, or synagogue will give you the use of the basement under certain conditions for a small monthly fee.

Do not try to fit ten or more dogs into a small place. You need about 2,000 square feet, so that the dogs are not all over each other and tempted to break away. Also, the floor surface of the room or area should not be slippery. Rubber makes the best floor material for this purpose, but it is not always available. If the climate permits or if you live in a warm-weather area, the outdoors provides the best training spot of all. A deserted baseball field on the outskirts of town, the playground of a school, or a cleared area where there are few distractions are all to be highly recommended. Incidentally, if you do run classes outside, try to hold down the distractions. The dogs will be difficult to train if there is noise or excitement nearby.

One person in the group should be assigned the job of secretary—his chief work will be to keep track of whatever money is in the kitty. Then you will have to find a trainer—perhaps from a local kennel—who is experienced with dogs. This will be your chief expense. If there are ten of you, each could put in five dollars, and from that get two or three lessons a week. If getting a first-rate trainer costs a little more, do not hesitate about the extra expense. A good trainer can make the whole enterprise valuable, while a poor or indifferent trainer can frustrate the enterprise from the beginning and perhaps destroy your initial enthusiasm. The trainer you select should be familiar with many breeds, since the dogs within your group will certainly vary according to the behavior of their own breed, and many will be mongrels.

Once you have the place, the secretary for the group, and the trainer, there are a few ground rules you and the other owners should agree on. Without such rules, there may be disharmony, particularly when something as sensitive as the behavior of one's own dog is in question. To keep yourself and your group happy, keep in mind the following general rules:

1. If you decide on a certain weekly or monthly fee, do not neglect a payment. Remember that financial arrangements depend on the fee of the trainer and the rent of a place—once they are agreed upon, you must be willing to meet your obligation.

2. If your bitch is in heat, you will not be able to enroll her in the obedience school, or else all the males in the class will be unable to concentrate. If her season occurs during the training course, you must withdraw until the bitch is back to normal—about 3 weeks in all. Bathe her before returning to class. You may, of course, continue to attend the class yourself and practice at home with your dog what you have learned. Provide for such eventualities when you work out the arrangements with your group.

3. Discuss among yourselves whether you wish to allow visitors or not, and whether they can be children. Some of the owners may have no one to take care of their children and will want to bring them along. Young children may be a disruptive element, particularly in the beginning classes, and the trainer might not want them around. Talk this out before starting the course.

4. Everyone enrolled in the class should have the correct equipment from the start so that no time is lost in trivialities. Each dog should wear a link collar, with heavy-link chain for a large dog scaled down to small-link chain for the toy sizes. The collar should fit, being neither too loose nor too tight. Each owner should also have a leash about 6 feet long made of flat leather or webbing. If there is any doubt, wait until the first evening of the class when the trainer can advise you.

5. Decide among yourselves precisely what you want to accomplish in the beginning course. There are several books on obedience which outline what the course can be—consult your local library for this information. If you prefer, break the course down into lessons and decide what you wish to get from each lesson.

6. Do not attempt to train a dog under 7 or 8 months in a class atmosphere. The young puppy is too frisky and playful, and too indifferent to commands. Also, the presence of other dogs will distract him. You may have trained your puppy in simple commands at home, but

in a training course the conditions are quite different and require an older, more settled dog.

7. There are certain procedures you should follow with your dog to prevent embarrassing accidents. Do not feed him before class; make sure he has relieved himself just before the class hour; keep good control of your dog in halls, on stairs, and in the training room itself to prevent clashes with other dogs; be prompt—an owner and his dog entering late can upset the delicate balance of a class; try not to be absent unless you have good reason, for example, when your dog is ill or in heat—if you are absent your dog falls behind and upsets the rhythm of the entire class; keep your dog in the room for the entire hour—coming and going can be very upsetting for the whole class.

8. If your dog cannot keep up with the required work, be willing to withdraw him. Some dogs are temperamentally unsuited for class participation and should not be forced. If you see from the way your dog behaves that further class work is impossible, don't love or respect him the less. And don't be worried or ashamed. Some dogs, like some people, are managed best by themselves.

9. Do not come to the training hour with pocketbook, hanging jewelry, long coat, etc. All these will provide distractions. Dress simply so that you can move freely. Wear comfortable shoes with rubber heels— they will give you a better grip on the floor and they won't distract your dog with any clicking sounds.

10. Be patient with your dog at all times. Some dogs learn more quickly than others for many reasons. If your dog seems to be falling behind, you won't help him by becoming angry. He will move at his own pace anyway, and you will probably just confuse him.

11. Be willing to supplement your dog's training with home lessons. All owners should follow up a lesson with home practice for ten minutes twice a day. Keep the lessons at home and in class spaced so that your dog doesn't become too tired. If for some reason your dog has to miss a class, you should attend and then practice with him at home.

12. You and only you must remain responsible for your dog. If there is any fighting—a possibility when so many dogs are assembled—you must take full responsibility for any injury inflicted by or on your dog. You must take this into account when you start a training club, or else owners may create an ugly situation by suing for damages. All the entrants in the class should agree to whatever arrangement the majority decides to make.

All of these and other rules are included in the agreement for professional training courses as well as for amateur ones. If you wish to enter your dog in a course given by your local SPCA or dog club, or start one yourself, you will find that obedience courses work best when there are regulations governing them. If run correctly, obedience courses can give you and your dog tremendous pleasure. And if you wish, such courses can be the first steps toward your dog's further training, leading ultimately to dog shows and exhibitions. But whatever your motives, you should approach the course with the desire to cooperate and to do the best you can for your dog.

SHOWS AND EXHIBITIONS

If you wish to enter your dog in a licensed dog show or obedience trial, he must be purebred. These licensed shows are held under the rules laid down by the American Kennel Club, and therefore all dogs must be among the 121 breeds currently recognized by the Club. There are, of course, plenty of shows and trials that the American Kennel Club has nothing to do with. Your local dog club or SPCA, for instance, might sponsor shows open to all dogs, whether purebred or mongrels. There is, clearly, something for everyone.

If your dog is purebred and you wish to show him, then write to the American Kennel Club for a copy of *The Complete Dog Book,* which it publishes. The standards for all 121 of its accepted breeds are described in the book. There are certain desirable and undesirable physical qualities for each breed, and if your dog does have undesirable characteristics, he will be disqualified. Such characteristics have to do with color, tail, and ears. Disqualification does not mean that there is anything objectionable about your dog, but simply that he cannot qualify under the rules agreed upon for his particular breed. Obtain from the Club at the same time a copy of the regulations governing dog shows and obedience trials. Once again, there is a precise procedure to follow, and if you cannot follow it, you should know this ahead of time.

Official dog shows include five basic classes for the individual breeds. The first is Puppy: for dogs under a year old, divided into two subclasses— 6 to 9 months and 9 to 12 months; second is Novice: for dogs who have never won a first prize or blue ribbon except in the Puppy Class; third is American Bred: for dogs (except champions) born in the United States or its possessions; fourth is Bred by Exhibitor: for dogs (except champions) owned and shown by their breeders; fifth is Open: for all dogs, including champions. There are also specialty shows, which feature only one breed.

Within each classification indicated above, there is a still further subdivision into male and female, or dog and bitch, as the professional calls them. Generally, a given breed is entered in only one classification at a time. If he wins within his classification, he then competes against the other winners in a special class. If the dogs are male, it is called the Winners' Dog Class; if female, it is called Winners' Bitch Class. Eventually the winners of these two classes will compete against each other for Best of Winners. The one who wins this competition then moves on to the heights of Specials Only Class, where he competes only against champions, although not himself a champion.

A dog which wins Best of Breed or Best of Variety (a term used to indicate varieties in a breed, as in Poodles) then competes with the winners of all the other breed competitions (Hounds, Working Dogs, Sporting Dogs, Terriers, Toys, and Nonsporting Dogs). The winning dog here is a super-champion of a sort, called Best Dog in Show or Best in Show. The champions of the opposite sex of Best of Breed further compete for the title of Best of Opposite Sex to Best of Breed.

I won't go into the details of this any further because the owner who has followed even a quarter of this distance is already familiar with the ins and outs of dog competition. All dogs entered into competition sanctioned by the American Kennel Club must meet the minimum standards of each breed. A dog with a serious organic defect is automatically barred from all competition. Castrated males and spayed bitches may not compete in a breed class, although they may in obedience trials. The dog's colors must conform to those set down as standard for the breed. Also, in a show, the judge will look for several other things: the dog's skin and coat, the way he moves, the firmness of his muscles, the formation of his bones, the soundness of his teeth, his general structure, his muzzle, and so on.

Obedience

In obedience trials, the judge scores dogs of all breeds solely on how well they perform a series of exercises. These exercises have been selected because they are the foundation for any useful work the dog may be called upon to do. Once again, the requirements for the professional obedience ring are set forth by the American Kennel Club, in a booklet called *Regulations and Standards for Obedience Trials.*

Dogs compete against each other in five obedience classes at dog shows and gain scores that can lead to obedience degrees: C.D. (Companion Dog), C.D.X. (Companion Dog Excellent), and U.D. (Utility Dog). The five classes are called: Novice Class A, Novice Class B, Open Class A, Open Class B, and Utility Class. Novice Class A and Novice Class B involve the same exercises, but in the first the dog is handled by his owner or a member of his family, while in the second the dog may be handled by professional trainers and kennel workers. This same distinction extends to Open Class A (dogs handled by owner) and Open Class B (dogs handled by a professional).

The Novice Classes, both A and B, are limited to dogs seeking the C.D. (Companion Dog) degree. There are, in all, six exercises, which are graded so that a perfect score would total 200 points. They are as follows:

1. Heel on leash	35 points
2. Stand for examination	30 points
3. Heel free	45 points
4. Recall	30 points
5. Long sit (one minute)	30 points
6. Long down (3 minutes)	30 points

In order to gain his C.D. degree, the dog must score at least 50 percent on *each* exercise and score 170 or more points at each of three obedience trials where the combined number of entries in Novice Classes A and B is six or more dogs.

Open Classes A and B are considerably more difficult. Dogs compete here who have already gained the C.D. degree, and they compete against dogs who may have also won the C.D.X. or U.D. degrees. Open Class involves seven exercises, as follows:

1. Heel free	40 points
2. Drop on recall	30 points
3. Retrieve on flat	25 points
4. Retrieve over high jump	35 points
5. Broad jump	20 points
6. Long sit (3 minutes)	25 points
7. Long down (5 minutes)	25 points

Of the possible total of 200 points, the dog, to win his C.D.X., must receive scores of not less than 50 percent on each of the seven exercises and attain a total score of 170 or more points at each of three obedience trials where the combined number of entries in Open Classes A and B is six or more dogs.

The Utility Class is open to dogs who have won the C.D.X., but dogs with the U.D. may also compete. The Utility Class involves five exercises, as follows:

1. Scent discrimination	60 points
2. Seek back for lost article	30 points
3. Signal exercise	35 points
4. Directed jumping	40 points
5. Group examination	35 points

Of the possible total of 200 points, the dog, to win his U.D., must receive scores of not less than 50 percent on each of the five exercises and attain a total score of 170 or more points at each of three obedience trials where the combined number of entries in the Utility Class is three or more dogs.

There is one further sanctioned obedience trial called the Tracking

Dog Test. Once a dog has been approved as ready by an accredited judge, he is given an outdoor test in which he is required to follow a person's trail over at least a quarter of a mile. The dog must already have his U.D. degree and must compete against at least three other dogs. Speed is a considerable factor in whether or not the two judges pass him. If he is passed, he wins his Tracking Dog degree, which combines with the Utility Dog degree to become U.D.T., or Utility Dog Tracker.

As you can easily see, the rules are strictly set down so that the dog who does win an obedience trial wins something worthwhile. Perhaps you started your dog in an obedience school without intending to enter him in competitions, but you can recognize that the future is almost unlimited. To train a dog to win awards and degrees is a marvelous accomplishment for both the dog and the owner. If you feel suited for such an assignment and if your dog responds correctly, then you have a wonderful future ahead of you. The disappointments that may occur along the way should not prevent you from going on, as long as your dog seems to be enjoying his work. Of course, if the dog finds it a burden and begins to balk, you must reconsider whether to continue. But a healthy dog given plenty of love and respect, and treated firmly but kindly, should take to shows and obedience trials with a minimum of difficulty.

GROOMING YOUR DOG

Grooming your dog will benefit not only his beauty but also his health and cleanliness. A well-groomed dog stands less chance of suffering from fleas and other external parasites than the dog whose coat is neglected. (External parasites, incidentally, can lead to skin troubles, which in turn may affect a dog's general health). A clean dog is also a happier dog. The time you spend on him each day—perhaps only ten minutes— indicates your interest in his welfare. He feels needed and wanted and takes pride in his appearance. Since a dog cannot speak his appreciation, he shows gratitude in his manner; your dog will gain in confidence and assurance. A well-groomed dog, furthermore, wins respect in the neighborhood and receives better treatment from all who know him.

In some instances, you can't avoid grooming your dog. If his coat becomes matted or picks up chewing gum or tar, you must brush it out to remove the foreign particles. Burrs and briars picked up by the country and suburban dog, or the city dog in the park, must be removed with a comb. Tangles, also, must be gently combed or brushed out.

Rather than wait until an urgent need arises before you groom your dog, start when the puppy is young. It's a good idea to get him used to grooming in its various aspects. Not all dogs need extensive grooming; most dogs, in fact, need only ten minutes a day. When the puppy is young, accustom him to standing on a low table or bench which you keep especially for grooming. If your dog is small, you can lift him on the table, and if he is big, in time he will jump up himself and wait for your attention. A table or bench is preferable to the floor because it allows you to work more comfortably and efficiently.

Who Needs Grooming and What Kind?

While all dogs regardless of their coat length need combing and brushing, some breeds obviously need more extensive grooming (such as clipping and stripping) than others. As a general rule, longhaired dogs need greater attention than shorthaired ones. Although breeds like the Collie, Old English Sheepdog, Shetland and Belgian Sheepdogs, Pomeranian, Samoyed, Chow Chow, and other longhairs of this type do not need clipping or stripping, to comb and brush them is quite a chore. They must of course be combed and brushed, so that their coats are kept free of mats, tangles, and foreign particles.

Still other longhaired breeds like the Afghan, Yorkshire Terrier, Setters, Cocker Spaniel, and Pekingese require stripping as well as combing and brushing. In addition, Terriers with rough hair, like the Airedale, Bedlington, Cairn, Irish, Kerry Blue, Scottish, Sealyham, Wire Fox, and Welsh, require clipping. The Poodle is in a class by himself. No fewer than eight ways of clipping him have been stylish: the English Saddle, Royal Dutch, Puppy, Continental, Shawl, Kennel, Terrier Dutch, and Corded. Some of course are more popular than others, but each needs a good deal of time, patience, and skill. The average owner should not even think of clipping and trimming the Poodle until he watches an expert on several occasions. With the other dogs that require clipping— like the Miniature Schnauzer and the Scottish Terrier—you should also not try it yourself unless you have attended a few clipping sessions.

What To Do

I indicated in Chapter 1 that you should not get a longhaired dog if you worry about having loose hair around the house, or if you do not have time to groom him daily. With a dog that presents no special grooming problems, start by putting him on the table or bench set aside for him. Speak to him gently and be patient if he resists at first. Reward him with a tidbit at the beginning if he holds still. In time he will connect grooming with your kindness and look forward to it.

The equipment you will need consists of the following:

a brush with short bristles for short- and medium-haired dogs;
a brush with long bristles for the longhaired dog
a fine comb for shorthaired dogs; a comb with widely spaced teeth for the wirehaired and longhaired dog
a stripping comb (a saw-toothed comb)

scissors
a plucking comb (for show dogs)
nail clippers
clippers (for the coat that is not to be plucked)

Grooming Procedures

Starting with the puppy (if you begin later, there may be an obedience problem—usually only temporary), place him on the table or bench chosen for his grooming. Comb his coat carefully to remove all loose hair and to unravel any snarls. Work rapidly but gently, all the time assuring the dog that you mean well. Once he gets used to the procedure, he will accept it as part of his daily routine. Keep working with the comb until the coat is smooth. If there is matted hair that the comb cannot part, cut out the mat with scissors. Do this by placing the scissors under the mat and cutting through. When cutting, always keep the point of the scissors away from the dog's body.

If there are burrs or spines or other sharp particles in the dog's coat, remove them by hand. Country dogs, in particular, pick up objects that might work their way in and injure the skin if they are not carefully removed. Once the combing has evened out the coat and removed all foreign elements, then use the brush. Always brush in the direction that you want the hair to lie. Brush steadily with sufficient pressure to smooth the coat, and do not miss any spots. *Do not substitute the brush for the comb.* The brush simply keeps the coat smooth and fluffy (depending on the coat itself, of course), but the comb does most of the grooming work.

In the summer months, do not cut the coat short. Instead, keep the dog's coat clear of dead hair by stripping it with a stripping comb. This comb has saw teeth that remove all loose hair. With this hair removed, the dog's skin can be cleaned more easily. Also, the stripping comb will come in handy when the dog sheds—usually in the spring and fall. If you run the comb through his coat several times a day, you will save yourself more troublesome work; a longhaired dog who sheds in an apartment will spread hair over everything. After stripping, use a regular comb and finish up with a vigorous brushing.

Bathing

If your dog is young—under 6 months—do not bathe him to keep his coat clean. The young puppy is subject to upper respiratory illnesses if he suffers a chill while wet. Don't take any chances. If his coat is very dirty, wash it off with a damp washcloth. In that way the moisture does not penetrate to the skin. Even an older dog should not be bathed often, and when you do give him a bath the room should be draft-free and the weather mild.

When bathing your dog (as a last resort), protect his eyes against soap, no matter how mild it is. Put some vaseline or eye ointment in the corner of each eye to form a protective film. Wash him in warm, not hot, water, and work up a good lather all over his coat. Remove the soap thoroughly with warm water. Do not leave any suds on him— itching or flaking may develop later. After his bath, rub him briskly with a large towel to remove most of the moisture. Then keep him indoors until his coat dries. Make sure he does not get into a draft while he is drying off.

If your dog somehow gets very dirty and you don't want to bathe him, try some of the dry shampoos which are sold commercially. Then, if your dog has a bad odor, you can keep him clean without the fuss of a bath. Follow the directions on the label.

Usually a "doggy" odor disappears with daily grooming, unless of course the odor is the result of an ear infection, an anal gland secretion, or messy toilet habits. If there is an ear infection, that is a matter for your veterinarian, as is an anal gland infection. A soiled coat, however, is another matter. Daily washing around the anus and the application of baby oil will prevent the hair from caking.

Ears

Normally the ears will not smell or give trouble if they are kept clean. Keeping them clean is part of grooming. Do not wash the ears out with soap and water, but apply baby oil or peroxide on cotton. *And never poke or probe.* Go only as far as you can without stretching the tissue. Probing can injure the delicate mechanism or push in dirt that should come out. Also, because his ears are very sensitive, a dog may resist even having them touched. If so, calm him by speaking to him and assuring him by your tone that you mean no harm. In some cases, dogs have to be restrained before they will cooperate. If you don't make it a big issue, the dog will eventually accept it as part of the grooming routine.

Eyes

Generally, a dog's eyes will not bother him, although occasionally foreign objects may enter, especially if he is a country dog who runs through grass and bushes. If your dog does have a foreign particle in his eye, restrain him with a mouth tie. Then using a clean handkerchief, as you would for a person, lift up the eyelid and remove the object. You may need someone to hold the dog's head still. If the eye appears irritated, apply a mild eye wash with a piece of cotton.

Teeth

Like the eyes and ears, the teeth usually need a minimum of attention. Since dogs do not ordinarily develop cavities, about the only thing they are subject to is a tartar deposit, unless they suffer an actual broken tooth. When the puppy is young, you might gently wipe off his teeth with a clean cloth or wet cotton. Tartar, incidentally, is often a cause of bad breath in dogs. If it develops in excess, your veterinarian can scale it off. If bad breath continues, it may be a symptom of decaying teeth, a digestive upset, infected tonsils, or a mouth infection.

Unusual Grooming Conditions

If your dog gets paint on his coat (not in his mouth—if he does that, he needs first aid), ordinary combing and brushing will do little good. If the paint is still wet or damp, remove it with turpentine. While applying turpentine, you must keep it from penetrating to the dog's skin, where it will act as an irritant. *Use with caution.* Once the paint has been removed, wash out all the turpentine with soap and warm water. If the paint is made with water and not oil, then soap and water will do, without the turpentine.

If the paint is dry, you may have trouble removing it. Then the only recourse is to clip the hair that is matted. Do not pull on the hair or you will irritate the dog's skin. Try to loosen the paint as described above before you begin clipping. If you must cut a good deal of hair, the dog will look funny, but his coat will grow in again rapidly.

Sometimes a dog will return home covered with road tar, especially in the summer when tarred roads partially melt. His feet and legs will be covered with the stuff, and the only way to remove it is with kerosene. Do not let the kerosene penetrate, because it is an irritant. As soon as some of the tar comes off, wash away the kerosene before it can soak into the skin. When the job is finished, and all the kerosene has been washed off, apply mineral oil. Also, if some discoloration from the tar remains on the dog's coat, do not worry about it. Eventually it will fade away. For chewing gum, follow the same procedure as for tar.

A further word on shedding. A dog accustomed to living outdoors sheds according to nature's plan. That is, in the spring he sheds his heavy coat, and in the fall he sheds his light coat to make way for his winter hair. Since the great majority of dogs no longer live outdoors, most owners will notice that their dogs shed over longer periods of time. There are several reasons: the heat of electric lights, excessive steam heat, lack of exercise. You might exercise your dog more, but that in itself will probably not help matters if your dog lives indoors. You might also comb and brush him several times a day. Generally, the best cure for shedding is to keep the dog outside where the coat develops as nature intended, but this is hardly practical for city people. Unless shedding is the result of illness, it is not a threat to the dog, although it is of course a considerable nuisance to you. As I indicated above, all you can probably do is to keep your dog well groomed and wait for his shedding season to end. Then hire a couple of people to clean out the house.

Care of the Nails

In Chapter 3, on the Puppy, I mentioned that the very young dog needs to have his nails periodically cut. The same is true for the older dog. The frequency of the clipping depends on how fast the dog's nails grow and how far he wears them down in normal usage. The nails of a puppy tend to grow rapidly since he goes out very little, and therefore his nails do not wear off with friction. This is also true of apartment dogs of any age.

Long nails are troublesome to the dog and to you. In the dog's case, a long nail can get caught and be pulled off, or may curve back and press into the toes, causing pain and even lameness. The dog will also slide on smooth surfaces and have difficulty in climbing stairs. As for you, the long-nailed dog will tear stockings, get caught in skirts and trouser legs, become snagged on rugs, sweaters, and other objects.

Most puppies do not like to have their nails clipped. If you are at all hesitant about doing it yourself, have the veterinarian clip the nails while you watch and learn. At the beginning, to play safe apply restraint (a mouth tie). You may also need an assistant the first few times. As with all other grooming, assure your dog with a gentle tone that you mean no harm. Remember, for all he knows, you plan to cut off his leg. To do the job, use nail clippers made especially for animals. Cut only the transparent part that projects past the foot pads. On black nails, you must approximate the length to cut—always too little rather than too much. If you should by error cut into the quick, place a piece of gauze or cotton against the wound until the bleeding stops. If it continues, call your veterinarian.

You follow the same procedure with older dogs, using the special nail clippers made for animals. They are available at most pet shops or pet supply stores. Be sure to cut only the transparent part of the nail—just the tip. As with the puppy, always cut too little rather than too much. If you have cut too little, you can always clip the nail again. As your dog becomes accustomed to the routine, he will cooperate without the need of restraint.

The dog also has a residual thumb just above the paws: what is called the dewclaw. If the dewclaws were not removed by the veterinarian when the puppy was a few days old, the nail attached to the dewclaw must also be clipped. Follow exactly the same method. Do not forget the dewclaw nail, for if neglected it can curve back and cause infection.

Ten minutes each day will take care of the basic grooming needs of most breeds and mongrels. If you want to provide a fancier treatment, you can give your dog's coat an occasional oiling—with lanolin or coconut oil. Rub it in well, and then rub it out with a heavy towel; otherwise he will leave grease marks on everything he touches. There are also commercial powders which you can rub into his coat to bring out his color or to give him a sheen. None of this extra care, however, is really necessary. The average dog will thrive with the minimum treatment indicated above.

Clipping, Plucking, Trimming

Do not have your dog's coat clipped in the summer. Giving him a short coat does not help him keep cool. The short, prickly hairs, in fact, may make him itchy and miserable. Instead, run a stripping comb (obtainable at most pet shops) through his coat to remove the dead hair.

The only dogs that should be clipped and trimmed are those whose standards demand a particular kind of coat style, but unless you have repeatedly observed a professional, do not attempt to clip, pluck, or trim your dog yourself. If you have such a dog and wish to exhibit him, show standards demand that a plucking comb be used to remove the dead hair. Stripping is the same thing, done with a stripping comb. After the dead hair is removed, the rest of the hair is shaped in accordance with the breed standard.

Procedures for Special Breeds

If you have one of the breeds that require the whole range of grooming—clipping, trimming, and plucking or stripping—and if you eventually intend to enter your dog in competition at dog shows, he requires particular care. Whatever your ultimate purpose, the dog who needs to meet a particular standard of appearance must be groomed professionally, with the Poodle, of course, requiring the most attention.

I doubt that you can acquire sufficient skill to do a good job on your Poodle without becoming a professional yourself. The other breeds—like several of the Terriers that require special attention—present less of a problem, and there is a good chance that after watching a few professional sessions you can have a try at it yourself. Of course, if you plan to have your dog compete, forget about doing the clipping and plucking yourself. All owners, certainly, can keep up the grooming by removing dead hair and by daily combing and brushing, but the standard cut itself is usually beyond their ability.

The cost may be considerable, depending on the skill of the professional groom. Show dogs are given very extensive care, while other dogs need not be groomed so meticulously. You may ask if it is absolutely necessary to make your dog conform to his breed standard of appearance. No, it's not absolutely necessary. The dog will live and even thrive without more than the usual daily attention to his coat. But it seems to me that your original choice of dog was made because you like his appearance. If you fail to give him the appearance that originally appealed to you, then your choice of dog would not seem to make much sense. Of course, in the long run, such matters involve personal decisions that only the individual owner can make.

The owner of a mongrel is obviously not concerned with such details. In fact, one reason you obtained a mongrel was that you didn't wish to bother with special grooming problems. The coat should be combed and brushed daily, and that is the extent of your worries. A mongrel's coat often has a beauty of its own, and a well-groomed dog is a delight whatever breed, crossbreed, or mongrel you own. It is not the kind of dog you have that counts, but the way you take care of him. All dogs, like all babies, are potentially beautiful—it all depends on what you do for them.

One further thought on grooming: There seems to be a small movement in several large communities to start classes in grooming dogs. That is, a professional groom opens a school in which he enrolls a certain number of dog owners as students at a fixed fee. The cost of the training course varies, depending on how far the owner wishes to progress, but in the long run the savings will be huge. Such courses are particularly appealing to owners of Poodles, as this breed requires the most attention.

Since these schools are still somewhat rare, I would suggest that several dog owners get together in their community and hire a professional to teach them grooming. Such courses can probably be easily arranged in most cities and large towns, and the benefit for the owner should be tremendous, not only in the ultimate savings but in the pride he takes in the knowledge that he can groom his dog himself.

6
Ailments

I suggest that you read the first section of this chapter so as to acquaint yourself with the symptoms of illness in dogs as well as with a dog's general structure. Then read the rest of the chapter a little at a time. Don't try to read it all at once.

Throughout the chapter, I advise that in most cases you should see a veterinarian when you recognize certain symptoms. However, a phone call will often dispel your fears; a visit may not be necessary. On many occasions, the veterinarian can advise you on what to do at home.

CONTENTS OF THIS CHAPTER

SYMPTOMS OF ILLNESS AND GENERAL STRUCTURE OF THE DOG

It is, of course, sad and depressing when those we love suffer from illness or disease. The entire household becomes disrupted, and we go through our daily routines waiting for the time when everything will return to normal. With the great recent advances in veterinary medicine, you can be certain that any illness or disease your dog suffers from will be treated with the finest medication and professional care. Whenever you recognize warning signs, call your veterinarian, describe the symptoms as well as you can, and be ready to take your dog to him for examination. Then be prepared to follow carefully what the veterinarian tells you to do.

The greatest disservice you can do your dog, or any other pet for that matter, is to attempt home cures, *unless there is an emergency.* Owners mean well in every instance; in most cases, they mean too well. When you see that your dog is in pain, you wish to do something for him, immediately. The best thing you can do is to make your dog as comfortable as possible and wait until the veterinarian is available. Many home medicines that you would give to an infant are dangerous for a dog. For example, some laxatives and tonics contain strychnine, which people can absorb in small amounts without any harmful effects. Your dog, on the other hand, is extremely sensitive to the smallest amount of strychnine and may react badly to what seems a mild medication. Although this is an extreme example, take no chances. Do not try what you think might work. Unless you have worked closely with dogs for years, you most likely won't know of their reactions to medicines.

Another danger in giving home cures is that people often forget that the average dog weighs one-fifth or less of what a human weighs. A dose of your own medicine as prescribed on the label would be an overdose for the average dog. It must be sharply scaled down. On the other hand, you might figure that whatever amount you give an infant surely cannot hurt a grown dog, or even a puppy. After all, what could be more delicate than an infant! Yet an infant may weigh only a few pounds, and the amount you give it will be meaningless for the big dog; or vice versa—what you call an infant may weigh twice and sometimes three times as much as the small dog, and therefore the infant's dose will be an overdose for the dog.

The chances of your killing your dog, or even severely hurting him, are small, but they are there every time you become your own doctor. Why, then, take the chance of prolonging the trouble, making it worse, or even creating new trouble? Your dog means far too much for that.

As I advised in Chapter 1, choose a veterinarian who has a good reputation and inspires confidence. Do not be impressed by the newness and slickness of his equipment if you think he will not give his full attention to whatever goes wrong with your dog. He should really like dogs and wish to help them, as we expect a pediatrician to take an interest in every child he treats. After all, it is the man, not the equipment or the office, who will care for your dog when he needs help. He should also know his business. He does not need a bedside manner to inspire confidence. But he should know what he is doing.

When you select a veterinarian, the one thing you must look for is cleanliness. His equipment—whether lavish or not—is a matter of his own method of practice. But cleanliness—of person, equipment, and office—will tell you that he respects his profession, himself, and his patients. You want your dog to be treated only in sanitary surroundings.

Most often you find a veterinarian through a friend or relative or neighbor who owns or has owned a dog. Almost every community has at least one veterinarian, and most have one who limits his practice to small animals. To guarantee competence, he should be a member of city, state, and national veterinary medical associations. If there seems to be none in your city or town, get in touch with your State, County, or City Veterinary Medical Society or your local Society for the Prevention of Cruelty to Animals (SPCA), who will put you in touch with veterinarians in your community. You can then make your own choice.

When your dog is ill, the best thing you can do is be patient with him, and give him love and reassurance. The chances of a serious illness are slight, unless your dog has been sickly from birth or is very old. And you know that new medical techniques and new drugs will help him get well all the faster. So do not panic—illness in dogs is usually less frequent than in people, and when it occurs, it is just as natural.

But how will you know if your dog is sick? Will there be clear signs? And how severe must the signs be before you should call in a veterinarian?

First, you may notice that he looks "unthrifty." Veterinarians and breeders use the words "thrifty" and "unthrifty" to indicate whether a dog is vibrant, alive, perky, or listless, dried out, lazy. A sick dog loses his usual vitality, responds less frequently to familiar sounds and calls. His eyes will appear dull. His coat may lose its gloss and appear dry and coarse. His appetite will decline, and if he does eat it will be without his usual enthusiasm. He may become altogether indifferent to food. His bowel movements may become irregular, and he will have diarrhea or constipation. With diarrhea there may be only looseness, or he may evacuate a watery, thin substance; there may be a change of color to yellow or black or red (from bleeding). Bloody diarrhea is very serious. His gums and tongue will appear pale or whitish, as though coated. His eyes may run with a thin, watery mucus, later perhaps with pus. Incidentally, his nose may be either hot or cold. Contrary to popular belief, a dog's nose does not necessarily indicate his state of health.

If any of these signs appear, your dog is probably suffering from an infection or coming down with an illness. Take his temperature. Using a regular rectal thermometer, lubricate the tip in vaseline and insert half its length in the dog's rectum for two minutes. First be sure to shake the mercury down to below the dog's normal temperature. Your dog will not particularly mind the thermometer, although it is a good idea not to let him move around. Don't let him sit on it. The average normal temperature of a dog is 101.5°F. Very small breeds may run up to 102°F. without having a fever, while very large breeds may run as low as 99.5°F. You have to use your own judgment here. Of course the best thing is to take your dog's temperature when you know he is well in order to see what is normal for him. But it would not occur to most of us to insert a thermometer in a healthy dog. A rule of thumb would be: over 102°F. for small breeds is definitely a fever; over 101.5°F. for large breeds (60 pounds and up) is a fever; and a temperature somewhere between for the middle-sized breeds (30 to 55 pounds) would be considered a fever.

Check every three or four hours to see if the temperature is either up or down. A degree or two in a day is a considerable increase. Also, write down the figures so that you will have them all should you decide to call your veterinarian. Be prepared as well to describe all other symptoms. Remember, you are on the phone and the veterinarian cannot see your dog. Many illnesses begin in the same way, so it is all the more important that you give a full and accurate description if you want a correct diagnosis. Of course no sure diagnosis can be made until the veterinarian sees your dog.

Your dog may have a running nose, for example, which may be the first sign of a number of ailments, from a mild upper-respiratory infection (a common cold in a person) to the dreaded distemper. Or he may have difficulty in urinating, which may mean a simple irritation, or diabetes, sand in the urinary tract, or cystitis. Your dog may be ill in any number of ways, although most of the complicated ailments are somewhat rare. The chances are that a running nose *is* caused by a mild upper-respiratory infection and that difficulties in urinating can be traced to a simple irritation. Nevertheless, the veterinarian must see the entire picture before he can prescribe treatment.

I will mention here some of the more common signs so that you can be on the lookout for them. Watch for sharp shifts in your dog's appetite. If his exercise is constant, his appetite after he is a year old should remain more or less the same. If he suddenly becomes ravenous and even an increase in his food does not satisfy him, there might be internal parasites. On the other hand, an unusually large appetite may have a natural reason: some females eat more when they go into their semiannual heat period; and a very happy dog who has just been given a lot of personal attention will eat more. A sudden indifference to food may mean infection or poisons in the system; or you may simply have changed the dog's schedule and he is protesting by going on a temporary hunger strike.

A dog may be such a creature of habit that he will lose his appetite if you change his food dish or put it in a different corner, or if you alter his sleeping arrangements in any way. If you move to a different house or apartment, or to a different city with a different set of smells and sounds, this too can affect your dog's eating habits. Eventually he will adapt to all these changes, just as he once adapted to his present home. And what you think is illness may simply be a temporary attack of nerves.

Coughing in a dog may result from a chill suffered in a draft, or it may be the first symptom of a whole range of possible ailments: worms, laryngitis, distemper, bronchitis. You can most likely rule out distemper if your dog has received his vaccination and yearly boosters. Worms, also, are less frequent in the dog over a year old, but they do occur. In itself, a cough may mean very little, perhaps a temporary condition that will clear itself. A cough combined with a fever, running nose, hoarseness, a lot of blinking or sensitivity to light, and abnormal breathing, however, indicates a severe illness that should be attended to by a veterinarian without delay.

Trembling and shivering in a dog may mean that he has been exposed to a draft, has become chilled and has a fever. Or it may mean poisoning. Has your dog been near fresh insect powder, or have you used a spray that is harmful for pets? Has your dog perhaps gotten into the medicine cabinet or into the soaps? Then again, trembling in a pregnant bitch or in a nursing dam (the bitch) may indicate eclampsia, a disorder caused by a severe calcium deficiency, which a veterinarian can correct only by immediate injections of calcium.

Convulsions and collapse in a dog are of course frightening to any owner. They can result from poisoning, a very serious matter, or from worms, also serious, especially in the young puppy.

Some symptoms, however, will point to only a single ailment. If you notice, for example, that your dog is shaking his head or holding it at an unnatural angle, you will suspect trouble in the ear. He may have an infection, which your veterinarian can correct, or fleas, mites, or some other parasites. The ear flap itself might be torn or irritated.

Certain other annoyances like excessive scratching may be cleared up by a medicinal bath (prescribed by a veterinarian) or by a lotion that you can apply.

There are specific ailments that a dog is subject to in old age—most kidney troubles, weakening of sight, partial loss of hearing—the same afflictions that plague the human race. Yet, as we know from our own experiences, many of these more serious ailments can be partially or completely controlled by medication or surgery.

Allowing for small differences in skeleton and muscles, the dog is in fact strikingly like the human being in his makeup and in the illnesses that afflict him. Of course some of his senses are keener than ours—his senses of hearing and smell, for instance, are infinitely keener. The dog's nose often serves him as a direction finder as much as his eyes do. A dog like the Bloodhound relies much more on his nose than on his eyes to take him where he wants to go. While we utilize all our senses, the dog focuses chiefly on two, smell and sound.

Although a dog's skin and hair are somewhat different from ours, nevertheless they serve the same purpose—to protect him against heat and cold. And just as the races of man differ from each other in skin texture and hair type, so does one breed of dog differ from another. Dogs who are forced to adapt to the outdoors from puppyhood on grow longer and thicker coats than dogs who live indoors. Of course don't expect a shorthaired dog to become longhaired if he lives outside, but his coat will thicken and lengthen. Dogs living in sub-zero temperatures, like the Alaskan Malamute and the Husky, grow coats that protect them when the thermometer reads 20° or 30° below zero. A dog of this type prefers to sleep outside and will curl up in a circle, generate the heat of an oven, and sleep blissfully with his long tail curled around his nose to keep it warm.

When a dog sheds (usually twice a year, although exposure to constant light and heat will intensify the shedding), he is renewing his coat for summer or winter. This is a natural process for him, no matter how much of a nuisance it may be to you. All dogs shed, as a way of ridding themselves of the old, dead hair. Some—like the Poodle—shed a minimal amount, while the Collie may shed a rug every six months. Dogs can also do one thing that many a small person must envy him for: the dog can make his hair stand out so that he will look bigger and tougher.

The dog's skin works somewhat the way ours does, but not to the same degree. While our sweat glands regulate the body's temperature, only to a limited extent does the dog's skin cool his body through evaporation. His cooling system works, rather, through radiation. Also, his tongue and the pads of his feet help him to cool off, but not enough to give him relief if he is closed up in a hot car or attic. A dog may die of heat prostration or exhaustion in a situation that would only make a person very uncomfortable. In an enclosed hot place—like a car under a hot sun, with the windows closed—there is no place for his body heat to go. A person can get rid of some of his heat by sweating. A dog does not sweat through his skin.

But these are matters only of degree. The dog's body makeup is similar to a human's once we allow for certain dogs that have been bred for particular jobs. Thus, the muscular system of hounds and sporting dogs is constructed to allow them to run rapidly and powerfully, and other breeds at birth have predilections for certain specific muscular developments. In this respect, these dogs differ from humans.

The general muscular system is of course only one similarity between dogs and people. The dog's digestive tract has the usual recognizable elements: from the mouth to the esophagus, stomach, small and large intestines, and on to the rectum. The digestive process is aided by bile from the liver (bile splits up fat into tiny globules) and a starch-digesting element from the pancreas. All this is quite familiar. However, the dog begins to digest food in his stomach, not in his mouth. If his body can make use of what he has eaten, the digestive juices get to work on the food. If for some reason the dog wishes to reject the food, he has the power of voluntary vomiting: he can regurgitate his food at will. You often see this when a nursing bitch wishes to feed her young some solids. Like a bird, she will vomit up some recently swallowed food, which the young pups then eat. Because of the dog's unique method of digesting, do not try to force on him the eating habits you demand of your children. Let him bolt his food; let him vomit. He knows what he's doing.

The principal difference between the nervous system of a dog and that of a man lies in the dog's reflex actions, which are faster and more coordinated and can be conditioned to a much greater extent than in man. Otherwise, the dog's nervous system is built on the same principles, with the brain serving as the source of learning and motivation and the spinal cord acting as conductor of impulses to and from the brain. As with people, there are several illnesses that severely strain and even damage the nervous system, among them dreaded diseases like rabies and distemper. Still other ailments are caused by the malfunction of a gland. We are all familiar with the symptoms of a thyroid disorder: When the gland secretes too much of its hormone, the dog becomes nervous, and when it secretes too little, he appears lazy. If other endocrine glands—the pituitary or the adrenals—or the pancreas fail to work properly, then he may go into convulsions or fits. We often see trembling when poisons enter the dog's system, either through an insecticide or a snake bite, for these directly affect his nerve apparatus.

The dog's urinary system is again quite similar to man's. The chief organs involved are the kidneys, the bladder, and the urethra. The kidneys filter waste material, the bladder holds the liquid matter, and the urethra carries the urine from the bladder. The urinary system of the dog, as in man, works with the digestive tract. If something goes wrong with any one part, the disorder usually disturbs the entire system. You know that your dog may have a kidney ailment not only by the change in his urine but by the general decline in his appearance, behavior, and health.

The reproductive system for both male and female dogs is very much like that of men and women, if we allow for certain small differences that originate from the dog's former primitive state. The organs are the same: in the male the penis, testicles, and prostate gland; in the female the ovaries, uterus, and vagina, and for nursing her pups the mammary glands. The rest of the bitch's internal organization is similar to a woman's, except for the uterus (which is Y-shaped), with the cervix and Fallopian tubes serving the same purpose. Of course the bitch's estrus or heat period differs, occurring twice a year. In her semiannual season, she ovulates from 3 to 5 days, and only at this time is she receptive to males. Those differences that go back to the dog's primitive state include the "lock" or "tie" (the dog locks inside the bitch) during mating to insure impregnation, the fact that the bitch can be impregnated by more than one dog during any given heat period, and other such considerations that insured the survival of the canine species.

This, then, is your dog in his general structure and development. He is not very different from us physically, and even psychologically he grows like us, assuming our nervous habits or sharing our gaiety. If we think about him this way, he is a remarkable phenomenon, the sole creature who offers himself completely to people without asking anything but love in return. When you see him coming down with certain ailments, you owe it to him to take care of them immediately. And even if you suspect no illness, it is always a good idea to have your veterinarian give him a checkup every six months. A healthy dog is a marvelous creature. You should help keep him that way.

I mentioned before that a good way for you to approach this chapter is to read it through entirely, a little at a time, so that you have the general "feel" of what a dog's illnesses involve. When a child is sick, we can usually find out directly from him what hurts, but when a dog is ill, we must work from external evidence. After you have read the chapter, you will have a much better idea of what a sick dog is like and what a healthy dog is like. Then if you think your dog has a specific ailment, you can, through the use of the index, turn to the explanation of that ailment and find out what you should do. In this way, you can alleviate the anxiety and nervousness that one usually feels when faced by the unknown.

VACCINATION AND THE "BIG FIVE"

VACCINES, VACCINATION, AND IMMUNITY

The following information on vaccines, vaccination, and immunity is especially important in connection with the big five canine diseases: distemper, canine hepatitis, leptospirosis (both types), parainfluenza (also to protect against tracheobronchitis), and rabies.

Vaccination is the method (usually by injection) of making an animal immune to disease. It is generally a preventative and is not permanent. Revaccination periodically (a booster) is a recommended procedure.

Types of Immunity

Temporary: This immunity is received through the milk by the pup while nursing an immune bitch and is called natural immunity. The immunity lasts only as long as the pup is nursing, or 4 to 6 weeks. After that, the immunity ends and the pup is given measles vaccine or distemper-measles vaccine.

Active (sometimes called permanent): This immunity is produced by exposure to the agent causing the disease. The agent may be living or killed. If living, it generally has been modified (by various means) so that it will confer immunity, but not produce the disease. The killed and modified agents are used for vaccination. Active immunity results from vaccination or from recovery from the disease.

Types of Vaccination Used in Dogs

Modified live virus: The virus has been lessened in strength so that it will produce immunity but not the disease. This is accomplished by growing the virus in an unnatural host (rabbit, ferret, or tissue culture such as dog kidney cells, swine kidney cells) or in eggs (injected into embryo or membranes of fertile eggs). The dog generally gets a satisfactory immunization with one injection after three months of age, which may be repeated as advised by your veterinarian.

Killed virus: The virus or bacteria has been killed by exposure to heat or to formalin, ultraviolet, etc. This type generally requires a series of injections to confer immunity.

DISTEMPER

Distemper is a virus infection that attacks the dog's tissue, particularly through the mucous membranes. The virus is spread easily to nonvaccinated dogs, and your dog may be exposed to it more often than you suspect. He can be infected through contact with the urine or feces of a dog suffering from distemper. Even the infected dog's saliva and nasal discharge from sneezing can spread the virus if they are airborne. While people cannot catch the disease, they may carry it on their hands and clothing and unwittingly infect their dogs. A dog with no distemper symptoms may be carrying the virus during the early days of its incubation period. Adequate preventive measures, therefore, are necessary. The best method of prevention is vaccination and revaccination.

A dog may contract the disease in any weather. The most common symptoms of distemper are similar to those of an upper-respiratory ailment, like a severe respiratory infection (influenza) in a person. Since the virus may incubate for about one week, no symptoms appear during this time. Some dogs, however, may show symptoms immediately after exposure. You may notice a running nose, a flat and dry cough, loss of appetite. The dog's bowels may be loose (diarrhea) and smell strong. Fluid will discharge from his eyes, and he will seem generally miserable and depressed. His temperature may rise two or three degrees above normal, to 103° or 104°F. You may also notice what we call photophobia, or sensitivity to light, especially when you suddenly turn on the lights in a dark room or take the dog into direct sunlight. He will blink excessively, as if trying to eliminate the light altogether. In some cases, he may suffer from fits or convulsions.

As the disease progresses, the dog's symptoms will get worse. He will sleep a great deal. The discharge from his eyes and nose may become thick, mucous, often bloody. The loss of fluid dehydrates the dog, giving him an overwhelming thirst. His bowel movements become watery and blood-flecked, another severe loss of his body fluids. Quite commonly distemper pustules (pimples with pus) are found in the abdominal area.

There will be no mistaking the dog's misery and depression. The mucus around his nose and eyes will cake, causing difficulty in breathing. When the nervous system is affected, he will champ his jaws, as though chewing on an invisible rope, and the muscles near the surface of his skin will twitch. In the last stages, the dog will be stiff, flat on his back, champing away. *At no time is he dangerous,* although in his anxiety he may bite.

Even if distemper symptoms are arrested by antibiotics, or whatever your veterinarian recommends, the virus so lowers the dog's resistance that he is open to secondary infections. He may develop pneumonia, tonsillitis, chronic diarrhea; he may develop encephalitis (inflammation of the brain, often resulting in permanent brain damage), meningitis (inflammation of the covering of the spinal cord), enteritis (inflammation of the intestine), and other afflictions that can affect his sight, hearing, and muscle tone. When the nerves are damaged, he may develop paralysis or weakness of the hind legs, or chorea, a spasmodic twitching of legs, head, or the entire body.

Often a dog with distemper will not show any discomfort for nearly a week. Then his symptoms may appear somewhat mild. Do not panic, however, if you see discharges from your dog's mouth and eyes—other canine diseases begin this way, and few of them are as serious as distemper. Your dog may have a simple upper-respiratory infection (as simple as the common cold), which treatment and time will cure. Or he may be suffering from a mild illness that will respond to home care. If you have given your dog protection against distemper, you are relatively safe in assuming that these symptoms are not from this virus. Although no vaccination is 100 percent effective, the incidence of a vaccination failure is very low.

The treatment of a dog with distemper should be left entirely to a veterinarian. He should be notified as soon as you see any of the symptoms. In most cases he will give your dog injections of antibiotics and oral medication to control the symptoms. Cures for distemper are still uncertain, although antibiotics and modern methods may arrest the secondary symptoms if a case is treated in time, and the dog can overcome the virus.

In the meantime, what can you do? If your dog's eyes are sore, keep them free of discharge by washing them with a warm eye wash. Keep his nose clear and open, and soothe it with cotton dipped in mineral or baby oil. His mouth may be tender and perhaps inflamed. Wash it out with a piece of cotton doused in bicarbonate of soda. If your dog has a fit or convulsion, leave him alone until he recovers—sometimes in a few moments. When he recovers from a fit, give him a sedative recommended by the veterinarian. If he has trouble with his breathing, ease it with a vaporizer.

Keep your dog out of drafts and dampness—it is best to keep him in a warm, dry room; cover him with a blanket or with his coat. Do not take him outdoors. The chances are that he will move his bowels on paper indoors since his diarrhea leaves him little choice. Feed him a mild diet. He may not want to eat, and you should therefore vary his diet, tempting him with several choices. Chopped meat, either raw or cooked, is fine, but if he rejects that, try some boiled chicken, a boiled egg, cooked fish, cereal, milk, fruit—until you find something that he will take. You must get some food into him because the strain of distemper on the body is tremendous. Vitamin and mineral supplements will come later. Food is the important thing. If he doesn't eat, force-feed him with broth, eggnog, strained baby food, or soups in small amounts at frequent intervals. Make sure his water dish is always filled with fresh water.

This is the time to give your dog a great deal of care and love. He is very sick and he needs attention. He also needs an even more generous proportion of your time than he is usually accustomed to. Nevertheless, he is in no condition to play—be sure not to make any excessive demands on his energy. Restrict his activity. If you have small children, warn them that their pet is not ready for exercises or roughhousing, although he would enjoy their attention. The care you give must be of the kind that reaffirms his faith in himself and that assures him you want his recovery as much as he wants it.

A sick animal loses confidence in himself. He has no way of understanding what is wrong with him, and he does not know that he will probably recover. It is up to you to give him assurance, to let him feel that his role in the house remains as firm and strong as ever. Only you can provide that continuity.

At one time distemper was, next to rabies, the most feared of all dog illnesses. With recent improvements in veterinary medicine, distemper can be prevented through vaccination and revaccination. While these are not foolproof, they do offer protection in the great majority of cases.

Most of the research that has effectively combatted distemper has been in the area of prevention. We know that the puppy who nurses at the dam's (mother's) first milk receives the mother's immunity *(that is, if she is immune)*, which lasts during nursing. Your veterinarian will probably give your puppy measles or distemper-measles vaccine at 6 weeks. Usually a dog is then given a DHL (distemper-hepatitis-leptospirosis [both types] vaccine), along with parainfluenza vaccination against tracheobronchitis, commonly called Kennel Cough. These are given at 12 and 16 weeks; thereafter, the dog receives a yearly injection. While puppies are more likely to get distemper, the older dog, if not adequately protected, can also contract the disease. It is up to your veterinarian to decide when and what type of immunization to use. *Distemper is such a difficult disease to treat that you should not hesitate to take any means to prevent it.*

CANINE HEPATITIS

Canine hepatitis is caused by a virus that attacks primarily the liver and the gastrointestinal tract, although it can affect other organs like the kidneys and the brain. While it can attack dogs of all ages, puppies are more susceptible to it than older dogs. Hepatitis has an incubation period of about one week.

The virus is infectious, which means that your dog can contract it from the urine, stools, or saliva of an infected dog. You may carry it on shoes and clothes infected with it. You cannot, however, catch it: Canine hepatitis is not the same as human hepatitis. Hepatitis, incidentally, seems to be on the increase, and for a while it was confused with distemper, since the symptoms appear somewhat similar. It is, in fact, worldwide.

Your dog may be perfectly well one day, very ill the next. Hepatitis develops very rapidly once the dog is infected. The more common symptoms are severe listlessness, extreme thirst and dehydration, diarrhea, vomiting, loss of appetite. The temperature will be high (104° to 105°F.), and there will be considerable abdominal tenderness as a result of the liver inflammation. The dog may even develop spasms, with his breathing becoming heavy and rapid.

One of the more obvious signs is that he may repeatedly hump his back or rub his belly against the floor in order to get relief from severe discomfort. The treatment of hepatitis is a matter for the veterinarian. The disease is very serious, and it spreads rapidly to other dogs.

Your treatment of a dog suffering from hepatitis will consist chiefly of following the veterinarian's instructions. After your dog returns from the hospital, you should, if necessary, force-feed him with a bland diet (chopped meat, raw or cooked, boiled chicken or egg) to keep up his strength. See the section at the end of this chapter on how to give pills and liquids to a dog. Keep his eyes clear of any discharge by washing them with a good eye wash.

Canine hepatitis is not a likely occurrence if your dog has been inoculated against it. A multiple vaccination provides immunity against hepatitis, distemper, and leptospirosis, although your dog should receive booster injections throughout his life. There is no permanent immunity against hepatitis.

One unusual feature of canine hepatitis is that a dog after being cured may still, for a time, spread the virus through his urine and feces. In the normal course of events, your dog may be exposed to hepatitis whenever he goes for a walk or runs around in the neighborhood. Clearly, prevention is the best possible course.

LEPTOSPIROSIS

In recent years there has been an important breakthrough in the diagnosis of the two strains of leptospirosis and in their treatment. It is an infectious disease caused by a spirochete (a spiral-shaped bacterium) that attacks the dog's kidneys and liver, creating some of the symptoms common to hepatitis.

The spirochete is transmitted by the urine of an infected dog or an infected rat. The dog licks the contaminated urine, which contains the spirochete. Or else he gets the contaminated urine on his coat or paws, which he then licks. Leptospirosis is more common where the dog has some contact with rats or rat droppings and urine. It is a world-wide disease, with an incubation period of 5 to 15 days.

Unfortunately, the dog can carry the leptospiral spirochete even while seemingly healthy or after recovery, and on very rare occasions can transmit it to humans. The best way to prevent the ailment is through inoculation, usually given now together with distemper and hepatitis. In this way you protect your dog, yourself, and your family.

The symptoms of leptospirosis were once confused with those of canine hepatitis and distemper. And they still are. One of the signs of the disease is a change in the color and smell of the dog's urine. Look for a deep yellow, even orange, color, and a strong, offensive smell. The dog may vomit any recently eaten food and will suffer considerable pain in the abdominal area. He will also be severely dehydrated and therefore very thirsty. The mucous membranes (of the gums and palate), the eyes, and the skin itself may turn yellowish. By this time, the dog's condition is very serious. Probably his kidneys have been permanently affected, and most of the internal damage has been done. At the onset of the illness, which is sudden, the temperature will rise alarmingly (perhaps as high as 105°F.), and then fall almost 5 degrees on succeeding days. In some cases the stools appear bloody, and there is a bloody discharge from the gums. If the dog vomits, the vomitus too may contain blood. He is very depressed and has difficulty in eating and swallowing. His muscles, especially those of the back legs, become stiff and sore. Most likely he won't get up from a sitting position.

Despite all these symptoms, the disease is very difficult to diagnose. Laboratory tests are usually necessary. Very early diagnosis may save the dog. Antibiotics seem to help kill the spirochete, and many dogs recover without any further damage. *It is best, however, to prevent this kind of suffering in your pet by giving him the inoculation that helps prevent the ailment.*

The treatment of a dog with leptospirosis is never left entirely to the owner. The ill animal may have to be kept in the hospital for a week or longer to receive medical treatment—usually antibiotics as well as vitamins and fluids by injection.

PARAINFLUENZA AND TRACHEOBRONCHITIS

Parainfluenza is the name given to assorted viruses of the upper-respiratory system that dogs may catch when they congregate together. Tracheobronchitis is better known as Kennel Cough (see page 321). It, also, is an inflammation, of the bronchi, and can result wherever dogs congregate. Any dog that is to be put in a kennel or boarded for a long or short time should receive an injection against these diseases.

RABIES

Rabies is a disease of the nervous system. It is a virus transmitted in the saliva of a rabid dog or another rabid animal. *The usual way in which a person or a dog can get rabies is through the bite of a rabid animal, although contact of infected saliva with any skin lesion can transmit the disease.*

Contrary to a popular belief, rabies does not come upon a dog when he is overheated or irritated. It is not more common in summer than in winter. There is no season for rabies, and there is no particular area for it. It is world-wide and especially prevalent in wild animals.

Rabies is something quite different from "unhappiness" or "discomfort" in a dog. An uncomfortable dog may be irritable and snappish because he is suffering from the heat. A rabid dog, on the other hand, has had the virus transmitted to his nerve tissues by the saliva from the bite of another rabid dog or animal, and this virus travels eventually to the brain, where it causes an inflammation called encephalitis. Once his brain is inflamed, the dog's behavior changes in one of two ways. He may be entirely lethargic—what is called the "dumb" or "paralytic" kind of rabies; or he may be overly excited—what is called the "furious" kind.

In the dumb kind, the dog will sit around listlessly, utterly depressed and incapable of action. Often, his mouth is wide open, and his lower jaw hangs as if useless. The tongue drools saliva. In furious rabies, the dog will be irritated by everything he sees that moves. He will race around, chase his tail, bite man or beast, and attack anything that moves. The dog is alert and very anxious, with his pupils dilated. There is no evidence of paralysis in the early stages.

Incidentally, a dog can sometimes transmit the virus three or four days before you see any recognizable symptoms.

What are the most common symptoms of rabies? The first signs may be no different from those you see in digestive disorders, injuries, poisoning, or any infectious disease. Before the dog becomes either dumb or furious, there is usually a sharp change in his behavior. A pleasant, friendly dog may become irritable, and an irritable dog subdued. In most cases, your dog will show extreme restlessness. His appetite will be disturbed, although it is difficult for me to predict exactly how. He may become ravenously hungry, and yet appear indifferent to food. After a while, he may lose all interest in his food. On other occasions, as the furious kind develops, the dog will show a perverted appetite for sticks, stones, wire, and other foreign objects. There will be frequent urination and sexual excitement in the male. Young pups will seek human companionship, only to bite when somebody comes near.

Some of the panic that a rabid dog shows comes from his difficulty in swallowing. The rabies virus paralyzes the nerves and the throat and jaw muscles—that is why we often see the jaw hanging open uselessly. Since the dog feels great thirst and cannot swallow, he may become alarmed. Rabies was once known as hydrophobia ("fear of water"), but the dog does not fear water. He is simply unable to swallow it. Frothing may or may not occur; it by no means always accompanies rabies.

As the disease develops, the dog's frenzy usually increases. In time, the brain is affected, but even before this happens the dog is filled with fear and frustration. Once the brain is inflamed, the dog usually dies shortly after. Rabies is considered 100 percent fatal in all animals and man if not treated immediately.

Because most owners have had their pets vaccinated and have continued with revaccination, canine rabies in the United States is now rare. *Be sure your own dog has been vaccinated. With this disease, prevention counts.*

Even though your chances of running into a case of rabies in a city or suburban dog are slight, if you do suspect a case report the dog immediately to the police, the health authorities, or a veterinarian. If a dog (or other animal) does bite you or your dog, or someone else, the suspected animal must be immediately reported and quarantined to see if rabies will develop.

Do not go near any dog that you suspect has rabies, and do not try to handle even your own dog if you should be in doubt. Warn your children. Prevention of a bite is all-important. If the suspected dog has been vaccinated (the owner should have a certificate to that effect), the possibility of his spreading rabies is small, although he will be kept in quarantine anyway. But often you do not know if he has been vaccinated unless you see the signed certificate. Your job is to protect yourself, your family, and your dog. All suspected dogs should be examined by a veterinarian and quarantined if necessary.

EXTERNAL AND INTERNAL PARASITES

EXTERNAL PARASITES

General Description of External Parasites

There are four external parasites that can make life hellish for your dog: fleas, lice, mites, and ticks. They are called external because they attach themselves to your dog's skin. In most cases, they burrow in deeply, and it is impossible for him to dislodge them by himself. In addition to the terrible annoyance, some parasites carry disease with them. The dog heavily infested by parasites may even come down with serious illnesses because his resistance is lowered.

Fleas, for example, carry tapeworm eggs. Ticks may carry blood parasites. Lice in great numbers may suck the dog's blood and cause anemia. Mites cause manges that can make a dog crazy with itchiness.

External parasites multiply incredibly fast. If a few find your dog, they attract all their relatives and their relatives' relatives. Everyone comes to the feast. Since the chief pleasure that a parasite gets is a meal and annoying your dog, he resists ferociously any attempt to dislodge him, all the time biting, nipping, and sucking. Many have built up a resistance to parasiticides.

Of course these parasites are by no means the only cause of skin trouble in a dog. There are several other kinds of skin ailments that are persistent and troublesome. For these, see pages 295–299 for my discussion of skin problems. Like the parasitic variety, most of the others need veterinary treatment and advice. The general rule to follow is not to attempt treatment yourself. Many of these organisms are difficult to identify except under the microscope. And if you cannot identify them, any home treatment is a hit-or-miss affair. You may feel that you are clearing up the condition when actually you are not. In the meanwhile, the organisms are multiplying. Ordinarily, a veterinarian can determine the kind of skin trouble your dog has and recommend the correct treatment, although some skin ailments persist even under treatment.

Characteristics of External Parasites

FLEAS

Fleas jump around, from one place to another, from one dog to another, or even to a person. You can find fleas on nearly any part of your dog's body, although they do prefer the hairiest places: the neck, head, tail area, and chest, depending on how the dog's coat is cut and kept.

Flea eggs are dormant during the cold weather, and even if they are in an area where the dog sleeps or lies, he will not be troubled. With the coming of warm and humid weather, however, the eggs hatch. You may have noticed that your dog does a good deal of scratching during the summer and seems to have most of his skin trouble then.

Once awakened by heat and damp, the flea egg hatches a worm. From this worm or larva eventually comes the flea, a very hardy fellow indeed. The flea simply waits until something warm comes along that he can jump on—either your dog or you or someone else in your family. The exception is the sticktight flea, which, instead of wandering around, lays its eggs deep down in the victim's skin, in little burrow-like ulcers it has successfully made.

Fleas will make your dog scratch furiously. In time, not only will he wear away the hair in several places; he will also damage the skin, in some cases giving himself a case of chronic parasitic dermatitis.

LICE

Lice, on the other hand, do not move around on the dog's body, but burrow into one place and remain there, sucking and biting until you flush them out. Once the louse settles, he makes the spot his permanent home, from egg state through adolescence and adulthood. Since the louse is so small, your chances of seeing him are slight. The louse is smaller than a pinhead, and it becomes lost in all that hair.

You can be pretty sure that your dog has lice or some other parasite when you see him using up several hundred calories a day burrowing into his coat with his paws, tongue, and teeth. His chances of finding such a small parasite are as slight as yours. Gradually his scratching may wear away the hair in the infested part, but by then the lice are deeply embedded. The parasites may also wear away the hair by attacking the follicles. The danger of a great number of lice is that because they suck blood, they can cause anemia in a puppy. Lice, too, can be passed on to members of your family when the dog sheds hair containing them or their eggs. They are harmless and will not stay on people, but may tend to irritate your nerves.

MITES

Mites are particularly troublesome because there are several varieties and they are difficult for the owner to detect. One type of mite—a cigar-shaped parasite—causes demodectic or follicular mange (red mange). A second type—a spider-shaped parasite with eight legs—causes sarcoptic mange or scabies. A third type, the ear mite, infests the dog's ear and may cause an ailment called otodectic mange. These manges are serious skin diseases that go further than discomfort for your dog. They can lead to serious complications. Demodectic mange spreads rapidly and may cause infections all over your dog's body. Sarcoptic mange results in a whole series of scabs, inflammations, and bloody lesions. Otodectic mange may lead to permanent ear damage if not treated.

The mange mite, like many other parasites, with the exception of the flea, works its way into the dog's skin. It burrows into the small sac containing the root of the hair, and the hair falls out. This sac is called the follicle, thus the word follicular mange for this particular kind. Many researchers believe that the mange mite can be passed at birth, though not by genes, but it cannot be passed across lines from one dog to another. Everyone agrees, however, that demodectic mange cannot be transmitted from a dog to a person. Unfortunately, sarcoptic mange may be carried from the dog's skin to children and adults. Children, in particular, are exposed to it when they roll and play with their pet. The result is an annoying rash.

In all types of mange, your dog will scratch violently at different parts of his body. Demodectic mange itself may be indicated only by general inflammation or by bloody pimples. Sarcoptic mange is evidenced by scabs, a thickening of the skin, and extreme shedding of hair in the afflicted area. The dog may begin to smell sour. With otodectic mange, a dog will carry his head at a strange angle, while the ear itself discharges a smelly fluid. The dog may even suffer loss of balance and show the symptoms of a general illness: listlessness, loss of appetite and weight.

The definitive diagnosis for all mites can be made only by skin scraping and microscopic examination.

TICKS

Ticks are an extremely annoying parasite, mainly because of their hardiness and endurance. The tick lives off three stages of hosts, and by the time it fastens on a person or an animal it is very practiced indeed. Once embedded in the skin, it resists removal with the ferocity of a squatter fighting for his rights.

Ticks can be rather easily recognized because they look like flat, blackish-brown seeds, giving the appearance of small warts. Often the seeds have become greatly swollen with blood and are an ugly dark red. A serious infestation may mean anemia for your dog. The most common type is called the American dog tick or the brown dog tick, and it can make its home in long grass or in crevices around your house or apartment. Ticks seek out certain parts of the dog's body: the stomach area, the pads of the feet, the feet themselves, and the folds between the legs and the body. Some varieties find the dog's ear a fine place in which to live. The tick searches for crevices in the dog, just as it looks for crevices in your house in which to lay its eggs and thrive.

A large infestation is indicated by the persistent scratching and general misery of your dog. Unlike most other parasites, ticks can be identified without microscopic examination. Also, ask your veterinarian about an internal medicine that may keep your dog free of ticks during the summer.

General Treatment of External Parasites

Although the treatment for each type of parasite is somewhat different, there are two general procedures common to all. First, a veterinarian must determine by examination exactly what parasite is involved. The treatment he recommends will depend on the diagnosis. Second, the owner must himself eliminate the source of the parasite by spraying, cleaning out the dog's kennel, laundering his bedding, and by breaking up the life cycle of the parasite.

The veterinarian will often recommend a flea or tick collar, powders, dips, or sprays to eliminate the parasites already infesting your dog. In some cases, he will advise internal medicine given by mouth. If the case is advanced, the treatment, unfortunately, may be lengthy. As a rule, the sooner an infestation is discovered, the faster it may be cleared up.

In addition, there is something that all owners can do to prevent parasites. The dog that is combed and brushed regularly will stand a better chance of avoiding parasites than one who is ungroomed. Regular combing and stripping (removing the old hair) will not only add tone to the dog's skin and coat, but it will also help remove parasites before they become solidly entrenched. Keeping a dog clean may not be the complete answer to parasites—certainly not if you live in an area where such parasites abound—but it helps greatly in keeping off these little armies of pests.

Cleanliness also means keeping the dog's sleeping area free of parasites, as well as his kennel (if he has one) and his run—*before* he is infested. The surrounding area—bushes and trees—should be sprayed with a nontoxic insecticide so that parasites do not gather there and eventually nest in your dog. Secondary carriers like field mice and rats are also sources of parasites that may in time find a home on your dog. They too should be sharply controlled if you wish to avoid later trouble. A few precautions may prevent infestations for the entire life of your dog. His happiness and good health—as well as your own protection—are certainly well worth the effort.

For a detailed description of each external parasite, along with the treatment for each, see the section on skin ailments, pages 295–307.

INTERNAL PARASITES

General Description of Internal Parasites

One of the more common afflictions that a dog may suffer from is worms. Perhaps 50 percent of dogs have worms at one time or another, in varying degrees of infestation. Most puppies, even when turned over to the owner from a kennel, where they may have been wormed, or when purchased elsewhere, need to be examined for worms. If you recognize some of the symptoms listed below, act immediately because your pet probably needs worming and the degree of infestation may be serious. In most cases, worming is completely successful, especially with periodic stool examinations, and your dog returns to perfect health in a short time.

There are several common symptoms of worms. When you notice these symptoms, do not try to do the worming yourself *unless you cannot take your dog to a veterinarian.* Certain worms are more dangerous than others, and a veterinarian's diagnosis is essential. Different worms have to be treated in different ways. The patent medicines available in your local drugstore are generally aimed at specific types. Thus, the patent medicine you choose may be for a type your dog does not have and will do no good.

One of the more frequent signs of worms—depending on the degree of infestation—may be that your dog becomes weak and listless. Actually he is, for the worms are parasites living off his body. His appetite may be affected; at times he will stuff himself and at other times he will seem indifferent to food. Or his stomach may become bloated, all out of proportion to the amount he is eating. He will usually have diarrhea: watery, thin bowel movements; at times his stool will be flecked with blood. This is always serious.

The dog's coat might be affected, becoming dry and coarse if the infestation is heavy and neglected. Or loss of weight can possibly result; the dog will actually appear shrunken because he has lost a good deal of fluid. Sometimes he will vomit the worms. In every case where worms are present in large numbers, your dog will not be the frisky animal who jumps all over you or tries to lick you. While he may not be in actual pain, he has lost some of his energy and may drowse for long periods or go through fits of rubbing his body against the floor. He is uncomfortable, and his discomfort will soon become apparent to you. At such times, when you suspect worms, be particularly gentle with him.

Stroke and reassure him. Do not ask too much of him, and warn your children that he is temporarily ill.

For other reasons as well your children should be kept from a dog suffering from worms. A child who touches the dog's excrement and then inadvertently puts his finger in his mouth may become infected with worms, especially roundworms and hookworms.

There are several types of worms, some relatively easy to treat and others requiring more care. If you suspect worms from the above symptoms, the best thing to do is to take a sample of the dog's stool (bowel movement) to the veterinarian for examination. The actual worming usually takes one day and may have to be repeated in ten days, and then the stool is rechecked. Usually, a puppy under 4 to 6 weeks is not wormed unless his stool and vomitus show signs of worms, and then only by a veterinarian.

Characteristics of the Various Internal Parasites

I take up internal parasites in detail when I later discuss each organ that they affect.

For *heartworm*, see Circulatory Disorders, page 275.

For *ascarid* or *roundworm ("puppy worm"), esophageal worm, fluke disease, hookworm, intestinal protozoans (coccidia), tapeworm,* and *whipworm,* see Digestive Disorders, pages 288–290.

For *kidneyworm*, see Urinary Disorders, page 328.

Heartworms (also called filariae) are usually transmitted to dogs by mosquitoes that have bitten an infected dog. They usually affect those dogs who are more exposed to mosquitoes than apartment and suburban dogs. The mature worm settles in the heart and interferes with the flow of blood, causing difficulty in breathing, loss of weight, a cough, and even convulsions.

The ascarid or roundworm (also called "puppy worm") is very common in puppies and grown dogs. It is a white, slim worm, about one to four inches in length, that develops in the intestine.

Esophageal worms are relatively rare, and are found only in the South. They are so called because they infest the dog's esophagus or gullet, causing difficulty in swallowing and frequent vomiting. Sometimes the dog becomes frantic because of his inability to swallow, and his symptoms might frighten you into thinking he has rabies.

Fluke disease is a type of poisoning that the dog gets from eating raw fish. Flukes are parasitic worms that harbor a viruslike organism that makes the dog very ill. The symptoms are somewhat like those of distemper: eye and nose discharge, diarrhea (often bloody), dehydration, loss of weight and appetite. The ailment is more common in Northwest coastal areas.

Hookworm is especially dangerous for puppies because the worm attaches itself to the intestinal wall and sucks blood. If neglected, the puppy or dog may develop anemia.

Intestinal protozoans (coccidia) are a particularly troublesome intestinal parasite because they lower a dog's resistance to disease. The symptoms of an infestation are similar to those of distemper, particularly in the dehydration of the dog, which will be severe.

The tapeworm is difficult to eliminate, for the head, which is attached to the intestinal wall, must be removed and the worm itself may be several feet in length. Or there may be more than one worm. Sometimes an infestation of tapeworms becomes apparent to the owner when he sees what look like little kernels of rice around the dog's anus. Actually, these are pieces of the tapeworm. Removal of these pieces, however, do not mean the end of the worm—the head itself must be removed.

Whipworms are round, tapered parasites that settle in the dog's colon and intestinal tract. They cause chronic diarrhea, loss of blood, and extreme irritation, particularly when the infestation is severe and neglected.

Eyeworms, kidneyworms, and lungworms make their homes in the organs they are named after. These worms, while rare, cause the same symptoms as other worm infestations and must be treated without delay.

General Treatment of Internal Parasites

1. All worming should be done by a veterinarian or under his direction. Give your dog a patent medicine only when you know the type of worm or when you are unable to see or talk to a veterinarian in the immediate future.

2. Between the time you notice the worms and the time you see your veterinarian, give your dog a bland diet of starch (rice, barley, or noodles) and cooked hamburger meat. Give him strong tea to drink—if he will drink it. Avoid bulky foods (raw meat, raw vegetables). During the actual worming, feeding will differ according to the medicines being administered by your veterinarian and according to the degree of infestation. Ask your veterinarian about fasting and feeding at this time. After worming, continue the bland diet suggested above for a week or for as long as your veterinarian advises.

3. For the protection of the dog as well as for the protection of everyone else in the house, keep your dog's living quarters clean. Scrub the floor with a strong (nontoxic) disinfectant. Change the dog's drinking water two or three times a day. Disinfect all pails and feeding dishes. Soak a solution of borax into the ground in his running area—or simply salt and hot water. (Use ½ tablespoon of salt per quart of water. This may, incidentally, permanently kill grass.)

4. Never worm a dog that is badly constipated because he generally will vomit. Give him milk of magnesia, or put him on a diet of buttermilk or skimmed milk for twenty-four hours before you have him wormed.

5. Do not worm a weak dog except under a veterinarian's supervision. It is difficult for the owner to ignore the fact that his pet has worms, for the dog will almost always call it to his attention. Worm infestations seldom leave any lasting effects if the worms are identified early and completely eliminated. One must be careful to continue treatment when necessary, for worms, like any other parasite, are persistent. With modern equipment and medication, however, the veterinarian can quickly determine what kind of worm is involved and prescribe the proper treatment.

THE SYSTEMS

CIRCULATORY DISORDERS
(Heart and Blood Vessels)

The circulatory system is comprised of the heart and blood vessels. Heart disorders and blood ailments in dogs are much the same as in people, and often the causes are similar. Some dogs have congenital heart disease (incomplete closure of blood vessels in the heart), creating a condition similar to that of the "blue baby." Some puppies are now operated upon for such ailments and recover.

One of the most common signs of a heart ailment in your dog is a cardiac cough, a sound similar to an upper-respiratory cough. When he is excited he may hack; when calm he may not. Or he may cough all the time. Also, your dog may become winded very easily or gasp for breath. Other symptoms include blue tongue and gums, lack of vitality, quickness to tire, weakness of pulse, collapse itself. When any of these appear, consult a veterinarian. Digitalis, which is prescribed for people, also works well with dogs, but do not give it without professional advice.

Sometimes you can feel sharp vibrations like trills (indicative of a murmur) in the dog's chest when you pick him up. This does not necessarily mean a heart disorder, but your dog should nevertheless be checked for a heart ailment.

An enlarged heart also causes a weakness. Enlargement means that your dog must cut down on his everyday activities, and this precaution may help him live to an old age.

An old dog, like an old person, should not suddenly be forced into violent activity. Old field dogs, for example, who are forced to be active in the field after long periods of rest, might collapse from a heart seizure. Similarly, the apartment dog over 7 or 8 years old should not be raced and exercised into exhaustion. He will not know when to stop, especially as he wants to please you, and will drive himself until he collapses.

Accidents that affect the heart are usually fatal. There is, as far as I know, no certain cure for heart injuries, although a breakthrough may soon be made. Occasionally, if the dog is operated upon and treated immediately, a heart injury might be handled successfully. In any accident involving the chest area, you should rush the dog to a veterinarian.

With modern methods of diagnosis by means of electrocardiographs and audio-visual recorders and with new medicines available, heart disorders can be successfully handled today. Many dogs can now live years with impaired hearts whereas only a few years ago they would have died.

Anemia

When the hemoglobin in the blood is reduced by illness, bleeding from an accident, hookworms, whipworms, or any other cause, the dog has anemia. It is, however, relatively rare. Since the red cells carry oxygen from the lungs, their breakdown leads to certain obvious signs: The dog's tongue and gums will become whitish, as will the mucous membranes of his eyes; his appetite may decline; he will be listless and sleep a great deal. His body becomes thin and drawn; his eyes sink into their sockets like pennies in loose sand.

Another cause of anemia is an intestinal protozoan known as canine piroplasmosis (also called babesiasis), a disease that is prevalent in Southern climates but almost unknown elsewhere. It is a tiny parasite spread by the brown dog tick. Since it lives in the red blood cells, it drains the dog's energy. A dog with this protozoan will fall into a lethargic and depressed state.

Some of the symptoms are similar to those of distemper: rise in temperature, loss of appetite, reddish discoloration of the urine, extreme listlessness, pale lips and gums, increase in pulse rate. The dog may also develop jaundice. Any of these symptoms should send you to a veterinarian immediately, for the death rate from piroplasmosis is quite high. To prevent the infestation, spray the kennel and yard as well as the dog with an insecticide safe for dogs. Once you get rid of the brown dog tick, you eliminate the source of the infection.

The treatment of anemia itself involves supplements of iron in the diet: plenty of meat (especially liver) supplemented by iron pills, liquid iron, or injections of B_{12}. Even a blood transfusion may be called for. Once the red cells are built up again, you will notice a steady increase in your dog's vigor. The bright look in his eyes will return, his appetite will pick up, and his body will begin to fill out.

Ascites

Ascites is an accumulation of fluid in the abdominal cavity. It usually results from a defect in the liver, heart, or kidneys. Usually ascites occurs in older dogs when their internal organs begin to work less effectively, although it can occur in the younger animal as well. In some cases, you may notice an unnaturally swollen abdomen and shallow breathing. The condition calls for immediate professional treatment, for ascites is not itself the disease, but simply a symptom of the disease.

Hemorrhaging, Clotting, Rupture of Blood Vessels

One of the most common and most recognizable blood vessel ailments is hemorrhaging or bleeding. When this happens, follow the directions in Chapter 7, on first aid.

In certain other cases, blood clots can form, especially after surgery or after an accident. A clot that is neglected in a vital vein can block the passage so that blood does not flow. Eventually the area without blood will become gangrenous. Blood clots in dogs, fortunately, are fairly rare. (For hematoma, a hemorrhage in the ear that clots, see section on Ear Disorders, page 293.)

A stroke, or apoplexy, is the result of a rupture of a blood vessel in the brain. The chief sign of a stroke may be that the dog circles in one direction and is unable to stand steadily on his hind legs. A stroke usually occurs in the old rather than the young dog. The aftereffects vary according to the severity of the stroke. A limb may be paralyzed either temporarily or permanently, depending on the severity of the circulatory disturbance. Of course many dogs may recover completely from a stroke. A good deal depends on the dog's age, general health, and, most important, the size of the brain area affected, which is usually unknown.

Edema

As part of a circulatory disturbance, large accumulations of fluid may form in the tissues—sometimes in the lungs but more often in the legs—causing a swelling of the tissue. If you push your finger into the skin, an indentation remains for several minutes. Edema requires immediate treatment, or else disintegration of tissue will occur. It is generally more common in older dogs.

Worms: Heartworms

Dogs who are exposed to mosquitoes may become afflicted with heartworms (also called filariae). These internal parasites are transmitted to dogs by mosquitoes that have bitten an infected dog. The mature worm settles in the heart, where it interferes with the flow of blood. A dog infested with heartworms may have difficulty in breathing, lose weight, seem nervous and irritable, suffer from a cough. If he exercises hard, he may faint or go into convulsions. These symptoms are similar to those of many ailments, but a periodic blood examination will tell you if your dog has heartworms.

Since mosquitoes carry the parasite, heartworms usually are found in hunting and working dogs and only rarely found in the apartment dog. If you live in a mosquito-infested area, be sure that your dog's kennel is screened. Keep him dusted with insect powder, and if necessary periodically dip him in a medicated or insecticidal bath as recommended by your veterinarian. If your dog has a running area of soil, keep it sprayed with an approved insecticide—one of the many containing chlordane or lindane; and cover any area where water accumulates, as it is a breeding spot for mosquitoes.

In recent years, heartworm disease has spread to many parts of the United States, and you should check with your local veterinarian to see if it has become a problem in your section or in a section you plan to visit. Remember, your dog may be infected with heartworms for a long period of time before the signs become visible to you, and by then the condition will have become dangerous.

The best procedure is to have a laboratory blood test done. If the results are positive, your veterinarian can begin a program of treatment to eliminate the condition. Once that is done, your dog will be put on a preventive drug to prevent a recurrence. If the laboratory test indicates a negative state, then your dog should be put on the preventive, as determined by your veterinarian. The procedure that I recommend strongly is:

1. Wherever you live, have your dog tested for heartworms.

2. If your veterinarian so recommends, put your dog on preventive medication.

You must be sure *not* to give your dog the preventive before you determine whether or not he is free of heartworm infestation by a negative blood test. The medication, if given to a dog with heartworm, will create a serious condition—even death.

Once the medication is begun, it is continued during the entire mosquito season.

DIGESTIVE DISORDERS

The digestive system of a dog starts with his mouth and ends with his anus. All ailments that have to do with his mouth and teeth, throat, esophagus, stomach, intestines, liver, or rectum are considered digestive disorders.

Several ailments affecting this system are localized—like trouble with the teeth—and can be cleared up with a minimum of difficulty. Others may require more extensive treatment and a longer convalescence. These ailments will be accompanied by many symptoms that you are now familiar with: drooling as a sign of nausea; vomiting, possibly blood-flecked;

LIFE CYCLE OF THE HEARTWORM OF DOGS

Dirofilaria immitis

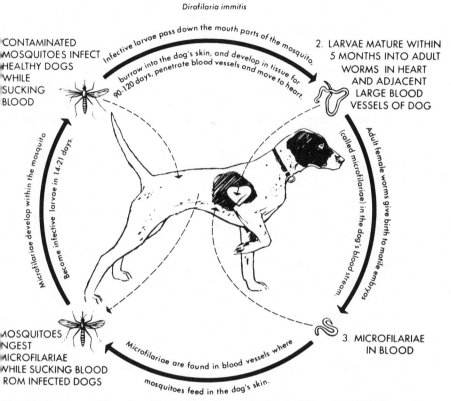

CONTAMINATED MOSQUITOES INFECT HEALTHY DOGS WHILE SUCKING BLOOD

Infective larvae pass down the mouth parts of the mosquito, burrow into the dog's skin, and develop in tissue for 90-120 days, penetrate blood vessels and move to heart.

2. LARVAE MATURE WITHIN 5 MONTHS INTO ADULT WORMS IN HEART AND ADJACENT LARGE BLOOD VESSELS OF DOG

Microfilariae develop within the mosquito

Become infective larvae in 14-21 days.

Adult female worms give birth to motile embryos (called microfilariae) in the dog's blood stream.

MOSQUITOES INGEST MICROFILARIAE WHILE SUCKING BLOOD FROM INFECTED DOGS

Microfilariae are found in blood vessels where mosquitoes feed in the dog's skin.

3. MICROFILARIAE IN BLOOD

(Reprinted courtesy of American Cyanamid Company, Professional Veterinary Pharmaceuticals Department.)

diarrhea, also possibly with blood; severe constipation; excessive gas, leading sometimes to bloat, a condition in which the abdomen swells and the skin becomes like the surface of a balloon; the presence of undigested bones or pieces of food in the stool; a strong or unusual odor in the feces and urine; a rise in temperature; possibly the presence of worms or pieces of worms in the feces; a general depression and unhealthiness in the dog's appearance; listlessness and exhaustion.

As far as his digestion is concerned, there are really few things that a dog should not eat if he is willing. You should, however, discourage bones. They may tear the throat or create an obstruction if swallowed whole; and they contribute to constipation even if chewed. If you must feed bones, give your dog a shinbone or a commercial biscuit in the shape of a bone. Try to avoid very spicy foods, or foods with too much salt or gaseous matter, although dogs have thrived on nearly any kind of scraps. An excess of spice will make him drink more than he usually does and urinate more often, a burden upon him and the owner. It may also create some discomfort and result in vomiting.

Abscesses (of Mouth)

The usual place for dental abscesses is at the very end of the tooth root, deep within the gum. The abscess itself is a collection of pus. Receding gums, a blow on the mouth, or broken teeth may leave openings for bacteria to enter, and sometimes tooth abscesses form. The condition is very painful, and if neglected, it may lead to general body infections. It generally occurs in the older dog.

When there is an abscess, your dog will almost always let you know it. He will try to avoid using the affected tooth when he eats and will hold his head at an angle while he chews. He will shake his head and paw at his mouth. Loss of appetite and some fever are often present. There may also be a discharge on the gum line of the tooth.

Also, dogs will sometimes develop a swelling under the eye which may rupture and discharge pus. This condition—called dental fistula—is mostly symptomatic of a tooth abscess, usually in the upper third premolar. Extraction of the tooth is the only cure.

Bloat

Bloat is rare but extremely serious, for unless it is quickly relieved it can lead to the dog's death. You will usually recognize bloat. The dog seems to be blowing up right before your eyes, as if you were pumping air into him. The cause may be violent exercise that results in a twisted stomach. Or the gas may come from a meal taken from the garbage can. As the gas expands, it forces the dog's stomach to swell, until he seems all stomach and all his other internal organs are constricted.

Large breeds seem to suffer more frequently from the condition than small ones, especially Great Danes and St. Bernards, perhaps because they are more violent in their exercise. Besides the swollen or twisted stomach and the taut skin, other symptoms are a great restlessness on the dog's part as well as difficulty in breathing. *The condition needs immediate treatment, or surgery, by a veterinarian.*

Although the exact cause is unknown, one way to avoid bloat is to keep your dog off large amounts of dry food in the warm weather when his tendency is to drink a good deal of water anyway. In addition, strong-flavored vegetables are not well tolerated. Also, do not exercise him violently either before or after mealtime. You should take particular care if you have a large dog, over 50 to 60 pounds.

Constipation

Constipation occurs when solid waste products build up in the dog's intestine and for some reason cannot be eliminated easily. There are several possible reasons for this condition. In the older dog, intestinal movement slows down and more fluid is absorbed from the feces. An enlarged prostate gland may make movement painful and the dog will not evacuate. For dogs of all ages, a poor diet can cause constipation—too little exercise, too much hard biscuit or constipating dry food. Another serious cause might be an obstruction in the intestine, either a tumor or some foreign object the dog swallowed.

When constipation occurs infrequently, your dog may need only a mild laxative—a teaspoonful of milk of magnesia for every 10 pounds of dog—or a lubricant: a teaspoonful of mineral oil. *Do not give other human laxatives or tonics,* as some contain strychnine, which even in small doses can be harmful. If your dog is still constipated after a couple of days, the waste product is probably so solid that a mild laxative will not penetrate. You should then consult your veterinarian. *Do not experiment with laxatives.*

When there is a prostate disorder in old dogs, keep the bowels soft with oil in his food, to reduce the pain of hard movement. A bland diet for this condition means keeping away from fillers (roughage and cereal). Of course, if the male's prostate is so enlarged that it causes chronic constipation, then you should consult your veterinarian.

If, however, the constipation comes from lack of bulk, you can rectify it easily by including roughage (leafy vegetables, cereals). If it is caused by old age or lack of exercise, use a lubricant like mineral oil.

When your dog swallows a ball or other toy, the object can partially block the passage from the stomach to the small intestine. Call your veterinarian immediately. *Never* give a laxative when you suspect a foreign body.

Sometimes constipation results from an illness. Depending on the particular ailment from which your dog is recovering, his treatment must be regulated by a veterinarian. After an operation, for example, a dog may become constipated for lack of exercise and because of a break in his regular feeding habits. In such a case or in a similar one, do not treat the constipation yourself.

Sometimes the cause of constipation is deceptively simple. Your dog's anus might be caked with feces attached to the hair, creating a wall which nothing can penetrate. A washing with soap and warm water will remedy the condition. Or your dog may need more exercise to give some tone to his system. A long run in the park or around the neighborhood, or a game of catch, may be all that he needs to regain regularity. On occasion, while the dog's diet and exercise may be adequate, what he requires is a change of food. Something as simple as a shift from one canned product to another, or from one meat to another, can bring results.

Diarrhea

A watery or bloody loose bowel movement is called diarrhea. If your dog simply has a softly formed stool, it is not diarrhea, although it may be a prelude to diarrhea.

Like vomiting that persists or recurs, continuing diarrhea is usually a symptom of a larger ailment, although it may be a temporary condition or result from a simple cause. Nearly every canine ailment may cause diarrhea: distemper, canine hepatitis, intestinal parasites (worms), poisons, foreign objects in the digestive tract, spoiled food, even nervous disorders.

If the diarrhea occurs as an isolated event and your dog otherwise seems healthy, it is probably a minor stomach or intestinal upset. Or it may be that for some reason unknown to you, your dog is emotionally upset. Also, diarrhea is not unusual in a very young puppy, say up to 2 months. Of course, if the puppy of that age, or older, has persistent attacks of diarrhea, you should be on the alert. If the elimination contains mucus as well as fluid, there is something wrong and you should consult a veterinarian. *And if the stool contains blood, your dog needs immediate professional care.* The normal color of the bowel movement is light to dark brown. It of course varies with the food that is eaten.

When diarrhea is infrequent, it may simply indicate a mild stomach upset—of the kind people occasionally suffer from after a heavy meal or a bout of drinking. A good remedy for control, recommended for both dogs and children, is Kaopectate or milk of bismuth. It helps settle the stomach and usually stops any minor diarrhea. Give a tablespoon of Kaopectate for every 20 pounds of dog three times a day and after each bowel movement. If Kaopectate doesn't do the trick in a couple of days, you know that the condition goes beyond the diarrhea itself. Neglect can lead to dehydration and depression.

Regulate your dog's diet during attacks of diarrhea. Do not give him liquid foods, like milk and broth. Feed him cooked starches like rice or macaroni with meat. These should cure simple diarrhea.

Sometimes the diarrhea is only one symptom among many, and you will see several other signs of illness. The diarrhea itself will be persistent, turning yellowish or tarry, while your dog also vomits, loses his appetite, has a fever, experiences mucous discharges from his eyes and nose, and seems generally depressed and miserable. When some or all of these signs occur, you should call in your veterinarian immediately.

Enteritis (Inflammation of the Intestine)

Infection or inflammation of the intestine may come from poisons or bacteria from putrefying food, or from worms, or from sharp objects that have been swallowed. Such an infection, whatever its direct cause, is called enteritis, and is usually accompanied by diarrhea or foul-smelling bowel movements. In his discomfort, your dog may assume a prayerlike position, like a Moslem at worship. All of these symptoms might not come at once.

The intestine is particularly sensitive and is therefore easily irritated. All food must be processed through the intestine, and it is the residing place of most worms when and if they exist. Whenever anything goes wrong in the intestine, there is indication in the bowel movements. They may show worms or mucus from the intestine itself; and they are good indicators of the condition of the colon. If food comes through in solid form in the stool, that will inform you that your dog is not digesting properly.

Most intestinal ailments require professional care. While your dog is recovering from an intestinal ailment, your veterinarian will probably recommend a bland diet. Rice, meat, and baby food are all safe for him to eat. The veterinarian may recommend a prescription diet especially made for this condition.

Disorders of the Esophagus

The esophagus (or gullet) is the passage down which food passes from the mouth to the stomach. If there is something wrong with the dog's esophagus, he will have a good deal of trouble swallowing, which is the chief symptom.

Some typical ailments involving the esophagus are inflammation or injuries caused by caustics (lye, rat and roach poisons), acids and poisons, the presence of worms, ruptures, and fistulas, foreign objects, a blow, or an enlargement so that pouches or pockets are formed. All these injuries or ailments require medical treatment outside the scope of the average owner. Dogs with such injuries should be given soft foods and liquids until the condition can be cleared up by medication or surgery. If you continue to feed your dog his regular diet, he may eat nothing, or vomit what he does eat.

Foreign objects caught in the esophagus and not removed may tear the lining and increase the damage. When such objects are caught in the throat, your dog won't eat. Esophageal injuries caused by objects in the throat, or by acids or caustics, and other similar afflictions are discussed in Chapter 7, on first aid. After the emergency treatment indicated there, call a veterinarian at once.

Fissures (Anal)

Anal fissures are cracks in the skin around the anus, the result of too much straining during a bowel movement or of an anal wound that fails to heal. Since constant bowel movements do not give the fissure much opportunity to heal, the best treatment for a case that does not respond is cryosurgery; but a soft diet—cooked oatmeal, rice, meat—will ease the bowel movements. Ask your veterinarian about a diet if this condition fails to heal. Mineral oil added to the food will also help to lubricate the stool. After a couple of weeks, the tear should be sufficiently healed to allow a return to the dog's normal diet. If not, consult your veterinarian; cyrosurgery may be necessary for persistent cases.

Flatulence (Gas)

Flatulence is simply a big word to indicate that your dog has an accumulation of gas in his stomach or intestines, which may make him pass wind a little more than he normally would. Very often large amounts of proteins—like hard-boiled eggs, meat, and cheese—will cause a buildup of gas. Also, strong-flavored vegetables like cabbage, turnips, cauliflower, and onions will produce flatulence. If you watch the proteins and vegetables in your dog's diet, you should normally relieve the accumulation of gas. Give small amounts of milk of magnesia as an antacid. Both you and your dog will feel happier for it. If your dog is old, however, expect flatulence as a normal part of the aging process.

Of course some dogs are more nervous than others. Nervousness can result in inadequate digestion, which in turn leads to gas. Some breeds—older Boxers and certain Terriers, for instance—seem to be bothered with gas more than the placid sporting and hound dogs.

If the condition persists and really becomes offensive, you should consult a veterinarian. He can recommend an antiflatulent. A chronic gas condition might indicate stomach or intestinal trouble that requires treatment.

Foreign Objects (in Rectum)

Sharp objects which have worked their way through the dog's body may become lodged in the rectum and do considerable tearing damage. A pin or needle, for example, may come through the stomach and intestine, become lodged in the dog's anus, and then cause an obstruction in the rectum. As the dog strains, the pin, or whatever it is, works into the rectal lining, causing severe pain. He may yell when he evacuates, and you may see blood dripping from his anus or blood in his stool.

Unless you know what is wrong, a professional check is necessary. Home remedies may only aggravate the condition.

Gastritis

Gastritis is an inflammation of the stomach lining caused by overeating, eating of spoiled food, or the presence of indigestible food in the stomach. It also accompanies leptospirosis, distemper, and rabies, and is often seen in advanced uremia. The symptoms are vomiting and an irregular appetite. In acute cases, the dog may feel pain when you touch his stomach. A veterinarian must determine whether the case is acute or chronic.

Treatment often includes the feeding of bland foods like broth, boiled chicken, soft-boiled eggs, Pablum and milk in small amounts three or four times a day. If the condition is acute, all food and water should be withdrawn for twenty-four hours. Give your dog ice cubes to lick to quench his thirst.

Infection of Salivary Glands

The salivary glands, which secrete saliva, might not function correctly for a variety of reasons. As the result of an injury, the ducts leading from the glands into the mouth can become infected with bacteria. Cysts may form under the tongue because of interference with the gland secretion. Or the glands themselves may become infected, equivalent to what happens to a person with mumps. If your dog's neck seems swollen, or if there is swelling under his tongue, a salivary gland infection may well be the reason. Only a veterinarian can diagnose the condition, which could also be a number of other things. Surgery is usually necessary in many of these cases.

Intestinal Impactions

Intestinal impactions are blocks or accumulations of undigestible material in the intestine. If left alone, dogs may indulge strange eating habits: They may eat straw, stones, pieces of metal, toys, hunks of rubber, leaves, cellophane, lengths of wire, knitting needles, Brillo, soap compounds, cigars and cigarettes, matches, rope, and other such delicacies. They will often consume these unlikely items even when they are otherwise receiving a well-balanced diet.

These objects can, understandably, cause a digestive problem. In fact, they may block the intestinal tract so that your dog is in real trouble. Treatment for impactions of this sort must be left to your veterinarian. A laxative here is useless and may falsely lull you into thinking you are helping the condition when actually you aren't. In very severe cases of intestinal impaction, surgery sometimes is necessary, especially when the foreign objects are tightly lodged and will not work free.

An impaction may be difficult to diagnose. Usually the abdomen is taut and hard, and the dog seems indifferent and depressed. He may assume strange positions to relieve the pain. Your chief clue, however, is constipation. After a couple of days, the condition may call for hospital care and surgery.

Intussusceptions

The condition known as intussusception means that the intestine has telescoped into itself. When this occurs—and the reasons for it are not always clear—the food passing through the intestine is blocked. The blood supply to the telescoped part is also cut off.

You will probably not know when a dog has this condition, but he will show many symptoms of illness. The symptoms, incidentally, are comparable to an appendicitis in a person. The abdomen itself will become very sensitive; the dog may vomit frequently, perhaps after every meal. As a result of the inflammation, the temperature rises. Dehydration occurs. The feces might be bloody and are almost always watery, or bowel movements may stop altogether. There will be pain if you touch the dog in the abdominal area. Correction of the condition calls for immediate surgery.

Jaundice

Jaundice occurs when some growth blocks the bile duct or disease interferes with the normal secretion of bile. The symptoms are orange urine and yellowish coloring of the skin and the whites of the eyes. Like all other liver ailments, jaundice requires professional care immediately.

Liver Ailments

Dogs generally do not have liver trouble unless they have a disease that directly affects the liver. Canine hepatitis, for example, prevents the liver from doing its job. Whenever your dog has something wrong with his liver, you can usually tell by the color of his eyes. The whites will turn yellowish, as will his gums and skin. Furthermore, the urine will be orange, and the dog's stools may be gray or black and sticky-looking. However, since certain foods will change the color of the stool, this is not always a dependable symptom.

Do not neglect any condition involving the liver. It is the largest organ in the body, and in the dog it is even larger, proportionately, than it is in people. Damage to the liver may create a chronic condition.

Some worming medicines when given in large doses, as well as certain toxins, can cause liver damage. Certain poisons, especially insecticides, may, if consumed over a period of time, cause liver trouble. The symptoms are gray or black stools, a yellowish color to the skin, and general depression and listlessness. See Chapter 7 for first aid in the event of an emergency. If there is no emergency and you see these symptoms, consult with your veterinarian.

Rectal and Anal Gland Trouble: Anal Gland Impactions

On each side of the anus, situated inside and below the anus, are the anal glands, which secrete a yellowish fluid. It is an accumulation that carries over from the dog's primitive state, what the skunk still retains to frighten away possible attackers. Because dogs today do not exercise much and do not usually lead hard, rugged lives, their glands tend to retain the secretion, causing irritation and sometimes leading to abscesses. When these abscesses form, they are obviously painful. The dog tries to help himself by rubbing and licking the affected parts or by skidding on his hindquarters. Sometimes the abscesses will burst open, discharging pus and blood. Take your dog to a veterinarian for the treatment of any swelling near the anus.

Do not break the abscess-filled sacs yourself. The secretion is particularly foul, and you will not remove all of it. Only a veterinarian should do this job. He will exert pressure in the right way to empty the sacs. This should clear up the condition, and your dog will stop irritating the area. If the glands fill up again, the symptoms may return and your dog may need further treatment.

Perianal tumors are prevalent in the older dog. Hemorrhoids as we understand them in a person are virtually unknown in a dog. Sometimes the veins in the rectal area will swell, but they almost always return to normal. Constipation may make the anus swell, but as soon as regularity returns the swelling goes away.

Throat Ailments

Inflammation of the pharynx (the link between the esophagus and the mouth cavity) is called pharyngitis. Inflammation of the larynx (the so-called voice box) is called laryngitis. Neither kind of inflammation will in itself indicate what is wrong with your dog. Usually pharyngitis and laryngitis accompany other symptoms of a larger ailment: distemper or a general infection in the system.

Probably you will not know precisely what is wrong with your dog's throat even though something is clearly bothering him. If he continues to eat, you know there is no foreign object caught in his throat and it may be an infection. There will surely be other signs of an ailment: vomiting, running nose and eyes, loss of appetite, fever, perhaps difficulty in swallowing, or general depression and lack of vitality. If you notice any of these signs, take your dog to a veterinarian, who can determine whether it is a purely local throat ailment or part of some other problem. Half a baby aspirin will provide temporary relief. Repeat as needed.

Tooth Problems

Your veterinarian should check your dog's teeth in his regular examination. The most common tooth problems are pits, discoloration, worn enamel, breaks, an accumulation of tartar, or calculus, where the tooth joins the gum, and gum abscesses. Cavities of the kind people have do not usually trouble dogs. Tooth problems in general—except for calculus, or tartar—are not frequent unless the dog gets into mischief and cracks a tooth on another dog or, as a puppy, suffers from a virus disease (like distemper) that pits the teeth.

A very bad mouth odor may mean a tooth problem. Or it may mean a digestive ailment, in which case the sour smell comes from the stomach. If the odor persists and your dog seems otherwise healthy, the problem is probably a dental one, particularly in an older dog. His teeth may need no more than a cleaning.

Your dog has all his permanent teeth by the time he is 6 months old. If he eats a reasonably balanced diet—including minerals—he should have no real trouble with his teeth until he is much older and most likely not even then. Even dogs on bizarre diets usually have few cavities, although they may have a lot of tartar.

A large accumulation of tartar or dental calculus on the teeth will often cause bad breath. If your dog gnaws on hard biscuits or a very hard bone—a knucklebone or shinbone—he may clean his own teeth with it. Soft bones, however, will do him no good. They are more trouble than they are worth. If you wish to keep your dog off bones altogether, substitute a hard rubber object or a synthetic bone, which will wear away the tartar accumulations. There is a chance that your dog may not take to the synthetic bone, and there is the further chance that tartar will develop no matter what you do.

Although a little tartar may be offensive to look at, it is otherwise harmless. A lot of tartar, however, can lead in time to further dental trouble—recession of gums and bacterial infection. Heart trouble and arthritis can result from a long infection. To remove the tartar, a veterinarian usually gives your dog an anesthetic first and then cleans his teeth until they gleam like those in a toothpaste ad. This should be done once a year if needed.

You can yourself try to keep your dog's teeth clean by washing them a few times a month with a piece of cotton dipped in milk of magnesia. If all this strikes you as too much trouble, you should let a veterinarian do the job his way. Also, your dog may resist your treatment unless he has been trained to it from puppyhood.

There is not much you can do about teeth that have developed pits or stains because of illness. If the stain is from plain neglect, then of course it can be removed along with the tartar accumulations. Distemper, however, usually permanently marks the teeth, particularly since the virus may strike the puppy at the very time his permanent teeth are ready to come in. When he recovers, his teeth are stained and pitted, even if the attack was so mild that it was not even recognized as distemper. Stains, incidentally, can be caused by any other generalized infection.

If your dog loves stones and other hard objects, he may over a period of time wear down his teeth. The best of teeth are no match for metal piping, nails, rocks, and other such items. Or you may have a terrier whose instincts are true: He will tear at anything to get at his prey, including objects that wear down his teeth—things covered with sand, rocks, pieces of wire. By the way, when the enamel is worn away, then cavities are possible in the small rutted areas where the surface of the tooth is gone.

There really isn't much you can do about worn teeth. If you notice that your dog has the strange habit of using his teeth where pliers and hammer are usually called for, you might try to stop him. But unless you devote a lot of time to watching him, he will do what he likes best and let you do the worrying. In fact, worn teeth do not seem to bother him.

Broken teeth, however, are another matter. If your dog cracks a tooth in a fight or in play, or in trying to get into one thing or another, then he should have professional treatment. A cracked tooth can often be saved, but if that is impossible it must be extracted before it causes infection and great pain.

Tonsillitis

When a dog's tonsils bother him, he may run a fever, refuse to eat, or gag and vomit a great deal. The ailment may of course go beyond the tonsils themselves. An infection in the mouth may cause tonsillitis (inflammation of the tonsils), a condition which can be treated with antibiotics: only in rare cases is surgery indicated. The condition needs professional care.

Tumors of Mouth

Although I discuss tumors in a separate category in this chapter, I mention mouth tumors because you possibly can recognize them yourself. Others tumors develop internally and are beyond your powers of diagnosis.

The dog's mouth, like a person's, is subject to tumors. If you see any growth or if your dog has any difficulty in eating, have your veterinarian check his mouth. Since gum tumors become easily irritated, they should not be neglected. The condition is generally seen in the older dog and frequently in the Boxer.

There are several types of gum tumor that are troublesome but generally benign. They can be removed if they interfere with eating or start to bleed.

Worms

Before I describe the important types of worms, I will repeat some of the signs that indicate worms in your dog. Also see pages 270–273.
1. Weakness and listlessness
2. Diarrhea, with or without blood, or thin bowel movements
3. Bloated stomach
4. Dry and coarse coat
5. Vomiting, with or without the presence of worms
6. Loss of weight and dehydration
7. Sleepiness, loss of vitality
8. Frequent rubbing of body against the floor

ASCARID OR ROUNDWORM ("PUPPY WORM")
One of the most common worms in puppies and grown dogs is the roundworm or "puppy worm," also known as the ascarid, which develops in the intestinal wall. The roundworm is white and slim, about one to four inches in length. In most instances roundworms infect the puppy before he is born. When taken care of early, roundworms are relatively easy to get rid of if the infestation is slight.

ESOPHAGEAL WORMS
Esophageal worms (so called because they infest the dog's esophagus) are found only in the South and may cause a malignancy in the esophagus. The life cycle of the worm is unknown.

The infested dog will have difficulty in swallowing and may vomit frequently. You may, in fact, suspect rabies because of the dog's coughing, labored breathing, and difficulty in swallowing. The dog will also lose weight, look unhealthy, and become lethargic and depressed.

FLUKE DISEASE
Flukes are parasitic worms that harbor a type of viruslike organism that makes the dog severely ill. In those parts of the country where dogs are fed raw fish—salmon, tuna, trout—they may get fish poisoning or what is called "fluke disease."

The most common signs are similar to those of distemper: discharge from the eyes and nose, swelling around the face, diarrhea (often bloody), dehydration with great thirst, loss of appetite, severe loss of weight. The disease is very serious, and the best prevention is not to feed your dog raw fish. Boil it, remove the bones, and then it becomes a fine, nutritious food.

HOOKWORM

The hookworm is so called because of its mouth (buccal) hooks, which clamp onto the dog's intestinal wall. The worm is most dangerous, especially for puppies, because when it attaches itself it sucks blood. If it is not removed, it may seriously weaken your dog by causing severe anemia.

A dog with hookworms will become listless and exhausted, suffer from anemia, and may have blood-streaked stool. In some instances—especially when the affliction has gone unnoticed for a long time—the dog may need a blood transfusion. Since hookworms multiply rapidly and deplete the dog's blood, the anemia that results can be severe. A puppy can have hookworms before he is born. Your veterinarian may advise an injectible worm medicine to treat hookworms.

INTESTINAL PROTOZOANS (COCCIDIA)

In addition to the hookworm, you should be on the lookout for coccidiosis, one of the most common of intestinal parasitic infestations. It is particularly dangerous because it weakens the dog by lowering his resistance to other diseases.

The symptoms are chronic diarrhea (often with blood), rough, unkempt coat, listlessness, and general lassitude. When the attack is severe, the dog will seem to have a cold. He will cough, his eyes will water, and his nose will run. He may also have a slight fever, about 103°F. After treatment, to prevent reinfection keep your dog's living quarters absolutely sanitary.

TAPEWORM

Difficult to eliminate is the tapeworm, which infects both younger and older dogs. The tapeworm is hard to get rid of because the head, which is attached to the intestinal wall, must be removed. The worm itself may be several feet in length.

The dog shows his discomfort with diarrhea. If not treated, he may vomit, become listless, and rub his hindquarters insistently on the rug or floor as though suffering from a perpetual itch. The proglottids (small flat white or pink pieces of the tapeworm ¼" in length) might be found in the stool. When they dry around the anus, they look like kernels of rice. Since the head remains attached to the intestinal lining of the dog, the appearance of pieces in the stool does not mean that the parasite has been eliminated. Infestations of tapeworms often call for periodic treatment (under advice from a veterinarian), for the worms are hardy and resist complete removal.

Since fleas are the carriers of one variety of tapeworm, eliminate fleas through spraying.

WHIPWORM

A more serious parasite, although sometimes less persistent than the tapeworm, is the whipworm. As the name implies, whipworms are roundish and tapered. They settle in the dog's colon and cecum (a pouchlike extension of the intestinal tract), where they multiply and may cause chronic diarrhea, loss of blood, and severe nervous discomfort. When the infestation is heavy, they must be treated by a veterinarian.

In nearly all cases of worms, medication can eliminate the parasites. For general treatment of your dog while he is undergoing worming, see page 272.

EYE DISORDERS

Ordinarily your dog's eyes are as hardy as your own. Certain breeds, it is true, are more prone to eye injuries than others. The popeyed breeds— the Pekingese, Boston Bull, the Pug, and some Spaniels—have larger surfaces of their eyes exposed and therefore are more subject to injuries. Otherwise, you should expect little trouble from your dog's eyes. A few eye ailments, however, are hereditary: in particular, glaucoma, cataracts, progressive retinal atrophy ectropion, and entropion affect the eyelids.

One of the first signs that something is wrong with your dog's eye is a sudden discharge beyond the usual "washing." Along with this discharge, the dog will paw and scratch his eyes and shake his head. A clear discharge may mean a vitamin A deficiency and can easily be corrected with a vitamin-mineral supplement. Scratching and pawing, however, may indicate that there is a foreign body in the eye, or a scratch on the cornea, or trouble with the "third eyelid," which all dogs have, or a simple inflammation of the eyelids.

If any of these symptoms appear, contact your veterinarian at once. Do not try any home remedies beyond wiping away the discharge with a sterile piece of cotton soaked in an eye wash. Until you know what the trouble is, you don't know what to do. And by giving home treatment yourself, you will probably only postpone a visit to the veterinarian.

Country dogs in particular might pick up several nuisance eye ailments, especially if they are of the bulge-eyed breeds. The country dog roaming free may have his eyes scratched by branches and twigs, or whipped by tall grass. While the city dog is exposed to chemical fumes and dust in larger doses than his country cousin, the city dog has fewer opportunities for direct eye injuries.

Cataracts

Cataracts are a partial or complete opacity of the crystalline lens, that part of the eye which is just behind the pupil, giving it the appearance of a china-blue color. Cataracts usually occur in older dogs, although not exclusively. They can also be inherited or caused by an injury, which is more rare.

In some cases, the cataracts may be slow in developing, but the condition often means a gradual worsening of sight until the dog goes blind. Since blindness develops very slowly, the dog may live out most, and perhaps all, of his life with some sight. Sometimes surgery provides relief, but there is always the possibility that the dog's sight will not be improved.

Conjunctivitis

On the inner surface of the eyelids is a mucous membrane that keeps the eye moist. When that membrane becomes inflamed, the dog is suffering from conjunctivitis. Usually the condition is caused by a foreign body (dust, smoke, pollen) or by bacterial infection in the eyelid.

Conjunctivitis is characterized by tearing, inflammation, and sensitivity to light—any one of these or all three.

If the cause is a foreign object and you can remove it with a piece of sterile cotton, wash the eye out with warm water or an eye wash after you have done so. Sometimes an eye ointment is soothing, but it is best to consult a veterinarian before you put anything in your dog's eyes.

Removal of the foreign object should clear up the inflammation in a day or two. If the redness persists longer, the eye needs a veterinarian's attention. If you see no foreign object in the eye, do not probe around and do not try any home remedies.

A particular kind of conjunctivitis is follicular conjunctivitis, a chronic type that is difficult to clear up. It is characterized by follicles in the conjunctiva (the mucous membrane lining the inner surface) of the third eyelid that do not respond readily to treatment and that may require surgery.

Glaucoma

Glaucoma involves an increase in pressure inside the eye. When fluid cannot escape normally, the eyeball becomes enlarged, swollen, congested, and painful. There is an accompanying impairment of vision and eventually a loss of sight. The disease may be congenital, and although it often appears only after a dog enters middle age—that is, after age 5—it can occur at any time. It may be traumatic or infectious. If glaucoma develops in only one eye, its removal may save the other. But even here there is no guarantee. Sometimes the condition responds to treatment and removal is not necessary.

Progressive Retinal Atrophy

Progressive retinal atrophy is a hereditary eye disorder and leads to blindness. Your veterinarian can check your dog for this condition.

Harder's Gland (or, commonly, Cherry Eye)

In the inside corner of the eye, next to the nose, is a gland called Harder's Gland. When the third eyelid (the nictitating membrane) becomes enlarged, the gland becomes visible as a small red piece of flesh, the size of a cherry, in the corner. Also, the eye may discharge profusely. This is a condition for your veterinarian to diagnose since the symptoms are so close to several other eye ailments. Surgical removal is the treatment of choice.

Eyelid Abnormalities

Inverted eyelids, or entropion, is a curious condition that is usually congenital. The eyelid is actually inverted, creating constant irritation on the ball of the eye. If diagnosed early, it can be surgically corrected before any permanent damage is done. Small or pig-eyed dogs seem more prone to this condition. Everted eyelids, or ectropion, is the opposite condition from entropion—here the eyelid turns out. It can occur in any breed but is seen more frequently in short-nosed, bull-type breeds, and must be surgically corrected before the eye becomes too inflamed.

Eyelid Ailments

There are few specific lid ailments; most of them are connected to eye trouble. If there are pimples, warts, ingrown hairs, infected glands, or other irritants on the lid, the problem may involve the entire eye, which will reflect the condition. You should not attempt home treatments.

Keratitis (or Blue Eye)

This ailment is so called because the cornea (the transparent tissue that covers the iris and the pupil) turns a bluish-white. The blue color indicates an inflammation. The white of the eye may turn reddish or red at the same time. If the cornea is ulcerated, you may see a small hole in it. This is a condition that usually accompanies a serious illness like distemper or hepatitis or derives from an injury. Keratitis needs immediate treatment.

EAR DISORDERS

If you suspect ear trouble, the best thing to do is to leave the ear alone and call a veterinarian. While many dogs do suffer from ear ailments, many thousands more have their ears injured by overanxious owners who probe too far and damage the sensitive ear canal. If you must do something, remember not to put anything in the ear, certainly nothing sharp or pointed.

If the surface of the dog's ear appears dry, you might wipe it with baby oil or some mild ointment. Or if the surface seems too moist (a mild discharge), you might dust it with antiseptic powder after cleaning with an ear wash. But you should go no further, and if either condition persists, the treatment is a matter for your veterinarian. Incidentally, if you suspect that the ear is infected (see the symptoms below), do not use any medication or insecticides you may have around the house. They may irritate the ear and will only intensify the condition or create a worse one.

Some of the more obvious symptoms of ear ailments are puslike discharge, black caking around the canal just inside the ear, frequent shaking of the head and pawing at the ear, holding the head at a strange angle so that you think your dog has suddenly lost his wits, a strong, cheesy odor coming from the ear, or heavy waxy material and matted hair on the ear surface. The ear is often red and inflamed.

Probably no single condition will present all these symptoms, but if you see one or more, suspect trouble. Sometimes the cause may be no more than an insect bite, whose minor inflammation upsets your dog. Or it may be a minor ulceration, a small pimple, that will clear up by itself. Nevertheless, the dog acts as if he has nothing left to live for and worries the ear until he and you are frantic.

With all ear conditions, however, it is better to be overcareful rather than nonchalant. *Neglect of a relatively simple matter may lead to something more serious and possibly to eventual deafness.*

Certain breeds are more subject to ear ailments than others. Those with floppy or pendulous ears—chiefly hounds and sporting dogs (especially Setters and Spaniels)—are predisposed to ear infections, for there is little circulation of air into the ear. A scratch or laceration that would ordinarily heal might become worse because the ear flap prevents circulation.

Likewise, breeds with prick or straight ears—Boxers, French Bulldogs, Schnauzers, German Shepherds, for example—may be subject to ailments around the ear rim, while suffering only infrequently from internal infections. Other breeds with a great deal of hair inside the ear—terriers and especially Poodles—retain dirt and wax that cling to the hair and may cause infection.

Hematoma

A hematoma is a swelling that contains blood. Hematomas sometimes occur in the middle of the skin of the ear flap. They result from a sharp blow that ruptures blood vessels in the ear. The shaking and scratching that accompanies otitis, or an ear infection, can lead to hematomas. The swellings, which may greatly distend the ear, must be operated on by a veterinarian. Your dog will show you his extreme discomfort by shaking his head, crying, pawing, and scratching at his ear(s). Long-eared or floppy-eared dogs in particular are subject to hematomas.

Expect your dog to run away from you if you try to examine the flap. The spot is sometimes extremely sensitive to the touch. If you do get close, do not be surprised to find the ear very large and inflamed. If you neglect a hematoma or any growth on the ear, your dog may develop permanent ear trouble. Often such ears resemble the cauliflower ears of a prize fighter even after an operation.

If you can't see a veterinarian immediately, put a stocking over your dog's head so that his ears don't flap when he shakes his head. Do not cover his nose with the stocking. Half an aspirin and swabbing with baby or mineral oil may provide temporary relief.

Infection (Otorrhea or Otitis)

Infection or parasites can cause a condition known as otorrhea or otitis, a painful inflammation of the skin of the external ear canal. The infection may come from irritation by foreign material like water, bacteria, or fungi, or as a result of excessive probing. Your dog will scratch and paw at the ear, shake his head, become irritable, even lose his appetite. He will also resent your attempts to help him because his ear is sensitive and hot. The inflamed skin bleeds easily.

You may relieve the pain temporarily with half a baby aspirin. Soothe the area with sterile cotton soaked in mineral oil, baby oil, or ear wash. *Do not probe the inside of the ear.* See a veterinarian.

Occasionally, a dog will suffer from an inflammation of the middle ear, or what is called otitis media. It comes from an infection of the external ear passage or from infection in the nasal passages by way of the eustachian tube. The most common symptoms are pain, fever, ear discharge, circling, head tilting, and possible loss of balance. Immediate veterinary treatment is necessary.

Mites

Ear mites are parasites that settle in the ear and lead to chronic irritation. The symptoms are practically the same as for otitis. The dog will shake his head and scratch violently, as though he wants to rip off his ear. Sometimes he will scratch until the whole area bleeds. There is a waxy, dark secretion, as well as a sour, cheesy odor.

Mites may crawl out of the ear, and even if a veterinarian has seemingly flushed all of them out, a few might come back to set up housekeeping again. Also, there is the possibility that the dog through excessive shaking and scratching will cause hematomas in the ear flap (described above). Prompt attention to mites will clear up a problem that makes your dog uncomfortable. You can temporarily relieve his misery with half a baby aspirin and by swabbing the ear with baby oil. This, however, will not effect a permanent cure. The only cure is to keep the ears scrupulously clean.

Wax

You may see that something is obviously bothering your dog's ear, although his symptoms are no more than an occasional shaking of the head and some pawing. The condition may be as simple as too much wax in the ear because of infection or inflammation.

You may have read that you can remove wax by pouring in some mineral oil and then massaging the outside of the ear until the wax softens and falls out. You may well succeed in dislodging the wax. But you might also injure the ear canal by rubbing the hardened wax against the sensitive interior. You may also be trying to remove wax in the ear when that is not what's bothering your dog. All your massaging and manipulating will do little good and perhaps some harm.

It is much better to have a veterinarian take a look. If there is an accumulation of wax, or an infection, he can tell you precisely what to do. He will show you what to use and how to massage the ear and what to watch for in the event of a recurrence.

INTEGUMENTARY (SKIN) DISORDERS

Skin ailments in dogs—as you can see from the table of contents— are as extensive and varied as those in people. Dogs are allergic, they suffer from infectious ailments, they draw parasites like fleas and lice, they can get serious afflictions like tumors and as well suffer less serious conditions like dandruff. On occasion they can even become bald. Sometimes their skin ailments can be traced to a hormonal imbalance. Sometimes they develop an eczema or dermatitis that defies diagnosis and treatment.

The dog's skin is a sensitive, accurate indicator of his health. Usually when his skin is clear and well-toned, you can assume that your dog is at the peak of his condition. A well-groomed dog—one who is combed and brushed daily—stands the least chance of suffering from a skin ailment, although even such a dog of course is not immune. Nevertheless, if you care for your dog's coat daily, you give him protection against parasites and other skin ailments.

Each skin ailment produces somewhat different symptoms, but there are certain signs common to all. When you see these signs, do not attempt home treatment. Such ailments are extremely tricky and often require

laboratory tests to determine their exact nature. You may seriously aggravate a condition by treating incorrectly an ailment that needs very different
handling.

Nearly all skin ailments are accompanied by some of the following
symptoms. There will be severe itching—the dog will be scratching almost
constantly, until often parts of his coat are worn away. You will notice
pus-filled pimples, inflammation in one or several areas. The skin itself
will thicken and coarsen, in time flake or scale. Sometimes you see no
more than an angry-looking rash, with little scabs forming, or else an
extremely dry spot which the dog scratches and irritates. One or all of
these are danger signals, which you should heed.

Allergies

A dog may be allergic to an endless number of things. If an allergy
does appear in the form of a skin condition, it may usually be traced
to something in his home or neighborhood: possibly a new food, perhaps
an insect, dust, pollen, a particular plant or flower, certain chemicals in
the soil or paint, even his own bedding. Some dogs are allergic to vaccines,
serums, and milk products. Others are literally allergic to themselves—
to certain chemicals that their own bodies produce. There seems to be
a higher incidence of allergies in light-colored or white dogs—Maltese,
white Poodle, Sealyham—than in dark dogs.

An allergy may be apparent in the same way as any of the other
skin ailments, with inflammation, swelling or puffiness around the face,
itching, hives, pus-filled pimples, irritation, thickening of the skin, flaking
or scaling, perhaps loss of hair.

The treatment may take some time since the veterinarian has to discover the specific cause. Very often an allergy will look so much like
other skin ailments that identification is almost impossible.

Often, too, allergies will disappear with time. To soothe the irritated
area while the cause is being determined, wash it with mild soap and
warm water and apply lotions or oils recommended by your veterinarian.
An allergy to flea bites can be effectively relieved by a flea antigen, which
sharply reduces the itching.

BEE STINGS

Sometimes a dog will be allergic to a bee sting, which can lead to
difficulty in breathing. Along with the breathing difficulty, the dog will
possibly show the classic symptoms of allergy: swelling of lips and face,
puffiness around the eyes, general discomfort and restlessness. If your
dog reacts in this way, you should call a veterinarian immediately. If
you have antiallergy pills or liquid on hand, check with him first to
make sure they are all right for a dog.

COLLIE NOSE (NASAL SOLAR DERMATITIS)

Collie nose is a form of skin inflammation of the nose (caused by the sun) which the dog aggravates by pawing at his nose. The condition is localized in his nose and eyes, and the skin surface around them. It is a rather rare condition that strikes only a few breeds: Shetland Sheepdogs ("Shelties") and Collies, as well as mongrels containing Shetland and Collie blood. Other light-skinned dogs have similar trouble.

You can recognize this type of eczema from the lesions or pustules (pus-filled pimples) that form in the area, as well as from the inflammation of the eyes and from scabs or scales on the nose bridge. There will probably also be a loss of hair in the region and even some bleeding. The very first step is to keep the dog out of the sun until the condition heals.

As with all types of eczema, there isn't much you can do yourself except relieve the dog's discomfort with applications of calamine lotion or mineral oil on the nose and skin surface, and a mild eye wash for the inflamed eyes. The actual treatment must be left to your veterinarian, who should be consulted as soon as you recognize the condition. When the skin is white after an attack, the dog may be tattooed to restore the color.

FLEA DERMATITIS

When a dog is infested with fleas, his furious scratching will wear away the hair in several places and eventually damage the skin. The result is often a case of chronic flea dermatitis.

You probably won't be able to diagnose this condition, although you will notice the severe itchiness as well as the damaged coat. The condition calls for professional treatment, which may involve dusting with powder or internal medication. Sometimes a powder or spray is recommended. See the section on fleas earlier in this chapter (page 267) for the details of treatment.

URTICARIA (OR HIVES)

Hives are large, inflamed areas on the dog's skin, like gigantic puffed-up pimples. They indicate an allergic reaction on the dog's part. You can relieve some of the itchiness caused by the hives by applying cold packs. But if they persist, you can correct them only by treating the allergy itself with antihistamines and by removing the cause.

Infectious Ailments

Infectious skin ailments in a dog are somewhat common, although some—like ringworm and chin infection—are more frequently seen than acne and impetigo. Like most skin disorders, the infectious type is characterized by pustules, inflammation, itchiness, and irregularities in the dog's coat. All these conditions—acne, pimples, chin infection, and impetigo— are basically the same.

ACNE (PIMPLES)

Acne results from an inflammation of the skin glands. Dirt may get into the pores and the bacteria will multiply, causing the red, pus-filled eruptions. It is not very serious in dogs, and nearly any recommended lotion should clear up the condition. If the eruptions occur where the dog wears his harness or collar, it may be that they are rubbing dirt into the skin and creating the problem.

CHIN INFECTION

In several different ways a dog can irritate the skin on his chin. When the irritation opens the surface of the skin and bacteria enter, an infection may result. The short-nosed breeds are particularly subject to this condition as they sniff with their chins close to the ground. Other dogs may suffer from the same condition from dribbling their food and drink, which dries, hardens, cracks the skin, and leaves it open to infection.

The infection is usually minor, and daily washing with a mild disinfectant soap and warm water will usually heal it quickly. If the infection persists and pus is present, a veterinarian should examine the dog.

IMPETIGO

Impetigo is not frequent in dogs—it is much more common in children. But it does occur in puppies, on their bellies, and you may recognize it by the isolated pustules or pus-filled pimples that characterize the ailment. Impetigo is not a long-term condition. Usually, the pustules break open easily and lend themselves to rapid cure. Your veterinarian will recommend an antiseptic powder or lotion to clear this trouble. Keep the dog clean and dry.

RINGWORM

At first you may confuse ringworm with one of the mange parasites (described below), but there are differences. Ringworm is more or less localized and is so called because the infected area is in the shape of a small ring or circle, perhaps the size of a dime at the beginning, growing larger and larger as the infection spreads. The ringworm lesion, however, may not be precisely a circle; it may be oval, although the general shape is roundish. Incidentally, there is no worm involved in ringworm. It is a fungus.

Your veterinarian has a piece of equipment called a Wood's light, which gives some lesions a greenish coloration under its glow and can identify a fungus. It can also be identified by growing the fungus in a culture in the laboratory.

Ringworm usually attacks the outer layer of the dog's skin. There it settles into the follicles or hair sacs. At first the hair may not fall out—which may distinguish ringworm from mange parasites. Instead, the hair in the infected area becomes dry and coarse; the skin underneath is also dry and scaly, like a person's scalp when he suffers from severe dandruff. Eventually the hair will fall out when the infection is neglected, but even then the affected area is left with small stubbles, like tree trunks in a cleared forest.

Before the hair falls out, the infected area usually looks like a slightly raised platform of scaly matter. It may also take the form of small, bloody pimples on the less hairy parts of the dog's body, like the abdomen. However, look for ringworm on any part of his body. When the hair falls out, by the way, that particular spot will probably not give further trouble. But then the infection spreads to another nearby area, with the same results.

If you suspect ringworm or fungus, be particularly careful because you and your children may get it. When you treat the dog, be sure to use rubber gloves, which should then be sterilized in alcohol or in hot water and soap. The best method of care, once your veterinarian has determined the condition, is first to clip the hair in the afflicted area for spot treatment. (The whole body may have to be so treated.) Then wash the lesions of the "ring" with mild soap and water in order to soften and loosen the scabs. The next step is to apply a fungicidal ointment or another recommended solution to the lesions and let them dry. If the dog tries to lick the treated areas, you might have to put an Elizabethan collar on him (see Chapter 7). Accompanying this treatment will be oral medication prescribed by your veterinarian. Both are necessary to gain a quick and complete recovery. Remember: Do not touch your face with your rubber gloves, and keep your children away from the dog and from any of the material you used to treat the dog.

Parasites

External parasites are one of the most common causes of skin disorders in your dog. Fleas, lice, mites, and ticks can create ailments that are difficult to treat and cure once the infestation becomes generalized. The chief sign of an infestation is scratching, persistent and furious. There may also be inflammation, lesions, and bald spots. All such parasitic conditions need professional treatment.

FLEAS

The chief characteristic of the flea is that it jumps around. In this respect it differs from the other external parasites, which burrow into a particular place and remain there until they are dislodged. If you have ever picked up even a single flea while traveling in a strange place, or even in your own home, you know how annoying those little bites prove to be. Imagine several fleas moving on your dog's skin and nipping him insistently. No wonder he scratches so angrily. And a few fleas may soon become dozens. Fleas also may carry the eggs that give your dog tapeworm—so that complications are added to mere discomfort.

There are four basic kinds of flea: the human flea, cat flea, dog flea, and sticktight flea. They will all hang on to any warm animal or person, with the sticktight variety finding the ears and their rims a most congenial part. But expect to find fleas in nearly any part of the dog's body, although they do prefer the hairiest places: the neck, head, tail area, and chest.

Flea eggs are incubated in heat and dampness, and they hatch during the summer. The life cycle of the flea is about thirty days, and the best way to treat your dog is to do two things: break up the cycle and get rid of those fleas that have already hatched.

Once a veterinarian has seen your dog and diagnosed fleas, there are several ways of dealing with them: medicated baths, a powder, or a flea collar (the recommended treatment). If your veterinarian recommends dusting, make sure that you work the powder into the skin. If it simply lies on the surface of the coat, it won't do much good. Avoid getting any in his eyes. And if you do use a powder without consulting a veterinarian first, be sure that the powder is safe for dogs. Remember that dogs will lick the powder, and if it is toxic they will absorb poison into the digestive system.

You may also dip or spray the dog. Once again, if you spray make sure you use one that is nontoxic, and be sure to protect your dog's eyes from the spray. If you use a dip, follow the same precautions. Let the solution dry. If you rub the dog dry right away, you eliminate the flea-killing power of the dip. Keep the dog in a warm, draft-free area until his coat is dry.

If you use a flea collar, be sure you read the label. Your dog may be allergic to it. Whichever method you use, you will have to comb out the dead fleas. Have the dog stand on some newspaper and then comb carefully. The dead fleas will fall out. When you think you have them all, wrap up the newspaper and burn it. You may have to repeat this treatment several times if the dog is seriously infested.

You must also disinfect all the spots where your dog might have caught fleas. If he sleeps in a kennel, spray this area, or wash it down with the same chemical compound you used on the dog. You should use the chemical in a stronger solution on the kennel. If your dog sleeps indoors, disinfect his sleeping quarters, his blankets and sheets (or whatever he uses), even the furniture. Everything that might harbor the fleas—rugs, couches, chairs, all crevices and corners—must be sprayed, and sprayed often, or else the fleas will continue hatching. Like roaches, they are difficult to eliminate once they have moved in.

It might be a good idea to spray your dog's living quarters even if you don't suspect fleas. A few minutes of prevention will serve you well. A fleabitten dog was once a source of amusement, but only to those who didn't know the misery that he suffered.

LICE

Unlike the flea, the louse burrows into one place and remains there sucking and biting until you flush him out. Since the louse is so small— smaller than a pinhead—your chances of seeing him are small. But your dog feels the louse in his skin and sometimes scratches violently trying to dislodge him. Gradually his scratching may abrade the skin, but the louse simply burrows more deeply, right into the hair follicles. When this occurs, the hair will be worn away in the infested area.

A large infestation of lice is dangerous for a puppy, for lice suck blood and can possibly cause anemia. The louse, if allowed, will live out his entire life cycle on your dog, with the female producing large numbers of eggs. Those eggs will then hatch in about a week and become adult lice in three weeks—a fantastic rate of multiplication.

A nursing bitch should be watched carefully for this and other parasites. If she has lice, her puppies too will become infested. While she may be able to cope with armies (although the infestation may weaken her), the puppies are in no condition to do so.

Frequently, you will not be able to discover the cause of the persistent scratching and biting. But your veterinarian can recognize the parasite and clear up the condition. One method is the use of an insecticide dip.

MITES AND MANGES

Mites cause two different kinds of mange: demodectic, from a cigar-shaped parasite, also called follicular; and sarcoptic, from a spider-shaped parasite with eight legs. (Another kind of mite may cause otitis, an ear inflammation which is described under Ear Disorders in this chapter, page 294.)

Both of these manges are serious skin diseases that go further than mere discomfort for your dog. They can lead to complications. Demodectic mange spreads rapidly and may cause infections all over your dog's body. Sarcoptic mange can lead to bloody lesions and scabs. (Otitis or otodectic mange may lead to permanent ear damage if not treated.)

DEMODECTIC OR FOLLICULAR MANGE

Demodectic mange can develop with either of two types of lesions. The first type, called squamous, is relatively mild, showing in most cases little more than loss of hair and some reddening of the affected skin area, or some general inflammation. The second type, called pustular, is more serious, for the pustules or bloody pimples may become infected. The irritation to the dog's skin can be severe.

The mite that causes demodectic mange burrows its way into the dog's skin, into the small sac containing the root of the hair, until the hair falls out. This sac is called the follicle, thus the name follicular mange for this particular kind.

The condition is not always easily recognizable. Often it does not even cause a great deal of itching or irritation, especially in its developmental stages. The only signs might be small, dime-sized lesions, with the loss of some hair around the lesion, or simply a bald spot.

The treatment for the lesions can be quite extensive and there is no guarantee of a cure. Your veterinarian will recommend a good lotion that you can rub into the affected spot. (He may also recommend injections and internal medication.) Rub it in well with your fingers, and cover the area surrounding the lesions, as those spots too may be affected. Keep in mind that squamous or pustular lesions are bacterial infections that accompany the mange.

A more progressive and widespread case of mange means a more extensive treatment. Usually the dog's hair is clipped short, and he is bathed in a medicated solution. Frequently this treatment must be repeated, for the mange may recur. Injections of antibiotics may also be used to help cure the mange when the skin becomes infected. Incidentally, if you do use a bath or spray, make sure the dog's eyes are protected. A few drops of mineral oil or an application of a mild eye wash in each eye serves this purpose.

You might find that your dog's condition is getting worse in the first stages of treatment. Hair may fall out, and the chances of baldness are ever present. If you begin treatment soon enough, the infected areas may soon grow the same fine coat that your dog always had, unless the mange becomes generalized. But if you postpone treatment, there is the possibility of permanent bladness in the spots where the lesions formed. Even when you catch it early, as soon as you see a rash, or itching, or the lesions themselves, a cure is often difficult and lengthy.

Demodectic mange is sometimes referred to as the red mange because of the red and inflamed lesions.

SARCOPTIC MANGE

Sarcoptic mange is sometimes easier to recognize than demodectic mange, for the dog is made more miserable by the mite that causes it and will scratch himself more violently. Fortunately, if you can spot it early, you can prevent your dog from becoming seriously ill and halt its possible spread among the members of your family and other dogs. This condition is highly contagious to people and to dogs.

An infestation of the spiderlike sarcoptic mites produces a series of scabs; thus it is called scabies. The condition is marked by severe itchiness, reddening of the affected area, and bloody lesions that form scabs. The skin itself thickens and coarsens, with a consistency of something like wrinkled leather. The dog's coat will shed, with whole areas becoming bare as the mange spreads. Sarcoptic mange spreads very rapidly, another reason for checking it in its early stages. The dog may come to smell like dirty feet or strong cheese. The definitive diagnosis, as for demodectic mange, can be made only by skin scraping and microscopic examination.

The treatment is much the same as for demodectic mange: clipping of the long hair, a medicated bath or spray, oral medication, or injections when recommended by your veterinarian. Keep in mind that open sores may become infected. The scabby areas should be washed with a disinfectant soap to prevent a secondary infection. As with all skin conditions, the best thing is quick recognition, followed by professional treatment.

You may have to continue the treatment for a while, with your veterinarian's advice, but your dog will probably return to perfect health.

TICKS

The tick is an annoying parasite because of its hardiness and endurance. Once it becomes embedded in the dog's skin, it hangs on tenaciously. The most common tick is called the American dog tick or the brown dog tick, and a severe infestation can cause anemia in your dog. It looks something like a small wart or a flat, blackish-brown seed, and in some stages becomes a dark red. Ticks look for crevices and corners in which to live, and these crevices may be in your dog or in parts of your house or yard. Their favorite spots on the dog are the stomach area, the pads of the feet, the feet, and the folds between the legs and the body. Some varieties make their home in the dog's ear.

The general treatment is to dip the dog in a medicated compound, one of those recommended for fleas and lice, and also give him oral medication. Or else you might try a tick collar. Do not, however, take any action without consulting a veterinarian.

When the infestation is small, some owners may try to remove the ticks themselves. There is a definite way of doing it to protect both your dog and yourself. If you reach into the dog's coat to pry off the ticks, you may break off the head from the body, or vice versa, causing a skin infection. Or else, you may have an opening in your own skin, and the tick may possibly be carrying a serious disease (Rocky Mountain spotted fever is a possibility).

First, wash the infected area with alcohol. The tick does not like to move, and it takes a strong liquid to loosen it. When you've loosened it somewhat, place the tweezers squarely over it and lift it off. Be careful not to pull off any part of the tick's body. It is best to place one leg of the tweezers under the tick's body, so that it is separated from the dog's skin by the width of the tweezer. Place the tick directly in the toilet and flush. Don't think it's dead simply because it appears dazed. Like other parasites, ticks have marvelous recuperative powers.

Tick control is the best way of dealing with the entire problem. Control of the tick will also probably result in control of other major parasites. Clean out the kennel, the area around the dog's run, and his sleeping accommodations. Spray the entire area—particularly grass and bushes—with a solution recommended by a veterinarian. Once you have done this, you reduce the chance of infestation and provide excellent protection for your pet and your family.

Traumas

Traumas are wounds, injuries, or breaks in the skin. They can result from accidents or simply be part of the daily life of the dog.

ABRASIONS
For abrasions, see Chapter 7, on first aid.

CAPPED ELBOW (OR HARD ELBOW)
Unless your dog lies on rugs and mattresses, he will probably develop calluses on his elbows from resting on a hard surface of wood or stone. Large, heavy breeds tend to develop calluses more readily than small ones. This thickening of the skin is normal and is nature's way of protecting the area from constant irritation. Occasionally, however, the hardening may make your dog uncomfortable. Should this happen, rub some mineral oil into the elbows to make them softer and more malleable. You might also give your dog something soft to lie on. If the thickening is severe, and fluid accumulates, surgery may be necessary to relieve the condition.

CUTS
For cuts, see Chapter 7, on first aid.

Tumors

Tumors in general are covered later in this chapter (page 330). A tumor—whether on the skin or elsewhere—is by definition an uncontrolled growth of tissue. Very often you will feel these growths or tumors right under the surface of the dog's skin. They seem like small, pliant, doughy balls which under pressure shift in the fingers. Whenever you feel one, call it to the attention of your veterinarian even though it may prove to be nothing serious. Any lump or growth is *potentially* serious, and if it grows, however slowly, then surely it should not be neglected.

BENIGN
If the tumor or growth does not spread or recur after removal, we call it nonmalignant or benign.

When a growth or tumor spreads or if it recurs, it is said to be malignant or cancerous.

Other Skin Problems

BALDNESS (ALOPECIA)

Dogs generally are not subject to baldness unless some internal or external parasite or disease has affected the skin and coat. A dog's coat on occasion will nevertheless become thin in several places without any apparent reason. The bald spots may be small, localized areas, or they may appear on whole sections of the body: the ears, hind legs, head.

Unless there is a specific cause—digestive trouble, diabetes, friction, internal or external parasites, contact with acids and other chemicals, dietary or hormonal imbalances—the condition may have been inherited. Certain short-coated breeds suffer from such baldness. There is nothing you can do in these cases. Sometimes, without treatment, the hair grows back, and the dog regains his healthy, smart look.

CHEMICAL BURNS

For chemical burns, see Chapter 7, on first aid.

DANDRUFF

When a dog's skin flakes, we say that he has dandruff or dry skin. It may be a perfectly normal thing—for when the skin replenishes itself the old skin flakes away. When you see dandruff on the dog's coat, give him a good brushing. In time, the dandruff should stop accumulating. In many dogs, it is merely a seasonal event.

If dandruff persists, then there is some reason beyond the natural shedding of skin. The cause may be dietary—is the dog receiving enough fat? Without sufficient fat, the coat will dry and peel. Or perhaps you have been washing him with a strong soap, which has irritated his skin and made it flake. Lack of sufficient exercise or sleeping in a warm house may also dry his skin.

If the dog scratches persistently at his skin and makes it flake, there is the possibility of parasites. If the dandruff persists, a veterinarian should examine your dog, as he would for any skin disease. Only he can tell if the cause is dietary, parasitical, or seasonal.

LICK DERMATITIS

Some dogs lick their skin so much that they create a serious inflammation that is difficult to cure.

NONSPECIFIC DERMATITIS (ECZEMA)

Eczema, or nonspecific dermatitis, is a catchall name for skin conditions or irritations that cannot be clearly defined. By general agreement, the word "eczema" is best used to mean an ailment in which the skin shows either wet or dry patches: what we call moist and dry eczema. The causes of eczema have not been fully determined, and therefore the term itself is arbitrary.

Moist eczema is a skin condition in which moisture is discharged. The afflicted area then becomes scaly and pimply. The dog scratches the spot and irritates it still further. Although it looks angry and painful, surprisingly, it is sometimes easier to clear up than the dry kind.

Dry eczema is a skin condition in which moisture disappears from a given area, causing an itchy spot that the dog scratches and irritates. It may spread rapidly, with the result that the hair falls out. In long-haired breeds it may spread invisibly for a long time. Both types of eczema seem to annoy terriers and toys more than other breeds, but that is not always the case. Moist and dry eczema may occur in all breeds and in mongrels, and both types appear to be more prevalent in damp, warm weather than at any other time of the year.

Eczema attacks your dog suddenly. One day his skin is normal and the next he is scratching away at an ugly red moist patch. While medicated powder or calamine lotion may soothe him temporarily by relieving the itching, he must be treated by a veterinarian. The treatment may take some time, for eczema frequently disappears only to reappear shortly afterward. It is easy to confuse eczema with other skin ailments, and even after the condition has been determined, it is still very hard to diagnose the precise cause.

Researchers have suggested several possible causes of eczema. Dietary deficiencies are one of the more obvious possibilities, particularly deficiencies of vitamin A and fats. Other theories claim damp and heat as a possible cause, while some believe a hormone imbalance or even an infestation of parasites to be the cause. When parasites are a definite cause, the condition is called parasitic dermatitis. Still others claim that an organic breakdown—say in the kidneys or the digestive system—may be the fault. A further possibility is an allergy, but little is really known on this subject. The allergy may be to a food, a particular soap, the dog's bedding, or the coat he wears. Such is the range of possibilities.

As you can see, eczema is a baffling condition. When a veterinarian says that your dog has an eczema, he really means that there is no other skin ailment present and the cause is unknown. He will try to cure your dog through internal and external treatment, but the condition may hang on for a long time. External lotions and medication might soothe the dog, but until the internal factors are diagnosed there can be no permanent cure.

While eczema is not transferable from a dog to a person, once the treatment begins your dog may possibly be covered with messy lotions and creams. If this is the case, you will want to keep him away from your best furniture and rugs. Don't isolate him—he doesn't know he is a menace to furniture—but try to keep him in a place where his coat cannot damage anything. If your dog persists in scratching his sores or licking away the medication, you may have to put an Elizabethan collar on him. (See Chapter 7 for a description.)

Dry eczema is never helped by frequent baths. Frequent bathing, in fact, will make a dog's coat more dry, and this may actually intensify the eczema. Regular combing and brushing will help keep his coat soft and "thrifty," but even such care cannot prevent eczema if there is an organic reason for it.

One further warning: Avoid bathing a dog with *any* skin disease, but if you must bathe him, do it with medicated baths as recommended by a veterinarian.

HORMONAL IMBALANCES

Sometimes a skin disorder can be traced to a lack of hormonal balance in your dog, especially when the ailment resists all other treatment. In such a case, your veterinarian may recommend injections of hormones in an attempt to clear up the condition. Or else he may recommend castration (of the male) or spaying (of the bitch).

NEUROTROPHIC DERMATITIS

Neurotrophic dermatitis is an inflammation of the nerve endings which causes extreme sensitivity and pain.

POISON IVY

Generally even a short-coated dog will not be affected by poison ivy. If he runs through poison ivy, the oil will usually rub off on his coat. Occasionally the oil may make contact with the skin of a short-coated dog, or a dog who has been groomed so that certain places are bald, but this is rare indeed. Of course you can catch it from him if the irritating oil remains on his coat and rubs off on you. If your dog does wander through posion ivy, give him a good bath with mild soap and warm water, and always use gloves when washing him.

MUSCULO-SKELETAL DISORDERS
(Muscles, Bones, and Joints)

Unless your dog suffers a serious injury or is born with a congenital defect, you should not expect any serious trouble with his muscles, bones, or joints until he passes middle age, at 5 or 6. There are of course many minor ailments like infections, abscesses, irritations, and sprains that you might expect if you have a very active breed. Accidents or infections may cause inflammation and loss of movement. But the dog's musculoskeletal system is hardy until it becomes subject to the degenerative processes of old age. See also Chapter 10, on old age.

Degenerative (Aging)

ANKYLOSIS

On rare occasions, a dog will suffer the loss of movement in a joint because of infection, accident, inflammation, or excessive connective tissue. Ankylosis, or stiff joint, the name given to the ailment, calls for professional care.

ARTHRITIS

Inflammation of the bone at a joint is called arthritis. Older dogs suffer from arthritis much more than do younger ones, although it may afflict dogs of any age. With arthritis, the dog feels pain on walking and jumping. Often there is swelling around the joint, and the dog's discomfort is more severe in damp weather.

The condition must be treated by a veterinarian. Home treatment consists of half an aspirin as a pain killer (repeated as needed) and warm packs on the sore joint. Restrict the dog's activity and keep him in a warm, dry room away from drafts.

BURSITIS

Inflammation of the capsule (the bursa) that the joint moves in is called bursitis. The treatment and home care are the same as for rheumatism and arthritis.

RHEUMATISM

Rheumatism is a constitutional disease that causes pain in the joints and muscles. This should not be confused with rheumatoid arthritis, a systemic disease involving the joints that is still poorly understood. The symptoms of rheumatism are very often similar to those of arthritis. The dog will experience pain on walking and jumping, and extreme discomfort in wet weather. The most prevalent types are inflammatory or acute articular rheumatism and muscular rheumatism, which is accompanied by muscular pain. In the rare case of pulmonary rheumatism, the dog's breathing may be affected.

Rheumatism must be diagnosed by a veterinarian. Home care consists of half an aspirin to relieve pain (repeated as needed) and heat pads on the afflicted area. Keep your dog in a warm, dry, draft-free room.

Developmental: Congenital Hip Dysplasia

Congenital hip dysplasia is a malformation of the ball and socket of the hip joint, existing at birth or before. The defect may vary from a bad fit to an outright dislocation of the hip. Saint Bernards and German

Shepherds seem to suffer from this condition more than any other breeds, but I have often seen it in other medium- and large-sized dogs (those over 30 to 40 pounds), and even smaller dogs.

I would say as a general rule you can recognize hip dysplasia when the dog is 5 to 6 months old, although the only sure way to know is to have a veterinarian x-ray the hip. Dogs with the disease are usually lame, unwilling to get up, and unable to stand straight when they do. When sitting, they often stretch their hind legs to the side. The defect varies from mild to severe and may cause great pain.

Dogs with hip dysplasia should be exercised only moderately and their weight kept down to a minimum. Also, they should not be bred because this is a genetically determined disease.

Infections
BONE

A bone infection (called osteomyelitis) is usually caused by the formation or secretion of pus. A dog may develop osteomyelitis from an infected bone fracture, from bone surgery, or from bites from other animals. Severe dental disease can also lead to osteomyelitis of the jaw.

Dogs with osteomyelitis usually have fever, pain, and swelling in the afflicted area, and they avoid moving the infected limb. Treatment should begin immediately if the dog's limb is to be saved.

JOINT

Bacteria lodging in a joint as a result of an injury may cause an infection. The enclosed area will generally swell, and the joint naturally becomes extremely painful. The symptoms will be the usual ones for an infection: pain (the dog may favor the area, particularly if it involves a leg), swelling or inflammation, redness (wherever you can see through the coat), and heat. If the infection is neglected, your dog may run a high temperature, lose his appetite, and become listless. Until you see a veterinarian, restrict your dog's activity and relieve his pain with half an aspirin (repeated as needed) and wet compresses or pads on the sore area.

MUSCLE ABSCESSES

A muscle abscess is a formation of pus in the muscle tissue as a result of an injury. It is caused by bacteria and often leads to the destruction of the tissue. The muscle itself is usually inflamed, swollen, and very painful; the dog will probably avoid using it. He may also run a fever.

You will have trouble recognizing this ailment as its symptoms are similar to those of many other musculo-skeletal conditions. If you notice any of the above signs, see your veterinarian at once. Muscle trouble—

even a bruise—needs immediate attention. If neglected, the unused muscle may cause a chronic lameness.

If your dog has a screw or twisted tail—as do some of the Boston Terriers, the Pug, the English and French Bulls—he may sometimes suffer from infection or sores under the tail. The tail might interfere with bowel movements in some dogs and the skin will become irritated. To relieve the irritation and prevent any possible infection, you should apply a mild antiseptic and medicated powder daily.

Nutritional: Rickets

Rickets is a bone disorder affecting both dogs and people, although rare in dogs. It is caused by a substandard diet, especially by a lack of vitamin D and calcium and phosphorus in the puppy's diet. It may also result despite the correct diet because the dog is unable to assimilate those foods that prevent rickets, although this is quite rare.

Rickets is characterized by irregular development of the bones, particularly the bones in the legs. A dog with rickets often has enlarged joints in his legs and walks on his wrists and ankles, like a cow: hind legs high, front legs low. When the nutritional disturbance is severe, other parts of the body are also affected: the head and jaw may bulge strangely, giving the dog an idiotic appearance. In addition, he will look unhealthy. His coat will lack gloss or sheen, and his eyes will be dull and bulged.

If caught early, rickets may be treated successfully with a balanced diet of mineral supplement, vitamins A and D, and meat, eggs, and milk. If the treatment comes too late, however, the dog's bones may remain soft and break easily.

Many owners will acquire a puppy with rickets and not know it until the dog is grown. In such cases, the dog must be protected against roughhousing. If his bones have been weakened by rickets, they will break with normal stress. Since the dog will not know this himself—he will always be ready for hard exercise—it is up to you to protect him.

Traumas
DISLOCATIONS

A dislocation is a displacement of one or more of the bones making up a joint, and it may occur at the hip, the knee, the toes, or the jaw, or any other place in which a joint is involved. For details of symptoms and treatment, see Chapter 7, on first aid.

FRACTURES

A bone fracture is a broken bone. For the different kinds of fractures, their symptoms, and their treatment, see Chapter 7, on first aid.

Hernias may be of several kinds, but all are characterized by soft swellings that appear in the general abdominal area. The hernia is itself a protrusion or bubble of tissue or organs working through a natural opening in the abdominal wall, the navel, or the diaphragm (the partition between the chest and abdomen). In an accident, a traumatic hernia may develop. Needless to say, all hernias need immediate professional treatment.

I will describe the different kinds of hernias so that you can be on the alert for any swellings that appear. The umbilical hernia is the most common in puppies and is generally hereditary. It is characterized by a lump or swelling that comes through the abdominal wall at the navel, where the umbilical cord was once attached. The lump may be a single small bubble or it may be extensive (several inches). The larger one usually requires surgery.

Car accidents may cause diaphragmatic hernia, a break in the wall between the chest and abdominal cavity. When this happens, the abdominal organs work their way through the tear in the diaphragm, exerting pressure on the heart and lungs and seriously interfering with breathing. There is no treatment except surgery, which should be performed as soon as the diagnosis is confirmed by x-ray.

The bitch and sometimes the male may suffer from inguinal hernia, the result of a tear from a structural defect that allows the intestines and often the bladder and uterus to pass into the inguinal region, sometimes called the groin.

While inguinal hernia occurs more frequently in the bitch, the perineal hernia is more prevalent in the older male. A tumor, an enlarged prostate gland, but most often chronic constipation may cause your dog to strain when at stool. Whatever the cause, the strain may create a tear in the rectal muscles in the pelvic region through which intestinal organs can pass. There is usually a large swelling around or on either side of the tail. By the time this happens your dog has the hernia. If you notice any excessive straining, or if you see your dog trying to move his bowels an excessive number of times, you should have him examined. He may have a perineal hernia.

A sprain occurs around a joint when, as a result of a sudden twist or wrench, the ligaments are stretched or torn. For details of the symptoms and treatment, see Chapter 7, on first aid.

Cancer

Bone cancer is rare, and almost always inoperable. Generally, if possible, the diseased bone is amputated. Many of these malignancies spread throughout the body if unchecked, carried by the blood, a process called metastasis. An abnormal swelling or an unexplained lameness may indicate this condition. The diagnosis is made by x-ray or biopsy.

In general, the overall incidence of cancer in the dog is approximately one-third greater than the incidence of cancer in humans. Dogs develop many different types of tumors, and some occur more frequently than others. Skin and skin-related tumors are the most common, but tumors of the mammary gland (breast cancer) are the single most common type of canine cancer. In contrast, the least common tumors are those of the lung and colon.

Canine tumors are similar in many ways to human tumors, which are thought to be caused by a combination of factors such as viruses, radiation, chemical carcinogens, genetic predisposition, hormones, nutrition, and the immunological status. Dogs with tumors can be treated with drugs, radiation, surgery, and by stimulating the natural defense (immunity) system of the body to attack the tumor cells. As with human cancer, the response of canine tumors to therapy varies, depending primarily on the tumor type and on the extent of the disease. Some tumors can be cured with therapy, while in others treatment does not result in cure and the best that can usually be achieved is an improvement in the quality and length of life.

The development and treatment of naturally occurring tumors in the dog are of interest to both veterinarians and cancer researchers, since dogs live in the same environment and are subject to the same tumor-causing agents as humans.

NERVOUS DISORDERS

The nervous system of the dog, like that of man, centers in the brain and spinal cord. From these central areas, like branches on a tree trunk, runs the complex network of the nervous system. The brain, of course, is the central repository of all motivation. What the brain commands, the rest of the body does. If the brain is troubled in any way, the entire body responds accordingly. Brain damage or inflammation (encephalitis) can throw the dog's entire nervous system off balance.

Certain diseases, like distemper and rabies, directly attack the dog's nervous system. Since the system is so delicate, prevention of such diseases is the only way to insure a healthy dog. Rabies leaves no survivors, and distemper may well leave a crippled dog. There are also diseases of lesser intensity that attack the nervous system only temporarily, such as eclampsia, the result of an imbalance of calcium and other minerals in the bitch's system during pregnancy or nursing. Poison may also attack the nervous system.

What are the signs that the nervous system has been affected? The clearest indications are excessive shaking, barking, fits, convulsions, paralysis. While many of these conditions are frightening, some may clear up, provided they are treated in time.

A new specialization in veterinary medicine concerns itself with nerves and nervous disorders. Such doctors are called canine neurologists.

Chorea

Sometimes as a result of distemper, your dog may suffer from chorea, a spasmodic twitching of his muscles, also called St. Vitus's dance. The area affected might be the jaw, a leg, the neck, or the whole body. If the chorea is limited to one area, your dog can live but with a twitch in that area.

Convulsions and Fits

A number of things can bring on convulsions and fits: disease, sunstroke, accidents, poisons, nervous ailments, inadequate diet, overexcitement, parasites, worms, high fevers. A fit is characterized by foaming or frothing at the mouth, champing of the jaws, as though the dog were chewing gum and salivating, thrashing of the feet for no purpose, stiffening of the muscles so that the body quivers and shakes, and even unconsciousness.

A fit is frightening to watch, but the important thing is not to panic. *The dog generally is not dangerous.* Nevertheless, you may be afraid that your dog has rabies, even though rabies is relatively rare. All dogs who have had a fit should be examined by a veterinarian.

The fit itself is not generally the disease or ailment, and there is little you can do except to make sure that the dog does not injure himself. Take precautions that there are no objects around which can hurt him, but otherwise leave him alone while he is in the fit. He may accidentally bite you. When the fit subsides, you should try to make the dog as comfortable as possible—give him a blanket to keep him warm and some fresh water. Do not give him any heavy food directly after a fit.

A fit may simply be from nervousness. On the other hand, it generally points to something more serious that needs professional care. A heavy infestation of worms, for instance, may lead to fits if not treated. Often you won't recognize the real ailment until your dog has the convulsion. And even then a veterinarian might have difficulty diagnosing the condition.

Encephalitis

Encephalitis is an inflammation of the brain that accompanies some of the more severe canine diseases: distemper and other viruses. When the virus reaches the brain, the result is inflammation. The dog may lie down and pedal with his feet, as though bicycling. The other signs are also obvious: convulsions, possibly with frothing; twitching of muscles; partial or complete loss of vision; rapidly fluctuating temperature, from very high to near normal; confusion for the dog as to where he is; partial (sometimes complete) paralysis; possibly excessive urinating and defecating.

By the time encephalitis has developed, your dog is already under professional care for the primary disease. The mortality rate is very high.

Seizures

Canine epilepsy is rare, but dogs do suffer from a condition like epilepsy. The chief sign is repeated seizures or convulsions brought on by nervousness or overexcitement, or for no apparent reason. It is thought to be congenital. During an attack, a dog should be left alone after you make sure that he cannot injure himself on any sharp or protruding objects. If you have children, keep them away. The dog will be thrashing wildly, without any idea of what he is doing.

When the fit is over, the dog may either run nervously or lie quiet as though depressed. Try to comfort him and make him feel that he has done nothing wrong. At this time he is frightened and needs assurance and love. Make fresh, cool water available to him in small amounts and feed him lightly on the following day. The veterinarian will, if necessary, administer anticonvulsive injections to quiet the dog.

Meningitis

Like the disease in people, canine meningitis is an inflammation of the material covering the brain and the spinal cord. It is a virus or bacterial infection that attacks the brain.

The dog may go into a stupor or become rigid. He loses all sense of direction, whines as if in pain, and seems to retreat into himself. All movement seems to be very painful. His eyes, too, may be affected, and he won't be able to control them. Meningitis is an ailment that needs immediate professional treatment, and even then it may last a long time and even be fatal. If the dog lives, convalescence is long and slow.

Neuritis

Inflammation of the nerves results in a condition known as neuritis. It may cause considerable pain in the dog. He will have difficulty in walking up or down stairs or climbing, particularly in cold damp weather. Your veterinarian will have to treat him. For temporary relief, half an aspirin is effective, about 2½ grains (half a normal adult aspirin) for a 30- to 40-pound dog; repeat as necessary.

Paralysis

An accident to the brain or spinal cord or a disease may cause paralysis, or immobilization.

Certain accidents can damage a section of the brain and the result is partial paralysis, depending on the extent of the damage. A sharp blow on the spine or a crunching smash that fractures a vertebra causes sufficient damage to bring on paralysis. A herniated disc that separates the vertebrae will also cause paralysis. The condition may appear in any breed, although the Dachshund has received the most publicity for it.

Paralysis may come on slowly as well, from distemper or from a cerebral hemorrhage. Recent advances in medicine, however, have made many cases treatable, whereas in the past such ailments were considered hopeless. The chief advance has been in surgery, which is still often the only remedy.

Convalescence from paralysis is usually slow, once again depending on the cause and the extent of the damage. For those cases in which surgery may help, the decision whether you wish to go through with an operation depends of course on you. If you do decide to see your dog through, even if there seems little chance of complete recovery, you should be prepared to give him plenty of time. In some cases, he must be helped in nearly everything he does, even to the point of helping him to have eliminations through stimulation. A dog convalescing from paralysis tests your love.

Poisoning

All poisoning, whether food or chemical, may affect the nervous system. For emergency treatment, see Chapter 7, on first aid.

Tetanus or Lockjaw

Tetanus is a severe infection that may occur when a puncture wound is cut off from the circulation of the air below the skin, as in a bite or a nail puncture. At a certain stage in its development, tetanus will cause a generalized muscle spasm. Very often in this state the dog will stretch in a grotesque way: lips, mouth, head. Everything stiffens unnaturally, as though he were turning to stone. Get him to a veterinarian immediately, but even then recovery is doubtful.

REPRODUCTIVE DISORDERS

Female

In the female, the reproductive system consists of all those organs that have something to do with giving birth: the ovaries, uterus, mammary glands, cervix, vagina, vulva, clitoris, and Fallopian tubes. When everything is going well for the bitch, all these organs work together in harmony. Her season of heat comes twice yearly; she conceives then, if you mate her, and 9 weeks later she whelps a healthy litter, which she proceeds to take care of. For most bitches, this is the natural cycle of life. It is only the exceptional case that causes difficulty, but it is the exceptional case that you are interested in.

There is little question that the bitch's normal cycle and conception have been disturbed by her enclosure in an apartment or house with restricted opportunities for exercise. When dogs ran in packs, the bitch enjoyed a great deal of exercise. She rarely became fat or ungainly, and she had numerous opportunities to make use of her heat periods to reproduce. Under such conditions, she lived a natural life as a dog. Most dogs are almost solely pets now, no longer hunting or working. Since the bitch's reproductive system is sensitive to radical changes, it is not unusual that difficulties should develop.

Most of these difficulties, however, can be effectively cleared up if treatment is prompt. While ailments in the reproductive system may occur more often than before, it is still the uncommon case when a bitch has severe trouble. Furthermore, many of these ailments usually do not affect the younger dog, although they possibly might.

ECLAMPSIA

Eclampsia is an ailment that afflicts pregnant or nursing bitches when their supply of calcium and other minerals is disturbed. When she is pregnant, the foetuses will absorb her calcium and other minerals for their own needs. Similarly, when the bitch nurses her litter, they will suck her breasts dry, and unless there is a calcium and mineral supplement she may lose what she herself needs. The chief preventative is to give a vitamin *and* mineral supplement, plus calcium, to the pregnant and nursing bitch. Also make sure that milk is available. The condition, generally, is more common in the nursing bitch than in the pregnant bitch.

The signs of eclampsia are clear and dramatic. The bitch will start excessive panting and shaking, and she may go into fits or convulsions. She will have a wild look in her eyes. The condition, obviously, is serious. Her temperature will rise, her mouth becomes rigid. You might think she is rabid, but of course she isn't. When you see these signs, be sure to call a veterinarian and describe the symptoms. He will sometimes have to inject calcium gluconate and sedatives to return her to normal. Relief is very rapid and dramatic in most cases.

If the nursing bitch has eclampsia, remove the puppies and do not let them nurse for two or three days. Feed them prepared bitch's milk with an eye dropper. When the condition occurs in the pregnant bitch, the puppies may be born with a mineral deficiency. Prevention, obviously, is the best treatment.

Strange as it may seem to you, the unspayed bitch may suffer from false pregnancy. If the condition recurs, you have a problem dog. In false pregnancy, the bitch shows all the symptoms of real pregnancy: expanded belly, swollen and sensitive breasts, a need to make a nest for her litter, even general nervousness as whelping time approaches. Only she is not pregnant.

Such a bitch needs special care, especially if the false pregnancies occur often, as frequently as every six months. Hormone injections might help the condition, but if not, she will have to be spayed. The condition may also occur with bred bitches. Ask your veterinarian about a new oral medication that can in most cases eliminate the condition. A hysterectomy, however, is the only permanent cure.

INFECTIONS (GENERAL)

While most female difficulties seem to focus on the uterus, the vagina occasionally will give some trouble, especially if there is an injury to the vulva that leads to vaginal infection. Since the vulva is exposed, it may be lacerated, probed, and irritated by foreign objects. The country dog may severely scratch her vulva on rocks or brush or even barbed wire. Or she may be probed with a stick by a child who has no intention of injuring her. The open wound might become infected, leading to infection of the cervix and the uterus. You will then see a discharge of pus and blood, and the bitch may have difficulty in urinating because of the pain.

There are also the usual injuries that a pregnant bitch might suffer when her breasts and nipples are filling with milk and hang low. Even before she is ungainly and slow, her nipples might be injured by sharp rocks, sticks, and other foreign objects. When she is pregnant, you should take particular care to see that she avoids injury. Any severe wound should receive professional care—there is always the danger of tetanus if the wound is of the puncture type. See Chapter 7, on first aid, for what to do if your pet, pregnant or not, suffers a cut or laceration.

MASTITIS

When the nursing bitch's teats become inflamed and swell up as a result of infection, she probably has mastitis. At first the milk may be removed easily, but then it suddenly stops; the infection follows.

If you touch the teat it will be hot, and the bitch may feel severe pain. This is a condition that needs immediate professional treatment. During the infection, the secretion coming from the teat may make the puppy suckling it sick. While most puppies will refuse the teat when the milk is infected, there is no guarantee that they will. Also, the bitch will be in danger, as the infection can spread throughout her body.

There is also a condition known as mechanical mastitis: the puppy's teeth, biting into the teat when there is no milk present can cause an inflammation or mastitis. The bitch needs professional care in this case also.

METRITIS

Metritis means the inflammation and swelling of the uterus. It generally occurs 6 to 8 weeks after heat. It may also occur during whelping, right after whelping, or at almost any time. It affects only unspayed bitches. One of the reasons for spaying a bitch, in fact, is to avoid ailments like metritis.

Its symptoms are common to many other ailments: increased thirst, vomiting, vaginal discharge, loss of appetite, general depression and listlessness. A veterinarian may clear it up with antibiotics if the condition has not progressed too far. A chronic or long-term metritis may require a hysterectomy (removal of female organs).

PYOMETRA

Pyometra is an accumulation of pus in the uterus, perhaps as a result of a hormonal imbalance. It occurs more often in unbred bitches over 5 years of age, most frequently in those between 8 and 9. It is accompanied by thirst and increased urination, vomiting (of solids and even of water), a rise in temperature, pain and bloating in the abdomen, loss of appetite. The bitch will sometimes have a discharge from the uterus, as though in continual heat. These are symptoms common to many ailments, but with pyometra the bitch's hindquarters may give off a sickly sweetish odor if she is discharging.

One symptom of pyometra is the distension of the uterus, which increases as the pus forms. If the condition is left untreated, the outcome is usually fatal. A bloody discharge with pus from the vulva will alert you to the infection. When this happens, the veterinarian will probably have to resort to surgery to correct the condition.

STRUCTURAL DEFECTS

Your bitch may have certain structural defects that you won't know about until she whelps. A bitch with a pelvic obstruction or with a uterus that cannot accommodate puppies should not have been bred. X-ray examination will reveal any pelvic defects before mating. In most cases, however, the mating will take place as most owners will not have the bitch x-rayed for this purpose. Therefore, it is always a good idea to have a veterinarian on call when your bitch is ready to whelp. Then if she does have trouble whelping, she can get professional help should she need it. The veterinarian may perform a Caesarean section if necessary.

See Chapter 9 for the details of what to do when whelping time comes near.

TUMORS

Tumors may appear in the mammary glands of the unspayed and unbred bitch particularly as she grows older—after 7 or 8. Such tumors are noticeable because of visible lumps or swellings in the teat area. You should have a veterinarian check them as soon as you notice anything unusual.

Tumors of the ovaries are also a possibility. With this condition, the female heat period is thrown off balance. There may be excessive bleeding or discharge, or no discharge at all. The heat may last an excessively long time, or there may be periods with no heat at all. You should call such an abnormality to the attention of your veterinarian.

Male

CRYPTORCHIDISM

Cryptorchidism means that neither testicle of the dog has descended. A dog with this condition is generally sterile because the undescended testicles have never developed or else bodily heat has destroyed the reproductive cells of the testicles. Otherwise, your dog is unimpaired—he simply cannot reproduce. This is an abnormal condition and these undescended testicles should be removed, for tumors may develop in them.

AILMENTS OF GENITAL ORGANS

Injuries to the testicles are rare, but occasionally they do occur and the testicles may become infected. If your dog has a serious laceration in the area, bacteria may enter, followed shortly after by an infection. There can be severe pain, and your dog will walk with his hind legs spread at an unnatural angle, with a stiff gait. The testicles themselves may become enlarged, a condition that is called orchitis. To relieve his pain temporarily, give him half an aspirin, either alone or mixed in his food, but call in a veterinarian to treat the infection without delay.

Injuries to the penis are also rare. Most of the time an injury will respond to first aid treatment (Chapter 7). There are few ailments to which the penis is subject, except perhaps for tumors, and these too are rare. Some males have congenital defects, such as having too small a sheath to allow the penis to come through for purposes of mating, a condition known as phimosis. Surgery can correct the fault.

Another defect may be that the dog's penis extends beyond the sheath and cannot be retracted, a condition known as paraphimosis. Both of these conditions are painful, and there is little you can do except divert his attention until you can get professional help. Fortunately, both conditions are rare.

Monorchidism means that only one of your dog's testicles has descended into the scrotum. The condition is hereditary, and there is nothing you can do about it without professional help. Such a dog, by the way, is not necessarily sterile, and he may pass on the defect to the male puppies in any litter.

The undescended testicle will generally give trouble, and your veterinarian should be consulted on what course to take. If there is a tumor, the testicle may grow to the size of a grapefruit, and emergency surgery will be necessary. Many times an operation is performed to remove the testicle before it gives trouble, and in some cases hormones help the testicle descend.

PROSTATITIS

The prostate gland may become enlarged, especially in the older dog, through either infection or hormonal imbalance. The resulting condition is prostatitis.

The gland normally rests in the dog's pelvic cavity below the colon (large bowel). As long as it remains normal, it serves its function in the reproductive system. When it swells or becomes inflamed, however, it compresses the rectum. The result is pain during defecation, and constipation. Other symptoms may include a reluctance on the part of the dog to sit down, because the whole area is sensitive. The dog may walk with a straddled gait, like an old man.

If there is an infection, there may be a rise in temperature. The dog will be restless, ill at ease, and generally unhappy. If you do nothing to relieve his condition, the dog may not have a bowel movement because the area is so sensitive.

The whole matter must be handled by a veterinarian. When the prostate is so large that massage and hormones will not work, surgery may be necessary. This is a very serious operation with a long recovery period. Consultation is suggested.

RESPIRATORY DISORDERS

The respiratory system consists of the nose, sinus, windpipe (trachea), pharynx, larynx, bronchial tubes, and lungs. Like people, dogs come down with respiratory illnesses of the most common kinds: coughs, sinusitis, bronchitis, laryngitis, tracheobronchitis, pharyngitis, and pneumonia. While dogs do not suffer from the common cold as we know it, they do get something very similar—an upper-respiratory infection. All these ailments, when severe, require professional treatment, especially now that antibiotics are used with such good and quick results.

Many respiratory ailments have common symptoms: discharge from the nose and eyes, rise in temperature, shallow and rapid breathing, generally a dry or hacking cough, loss of vitality, lack of interest in food. There may also be sneezing, although sneezing in itself can also mean an allergy or a sensitivity to dust rather than an infection. A warning: Your dog may have a dry, hot nose without being ill and a cold nose when ill. Don't use his nose as an indicator.

Asthma

Asthma is a chronic breathing difficulty that occurs more often in the old dog, although it is by no means exclusive to him. It is characterized by wheezing, and a deep-seated cough that seems to come from the dog's toes. Breathing may also be shallow, interrupted by bouts of coughing. A damp climate can intensify an asthmatic condition.

You should try to comfort your dog during an attack as much as you can. Since fright may prolong a coughing attack, the dog is assured by your kind words and tone. Pat him, speak to him quietly. Let him sniff aromatic spirits of ammonia, and rub his throat until the attack passes. Sometimes a sedative will help relax your dog. Injections and oral medication may relieve the condition temporarily.

Certain breeds seem to be more subject to asthmatic attacks than others, particularly the short-nosed ones, like the Bulldogs (English and French) and many of the toys. Also, the overweight dog is more disposed to asthma, no matter what his breed.

Do not confuse this asthmatic cough with the hack that many dogs get when pulling on the lead with a choke collar. Often they are simply clearing their throats or indicating nervousness. You may relieve that cough too by stroking the dog's throat.

Inflammation

If your dog has a persistent cough, it may mean inflammation of the trachea, pharynx, larynx, or bronchi. The most common is tracheobronchitis, or an inflammation of the trachea (windpipe) and bronchi (the two branches of the trachea). Some dog people refer to the ailment as Kennel Cough, probably because the disease afflicts dogs kept for long—or even short—periods of time in a kennel.

The cough is a scooping, wheezing one in which the dog seems to be trying to bring something up or to have something stuck in his throat. He may, indeed, foam or froth at the mouth in his frenzy of coughing or gagging.

All these respiratory ailments are generally infectious. They may last for several weeks or months, and if neglected can lead to complications. If tracheobronchitis is not treated, pneumonia is a distinct possibility. When neglected, the cough irritates the already inflamed areas, which in turn causes more coughing.

Do not give home remedies, but let a veterinarian prescribe what is best. Since the cough can indicate a variety of ailments—distemper, pneumonia, pleurisy, as well as tracheobronchitis—it should be attended to as soon as you recognize its persistence. Give it two days at most to clear up. In the meantime, keep your dog in the house, and cover him with a coat for his walk outside in cold weather.

If the condition is bronchitis or tracheobronchitis caused by a stay in a kennel, try to prevent its recurrence by yearly revaccinating your dog for distemper, hepatitis, leptospirosis, parainfluenza and tracheobronchitis. You may also give him therapeutic vitamins on the recommendation of a veterinarian.

Lung Ailments

There are several lung ailments that a dog can suffer from. Since you will not be able to diagnose any of these conditions yourself, I will give a short rundown on the possibilities. All are characterized by difficulty with breathing—usually short and rapid breath accompanied by a rasping sound—and by coughing.

Two very rare lung ailments are canine tuberculosis and emphysema. I mention them only in passing because you should not expect your dog to have either one. Canine tuberculosis is generally not recognized even when it is present unless it is confirmed by x-ray and other laboratory tests. Its chief symptoms are coughing, loss of weight, listlessness. Emphysema involves the breakdown of the lung cells, or dilatation, as they accumulate air pockets. This rare ailment usually only appears after other lung conditions.

If your dog has either of these lung ailments or any of those mentioned below, it will be hard for you not to notice them. In addition to the labored breathing and hacking cough, your dog will appear unhealthy and depressed. Much of his energy will be going into the sheer effort of breathing, and his heart will be under extra strain. Exercise will tire him rapidly. He will probably not feel like running around or even walking. He needs immediate professional care.

Pleurisy

An inflammation of the membrane covering the lung and adhering to the chest cavity is called pleurisy, and it is characterized by sharp, harsh respiration. Sometimes pleurisy follows or is present at the same time as an attack of pneumonia. Such inflammation of the lung area generally produces a cough and often fever. In another form of pleurisy, the chest cavity may fill with fluid. This is known as hydrothorax or chest-fluid. It is accompanied by shallow breathing, as though the dog cannot get enough air no matter how hard he tries. Fluid presses the lung so that it can't expand to its full capacity.

Pneumonia

Pneumonia is a lung ailment in which the tissues become inflamed, thickened, and watery. At one time pneumonia was a persistent killer of dogs, but antibiotics and prescription drugs have prevented many fatalities. The important thing is to treat pneumonia early.

There are several kinds, but all are characterized by a rough, hacking cough, discharge from the nose, shallow breathing—like a kind of chest vibration—loss of appetite, and a high fever. Frequently the nasal discharge will be ropy and greenish, perhaps even flecked with blood when the infection is severe. These are your danger signals. The dog needs prompt professional attention.

In the meantime, when you notice any symptoms of a respiratory nature, keep your dog warm—put on his coat and cover him with a blanket if he seems chilled. Make sure his chest is covered. Feed him an easily digested diet and try to make him eat. Baby foods are fine at this time, including protein cereal mixed with milk (warmed), and also yolk of egg and milk.

These are temporary precautions. Only a veterinarian can tell if the pneumonia is accompanying another illness or whether it exists alone.

Tumors

Tumors in the lungs or general chest cavity may have the same symptoms as tuberculosis: shortness of breath, coughing, loss of weight, listlessness. They are diagnosed by x-ray and by laboratory blood tests.

Upper-Respiratory Infections

Dogs do not suffer from what we call a cold, although the symptoms are similar. Generally, the dog's nose and eyes run with a thin mucous discharge; there may be a slight fever and chills. Your dog may also cough and sneeze. If there is no more than a slight upper-respiratory infection, the condition may pass in a few days. Keep your dog warm, out of drafts, and do not walk him in cold weather. Put a coat on him if he must go outside, and make sure the coat covers his chest.

The symptoms of an upper-respiratory infection can indicate something more severe: distemper, for example. Then, however, the symptoms might be much more intense, and your dog's misery will be obvious. He may not eat or want to move, and he might sleep constantly.

URINARY DISORDERS

The dog's urinary system consists of the kidneys, ureter, bladder, and urethra. The kidneys filter waste material that would otherwise poison the dog's system; the ureters carry the urine from the kidneys to the bladder; the bladder in turn holds the liquid matter, which is carried away in the urethra and eliminated as urine.

Kidney Troubles

In the normal course of events, your dog should not suffer from a kidney ailment until he is old. In dogs over 8, the incidence of kidney ailments rises, although in some shorter-lived dogs the condition may appear before 8. In those cases where age is not a factor, kidney trouble may result from a severe illness like virus distemper or leptospirosis. These diseases place an excessive burden on the kidneys, sometimes leading to kidney trouble.

Other factors that might cause kidney ailments are food poisons in the system or poisons or insect spray the dog has swallowed. Although he recovers and seems well, his kidneys may be affected because the poison has damaged the kidney cells. Since this organ is very delicate, it can be permanently damaged even while your dog appears perfectly well for some time. A very sharp blow like a kick may injure the sensitive tubules of the kidneys. When some are destroyed, a greater burden is placed on the rest, and the kidneys are unable to function properly.

INFLAMMATION OF KIDNEYS (NEPHRITIS)

There are many symptoms of inflamed kidneys (also called nephritis): chiefly, vomiting, as well as increased thirst and increase in urination, sensitivity in the general back area, actual pain when pressure on an area around the kidneys is applied, loss of appetite, general "unthriftiness" in the form of blurred eyes, depression, listlessness. The dog's urine may turn orange or red. In some instances, when stones are present, the dog may have difficulty in urinating. He might strain a great deal in order to pass a few drops. When the condition worsens, the dog may stagger or faint, or go into a coma. With neglect, nephritis becomes chronic or long-term, and your dog's chances of complete recovery are lessened.

If you notice any of these symptoms, call your veterinarian. Your dog may not have a kidney ailment at all. Your only signs may be thirst and difficulty in urination, and these can indicate many other conditions, or simply nervousness. Some bitches when they go into their heat periods urinate very frequently, often apparently without control. This may last for only a short period or for a week or two.

When an acute kidney ailment passes into a chronic condition, the attacks are frequent over a long period of time. There may also be difficulty in walking, as though the dog's entire back area were in pain.

Kidney ailments, whether from inflammation or other reasons, will probably throw your dog off his house-training. Since he already feels bad enough, your tone and attitude are important. Bear with him. He feels guilty about his lack of control, and he would do much better if he could. But there is little he can do. His kidneys are not functioning the way they should, and irritation may make retention of urine impossible.

There are certain dietary precautions you should take with kidney trouble. Highly seasoned food is generally not recommended for even a healthy dog; it should never be given to a dog with a kidney ailment. Since table scraps usually contain salt and pepper, avoid giving them if the dog is ill. A heavy meat diet is not recommended either because large amounts of protein will excessively burden the kidneys.

Consult with a veterinarian about your dog's diet. Now available are prescription diets specifically made for dogs with kidney ailments. These have been laboratory-tested, and they will give your dog all his nutritional needs without upsetting the delicate balance of his system. They are far better than a hit-or-miss diet of table scraps, which may contain spices, or the dog's usual diet, which may be too high in protein and fats. The only trouble with prescription diets is that some dogs do not like them, and the owner may have to resort to tricks to persuade his dog to eat. One method is gradually to remove the regular food and replace it with the special diet.

STONES

Some dogs carry kidney stones for years before showing any signs. Then suddenly they begin to pass blood in their urine, or they find urinating extremely difficult. At this time, your dog may whine when he urinates, or walk with a humped or arched back, indicating the pain he feels. He may even hold himself in a urinating position most of the time, but without being able to urinate. Kidney stones, however, are rare in dogs.

Do not confuse kidney stones with bladder stones, which are much more frequent and which collect in the bladder, where they may occlude or close off the urethra and prevent urination. Kidney stones have to be removed by surgery if x-rays show them to be present. Usually, attacks are recurrent. On occasion they will be aggravated by violent exercise or roughhousing, which results in the shifting of the stones and pain in the dog. Of course the stones can move at any time, even while the dog is sleeping.

Like all kidney ailments, kidney stones have symptoms similar to those of many other conditions. If your dog whines when he urinates or if he humps over when walking, he may well have some other illness. In any event, you should call your veterinarian, for your dog is obviously suffering and in need of medical aid. The veterinarian can give treatment to relieve pain temporarily. But the only permanent cure is an operation to remove the stones, followed by a special diet and medication after the stones have been analyzed.

Bladder Ailments

There are several bladder ailments, most often found in the older dog. Unless your dog is hurt in a fall or an automobile accident, or possibly is kicked hard, the chances of a bladder ailment are slight. However, any dog may suffer a bladder disorder if he gets chilled or wet. For this reason, hunting dogs, particularly when they are old, are kept from hunting in damp, cold weather. You should follow the same procedure with your own dog.

The most common bladder ailments involve dribbling, stones, and infection (called cystitis). Dribbling usually occurs in the older dog, but it may also afflict the younger one, and both sexes indiscriminately. It may also occur in spayed bitches, usually as they grow older. Dribbling results when the dog is unable to hold his urine. The reason is generally a loss of tone in the sphincter muscles of the urethra controlling the urine. It may be caused by a stone in the bladder, or possibly by an infection.

Dribbling is of course a nuisance for the owner. It is also a source of embarrassment for the dog. Before you can do anything about dribbling, a veterinarian must determine the cause. If the condition results from loss of tone in the sphincter, the chances are the dog is old and there isn't much that can be done except diet and water control. Sometimes medication works. If the cause is stones, then surgery is necessary. If the reason is that the bitch has lost control as a result of spaying, then hormones may be injected or given orally. This injection provides a substitute for the secretion of the now missing ovaries, and it may help. If your dog dribbles because of an irritation or an infection, your veterinarian may give antibiotics or some other medication to try to correct the condition.

Along with dribbling, the presence of stones in the bladder is fairly common in dogs of all ages. The most obvious symptom is that the dog will have trouble urinating, or there may be blood in the urine. The male may lift his hind leg and hold it raised while he tries to expel the urine, but only a few drops may come out, and often with blood. The bitch will squat and strain, only to release a few drops, or may pass blood with the urine. The fact is that the stone or stones are plugging the small opening between the bladder and the urethra, like a rock rolled into the mouth of a cave. Or in the male, several stones may enter the urethra and serve as a dam shutting off the passage of urine, especially where the urethra passes through the bone in the penis.

All this of course is very painful for your dog. A mild sedative like half an aspirin (repeated as needed) may temporarily relieve the discomfort. Usually the bitch will find it easier to pass small stones from the urethra than the male will.

Not all bladder stone conditions are the same, however, and each case needs separate treatment. The stones themselves (or calculi—accumulations of mineral matter) differ greatly in size, from gravel to a hen's egg. The stones also differ in smoothness and roughness, and they do not always settle in the same place in the dog's urinary tract. That's why some dogs can live comfortably with bladder stones, while others must have the stones removed. You probably will not notice their presence until your dog has trouble urinating or urinates with blood, and by that time the stones will most probably have lodged in the urethra. When that occurs, surgery is the only way to relieve the condition. Incidentally, the stones may be found only by accident when your dog is x-rayed for some other condition.

Cystitis is a severe inflammation of the urinary bladder—caused by infection, stones, diet, or chill. It seems more prevalent in bitches than in males. With cystitis, your dog may whine or cry when he urinates and he generally urinates frequently, possibly with blood. Often, increased urination is the only symptom.

As the inflammation worsens, your dog will develop the general symptoms of an infection: perhaps a rise in temperature, loss of appetite, general listlessness. Quite often, however, cystitis is a local infection without any fever. Some of these symptoms are so general and so applicable to other bladder conditions that you should have a veterinarian diagnose the condition with laboratory tests before you jump to any conclusions. Antibiotics may clear up the inflammation in short order, provided there are no other complications.

Bladder rupture may occur when a dog is kicked or struck by an automobile. This is very serious and if not treated immediately is usually fatal. The dog will react by losing his sense of equilibrium and collapsing. Surgery and antibiotics may give him a chance. Equally dangerous is the type of hernia in which the bladder itself passes through the hernia. Surgical care is needed quickly.

Renal Dropsy (Hydronephrosis)

Hydronephrosis is a collection of urine in the pelvis of the kidney. This condition leads to an impairment of the organ, which in time leads to atrophy of the kidney structure. The basic cause is an obstruction to the flow of urine, whether congenital or acquired. One kidney or both may be affected.

The chief symptoms are difficult to distinguish from other ailments: vomiting, pain upon touch, enlargement of the general area. Treatment must come from a veterinarian as soon as you notice any irregularity. Surgical removal of the kidney may be indicated, provided the other kidney remains unaffected.

Uremia

Uremia is a condition caused by the accumulation in the blood of waste products normally removed by the kidneys. The dog continues to urinate—in fact, generally more than normal.

Uremia usually causes a severe reaction on the part of the dog: nausea, vomiting, dizziness, and, in its final stages, convulsions and coma. His breath may take on an acrid odor, somewhat like ammonia. The older dog in particular is subject to uremia. When the condition develops, your veterinarian is the best judge of whether treatment is possible.

Worms: Kidneyworms

If a dog eats raw freshwater fish, he may develop kidneyworms, which almost invariably settle in the right kidney. This parasite causes loss of weight, frequent urination (often bloody), abdominal pain so severe that the dog may cry out, nervous trembling, and anemia.

The condition may be diagnosed by the parasitic eggs in the urine. Surgery is often necessary, to remove the infected kidney.

SPECIAL CATEGORIES

ABSCESSES

Abscesses are swellings caused by a collection of pus, and are quite common. They may appear nearly anywhere. They may result from several things: accidents, insect bites, dog and cat bites, vaccinations, or improperly draining wounds. A dog will usually run a fever when abscesses are present, and you can be sure that the general area will be sensitive. He will shy away whenever you attempt to see or touch it. He may also be irritable. If anyone happens to touch your dog on or near an abscess, he may snap or bite.

Abscesses must be treated by a veterinarian, who knows how to drain them properly. You may squeeze the sore spot yourself, but if you extract only part of the accumulated pus, the abscess will recur.

CYSTS

Cysts are not to be confused with tumors, even though the cyst takes the form of a growth. The cyst is a capsule or saclike body that is filled with fluid. It occurs in the tissues and forms lumps that appear right under the dog's skin, most commonly in the throat and jaw area. Cysts may also form in several organs, particularly in the ovaries and sometimes the kidneys. There they settle into the tissue of these organs; when in the ovaries, they sometimes cause partial or complete sterility.

Cysts do not necessarily upset your dog's health, although they will upset the bitch's powers of reproduction when they form in her ovaries. Some outward signs may be frequent heat periods or heat of long duration (beyond the usual 3 weeks), or no heat for up to 2 years, and sometimes frequent urination. When large enough, cysts may interfere with your dog's normal functions, especially if they are sub-lingual, under the tongue. Your veterinarian will decide whether they must be surgically removed.

DIABETES

A dog may suffer from two kinds of diabetes: diabetes insipidus and diabetes mellitus.

Diabetes insipidus is a serious and prolonged disease of the hypothalamus and pituitary gland characterized by excessive discharge of urine of low specific gravity. In most cases this form of diabetes occurs in dogs when a tumor damages his posterior pituitary gland, preventing the proper hormones from controlling urination.

This condition occurs most frequently in older dogs and comes upon them gradually. As the disease becomes more pronounced, a large dog may drink excessive amounts of water daily and urinate often. He may also become enlarged in the abdomen, sleep a lot, and have frequent and loose bowel movements.

The second type, diabetes mellitus, is a chronic disease of the metabolic system associated with insufficient insulin. This results in too much sugar in the blood and urine, progressive loss of weight, extreme hunger and thirst, and exhaustion. Eventually the dog will begin to shrink or waste away, becoming gaunt and unsightly. There are many causes of diabetes mellitus, most of which involve damage to the pancreatic islet cells, usually from disease. The disease is generally much more common in middle-aged and fat dogs and nearly always more common in bitches than in males.

Your veterinarian may keep your dog alive by checking his urine and blood regularly, prescribing a diet already prepared, giving injections of insulin or oral medication, and instructing you on how to do this. In most cases of diabetes mellitus the dog can resume a normal life with proper medication.

FROTHING

Frothing in itself is not an ailment. Motion sickness may bring it on, even on a short car ride. Occasionally frothing accompanies an ailment or it may simply be the dog's way of reacting to fright. Sometimes frothing will occur during a fit. If this is the case, let the dog alone until the fit is over, and then call your veterinarian. The fit is probably indicative of a serious disorder, which needs immediate treatment.

TUMORS

Tumors or growths may appear on nearly any part of your dog, but particularly on the breasts of bitches. A tumor, by definition, is an uncontrolled growth of tissue.

If the tumor or growth does not interfere with the workings of any vital organ and is not spreading, it may be nonmalignant, or benign. Very often you can feel these growths or tumors right under the surface of the dog's skin. They seem like small, pliant, doughy balls that under pressure shift in your fingers. Whenever you feel one, call it to the attention of your veterinarian even though it may prove to be unimportant. Any lump is potentially serious, and if it grows, however slowly, then it should surely not be neglected.

The older dog, in particular, is subject to growths, whether nonmalignant (benign) or otherwise. If your dog is over 7 or 8, you may find some growths under the surface of his skin without any further symptoms. They should nevertheless be checked. All old dogs are subject to warts, for example, another kind of growth which is usually not dangerous. They should be removed where possible. Warts are generally nonmalignant growths, usually rough to the touch. Sometimes your dog will scratch the wart until it becomes raw and bleeds and surgery becomes necessary.

When a growth or tumor spreads, it is said to be malignant or cancerous. Not all such tumors are of equal seriousness, and some dogs—like some people—who had them removed have gone on to long, rewarding lives. Malignant tumors can take several forms, depending on what kind of tissue is involved. Sarcomas, for example, are made up of embryonic connective tissue from the mesoderm, while carcinomas are malignant growths of epithelial cell origin. Cancer is a term applied to all malignant growths.

All bitches are subject to breast tumors, and therefore as soon as you see any signs of a swelling, call your veterinarian. I certainly recommend regular examinations of your dog after he passes 6 or 7, and not only as a way of checking for tumors; you never know what illness might be detected that could be corrected in its early stages. If your dog appears to be losing weight and his coat has no luster, these may be other symptoms of a tumor. X-rays of the lungs will generally show if a tumor is invading other organs.

VOMITING

Most owners worry when their dogs vomit. It is, perhaps, one of the most disturbing of sights and leads the average owner to feel that something dreadful is wrong.

Many things may cause vomiting, among them stomach or intestinal ailments of various kinds. Some occasional vomiting, however, is usually nothing to worry about. As I said before, the dog has the power to vomit whenever he wishes. Many times he wants to regurgitate something that is irritating, and he does so. Or he may eat grass, which usually causes vomiting. Or he may have swallowed something distasteful and brings it back up to have another look at it. If your dog is naturally nervous, as some terriers and many toys are, he may demonstrate his nervousness by vomiting whenever something bothers him.

This kind of vomiting is not serious. If your dog seems fine and settled after he has vomited, you know that the cause is isolated and temporary. You might skip his next meal if it is to come soon, and cut down on water for a few hours. If, however, the vomiting persists or falls into certain clear patterns (after eating or drinking), he is probably ill.

Persistent vomiting, with or without blood, is a symptom of nearly every dog disease, from kidney trouble to inflammation of the intestine. Vomiting may accompany worms, obstructions in the digestive tract, poisons or toxins in the system, nearly every kind of liver, stomach, and digestive ailment. If the vomiting is caused by poisons, follow the first-aid procedures outlined in Chapter 7. Usually when vomiting indicates a condition that needs immediate attention, it is associated with a fever or with some inconsistency in the dog's bowel movements (possibly diarrhea). Also, your dog may appear depressed or unusually quiet. All these signs add up to the fact that he needs treatment by a veterinarian.

ACUPUNCTURE

Acupuncture, or the system of treating the energy flow and balance in an ill person, has now become part of the practice of veterinary medicine. Considerable research has gone into the attempt to discover the chemical, biophysical, and neurophysiological mechanisms that will explain acupuncture therapy. The aim of all such research is to see how effective acupuncture treatment can be in veterinary medicine as well as to collect data on treatment procedures. Such material has been increasingly disseminated to other researchers and to veterinarians. So far, it has become clear that many ailments of all kinds—from hip dysplasia and arthritis to skin diseases and diarrhea—have been aided by acupuncture, even after other more traditional forms of therapy have failed. Exactly why this ancient treatment succeeds while other methods fail is still not clear, but research into acupuncture analgesia is as yet in its early stages.

THE SICKROOM

Like a sick person, a sick dog needs quiet and rest. Unlike a person, however, a dog does not know the limits of his energy, and he will try to take part in all the activities he sees around him. When he is convalescing or receiving home treatment, it is better for him to take it easy—so you must restrict his activity. And then, as he begins to get well, let him, little by little, do most of the things he used to do.

Very often your dog will be sent home from the hospital with a definite routine to follow. You will be under instructions from the veterinarian that should be carried out with a minimum of interference. If you can isolate your dog, so much the better for you and the dog. Children will of course want to play with their pet, but they should be discouraged from any roughhousing. If they offer sympathy, that will be welcome to the dog and build up his morale.

If an isolated room is out of the question, then a quiet corner is fine. Even a basement will do if it is warm and not drafty. Make sure that plenty of air is circulating and the area is clean. Also, remove all rugs and valuable furniture. Keep in mind that the convalescing dog may not have full control over his elimination. And he may not be able to go outdoors regularly because of the weather. Expect the dog, then, to urinate and have a bowel movement in the general area where he is convalescing. Make it as easy as possible for him. In some cases, he may not be able to get up readily, and if he fouls his nest be sure the material is changed. Newspapers are the best covering for your floor, and old sheets or blankets for the dog's bed. Unless there is a specific reason for him to sleep on a mattress, remove it for the time being so that he doesn't soil it.

If the area is excessively light, make sure that curtains cover the windows. Many illnesses—and particularly distemper, upper-respiratory infections, and conjunctivitis—make your dog's eyes sensitive to light. On the other hand, the room or corner should not be completely dark and depressing. Try for a happy medium between streaming, bright light and oppressive blackness.

The temperature of the room or corner should be about 70° F. Do not overheat the room or the dog may catch cold when he leaves. The

DAY	TEMPERATURE		BREATHING	BOWELS	APPETITE	URINE	EYES	MUSCULAR CONTROL	GENERAL CONDITION	NOSE	VOMITING	GENERAL COMMENTS
Monday (date)	A.M.	P.M.										
Tuesday	A.M.	P.M.										
Wednesday	A.M.	P.M.										
Thursday	A.M.	P.M.										
Friday	A.M.	P.M.										
Saturday	A.M.	P.M.										
Sunday	A.M.	P.M.										

SICK ROOM CHART

room should not be cool either, or your dog might contract an upper-respiratory infection in his weakened condition. Drafts should be avoided at all costs. If the room must be aired to eliminate a musty or bad odor, take the dog into another room of the same temperature. Then bring the original room back to 70° before returning the dog.

These and other precautions may seem bothersome, but they are certainly worth the trouble. The more careful you are and the more closely you follow your veterinarian's advice, the sooner your dog will return to health.

The room itself should be organized something like a hospital room. A good deal depends, naturally, on the length of the home treatment and on what the veterinarian tells you to do. If the illness is severe or if the operation requires a long convalescence, you should follow through on everything outlined here. If, however, the period of home treatment is to be only a few days, you might not wish to shift your house around.

And then there is the primary consideration of the dog himself. Does he need complete peace and quiet? Is he particularly nervous? Was or is the ailment severe enough so that isolation is absolutely necessary? What about your own needs? If you are already burdened with children, can you take on a "patient"? Many an owner has to leave his dog in a hospital because there is no one at home who can spare as much time for the sick dog as he requires. These are some considerations to keep in mind before you undertake home nursing, rewarding as you expect it to be. If you cannot devote all the necessary time to your dog, he should remain hospitalized, where you know he will receive good treatment.

There is one final consideration. Will your dog so pine for you when he is away that he will refuse to get well? Some dogs with a particular temperament need familiar surroundings and will not do well if left alone in a hospital even if the owner is allowed regular visits. In such an event, you must take care of him yourself.

In my chapter on first aid, I mention what a dog's typical medicine cabinet should contain. I refer you to Chapter 7, the final pages, for this information.

A Warning: Do not haphazardly administer any medicine that you happen to have around and think might be useful. Every medicine that you keep in your dog's medicine cabinet or first-aid kit must be specifically for dogs if it is to be taken internally. I do not mean medication like Kaopectate, which is safe for infants, and milk of magnesia, which is a very mild laxative. But medicines and tonics which you might yourself take are not to be given thoughtlessly to your dog. Some tonics, for example, contain small amounts of strychnine, which a person might absorb with no ill effects but that can be harmful to a dog.

Furthermore, do not use old medicines and pills that you have felt reluctant to throw out. You might make your dog worse by administering them as a possible cure. Also, make sure you scale down the dosage of any of your own medicines you give your dog. Thus, a small dog should be given far less of a laxative than a large dog. Do not use your own measurements as an example—the chances are you weigh several times what your dog weighs, unless you have a very large breed. Remember that the most popular size of dog in the United States is the terrier—a dog of 20 to 30 pounds. This means that the usual average human dosage (for a 150-pound person) must sometimes be cut to a fifth to suit a dog.

Above all, follow precisely the directions that the veterinarian gives you. If he tells you that your dog should receive medication at certain hours, you cannot skip one time and give a double dose at another. The dosage is set so that a uniform amount of medication is maintained in the dog's blood system at all times. If you forget his medicine at the proper time, the required amout decreases, and the dog receives less benefit from the medication for several hours. During that time, his illness has a chance to regain a foothold. In some instances, you may have to get up at night to give him his medicine, although usually this is seldom necessary over a long period. For the sake of your dog's health, you must be precise and prompt, and you must want to do everything possible to help him.

If you have any doubts about your ability to handle your dog during convalescence or during the necessary period of treatment, you should leave him in the hospital.

PROCEDURES

There are several checks you can make on your dog to see if he is recovering. If you telephone your veterinarian, he will want to know several things. It is a good idea to keep a chart—something, perhaps, that approximates the chart of the doctor and nurse in a hospital. You can make it a simple affair, or you may wish to make it more detailed.

In any event, some of the items you should note daily are the dog's temperature (taken rectally—leave thermometer in for 2 minutes) in the morning and evening, his breathing (rapid or slow?), his bowel movements (how many, loose, hard, bloody?), appetite (good, poor, fussy?), urination (frequent, infrequent, color, smell?), eyes (sensitive to light, discharge, inflamed?), muscular control (weak, able to move?), general condition (alert, interested?), nose (any discharge, bloody?), any vomiting? These are the most common signs in a dog who is now or who has recently been ill. There may be still other things that you notice. Write them down in a separate column and mention them to your veterinarian. He may not think of everything to ask, and if you can tell him of other symptoms you have observed, by all means do so.

TAKING THE TEMPERATURE

You take a dog's temperature the same way you would take a child's. Use a regular rectal thermometer. Shake it so that the mercury is below the dog's normal temperature. Dip it in vaseline so that the tip is covered. Insert it gently in the dog's rectum and make sure he does not sit on it. Leave in for 2 minutes. Wash it in cool—not hot—water when you have finished.

GIVING AN ENEMA

You need the following equipment: a regular enema bag, with hose and nozzle (if the dog is very small, the regular nozzle may be too big: in that event, use a small syringe that can be inserted without forcing); soap (mild or not, depending on what the veterinarian tells you and depending on the severity of the constipation); vaseline or mineral oil— for lubricating the nozzle before you insert it. You probably have all this on hand.

Before you give your dog an enema, however, you should have a go-ahead from the veterinarian. Many sick dogs may need only a mild laxative, and that might be the first step. If that fails, you may have to follow with a suppository or an enema. Also, not all sick dogs need an enema. You should keep a check on your dog's bowel movements to make sure that he has not had an elimination. Then after consultation (a phone call) with your veterinarian, go ahead with the enema if necessary.

If your dog is well and strong enough to resist, you will need someone to help restrain him. Most sick dogs are too weak to resist, but this is something you have to determine. The dog who is unable to stand will probably give in quietly. The dog who can run away, however, may present a problem unless you have help.

Use a Fleet enema for infants, which is complete with everything you need, and obtainable at nearly all drugstores. The nozzle, incidentally, is already lubricated. Place your dog in the bathtub. Since the enema usually results in fast action, the best place is the tub, which you can wash out right after the dog has an elimination. If you have a large, portable rubber tub, such as those used for infants, you may prefer that, provided the dog fits. The bathtub is best, however, because there is space for the dog to move, and he will not foul his coat, as he might do in a smaller space.

Insert the nozzle carefully and gently in the dog's rectum and administer the contents of the bag. Try to reassure the dog as you give the enema; this is a novel and perhaps threatening experience for him. When the bag is empty, remove the nozzle rapidly from his rectum, which should be elevated at a 90° angle. If his legs will hold him after the enema, make him stand up so that the bowel movement does not soil his coat.

If the dog's coat has been soiled, do not give him a bath. Soak a washcloth in warm water, wring it partially dry, and wipe off the coat until it is clean. Dry with a towel. If his skin becomes wet, make sure it is thoroughly dried. Before taking the dog from the bathroom, check to see that there are no drafts or windows open near his sleeping area.

FEEDING A SICK DOG

A sick or injured dog often presents a problem in feeding. You may be surprised at your dog's loss of appetite, for you are probably accustomed to having him eat voraciously and then beg for more. Nevertheless, the shock that accompanies many illnesses, the lack of exercise, the general depression that goes with inactivity and loss of muscular control, the weakness that follows upon an operation or a serious ailment—all these will destroy the healthiest of appetites.

Since the recovery of your dog often depends on his eating well, he must, if necessary, be force-fed. Usually such a drastic step is not necessary. You can encourage him to eat by simply varying his diet and giving him more tempting foods than usual. Try chicken, chicken liver, steak, and boiled beef before you force-feed him.

On many occasions your veterinarian will recommend a diet. There are prescription diets, obtainable only from a veterinarian, for various ailments. These diets are for dogs with heart trouble, weight and skin problems, kidney ailments, for dogs after surgery, for those with intestinal trouble and those who require rehabilitation after a severe illness, and for very old dogs. If your veteranarian puts your dog on one of these diets, or on a similarly controlled one, keep him on it until his recovery is complete. For special reasons, the diet may be a liquid one, or it may be high in protein or in calcium. Whatever it is, you should not add or subtract from it. Most of these diets cost somewhat more than regular dog food.

If the diet is a liquid one, you may have to feed your dog teaspoonful by teaspoonful, for he may not want to eat if he is very sick. In that case, the liquid, whether beef broth, milk, or soup, must be forced in—gently but firmly. The very weak dog might even have to be bottle-fed. On other occasions, you might have to feed by the lip-pouch method (see below for detailed instructions), the same way in which you usually give him liquid medicine.

With a soft or solid diet, small amounts of food placed on the back of the tongue will often force him to swallow. Stroke your dog's throat if he has difficulty in getting the food down or tries to spit it out. You might even put food on your finger and let him lick it off. Sometimes an appealing, aromatic piece of food in the palm of your hand will do the trick.

If you feel that this is a trying time for you, remember that it is also a difficult period for your dog. If you have to feed him in this way, you can be certain that he is unhappy; he doesn't want to make trouble for you. Treat him calmly and gently. You can be firm without making the dog more miserable than he already is. Take the situation as a matter of course, or else he will suspect you are upset and perhaps fight back. Tension and anxiety are usually contagious. Don't jam the food into his mouth, don't scream at him, don't push him around. He is doing the best he can.

If you are under no special orders from the veterinarian about feeding, there are several ways you can make your dog's food more attractive. Mix whatever you happen to be giving him in beef bouillon or in chicken broth. If you want him to have chopped meat, shape it into small balls and let him eat it out of your hand. If you give him solids, soak them well in beef broth or milk. Keep whatever he eats at room temperature.

For the dog who has trouble keeping his food down, a beef bouillon diet is nourishing and usually easy to digest. Do not try to give large quantities at any one time if your dog has trouble in holding his food. Feed him often—four or five times during the waking day. If the vomiting continues, of course consult your veterinarian. Usually, however, the vomiting lasts for a short time, and then the dog can gradually be put back on solids—mushy cereals, baby food, chopped meat, boiled chicken, even regular canned food if he can retain it.

During the convalescence, give your dog a vitamin and mineral supplement. If he doesn't mind having it mixed with his food, give it to him that way. If he objects—by refusing to eat or by vomiting—give the supplement as you would medicine, by the lip-pouch method (see below for details of the procedure).

Some ailing dogs suffer from diarrhea, and their diet should attempt to curb the diarrhea while providing nourishment and strength. Such foods as boiled rice, cheese (especially cottage cheese, which is easy to digest), and boiled milk generally serve this purpose. Your veterinarian will probably recommend special treatment or a prescription diet if the diarrhea continues.

On occasion the convalescing dog will regurgitate his food right after eating, become interested in it, and begin eating it again. While this is obviously nauseating to you, it is perfectly natural for the dog. You should not interfere with him—he regains the nourishment from his food in this way. If he has vomited because his digestive system is upset, he will not go near it. But if he is interested in the food, then he should be allowed to eat it. Many puppies of course eat the voluntarily vomited food of the mother. If this method, however, becomes the *sole way* in which your dog will eat, then there is something wrong, and you should consult your veterinarian.

The most important thing for you to keep in mind is that a sick dog must eat, and he must do so with a minimum of anxiety and nervousness. Your job is to be sure he gets his necessary nourishment without upsetting him, or yourself.

ADMINISTERING LIQUID MEDICINE

The best way to give a liquid medicine is to have your dog run up to you, open his mouth wide, and let you pour it down toward the back part of his tongue. The only difficulty is that most dogs who are otherwise very reasonable will do no such thing. If they permit you to pour in the medicine, they will calmly spit it on the floor, or on you if they are given the chance.

The second-best way is to mix the medicine with the dog's food, or mix it with other liquids that he generally likes. If the medicine is not bad-tasting, this method might work. The chances are good, however, that it won't. Dogs are very suspicious creatures, particularly when their noses tell them that something foreign is in their food. They will pass up the food, and with that pass up the medicine. If you have a lot of extra of both, you might try the method, but don't be too optimistic about the results.

The third method is the "force" method. Incidentally, whatever you do with liquids, make sure that you don't throw them down your dog's throat. They may get into his windpipe and cause considerable trouble. Liquid in the lungs can cause pneumonia, or at best a serious congestion. The "force" method is the lip-pouch way, which is safe and virtually infallible unless your dog is particularly devilish. First, place the medicine in a spoon, or better yet in a small bottle. Grab his lower lip (without hurting him) in front of the corner of his mouth and pull it out, without forcing. This forms a pouch or pocket. Pour the medicine slowly into the pouch, a very little at a time, close the pouch, and let the dog swallow. Lift his muzzle up if he hesitates about swallowing, and then he has little choice. The liquid will go through his clenched teeth down his throat. Repeat until all the medicine has been swallowed.

Sometimes a dog will see that it is useless to resist after he receives the first dose, and thereafter he will open wide. Consider yourself blessed when this happens. Conversely, some dogs will see the medicine coming and, sick or not, will fight like demons to avoid it. For some, it becomes a form of play. Then you will need a second person to hold the dog's head while you form the pouch and pour in the medicine. Do not, in any case, wrench the dog around or wrestle with him. Also, do not be timid. If the dog sees that you are a coward or unsure of yourself, he has an immediate urge to take advantage of you. Go about your business in a kind but firm way.

Some measurement equivalents are as follows: A teaspoon of liquid is about one-sixth of an ounce; a tablespoon is about one-half of an ounce or 5 cc.; a dram is about the same as a teaspoon; an ounce is 30 cc. and a cup is 8 ounces.

GIVING PILLS AND TABLETS

When the time comes to give a pill to your dog, you might try to sneak it in. Put it in his food and hope that he gulps down the pill with his filet mignon. Some dogs will, and some won't. Those who won't usually smell the medicine (it may have no odor to you, but a dog is much more sensitive) and eat all around it, looking up in triumph when they have finished and isolated the pill.

The next step is to "force" him, once again taking care not to hurt or upset him. If you get frantic about his pill, the dog will also become hysterical, and your job will be twice as hard. Simply do not let on that he is giving you trouble. Hum a little tune, as though you are accustomed to giving pills to lions as well as to dogs. The dog may not be fooled, but it will keep your blood pressure down.

Once you have his confidence, grasp his muzzle and squeeze his lips against his teeth, your thumb on one side and your fingers on the other. As you apply pressure just forward of the corners of his mouth, he will open his mouth. He has little choice, for resistance begins to hurt him. Push his lips between his teeth so that if he decides to play rough and bite (very rare), he will bite his own cheeks. You now have his mouth open, and you will have one hand free.

Tilt his head backward and upward. That will open the lower jaw and give you an excellent target. Make sure his teeth are covered by his lips, and with your free hand place the pill, capsule, or tablet well back in the mouth, toward the base of the tongue. Don't throw the pill in, or you may flick it into the windpipe and choke him. After the pill is settled on the back part of the tongue, close his mouth firmly. When his mouth is closed, hold it tight to prevent him from spitting out the pill. Then rub, stroke, or massage his throat. Lift up the muzzle at about the same time. The dog will have little choice but to swallow. When he does, the pill goes down with the swallow.

Admittedly, all this is easy if you have a small dog. I know that many of you can't imagine holding down a Mastiff or a Great Dane when he outweighs you by fifty pounds and is ordinarily twice as strong. But your dog is sick and probably weaker than you. If you can get help, so much the better. If you can't, you can always put on his collar and leash, and then fasten the leash to a stationary object or sit on it. That restricts his movement and gives you a better chance of winning.

Certain breeds, I should mention, can create special difficulties. The short-nosed breeds, for instance, like the Boxer, English Bull, and Boston Terrier, have thick tongues and wide mouths with narrow passageways to the stomach. But if the owner of such a dog is persistent, he will learn the technique necessary for giving the pill.

KEEPING THE SICK DOG CLEAN

Your problem in keeping the sick dog clean depends on how sick he is. If he can get up and walk, he probably will evacuate and urinate on newspaper that is several feet from his bed or nest. If he cannot walk, he may urinate and move his bowels right in his nest and soil himself.

First, make sure the dog rests on a washable material—rubber sheeting or washable sheets and blankets. These may have to be changed often, particularly if your dog has diarrhea or urinates frequently. Of course you might put a diaper on him, or better yet two diapers. You may find this idea absurd, but it will save you a lot of work. The dog might not like it at first either, and therefore make sure you fasten the diaper securely so he can't pull it off, which he'll try very hard to do. Change the diaper as soon as it gets soiled, or the dog, like an infant, will get a diaper rash to add to his woes.

The dog himself now has to be cleaned. If he soils himself or if he wears a diaper, there is still the problem of cleaning him. You cannot bathe him while he is undergoing treatment. Bathing is a dubious business even under the best of conditions, and you certainly shouldn't think of it now. Wherever he is soiled you should wash him off with a mild soap and warm water. After you've dried all wet spots, comb him.

If your dog has diarrhea, his hindquarters will probably be matted and dirty. This area requires frequent washings to prevent discomfort or a rash. You might, under these circumstances, trim the hair. It will grow back in due time.

The dog's nose and mouth should be kept clean of discharge, particularly if he has a respiratory ailment that keeps a mucous discharge on his face. With warm water, clear away any hard or caked matter around his eyes, ears, or nose. If the eyes are inflamed, apply a mild eye ointment. If your dog has a condition that causes vomiting, keep his mouth area fresh and clean, and wash out his mouth and teeth with a cloth. He will feel better after this attention.

Keep his coat combed and brushed. The care he gets will assure him of your love, and the coat itself will benefit. A dog who is well-groomed even while sick has received a lift in morale. Don't be severe, and don't strain him if he wishes to rest, but let him know through your care that his illness has not changed anything in your relationship.

A sick dog, like a sick person, may develop bed sores. The only way to avoid them, particularly in the dog who is bedridden, is to turn him over many times a day. The chances are that your dog will not be so sick that he cannot move himself. But if he is, you should move him around so that all areas of his body are relieved of the pressure that causes bed sores, which are hard to cure.

If he is very uncomfortable from the heat, sponge him off with a wet washcloth, and dry him with a towel. Do not soak him, and keep him out of drafts. This is, by the way, a good method with which to cool off the well dog also.

BANDAGES

For the application of dressings and bandages under emergency conditions, see First Aid, Chapter 7.

If your dog has been bandaged, and the bandage works loose, you should get in touch with your veterinarian. Dressings and bandages are a tricky business, and you may not replace them correctly. Unless there is no opportunity for professional help, you should not attempt to rebandage a dog.

Usually the veterinarian has arranged the bandage so that it cannot be torn or pulled off. Occasionally the dog, through sheer persistence, will be able to break through the bandage and get at the wound. The danger then is not always from the dog's mouth, but from bacterial infection in the general area. Sometimes the veterinarian will provide a collar for the dog—the well-known Elizabethan collar is one type—and the collar prevents the dog from getting at the wound with his mouth. When there is a face wound, this collar also keeps the dog's nails from his face.

You should keep bandage and tape available in the event the original packing comes off. But after rebandaging your dog, do not assume you have done what the veterinarian did. Your job is only temporary. Sometimes the bandage comes off, and bleeding starts. This is an emergency situation, particularly if the bleeding is heavy. In Chapter 7 on first aid, read about how to apply pressure directly on the wound. The chances of your having to do this except in accidents are rare. Usually when a veterinarian has finished with the dog, the bandages are solid and firm. Also, the dog is generally in a weakened condition, and too much pulling and tearing will tire him. As he recuperates, however, you may find him working at the bandages more and more.

A sick dog is a large responsibility. You must do everything for him, and he can help only by offering you affection in return. Surely the exchange is a worthwhile one. When your dog has recovered and regained his vitality, his gratitude will more than repay you for the trouble you took.

7

First Aid

F IRST AID is the emergency treatment you give your dog until you can get him to a veterinarian or a veterinarian can come to him. *First aid is not complete treatment, but only the stopgap measures you take before professional help is available.* The purpose of first aid is to save your dog's life. Always think of first aid as the first step toward his recovery, rarely as the final step. In almost all cases, your dog will need further treatment, sometimes extensive treatment.

First aid will be needed after automobile accidents, in hemorrhaging (bleeding), for broken bones, animal and snake bites, eye injuries, cuts and burns, electric shock, drowning, and insect bites and stings. One of the most important things to remember in giving first aid is that you must control the panic you may feel and remain calm. You should know your own limitations and not try any daring treatment that only a professional can administer. Nevertheless, you must have confidence in your ability to give temporary help. And you can certainly build up this confidence if you have some knowledge of the physical makeup of your dog and information about first aid itself. Always remain patient with your dog, soothing him with a soft, reassuring tone, for this too helps a good deal when he is in pain.

When you give first aid, begin with first things first. That is, you must be able to see what needs immediate attention. You must also be able to give accurate information to the veterinarian when he arrives. *In administering such aid, do not give up on your dog simply because the usual signs of life are absent.* Many dogs seem dead, but can be revived after many hours of hard work.

1. All severe bleeding must receive immediate attention, no matter what other injuries are present. Bleeding or hemorrhaging will be discussed in great detail later, but here it is enough to say that it may be either internal or external. Whenever you see heavy bleeding, stop it in any way you can. See directions in the section on bleeding, page 346.

343

2. The dog must be able to breathe freely. His nose or mouth must be clear to allow the passage of air, and his neck should not be constrained in a collar.

3. Do not change your dog's position. The chances are that he has chosen the most comfortable one. Make sure all injured parts are supported, as described later in this chapter.

4. Make sure that the dog is warm. Shock usually accompanies an accident or injury. In an emergency, cover your dog with sweaters or coats or any other garments available.

5. Cover any wound with a clean dressing. More on this later.

6. Do not give water. The injury may be internal, and water will only aggravate it. Furthermore, the dog may be groggy, and the water will run down his windpipe and get into his lungs.

7. While you are giving emergency treatment, be sure that someone is calling a veterinarian or making arrangements to take you and the dog to a veterinarian. This is very important, for it may mean the difference between life and death for your dog.

RESTRAINT

All injured dogs need to be restrained. You have restrained your dog in several ways before. When you hold him on the leash, you are using restraint. When you keep him in the yard or in his room, you restrain him. When a dog is injured, he must be more strictly restrained because he is frightened, and when he is frightened he may do things he has never done before—bite, snap, kick, and lunge. Remember, however, that he is injured, that he is suffering pain, and that he is probably in a state of shock and doesn't know what he is doing.

At first, you may talk to him, call him by his name, and try to calm and reassure him. But this may not be enough. Usually it isn't.

The most common form of restraint is used to prevent your dog from biting. Once you feel safe from his teeth, you will be able to treat him until the veterinarian arrives. The first step, then, is to make a mouth tie. The best material for this is a strong strip of cloth about 3 to 5 inches in width and about 2 feet in length. Make a large loop or lasso and slip it over the dog's nose, over the bones, so that it rests just behind the soft part of the nose and does not block his breathing. *Keep his nostrils free at all times.* Pull the loop tight and run the ends under his ears so that you can tie them behind his head.

A head tie or muzzle must be removed if the dog vomits, or else he may choke to death. Watch out for this situation. The dog will start to choke and the membranes around his mouth and eyes will turn blue.

Of course, you probably will not have a piece of cloth with you in an emergency. As a substitute, use a belt, a tie, a strip of material from your shirt or underwear, a large handkerchief, a sock if the dog's muzzle is small, even the leash if it is leather. Do not worry if you can't fasten the ends under his ears—the important thing is to prevent biting. Remember, no matter how well you think you know your dog, it is always dangerous to try first aid without restraint. Your dog may be half out of his mind and simply not know what he is doing.

All this is easy if the dog cooperates. How about the injured dog who will not cooperate—the one who thrashes and becomes vicious when you try to restrain him? In such an event, you will need someone to help you, especially if your pet is large and strong and has big teeth. The best thing to do if he is standing (unlikely) is to grab his collar and pull up on it while straddling him from behind. If he is lying down, do the same thing while squatting over him. Place his neck between your legs and hold tight. Do not at this stage be afraid of hurting him— your job is to restrain him so that you can treat his major injuries. While you are holding him, have the other person put on the mouth tie. If your dog tries to pull away, tie his hind legs.

Once his mouth is restrained, you may have to tie him to a tree or pole to prevent him from injuring himself further. This is by no means easy to do if he is a strong dog, but it may become necessary if he is really crazed. First, of course, make sure that the mouth tie is secure. If you cannot get close enough to grab his collar, you may have to lasso him and fasten him to something stationary. In extreme cases, you have to lasso him before you can attach the mouth tie. Most of the time, however, a dog will not resist to this extent.

AUTOMOBILE ACCIDENTS

Automobiles cause more injuries and deaths to dogs than any other kind of accident. When a dog is hit by a car, you can expect the following injuries: shock, internal bleeding, cuts that bleed profusely, broken bones, concussion and brain hemorrhage, perhaps unconsciousness. There are also injuries of a more minor nature: bruises, abrasions, contusions, superficial cuts, lacerations, dislocations. These minor injuries require treatment, but not immediate first aid because none of them will lead to a dog's death, no matter how much pain and discomfort they appear to cause.

In this chapter, you will find these and many other injuries described, with emergency treatment recommended for each. It is a good idea for the new owner to read through the entire chapter to understand the nature of a dog's injuries and to gain some information about his body under stress. Also, this general reading will be of great help if you must give first aid when the book is not available. Then you must act quickly and surely, especially if your dog has been in an automobile accident.

Bleeding

Let us follow through on an automobile accident, since it is the most common and probably the first fear of owners. What do you do if your dog is hit by a car? *Do not move the dog. Then apply restraint,* as described in the previous pages, to make sure that he cannot bite. Try to find out what is the matter without moving him. If you see a lot of blood, you must act immediately to stop it. If bones are broken or if there is internal bleeding, take care not to shake him. Lift the upper lip to look at the gums. If they are whitish or gray, there may be internal bleeding from a ruptured organ. In such an event, the eye becomes white—even the normally red part.

Other signs of internal hemorrhaging are changes in pulse to either feeble or rapid, coldness and clamminess of the skin of the legs, feebleness and listlessness, temperature falling well below normal, resulting in cold ears and extremities, respiration becoming rapid and shallow, as well as gasping, shivering, and shaking.

If there is internal bleeding, you must move quickly; the dog will bleed to death without immediate professional care. Find a flat surface— a board is best, second-best is a blanket used as a hammock—on which to lay him so that he will lie straight, and take him immediately to a veterinarian or to a hospital. If nothing is available, then lift him in your arms, keeping him quiet because agitation will only increase bleeding.

In case no veterinarian is immediately available, keep the dog quiet and give him nothing to drink. He will probably stay quiet because he is in shock. Try no other treatment until he can receive professional care.

If you notice abundant external bleeding, that must be taken care of if the dog is not to bleed to death. Do not bother with minor cuts, lacerations, and bruises that are seeping blood. You should here be concerned only with those wounds that will result in a severe loss of blood. There are three different kinds of bleeding:

1. ARTERIAL: bleeding from an artery. The color of the blood is bright red, and it spurts out in jets. If the cut artery is at the bottom of a wound, that is, deep inside it, the wound will fill rapidly with blood, like a cup with water. This is the most serious kind of external bleeding.

2. VENOUS: bleeding from a vein. The blood is dark red and flows steadily with a seeping movement.

3. CAPILLARY: bleeding from a capillary. The blood oozes steadily from several spots on the surface of a wound.

TREATMENT OF ARTERIAL BLEEDING

Since this bleeding is by far the most dangerous, you must give immediate first aid. One method is to apply direct finger pressure. Place your finger directly on the cut artery within the wound and apply pressure.

This is a fast and effective method. If your hand is dirty, place a clean handkerchief or other clean material over your finger first. Remember, your aim is to stop the bleeding. If infection does follow, at least the dog has lived.

A second method is to apply a pad and bandage. Bleeding from a small artery may usually be stopped by placing a pad of gauze and a bandage over the wound.

A final and the least effective method for the layman is to apply his finger at a pressure point. The dog has only three points at which pressure may easily and successfully be applied, and these are not easily located by most owners. The first pressure point occurs an inch or so above the elbow joint. Pressure on this point will stop hemorrhaging from wounds below the elbow by controlling the brachial artery. A second point is found on the femoral artery as it passes over the thighbone, on the inside of the thigh. Pressure here prevents bleeding below the thighbone. the third point is on the carotid artery and jugular vein which pass on each side of the neck above the shoulder. If you apply pressure here, you can stop hemorrhaging in the extremities.

TREATMENT OF VENOUS BLEEDING

The application of a gauze pad and a tight bandage directly over the wound is usually sufficient to stop bleeding from a vein.

TREATMENT OF CAPILLARY BLEEDING

If the bleeding from a capillary doesn't stop by itself—as it usually will—you can try any of the following: Apply gauze and bandage; use a styptic pencil (a specially medicated stick that contracts the blood vessels); bathe the wound with cold water or apply ice.

Once severe bleeding is under control, you should do the following things until the veterinarian can examine your dog to diagnose the extent of his injuries. Keep your dog quiet. He will rest if you place him in a confined, isolated area. Treat him for shock, which often accompanies bleeding, according to the steps I outline below.

Shock

Shock is a condition associated with some failure in the circulation of the blood. There are many causes of shock. It may result from a loss of blood, or from emotional upset, great pain, severe vomiting, exposure to extreme cold, fear, starvation, damage to tissues, or from a blow to a vital organ. An automobile accident often causes several of these conditions.

A dog suffering from shock may look as if he is asleep or may appear semiconscious. The gums and inside of his lips are usually whitish, his breathing rapid and shallow. Signs of course vary according to the severity of the condition. The dog's body may be cold, his pulse feeble and rapid, his temperature subnormal. Since his muscles will relax during shock, he will have no control of his bladder and bowels.

Shock is extremely serious, a frequent cause of death regardless of other injuries. It must be treated immediately. Make sure your dog's head is lower than his body. To raise his temperature, keep him warm with blankets and, if available, a hot-water bottle wrapped in a towel. Keep him quiet and try to eliminate any excitement or disturbances by putting him in an isolated, confined place if he can be moved.

If he is fully conscious and able to swallow, give him small amounts of fluids like warm milk and sugar, hot water and glucose, weak soup. Water should always be available if he wants it. Try to relieve any pain by comforting and soothing him.

Do not give stimulants like brandy or whiskey unless the dog's breathing becomes very weak, shallow, and irregular. You can recognize this condition when there is a long time between breaths. If the dog can't or won't swallow, let him sniff aromatic spirits of ammonia. If there is shock without bleeding, give warm coffee (figure a cup for a 60-pound dog and scale the amount up or down according to his weight). *You can do this only if the mouth tie can be safely removed.* If he is too weak to lap, form a pocket of his lip and pour in the coffee (make sure it is not too hot). See Chapter 6 for the lip-pouch method. Make sure the liquid doesn't go down his windpipe, or trachea. If he starts to cough or gag, remove the mouth tie if you have replaced it.

Fractures (Breakage of Bones)

A frequent injury in automobile accidents as well as in many other kinds of accident is a broken bone. Dogs are very durable, but when they are hit by two tons of steel their bones are unequal to the contest, and the result is a fracture.

A bone can be broken by a severe blow like a kick, the weight of a wheel, or the impact of a bullet. Furthermore, a dog may break a leg when he takes a big jump.

TYPES OF FRACTURE

Fractures fall into three types: simple, compound, and comminuted. A simple fracture means that a bone is broken; compound means not only that a bone is broken, but that skin and muscles are punctured or torn, allowing bacteria to enter and cause possible infection; comminuted means that a bone is broken into several pieces. There may be additional factors such as an injury to some organ (brain, lung, kidney) or to an important nerve, blood vessel, or joint.

SIGNS

How, you may ask, do you recognize a fracture? Generally, you won't have much trouble, especially if you are present at an accident and already suspect an injury. The dog will lose the use of a broken limb. Or if there is a fracture to bones other than the legs, the dog may not be able to walk, or else walk unnaturally. Further, there will be swelling and inflammation in the vicinity of the fracture, with bleeding occurring in a compound fracture where bones come through the skin. Usually there is pain, but that is not always so. The dog may go into shock and not feel much pain. If these signs are not sufficient, you may also look for a deformity at the point of fracture—the limb may hang strangely. Dogs who have suffered broken bones and do not receive adequate professional care often have deformed limbs, because the contracting muscles cause the bone ends to override each other. When this happens, the limb is shortened.

When you administer first aid to a dog suffering from a fracture, be sure to guard against further injury. The broken bone is a potential source of danger. A broken rib, for example, can pierce a lung. Or a simple leg fracture might become compound or comminuted if the leg is not immobilized. Most of the instructions below will show you how to prevent the fractured limb or bone from doing further damage while you await professional help. Further, you should try to reduce the dog's pain by making him comfortable, covering him with blankets, giving him half an aspirin if he is able to swallow, or a teaspoonful of whiskey diluted in water with sugar (for a 25- to 30–pound dog; for other dogs, scale the amount up or down as necessary).

GENERAL FIRST AID

Any dog who has suffered a fractured bone cannot be handled until restraint is first applied. Use the mouth tie as described earlier in this chapter. Approach the dog with the greatest of caution, for if the pain from his fracture is great he may try to bite. Once he has been restrained, determine if a fracture does exist by looking for any unnatural formation, lameness, inflammation, bleeding (from bone coming through the skin), inability to move the limb. If a fracture is present, handle the broken limb as little as possible. You only aggravate the condition by shifting it around or moving the dog. Keep him comfortable and treat him for shock, as described above.

If you cannot reach a veterinarian to treat your dog, you must immobilize the limb or limbs with a splint. You can improvise a splint from tree branches, pieces of wood, metal, leather, pipes, heavy cardboard, even pencils if nothing else is available. As long as the object is firm and long enough to keep the joints above and below the fractured bone from moving, it will do.

First wrap the limb itself in a layer of cotton or bandage. If you don't have these, use newspaper. Pad the splint with soft material so that pressure can be applied evenly; the bare splint is too hard and straight to fit snugly against the broken limb. Then place the padded splint against the limb, making sure that the splint ends extend above and below the fractured part. Bandage the splint and the limb together firmly, but not tightly. Do not restrict blood circulation, or you may cause gangrene. Remember that this treatment is only temporary. A veterinarian may apply traction and set the bones, or he may operate. If bandages are unavailable, use whatever is at hand: tape, strips of cloth, socks, handkerchiefs, a tie, a belt. If the accident occurs away from your home, you will have to improvise.

Sprains

Although a sprain is distinct from a fracture, you may not recognize the difference and should treat the condition in the same way. A sprain occurs around a joint when a sudden twist or wrench stretches or tears a ligament. The signs are tenderness and swelling at the joint, and evident pain when there is sudden pressure on it.

The treatment follows that recommended for a fracture. That is, restrain the dog, confine him, keep the affected joint immobilized by applying a splint, and call a veterinarian.

Dislocations

Sudden violence, like being hit by a car, can cause a dislocation. It means that one or more of the bones that form a joint is out of place. The most frequently dislocated bones are at the hip, knee, toe, and jaw.

The chief signs of dislocation are loss of movement or use of the limb; deformity—that is, the limb assumes an unnatural position, bulges, or sticks out; possible swelling around the joint; considerable pain if the bones around the joint are moved. With a knee dislocation, the dog holds his leg up in a flexed position or will not put any weight on it if he touches it to the ground. With a hip dislocation, one leg appears shorter than the other, and it swings when the dog walks.

The most you can do for a dislocation is to make your dog comfortable until you can see a veterinarian. Do not attempt to remedy the dislocation. Unless you know precisely how to do it, you can injure the ligaments and muscles in the area. Place your dog in a comfortable position in a quiet place. Apply cold compresses—ice-cold water, a cold-water bag, or ice cubes wrapped in a dish towel or wash cloth—to relieve pain. These are all temporary measures, and you should not attempt further treatment.

Incidentally, certain breeds seem more disposed to dislocations than others. Toys may suffer from dislocation of the knee joint, a weakness that can be present at birth. This is also true of Bulldogs and Boxers, as well as of several short-legged breeds like Scottish Terriers, Pekingese, and Sealyhams. Greyhounds and some sporting breeds show a high incidence of dislocations of toe joints as compared with other breeds.

Strains and Ruptured Muscles

A stretched muscle or tendon is a strain. When the muscle is torn, we say it is ruptured. For the layman, the signs of fracture, sprain, strain, rupture, and dislocation may be about the same, unless a bone is protruding through the skin. There is lameness present, as well as tenderness, and the dog will hold his leg up, fearing to put any weight on it. If the back muscles or tendons are injured, the dog may become partially paralyzed.

Since your dog is probably in great pain, do everything you can to make him comfortable. Give manual support to the injured area or use bandages so that it doesn't hang free and increase the pain. Also apply cold compresses, as suggested above for dislocations. Cold tends to reduce pain. Do not apply heat—it is for swelling, not pain.

Dressings and Bandages

Before you read the section on wounds, you need some information about dressings and bandages. I don't want to give you a lot of complicated directions because most owners, fortunately, will never have to bother with either dressings or bandages. What I tell you here, nevertheless, is important just in case the need does arise and you must do something to help your dog until you see a veterinarian. Everything that I describe involves temporary treatment of general conditions. A veterinarian will inform you of what to do in the particular case.

A dressing, whether wet or dry, is a covering applied to a wound or injury. The dry dressing usually consists of folded pads of gauze and is used to protect a wound, to prevent infection, or to apply pressure to stop bleeding. The ideal dressing is sterilized, but in the absence of one you can improvise with a clean handkerchief or any other sanitary piece of cloth. The dressing should be held in place by a bandage.

The wet dressing (often called a compress) may be applied either hot or cold. When applied to an open wound, the wet dressing is usually first soaked in an antiseptic solution (boric acid solution or half peroxide and half water). When there is no open wound, a cold compress or dressing is applied to lessen pain and control any internal bleeding. A handkerchief or dish towel folded several times to give some thickness serves the purpose. Make sure it doesn't drip after you soak it in cold water. Hold the compress in place with a bandage. A hot compress is used to relieve or reduce swelling. Follow the same procedure as with the cold compress, except that you substitute very hot water. Be sure to wring the cloth dry.

The most frequently used bandage is called roller bandage, usually

4 to 6 yards long and 1 to 6 inches wide. Bandages are used to keep dressings or splints in position. They also exert pressure and help reduce or prevent swelling or bleeding. In some instances, they give support when a bone is dislocated or strained.

Before applying roller bandages, be sure that they are tight and evenly rolled, and never allow more than a few inches to unroll at a time. Bandage from below upward and from within outward, over the front of the injured limb. In this way you can be sure you are making the bandage an even spiral. As you roll the bandage over the limb or splint, apply each successive layer so that two-thirds of the preceding layer is covered. Apply firmly, but never tightly enough to stop normal blood circulation.

WOUNDS

CLOSED WOUNDS

Closed wounds do not penetrate the entire thickness of the skin. A contusion or bruise caused by a blunt object is a closed wound. Here small blood vessels are ruptured and the soft tissue beneath the skin is damaged. The most common signs are pain, swelling, heat, and discoloration. Where the skin is normally loose—the fold in front of the hip—the swelling may be great, although pain is possibly slight. Where the skin is normally tight—the lower part of the leg—the swelling may be slight, but the pain great.

For treatment, apply a cold compress and bandage the part firmly to limit the area of swelling. If the swelling has already developed and pain is great, apply the cold compress to relieve the pain, but do not bandage.

Another kind of closed wound is the abrasion or sore. It is not dangerous, usually only involving the loss of some surface layers of skin. In a severe abrasion, the nerve endings in the skin may be exposed, and the dog will be in great pain. Such wounds are often soiled with dirt, grime, and matted hair, and are therefore open to infection.

After restraint with a mouth tie, clip away the hair around the abrasion with scissors, and wash with mild soap and warm water all loose hair on the wound. Then apply boric acid solution or half peroxide and half water, or other mild antiseptic solution.

OPEN WOUNDS

In an open wound the break in the skin or mucous membranes leads to a break in the soft tissue immediately beneath it. Open wounds can be of several kinds.

1. INCISED WOUNDS are made by a sharp cutting instrument such as a knife or glass. The edges of the wound are clean-cut, and it bleeds freely.

2. LACERATED WOUNDS are the most common type of wound, made by a tearing or bursting force. Lacerations may come from kicks by people or horses, from barbed wire, from collisions with a car, or from bites of other dogs. The wound is irregular in shape, with the skin edges ragged and uneven. The amount of bleeding depends on the vessels that are cut.

3. PUNCTURE WOUNDS come from sharp-pointed instruments like nails, pins, thorns, porcupine quills, hay forks, bullets, fishhooks, and similar objects. The bleeding in a puncture is usually slight, and therefore the wound might be overlooked. Examine the skin of the dog carefully, or through neglect the wound may become infected.

TREATMENT

A dog with an open wound is normally frightened and in pain. Before you examine him and attempt first aid, use restraint with a mouth tie as described above.

First, if the object that has caused the wound is still in the wound and can be removed easily, do remove it, particularly if it is likely to do further damage. Second, as soon as you've removed the object, control the bleeding by following the directions given under "Bleeding" on page 346 of this chapter. Severe bleeding must of course be stopped.

As part of first aid for wounds, whether open or closed, you must try to prevent infection once the bleeding has been stopped. Most wounds have been caused by objects that are themselves full of bacteria. Whenever possible, cover the wound with a sterile gauze pad soaked in antiseptic, and bandage it to keep it on. If no gauze pad is available, use a clean handkerchief.

In case of accident, then, *remain calm, and do what you can to help your dog*. First aid applied rapidly and expertly is often the difference between life and death. And remember that first aid—during an accident or otherwise—is only the first step toward treatment. While handling a relatively minor matter, you may overlook a major injury and falsely believe that your dog is on his way to recovery. You must call in a veterinarian to make a full diagnosis and to prescribe treatment.

HOME ACCIDENTS: POISONING

Unless you are careful, your dog may poison himself with one of the many germicides, insecticides, detergents, corrosives, or medicines on the market. If you leave them lying around, your dog will nose into them, perhaps sample them, and then need first aid.

No matter how careful you are, it is a good idea to keep a medicine chest or cabinet stocked for an emergency. At the very end of this chapter, I list several items for a well-stocked cabinet. Consult the list, and provide as many of these medicines and antidotes as you think necessary. Ideally you should have everything on hand. Many of the articles listed are of course also useful to have around for yourself. For first aid in the event of poisoning, certain antidotes and emetics like activated charcoal, mustard powder, and common table salt should always be available.

When a dog is poisoned, it is nearly always by accident. He may eat garbage that is poisonous refuse, or chew plants that have been sprayed, or eat poisoned food intended for insects and rats or other rodents. *The symptoms of poisoning often resemble the symptoms of several other dog ailments: a drooling mouth, trembling, abdominal pain, cringing, rapid, shallow breathing, vomiting, convulsions, depression, eventually coma.* The severity of the reaction depends on the amount of poison eaten. With some poisons, the symptoms appear suddenly and dramatically, while with others weeks may pass before you know your dog is poisoned. That is, the symptoms appear gradually as your dog eats small amounts of poison from day to day. He may be chewing on painted objects and swallowing small amounts of lead, which progressively poisons his system.

When you suspect poison, act rapidly. While with a mild case the dog recovers swiftly, recovery in severe cases depends on how quickly you get your dog to a veterinarian. Some poisons enter the bloodstream almost immediately, and any delay will prove fatal. *There are three things you must do at once, except in the event of strychnine poisoning, which must be treated by a veterinarian.*

   1. GIVE THE DOG AN EMETIC—SOMETHING TO MAKE HIM VOMIT. AND KEEP GIVING HIM THE EMETIC UNTIL HE VOMITS.

   2. GIVE AN ANTIDOTE.

   3. GIVE AN ENEMA.

If there is someone else around, have him call the veterinarian while you administer the emetic.

Emetics (to make the dog vomit)

   1. HYDROGEN PEROXIDE: Mix equal parts of hydrogen peroxide and water and administer 1½ tablespoonfuls for each 10 pounds of the dog's body weight. Vomiting should occur in a few minutes. This is possibly the best of all emetics.

   2. COMMON SALT—Dissolve 2 teaspoonfuls in a cup of warm water.

   3. MUSTARD POWDER—Dissolve 1 tablespoonful in a cup of warm water.

   4. WASHING SODA (SODIUM BICARBONATE)—Push a piece the size of a small nut down the throat like a pill.

Antidotes

If you know that your dog has been poisoned by some substance used in your household, the specific antidote for the poison may be printed on the container. Otherwise, activated charcoal will be effective.

Activated charcoal (available at all drugstores) is excellent to combat the poison after vomiting has taken place. Stir 3 or 4 tablespoonfuls into a glass of warm water and force it into the dog. Use the lip-pouch method, as described on page 339, if the dog will not swallow normally. The charcoal neutralizes much of the poison's power. Activated charcoal is particularly recommended if you do not know what specific poison is involved and therefore do not know what antidote to give, which is usually the case. *Follow this immediately with an enema.* If you have never given your dog an enema, see Chapter 6 for instructions on how to do it.

Identifying the Poison

When you call a veterinarian, tell him the source of the poison if you know it. In the rare case that you cannot get in touch with a veterinarian and you don't know what poison your dog has swallowed, the following symptoms may help you to determine what poison is involved. I repeat: You must act swiftly with emetic, antidote, and enema.

COMMON POISONS

1. ARSENIC occurs in rat and insect poisons. The symptoms include loss of appetite, intense thirst, pain in the abdomen, vomiting, bloody diarrhea, depression, rapid breathing, complete collapse. Give the dog an emetic (see list above). Follow with the antidote: activated charcoal. Then the enema.

2. WARFARIN and ANTU are rat poisons. Symptoms of Warfarin are bleeding from the nose, bloody vomit, bloody diarrhea, loss of hair after 4 or 5 days. Give emetic as listed above and follow with antidote of activated charcoal. Take the dog to a veterinarian. Symptoms of Antu are vomiting, progressive weakness, difficulty in breathing, diarrhea, collapse. Give emetic as listed above and follow with antidote of activated charcoal. Get the dog to a veterinarian.

3. PHOSPHORUS is found in rat and roach poisons. Poisoning usually develops slowly, sometimes taking several days. The symptoms include extreme restlessness, stomach pains, vomiting of greenish-brown material, a garlic-like odor of the breath, bloody diarrhea, swelling of the tongue, jaundice (yellow skin), and weakness. As a result of the phosphorus, the vomit will glow in the dark. First give the emetic as directed above. Then follow with the antidote: The best is a one-tenth of 1 percent solution of potassium permanganate.

If your dog will eat, barley soup or oatmeal may absorb some of the phosphorus in his system. *Warning:* Never give castor oil or other oils with a laxative effect.

4. LEAD is an ingredient of paint, and poisoning usually comes from licking wet paint or drinking out of old paint cans. Your dog may also

get lead poisoning if he absorbs the lead arsenate in sprays used to kill insects and vermin. There are two kinds of lead poisoning:

A. ACUTE: The symptoms are trembling, labored breathing, cramps, bloody diarrhea, muscular weakness, convulsions, and coma. The acute form occurs if your dog has consumed large amounts of a lead compound at one time. Give an emetic as directed above and follow with the antidote of activated charcoal. Then give an enema and take the dog to a veterinarian.

B. CHRONIC: The chief symptom is a bluish discoloration at the margin of the gums. This occurs when small amounts of lead are consumed over a long period of time. Chronic poisoning is relatively rare among dogs; it is more common among children. Take your dog to a veterinarian as soon as you notice the condition.

5. STRYCHNINE is contained in some rodent poisons, in poisoned bait, in poisoned rabbits and rats, and in some medicines which people thoughtlessly give to dogs. Small amounts of strychnine found in certain tonics are harmless to people but often fatal to dogs. Do not give medicines that are not directly prescribed for your pet. The symptoms of a small dose of this poison are increased respiration, frequent yawning, nausea and vomiting, spasmodic twitching of muscles, convulsions, the corners of the mouth will be drawn back, or the jaw locked, the eyes—with pupils dilated—will protrude, head and tail will be drawn upward in pain, and he will wear a vicious look. If he has a rapid series of convulsions, the dog is near death. Any sharp sound will make the dog go into convulsions—in fact, this is the way a veterinarian may diagnose strychnine poisoning.

If a veterinarian is immediately available, he will inject medicine to make the dog vomit. If the dog is in convulsions and shows nervous signs, the veterinarian will inject a sedative. If you *see* the dog take the poison, give emetic (see list above) and then antidote of activated charcoal. Follow with strong, warm tea. Take the dog to a veterinarian.

6. ALKALIES (corrosives) are found in cleaning preparations and drain cleaners. The symptoms are like those found in other cases of poisoning, plus the fact that the dog's mouth and throat are burned. You probably cannot get an emetic into him. Take your dog to a veterinarian.

7. MEDICINES AND TONICS (intended for people)—The symptoms may be any of those described above. Give an emetic and follow with the antidote of activated charcoal.

8. DDT is contained in flea powders and in insecticides. Such poisoning is rare. The symptoms are similar to those found in other cases of poisoning, with the addition of muscular twitching. Give an emetic and follow with the antidote of activated charcoal.

Remember: Do not hesitate with a case of poisoning. The recovery of your dog depends on your fast action and, of course, on the amount of poison swallowed. First give the emetic, follow with the antidote, and then with an enema. Have someone call a veterinarian while you are working on the dog. Be ready to describe the case in detail: the kind of poison if you can determine it, the symptoms, reactions, and whatever else he may need to know.

HOME ACCIDENTS: BURNS AND SCALDS

A thick-coated dog is usually protected against most of the minor burns that a person may suffer. There are, nevertheless, several situations which can lead to burns and scalds in varying degrees of severity. A child may knock some boiling water, soup, or coffee from the stove onto the dog, or the dog may himself nose into something that burns him.

Burns and scalds come from three basic sources:

1. Excessive heat from direct flame, hot solids, steam, boiling liquids like water, coffee, soup, oil, tar; or from a fire in the apartment or house.

2. An electric current—the dog chews through a wire that is connected.

3. Chemicals in sprays, acids and alkalies, or corrosives.

Types of Burns and the Reaction

Burns of course vary greatly in their surface extent and depth. You judge by the surface damage, for unless the surface is badly burned or scalded, the skin and muscle underneath cannot be severely burned. If a large skin surface is affected, the burn is considered a major one. If, however, the burn goes no deeper than the thickness of the skin, it is superficial. Deep burns extend through the skin and may involve muscles, fatty tissue, and even bones. Burns that cover a large surface and go deep are extremely serious, and the dog's general reaction will be severe.

1. The dog with severe burns will go into shock. For a full description, see the section on shock in this chapter.

2. Toxic poisoning and infection are always potential dangers from burns and scalds. The body absorbs the poisonous products of the cells damaged by the burns; or poisons from the organisms that multiply on the surface of the burn may spread throughout the entire body. What starts out as a burn can lead to a general poisoning of the entire body.

3. Death may follow severe and extensive burns as a result of shock, toxic poisoning, or infection—or from a combination of all three.

Treatment

The treatment of course varies according to the degree of the burn. For superficial burns, simply cut away the hair in the area, and with sterile cotton apply vaseline, burn ointment, or a similar preparation that you can obtain in the drugstore or already have in your dog's medicine kit. Tannic acid jelly is very useful here.

First-degree burns usually consist of a few blisters on a small surface of the skin. Give the same treatment as for superficial burns. If you have any doubts about the severity of the condition, see a veterinarian.

For extensive burns—that is, when a fourth or more of the dog's skin surface is damaged—you must see a veterinarian immediately. First aid in the meanwhile includes protection against infection and treatment for shock. The treatment for the burns themselves must be left entirely up to the veterinarian. You can do serious harm by applying oil, grease, flour, baking soda, iodine, hypol, or any ointment you may have on hand. You should cover the burned or scalded area with a clean, dry dressing—sterile gauze, a handkerchief, sheet, or towel—and bandage it to keep it in position. To treat the shock accompanying the burns, keep your dog warm, dry, and quiet.

Burns Caused by Chemicals

Chemical burns should be treated differently from burns caused by direct flame, boiling liquids, or hot solids. If the burn is caused by a corrosive acid—such as an alkali—bathe the affected part with an alkaline (*not alkali*) solution. You can make an alkaline solution by adding a tablespoon of baking soda (bicarbonate of soda) to a pint of warm water. Washing soda (sodium carbonate) can be used in the same strength. If you have neither one, wash the afflicted area gently with milk of magnesia.

If the burn has been caused by a corrosive alkali—such as a lime product, especially one used for the garden—brush out the alkali from the dog's coat. Be careful not to get it on yourself—use long rubber gloves if you have them. Bathe the affected area with a solution made by mixing equal parts of vinegar and water.

In either case, when the acids and alkalies have been neutralized, apply on the burned area tannic acid jelly or hypochlorite solution, which you can get in any drugstore. As with all burns, take your dog to the veterinarian. Depending on the depth and extent of the burn, as well as on the treatment, infection may set in without professional care.

HOME ACCIDENTS: LOSS OF CONSCIOUSNESS

A dog may lose consciousness for a number of reasons, some of them very serious, some only moderately so. I have already discussed shock, which can result in loss of consciousness or in semiconsciousness. In other parts of the book, I have discussed eclampsia (caused by the lack of calcium or a mineral imbalance in the pregnant or nursing bitch), which often results in fits of fainting. Poisons in the dog's system can have the same consequence, as can severe bleeding.

There are several other possible causes of unconsciousness in your dog.

1. BRAIN INJURY: This is obviously one of the most common causes of loss of consciousness. If your dog suffers a concussion—the result of a blow, fall, or kick—he will fall on his side, and his breathing will become slow and shallow. His pulse will be weak, his pupils enlarged. His body may feel cold, the inside of his lips becoming pale and whitish. The treatment is complete rest until the veterinarian can examine the dog.

A blow or fall can also cause compression, a very serious condition. The signs of compression depend upon the part of the brain affected, but usually there is a radical interference with the dog's sense of balance, and he may not be able to walk straight. Also, he may bleed from the ears and nose, and vomiting is common. His pupils may be unequal in size, and he may show sensitivity to light. The treatment is the same as for shock: Keep your dog warm (with a blanket or hot-water bottle wrapped in a towel) and allow him to rest in a quiet place. Call a veterinarian immediately.

Hemorrhaging or bleeding in the brain causes what is called a stroke, or apoplexy. A stroke comes on rapidly, with partial or full loss of consciousness. If only partially unconscious, the dog may vomit, become very excited, and try unsuccessfully to stand. Usually he holds his head to one side, while his eyeballs move uncontrollably in their sockets. There is of course no sign of external injury to the skull with this condition. The treatment is similar to that for all brain injuries: rest and quiet. Do not give stimulants. Allow him small amounts of water if he can swallow. Call a veterinarian immediately.

2. SUNSTROKE AND HEATSTROKE: The most common signs are rapid breathing, severe and loud panting, vomiting, rapid pulse, weakness in the legs, staggering, inability to focus on anything, collapse. A dog may suffer heatstroke when he is left in a closed car in the sun. Fat and old dogs are particularly subject to sunstroke and should be kept indoors during the hot hours of the day when the sun is shining.

The first thing to do is to place the dog in the shade and cool him off by sponging him with cold water; if practicable give him a cold-water enema. If you have a tub available, fill it partially with ice-cold water and put the dog in. The bath should be shallow; otherwise in his semiconscious condition he may swallow water, which will get into his lungs and may cause pneumonia. Whatever you do, dry him off thoroughly.

3. ELECTRIC SHOCK: Many dogs, especially playful puppies, bite through attached electric wires and suffer shock. The dog will become paralyzed if the shock is strong enough. *Do not touch him* until you've unplugged the wire or unless you are wearing rubber gloves. Keep children away.

Small dogs may be pushed away from the wire with a stick. The treatment is for shock: Keep the dog warm and give him warm liquids if he is able to swallow. If he has stopped breathing, give him artificial respiration, which is described below under "Suffocation." If the dog is burned, treat the burns according to the directions in the section on burns.

4. SUFFOCATION: Exposure to smoke or gas may cause suffocation. Remove the dog to the fresh air immediately. If he has stopped breathing, or if his breathing is very feeble, give him artificial respiration according to the following directions.

The best method of artificial respiration is to apply mouth-to-mouth breathing. Cup your hands to form a cone and breathe directly into the dog's mouth and nostrils. Continue until the dog starts to breathe.

The other method is to place the dog on his right side with his head and neck extended and his tongue drawn forward. Place your hand over the dog's ribs right behind the shoulder blade. With a sudden but gentle movement, press downward, and this will compress the chest and expel air. After this sudden movement, relax immediately to allow the air to go back into the lungs. Wait about five seconds (count one-two-three-four-five) and start again. Keep up the pressing and release at 20 to 30 times per minute until the dog begins to breathe. If you have experience in giving artificial respiration to people, follow the same procedure with a dog. The rhythm should be smooth and steady.

Once the dog is breathing, treat him for shock: Cover him with blankets, a hot-water bottle; give him something warm to drink if he can swallow. Do not force stimulants down the dog's throat. Unless he can swallow, the liquid will go into his lungs and may cause pneumonia.

5. HEART ATTACK OR CIRCULATORY FAILURE: When a dog suffers a heart attack or circulatory failure, he suddenly loses consciousness. This type of failure is prevalent in old dogs. In many cases, a heart attack will be accompanied by slight coughing, as though the dog were trying to clear his throat. This is not always serious, except in hunting or working dogs who may have overextended themselves and will not recover. Often the dog may stand perfectly still or sway a moment, with his eyes glazed.

In more serious cases, the dog falls as if stoned and may scream. His pulse is very rapid, and his breathing at first is shallow. His tongue, if you can see it, will be dark, turning lighter as the dog's condition improves and his blood circulation returns to normal. The treatment is to wait until the dog regains consciousness and then to give him a stimulant like whiskey or brandy diluted in water. Check with a veterinarian for further treatment.

6. FITS OR CONVULSIONS: Although I describe fits and convulsions in Chapter 6, on ailments, I will repeat some of the information here since the owner witnessing a fit will want to apply first aid.

Fits may come from several causes: distemper, hysteria, worms, epilepsy. A fit can come on suddenly, with the dog either barking furiously or going into a convulsive spasm. His jaws may chatter—what is called a "chewing gum fit." He may foam at the mouth or not. In many cases, the dog will lie on his side and "run"—that is, his feet will paddle away in the air. Breathing often becomes agitated and rapid; muscles may twitch. The dog may or may not lose consciousness. During a fit, a dog is unable to control his bladder and bowels and will probably soil himself. The fit itself may last a few moments or 5 to 10 minutes. One fit frequently follows another rapidly.

A dog in a fit is no more dangerous than he normally is. If he is outdoors when a fit comes on, keep your dog leashed. Speak to him reassuringly and calmly. Don't panic. When the fit is over, get him home or to a veterinarian. If you are at home, move the dog into a dark corner and keep the children away. To pick him up, cover him with a blanket—just in case he may try to bite. Put ice packs on his head, and call the veterinarian at the first opportunity. There are anticonvulsive injections and medicines that can help your dog.

OUTDOOR ACCIDENTS

If your dog runs free—even if he is a city dog—there will be occasions when first aid is required.

Drowning

In the event of drowning, your first step is to open the air passages. Hold the dog up by his hind legs for a few seconds to let the water run out of his nose and mouth. Keep his tongue out to help him breathe. Swing him around if necessary. Then apply artificial respiration as described on page 360. When the dog is breathing regularly, dry him thoroughly with brisk rubbing to prevent pneumonia. If he can swallow and will drink something, give him warm liquids. Keep him warm with blankets, and with a hot-water bottle if one is available.

Bites and Cuts

Bites, cuts, and abrasions are common among dogs. If they look like mere scratches that the dog continues to lick, don't bother with them. More serious bites and cuts, however, must be treated. If your dog, for example, has been in a fight, let him lick his wounds, for his saliva washes out the area. Then wash the wounds with soap and water and apply a good antiseptic like peroxide.

If the wound refuses to heal because the dog continues to irritate it, you may have to fit him with an Elizabethan collar to keep his mouth away from it. Let your veterinarian be your guide here. An Elizabethan collar fits snugly around the dog's neck and provides a protective shield. To make one, cut out a large circle from heavy cardboard. In the center cut out a smaller circle that will just fit over your dog's head. Be sure that the collar is wide anough to prevent the dog's muzzle from reaching his body. Make some holes in the collar, and with strings fasten it to his regular collar. If you are not good at making things with your hands, ask your veterinarian where you can buy rubber ones that inflate.

If your dog is bitten by a cat, the wounds can be more serious because they generally become infected. Cat bites superficially look like small, harmless punctures, which they are, but they close up easily and therefore do not drain. The result may be abscesses or tetanus. In some cases, veterinarians recommend an antitetanus injection for the dog. Try to let cat-bite wounds stay open and bleed freely. If possible, after you apply a mouth tie, insert round toothpicks with cotton tips dipped in Metaphen into the cat bites, although the dog will not like this. Take off the scabs to prevent surface healing. If your dog is bitten by a cat or dog, or suffers any other kind of puncture wound, you should always see a veterinarian.

Bee and Wasp Stings

If your dog is stung, there may be shock and considerable pain. Restrain him with a mouth tie before treating the painful area. Put a cold compress on the bite to help relieve the pain from the sting. If there is considerable swelling, put on a warm compress. Then cover it with Nupercainal or Caladryl.

If your dog seems to be having trouble with his breathing or appears to be passing out, give him whiskey as a stimulant, and then take him to a veterinarian immediately. He is probably reacting violently to the sting, as some people also do. If he is allergic—which a dog rarely is— he may need an injection to counteract the toxic effect.

Snake Bite

While most dogs bitten by snakes are country dogs, many city people now travel so much that their dogs spend a good deal of time in the country. If you suspect you are in snake country, you should be prepared. The chief dangerous snakes in the United States are (1) copperhead— poisonous and dangerous; (2) cottonmouth, or water moccasin—poisonous and dangerous; (3) coral—poisonous, very dangerous; (4) rattlesnake— deadly. Find out what snakes are in your part of the country or in the part you plan to visit, especially if you are going to camp out for any length of time. Also, determine what veterinarians are in the area should an emergency arise.

The venom of a poisonous snake travels quickly to the nerves of the dog and is followed by severe pain and swelling. *In all cases, immediate action is necessary.* The old method of treatment called for expelling as much poison as possible and then trying to keep the remaining poison from spreading to other parts of the body. This was usually done by making an X-shaped incision over each fang mark with a sterilized knife or razor blade. The cuts were about one-eighth to one-quarter of an inch deep. You then squeezed out the blood, or if you had a suction cup you drew out the blood. The prepared owner then dropped potassium permanganate into the wounds and applied a tourniquet to stop the bleeding.

I assume, however, that most owners will not be prepared to perform such an "operation." Most owners, in fact, won't be able to find the fang marks because of the hair coat. The only thing you can do is to get your dog to a veterinarian for an antivenom injection and further therapy. If the dog has been bitten on the leg, the chances of recovery are greater than if he is bitten on the face. In any kind of bite, *you must act immediately.*

Frostbite

Bring your dog into a warm area and *gradually* thaw out the frozen part. If there is no warm shelter available, warm the frozen part with hand, blanket, or whatever soft object is available. *Do not rub the frozen area with any rough material and especially not with snow or ice.* You can easily bruise or tear frozen tissues, and the result can be gangrene.

Porcupine Quills

The country dog will frequently attack a porcupine, only to discover that he gets more than he bargained for. The quills are very painful, especially if many of them are imbedded in the dog's muzzle, a particularly sensitive area. Removing the quills is difficult and dangerous because the dog is in great pain and can hardly be restrained.

Should your dog become stuck with quills, take him to the veterinarian. If no veterinarian is immediately available and only a couple of quills are imbedded in his skin, apply a mouth tie and try to ease out the quills. If this is impossible—as it is likely to be—wait until a veterinarian can remove them. He will have to give the dog an anesthetic for this operation.

Poison Ivy

Poison ivy will not usually penetrate a dog's coat. But to protect yourself when you touch the dog, wash him thoroughly with brown laundry soap or tincture of green soap. Wear rubber gloves when washing him.

Skunk Odor

The dog who meets and attacks a skunk will smell like one. Usually the odor takes time to wear off, and in the meantime the skunk's spray may bother the dog's eyes. If so, wash out his eyes with a solution of boric acid and apply an eye ointment. To relieve the odor, wash the dog thoroughly with tomato juice; follow this with a washing of soap and water, and this with a washing of a 5 percent solution of ammonia. These three washings will not work wonders, but they will help your dog to become a welcome part of the family again.

Lameness

A dog may become lame if a foreign object becomes lodged in his paw. Although this can happen in the house, it is more likely that an object outdoors will injure his foot. You will quickly notice lameness. Your dog will whimper or whine and hop on three feet. Also, the injured paw may bleed and swell, although not always.

If the lameness is from a foreign object and not from a leg fracture, remove the object gently after first restraining the dog with a mouth tie. Reassure your dog with a sympathetic tone that you don't intend to hurt him. Make sure you get the entire object out. Use tweezers or pliers for glass, thorns, nails, tacks, sharp splinters, etc. Wash the part thoroughly with mild soap and warm water. If the dog wants to, let him lick the area. If there is swelling, apply warm compresses. Most minor cuts will heal without further treatment.

If the cut seems to need further attention—continued swelling, exudation of pus, failure to heal—check with your veterinarian. Of course, if you discover a fracture or a sprain (see description of these conditions earlier in this chapter), you should take your dog to a veterinarian immediately.

Injured Tail

Your dog's tail can become injured in a variety of ways. Usually the worst to expect is a bruise, which can be treated with compresses soaked in boric acid or epsom salts (follow the directions on the label for the proper solution). If the skin is broken, wash out the area with peroxide or a boric acid solution and apply an ointment.

If the tail is caught in a car door or if a heavy object somehow drops on it, it may be broken and a veterinarian must set it. Or someone may step heavily on the dog's tail when he is lying down and severely crush it. This too is a matter for the veterinarian.

Objects in Mouth and Throat

A puppy will put nearly anything in his mouth and try to swallow it. Usually dogs outgrow this tendency, although many will still tempt fate and try to swallow nails, screws, spark plugs, rubber balls, children's jacks, and nearly anything else that attracts them. If the dog is choking or gulping hard, force open his mouth by pressing the thumb and fore-finger of one hand into his cheeks. If you can't reach the object with the fingers of your other hand, then he's swallowed it.

Sometimes a dog will have a sharp object caught in his throat, objects like chicken bones, fish bones, rabbit bones (in the case of the country dog), and needles (puppies, in particular, have a taste for needles). The dog will gulp repeatedly and refuse food or water. Have someone hold the dog while you grope for the object with your hand. If you can see it and remove it gently, do so. If a needle is involved, call a veterinarian immediately. And if any other sharp object does not come out easily, you should call for professional help.

If your dog swallows a foreign object, *but not a needle,* you must make him vomit. Mix equal amounts of hydrogen peroxide and water. Give 1½ tablespoonfuls of the mixture for each 10 pounds of the dog's body weight. Use the lip-pouch method to make him swallow. See page 339 for a description of this method.

Eye Injuries

Injuries to the eye vary from simple bruises and lacerations to severe accidents in which the socket bone is fractured or smashed. Scratches on the cornea are frequent—from fights with cats (who usually go for the dog's eyes) or from brush and tree branches. Small dogs with promi-nent or bulging eyes—like the Pekingese—are particularly subject to eye injuries. If the injury is only a scratch or minor laceration, bathe the eye in a solution of boric acid. Follow directions on the label. Call your veterinarian if you have any doubts about the severity of the injury.

When the dog has a foreign object in his eye, simply wash it with sterile cotton soaked in a boric acid solution. If it still bothers him, see your veterinarian. Eye injuries may cause serious trouble.

In most injuries, the eye should be kept moist until a veterinarian can examine it. If you have nothing else, pads of cotton dipped in warm water will serve the purpose. If you have an eye ointment, apply it to the eye to keep the surface moist. Pull the lower lid of the eye down and apply a little ointment on the lid or in the eye.

A severe accident may force the eye out of its socket, either because the protective arch bone is fractured or because of some other injury.

The most you can do is to keep the eyeball moist until a veterinarian examines the dog. If the socket itself becomes filled with dirt or grime, wash it out with warm water. In all such cases, the dog will have to be restrained with a mouth tie.

Ear Injuries

Ear injuries are usually in the form of lacerations and bruises on the flap. Hounds, with their low-hanging floppy ears, are particularly subject to this kind of trouble. If the condition is minor, wash the injured area with mild soap and warm water and apply an antiseptic. If the bleeding continues or if the healing seems slow, see a veterinarian. Also, if the cut is deep or looks particularly inflamed, your dog needs professional treatment, but first clean out the wound and apply an antiseptic.

OTHER INJURIES—INDOOR AND OUTDOOR

Abdomen

An accident or a gunshot wound may open the abdominal wall so that a section of the dog's intestine emerges. This is of course very serious—most times fatal. Such an injury should be treated by a veterinarian immediately. In the meantime, if there is any delay, wash the protruding section carefully with a mild antiseptic or with water and push it inside. Use your hand or a towel or sheet as a sling to keep the organ in place. The dog may begin to vomit blood. After a wound like this, your dog may be unconscious or in shock, but if not, you must apply restraint to keep his mouth from the wound.

Keep the dog quiet and calm. Cover him with a blanket because he is probably in shock. Give him no liquids or food. If he shows great thirst, let him lick ice, but nothing else.

Nose

A sharp blow, a kick, or an accident may injure the dog's nose, causing pain and swelling. Keep the dog quiet and apply cold water on a compress or handkerchief. If there is bleeding, the cold should stop it. If bleeding continues, call a veterinarian.

Larynx (Voice Box)

A blow, kick, or accident can cause swelling in the larynx and difficulty in breathing. Since the larynx is the passage through which air reaches the lungs, a severe blow might lead to suffocation.

The most common signs of injury are pain and swelling, noisy and difficult breathing. If the larynx is punctured by a sharp object or a bullet, you will hear the hiss of air escaping. Also, bubbles of blood will ooze out of the wound, and air will collect under the skin.

For treatment, first restrain the dog and then apply a hot compress. Make sure that the dog has plenty of fresh air. If there is an open wound, take care that no liquid gets into the air passage; otherwise coughing will follow. Furthermore, pneumonia can result if liquid gets into the lungs. For this kind of injury, the dog needs professional care once first aid is applied.

Lung

A lung can be injured in many ways: from a kick, a gunshot wound, an accident, or the penetration of a broken rib. In a lung injury, bleeding may occur inside the chest cavity without any external hemorrhaging. The most common signs are difficulty in breathing or irregular breathing, chest pains, general symptoms of shock, and coughing of frothy, bright red blood.

A lung injury is obviously a matter for the veterinarian, but there are some things you can do. Allow the dog to choose his own position— he will select the one most comfortable for him. Treat the external wound. If it is serious, you must first restrain the dog with a mouth tie. Wash out the wound with mild soap and warm water and then apply an antiseptic. If the wound is bleeding heavily, follow directions above for treating a wound. Since the dog will probably be in shock, keep him warm with blankets, and with a hot-water bottle if one is available. Give no liquids.

DIGESTIVE UPSETS

I treat digestive upsets at much greater length in Chapter 6, on ailments, and elsewhere through the book (see the index). I mention here only those digestive troubles that may require first aid.

Indigestion

Indigestion—principally seen when the dog vomits—occurs most frequently in puppies and young dogs, especially in those whose vitality is already low because of a weakening condition like worms. Since worms are more common in puppies than in older dogs, they naturally suffer more from indigestion. Also, certain breeds more than others seem subject to indigestion—Boxers, Bulldogs, Boston Terriers, and small, nervous dogs.

Unless there is something structurally wrong with the dog's internal organs, the usual cause of indigestion may be one or more among the following: overeating, eating too fast, overactivity, motion sickness, a case of nerves, an excess of fluids, the irritation of foreign material in the stomach. A dog with a perverted taste for chair stuffing, rug padding, newspapers, cigarette butts, plaster, and books will frequently have stomach disorders.

In mild digestive upsets, the dog is uneasy after eating. He will run around the room, occasionally lying down on his stomach, or crouching with his head and forefeet low and his hind parts in the air, in a praying position. His abdomen is usually swollen and painful. If the upset continues, the dog's appetite will fail.

Give milk of magnesia—one tablet or one teaspoonful of liquid for every 10 pounds of the dog's body weight. If the discomfort remains after several hours, give an enema of mild soap and warm water.

A neglected mild attack may be followed by a more severe one. Your dog becomes even more restless, chasing around after his tail, as if stung by a bee. He may throw himself on the floor and then start running again in a succession of such restless moves. There might be bloody vomiting and diarrhea. His abdomen may be very swollen, very hard and painful. An attack of this severity needs prompt professional treatment or your dog may go into convulsions and die.

Bloat

For a fuller description of bloat, see Chapter 6, on ailments. Bloat occurs when a dog's stomach fills with gas, usually after severe exercise or after he has eaten a lot of food rapidly. The condition is serious. First aid involves giving an enema (mild soap and water at room temperature). If this does not relieve the pressure, call a veterinarian.

Constipation

For a full description of constipation and its treatment, see Chapter 6 on ailments.

Diarrhea

For a full description of diarrhea and its treatment, see Chapter 6, on ailments.

Hot Foods

Given the opportunity, your dog may grab a very hot piece of food off the grill or stove and bolt it without chewing. The piece of food—a frankfurter, potato, or something of the sort—will then release its heat in his stomach and burn the lining. The dog will be in considerable pain from cramps, and perhaps vomit food, mucus, or blood. You must soothe the lining of his stomach by giving him milk or cream, Kaopectate, Pepto-Bismol, or any other creamy liquid you have available. Take your dog to a veterinarian immediately.

MISCELLANEOUS INCIDENTS

Swallowing Sleeping or Reducing Pills

More and more people take sleeping and reducing pills, with the result that a curious dog, especially a puppy, may find them and eat them in the mistaken notion that they are candy. The seriousness of the consequences depends on the nature of the pills and the number the dog has swallowed. If you think that the dog has eaten any, make him vomit at once. If the dog is knocked out from sleeping pills, or if he is climbing the walls and is overstimulated from the reducing pills, take him to the veterinarian for treatment. Be careful in trying to make an unconscious dog vomit—if you force liquid into the back of his throat, it may go down his windpipe into his lungs. Use the lip-pouch method (see page 339).

Car Sickness

I treat car sickness at some length in Chapter 2, on the puppy, and in Chapter 11, on the problem dog. Here, let me say that the most common symptoms are drooling and vomiting. Try to prevent car sickness by withholding the dog's food for an hour before starting on a trip, by giving him frequent opportunities to relieve himself during the trip, and by restraining him from drinking too much water. Don't feed him until after the trip (at night). If by experience you know that these methods don't work, consult with a veterinarian, who may give your dog a Dramamine tablet or other motion-sickness pill. Give such medication about an hour before the trip.

A FIRST-AID KIT FOR DOGS

(The starred items are especially important in the event of an emergency.)

1. Keep a GERMICIDE for disinfecting all dishes and pans that come into contact with the sick dog. This is a safety precaution for you and your children. Also, a good DETERGENT should be handy to wash whatever surfaces the dog may soil if he cannot evacuate outside.

2. A RECTAL THERMOMETER (Wash it in cool, never hot, water.)

3. PETROLEUM JELLY OR VASELINE for lubricating the thermometer (Vaseline, incidentally, is simply a solidified form of mineral oil.)

*4. STERILE COTTON (You will find several uses for this—in washing out eyes and ears, in removing external parasites, in washing sore areas on the dog's skin.)

5. A good eye wash of jelly (You will find this a handy item for eye washes and for sores that need washing.)

6. MINERAL OIL (This is excellent for enemas or as a mild laxative.)

7. KAOPECTATE as a fine control for diarrhea

8. RUBBING ALCOHOL as a disinfectant and Nupercainal or Caladryl to soothe stings

9. ASPIRIN as a pain reliever

10. GERMICIDAL SOAP, like Phisohex, for washing parts of the dog's skin and coat that have been infected (TINCTURE OF GREEN SOAP is also good, particularly if the dog has been in poison ivy.)

11. MILK OF MAGNESIA as an excellent mild laxative

*12. MUSTARD POWDER, SALT, and HYDROGEN PEROXIDE to induce vomiting (in the event of poisoning or stomach upsets)

*13. TANNIC ACID OINTMENT for burns, or any other ointment for treatment of minor burns

*14. ADHESIVE TAPE; one-inch and two-inch roller BANDAGE—in case of open wounds

15. COTTON SWAB STICKS for cleaning out eyes and nose

16. PAREGORIC to kill pain and to check diarrhea, if prescribed

17. DRAMAMINE (liquid or tablet) to control car sickness

18. YELLOW OXIDE OF MERCURY for minor eye irritations, if prescribed

19. TRANQUILIZERS for trips and for use after a dog has convulsions or a fit, if prescribed

*20. PEROXIDE, METAPHEN, or any other antiseptic to be used in dressing wounds

*21. SCISSORS (with blunt ends), for use in bandaging

22. (Optional—SUCTION CUP for snake bites, especially for country dogs)

23. FLEA POWDER and LICE POWDER, for external parasites

*24. ACTIVATED CHARCOAL as an antidote in all cases of poisoning, available at the drugstore

25. MEDICATED POWDER, for soothing irritated areas

26. PLIERS and TWEEZERS, for removing porcupine quills and fishhooks, especially recommended for the country dog

27. (Optional—SNAKE SERUM for country dogs)

28. (Optional—RAZOR BLADES, a sharp POCKET KNIFE, in case of a snake attack on the dog)

*29. ENEMA BAG (regular or disposable kind), for cases of poisoning and digestive upsets

*30. AROMATIC SPIRITS OF AMMONIA, for shock treatment

HANDY MEASUREMENTS: 1 TABLESPOON $= \frac{1}{2}$ OUNCE

3 TEASPOONS $=$ 1 TABLESPOON

1 CUP $=$ 8 OUNCES

8
Spaying and Castrating

THE BITCH

WHEN A veterinarian spays your bitch, he removes her ovaries and uterus, what is called a panhysterectomy. In this way, he makes it impossible for your bitch to come in heat or have any puppies.

The operation, of course, stops the discharge which the bitch has every 6 months. Many owners want their bitches spayed to avoid those two seasons each year, each period lasting about 3 weeks. At these times, the bitch goes into heat and becomes receptive to males, who smell her vaginal discharge. In the middle week of the 3 weeks, she will allow any male to mate with her. The result is usually a litter of puppies 9 weeks later. You may, as many owners do, board out your bitch at this time—at a cost, however, of about $25 to $75 depending on her size. Or you may, instead, give her a tablet medication at the onset of heat that provides estrus (or heat) control. Such medication, however, must be administered under the guidance of a veterinarian, for it is a powerful drug with possible side effects. This method is particularly attractive for those owners who wish to show a bitch while she is in heat.

There are other considerations involved in spaying besides the desire to avoid the season: 1) There is a tendency for the bitch to wander (if you live in the suburbs or country) when she is in season, seeking gratification where she can. Spaying will cut down on roaming for this reason. 2) Even if the owner does not particularly worry about the season, he may not wish to be presented with a litter, particularly if he feels that he may have to destroy the unwanted pups. Taking care of a pregnant bitch and then the puppies is more than many owners wish to face, especially those who want a dog simply for companionship. There is, further, the increase in food intake of the pregnant bitch, the cost of raising the puppies, the need to buy certain (small) items of equipment. There is even the (remote) danger that the bitch may die during whelping.

3) In some communities a license for a spayed bitch is less expensive than for an unspayed one—this may make a small but appreciable difference over the years. 4) Some bitches calm down, become more gentle, once they are spayed, although there is no guarantee of this.

Sometimes spaying is advisable for medical reasons. The unspayed bitch may suffer from false pregnancies, when she has all the symptoms of a pregnant bitch except that she isn't pregnant. This will generally be caused by cysts in her ovaries, which are not dangerous but may require surgery. Also she is subject to breast tumors in relatively higher incidence than is the spayed bitch. Similarly, the unspayed bitch might be troubled by metritis, or infection of the uterus. This too may require surgery if antibiotics don't cure it. Many of these ailments, incidentally, will not trouble the bitch as a puppy or in her middle years, but as she gets older she becomes more prone to several female ailments. It is to protect her in these years—perhaps the very best ones of the relationship between owner and pet—that many an owner has the bitch spayed early.

Many of the female difficulties that bitches currently suffer may be the result of their domesticated state. Most dogs (both male and female) now live in apartments or in suburban homes where their activities, even with the best of owners, are somewhat limited. A dog adapts easily to the kind of life his owner expects him to lead, but even as he adapts, his system is to some extent thrown out of kilter. We love the dog for his very ability to accommodate us, but we often fail to realize that he is meeting conditions that are different from those under which he thrives. In her primitive state, the bitch roamed with the pack, went through her normal semiannual season, and gave birth to litter after litter. The chances are that she suffered from few of the female disorders that result from her present inactivity. She exercised more, she ate according to her needs, she satisfied her physical desires.

In any event, the spayed bitch has a better chance of avoiding female ailments—she is generally less subject to tumors or growths of the breasts, her ovaries will not develop cysts, since they will have been removed, her uterus cannot become inflamed because it too has been removed, and false pregnancies are impossible. If you never intend to have puppies, it may be advisable to have your bitch spayed.

The arguments against spaying the bitch are several. Once she is spayed, you can, of course, never have a puppy from your own bitch. If you are at all undecided, do not take this drastic step. As your bitch gets older, you may wish to perpetuate the pet you have come to love, and if you have a purebred you can duplicate her appearance by breeding her with a purebred male. Even if you have a mongrel, you can mate her and know that the puppy—whatever he happens to look like—comes from your great and good companion of former days. Also, if you have a purebred bitch, you may at some future date decide to enter your bitch in a show, and if she has been spayed, she will not be eligible for showing.

It is just such considerations that stop people from having their pets spayed.

A few final words on the problem: A spayed bitch may tend to lose control of her sphincter muscle and urinate or dribble uncontrollably. But this reaction is one that may well occur with old age, whether the bitch has been spayed or not. There are, fortunately, hormone treatments which may control dribbling when and if it occurs.

Spaying, incidentally, does not hurt the hunting instincts of a bitch. If you use her for that purpose, you may, in fact, find spaying a relief, for you can use the bitch all the year around without worrying about her season, when she must be put into isolation to keep the males from her. Also, a further consideration: During her first season, when she is 8 to 10 months old, the bitch may have to interrupt her hunting training at a crucial time, and fall behind the other dogs in her group.

If you decide to have your bitch spayed, it is best to have it done early. Several veterinarians argue that spaying should be done after the bitch has experienced her first season (at about 8 to 10 months). At this time, so the argument runs, she is full-grown and there is no interruption in glandular development, something that could happen if she were still growing. These veterinarians claim that early spaying—that is, before the first season—results in a fat, waddling, ungainly bitch who is really neither female nor male when she grows up. I don't agree. If you want your bitch spayed, have the operation performed before the first heat, at about 6 to 7 months.

At this time there is little chance that the bitch will be too close to her first season, and also she is strong enough to withstand the necessary surgery. If you spay before the season, you do not upset the endocrine gland system on which the ovaries depend. The whole circuit of actions and reactions involved in this system is never activated, and the bitch, consequently, does not suffer from having it suddenly curtailed. If you spay after the first season, the bitch has already entered into her phase as a functioning female. The shock to her system at this time is naturally greater than it would be if the operation were performed before she is mature.

For these reasons I recommend early spaying by your veterinarian. Also, for individual bitches who may be nervous, early spaying generally calms them down, makes them more responsive and gentle. Spaying can of course be done at any age, but the longer you put it off the more complex the operation can become. Do not postpone your decision past the time your bitch is 2 or 3 years old.

The spayed bitch will not suddenly become fat if you watch her diet (as you would watch the diet of any dog) and exercise her reasonably. If you notice that she is putting on weight, simply cut her food intake, particularly the fat content. If that doesn't work, consult with your veterinarian about a special prescription diet. As for exercise, if you wish to keep her weight down, increase her activity without increasing her food. I discuss these considerations more fully in Chapters 3 and 4, but I mention them here because I know that many owners fear their spayed bitch will suddenly put on weight. They will not, any more than a woman will after a hysterectomy if she watches her diet and exercise.

If you are considering spaying your bitch for the sole reason of preventing her from coming in season, remember that there is an alternative. As mentioned before, there are ways of preventing the season altogether. On the market now there are tablets that you can give your bitch before her heat. They are available only on a veterinarian's prescription.

THE MALE (OR DOG)

The male is sexually willing to mate with a bitch from the time he is a few months old. But he is usually incapable of impregnating her until he is a little older, generally about his 8th or 9th month. The male through his entire adult life is sexually aggressive, unlike the bitch, who is receptive only during her season.

From the age of a few months (sometimes even younger), the male will experiment with his sexual powers by climbing on you, the children, the chair legs, and by rubbing himself, even pumping. Wherever there is a raised object—a blanket roll, a pile of newspapers, or a mattress—the male will rub himself and try to go through the motions of mating. Do not be upset or worry that you have a sexually abnormal or oversexed pet. All males do this, as do many bitches until they reach puberty, and even later.

As the puppy gets older, he will frolic with other dogs and practice on them—both males and bitches. He will also lick the genital area, ride (on males also), and pump, until the other dog gets tired of it and throws him off. All this is perfectly normal, the regular activity of a puppy growing up. If you find it personally distasteful, you can, of course, control it. Do not yell or scream at the dog because he will not understand why you are displeased with him; as far as he is concerned, it's all a great deal of harmless fun. Keep your dog firmly leashed, but if he does cavort sexually with other dogs, simply separate them with a minimum of fuss.

If he is young and starts to sniff around bitches who are out of season and wish to have nothing to do with him, he may be bitten or at least frightened. And if the object of his desires is in heat, he may soon find himself the center of a riot as every male in the neighborhood—all those toughies—will also be seeking her favors.

Although you may not like it, this is part of the growing-up and learning process. The most you can do is to be prepared to expect it and then act according to common sense. Remember that your dog is a dog. You make him less than he is when you try to make him conform to standards of human behavior. As a dog he has his own way of life, his own style. The greatest thing you can do as an owner is to honor it.

Depending on your situation and your own feelings, you may wish to have your dog altered or castrated. He may gain in stability, but *it is not generally recommended unless you have a problem dog.* If you decide on castration, the best time is at 6 months, before the dog becomes potent (8 to 12 months).

The "entire" male may create problems, especially if he is allowed to roam in the suburbs or in the country. An apartment dog of course is more controllable since he has no access to the outdoors without you. But if the country male runs free, he may disappear for days at a time, as soon as he picks up the scent of a bitch in heat. He will follow the scent and simply vanish until he is satisfied, gets hungry, or loses the object of his affection. One of the chief causes of roaming in a male is the sexual instinct, provided that the dog is not, for psychological reasons, a roamer to begin with.

While a dog may not harm a bitch who rejects his advances, he will fight savagely with other males for an available bitch. In this respect, dogs revert as close as they ever will to their primitive state, when the strongest of the males won the bitch in season. If your dog is small, or dainty, or otherwise unaggressive, he may well be hurt badly when he tangles with more experienced street fighters. Ears, muzzles, paws, neck, and other parts can be torn, scratched, bitten, or mauled. The castrated dog obviously will not get involved because he is not interested.

If, by chance, you have a male who is bad-tempered, castration may improve his character. Many owners have found this a good enough reason to have their dogs altered. Of course, if you have a dog who is really vicious toward other dogs and toward people, you should get rid of him, especially if you have children. But some dogs simply become snappish and testy as they grow older, and more possessive, and it is sometimes advisable to castrate if they cannot be controlled.

Incidentally, neither castration nor spaying prevents your pet from leading a healthy and happy life. Losing his sexual capacity does not lead to emotional insecurity, anxiety, psychopathic tendencies, or anything of the sort. Even in their wild state, many dogs simply did not have the opportunity to mate, for the simple reason that the small dog could not compete with the larger ones for available bitches. Apartment dogs, in particular, are fully domesticated, and the absence of a sexual life is more than compensated for by the love and affection they receive in the family group.

For many owners, of course, there is something distasteful about castrating or spaying a pet. They feel that they would be interfering with nature or removing some of the animal's personality. Such feelings should be the chief consideration in your decision whether to spay your bitch or castrate your dog. If you feel that only a "complete" dog can satisfy you, then don't tamper with nature.

Only a veterinarian should castrate or spay a dog. No owner should attempt spaying, and even those who have had some experience with farm animals endanger the life of a dog if they attempt castration.

Much has been written about spaying and castration, and so many tall tales have been spread that I feel obligated to comment on them.

1. Spaying or castrating does not affect a dog in any negative way except in his ability to reproduce. With proper food and exercise, he will not gain weight and become ungainly, nor will he become sluggish. And both bitch and dog will retain their separate personalities.

2. If your bitch is in heat, she can be impregnated by more than one dog, so that the litter is a combination of the sires. That is, the sperm of several males can fertilize her eggs and form puppies of distinct but different breeds. If your Beagle is impregnated on successive days (or in the same day) by a Beagle and a mongrel, she may have a mixed litter of Beagle and mongrel pups in whatever proportion the fertilization took place. This particular pregnancy, by the way, has no effect on future ones. Each pregnancy results in its own kind of litter.

3. A male will not ordinarily try to mate with a bitch who is not in heat. Further, a male will not fight with a bitch who has discouraged his advances but will honor her wishes—unless the particular male is so vicious that he shouldn't be out on the street at all.

4. The bitch herself makes no aesthetic judgments about a partner when she is in heat. She will usually take on every available male. If you wish to prevent this activity, keep her locked up, or board her out to a kennel, or give her tablets to prevent her season.

5. A male, once he has mated, does not turn vicious. He may indeed think of himself as a Don Juan and try to force away all other males when a bitch approaches. But this reaction is true of nearly all males, whether they have ever been mated or not. A stud dog may be tougher than most males in this respect, but a stud is kept under close watch and has little opportunity to become embroiled in a free-for-all.

6. When the bitch is in heat, she will become familiar with people as well as with other dogs. Expect her to become coy with you, raise (or "flag") her tail, and rub against you. The male will do this at any time, depending on the degree of his excitement.

7. Not all bitches have exactly the same kind of heat. Some stain very little, others a great deal depending on the individual. Some bitches do not stain at all and therefore are problems to breed. (Such a bitch must be checked by a veterinarian during her heat, and he can tell you when to breed her.) Some bitches lick up the discharge, others don't. Whatever your bitch does is normal for her. These matters are unpredictable, so don't worry if the behavior of your bitch is different from that of your neighbor's. Each bitch has her own style.

8. The pregnant bitch may pass along to her puppies any of her own deficiencies (if she has worms, the puppies are almost certain to have them), but she cannot pass along any characteristics that are a result of changes you may have made in her appearance. That is, a bitch whose tail has been docked will bear puppies with normal tails. And the cropping of her ears will have no effect on her puppies' ears.

9. Spaying and castration will in most instances cut down on a pet's wanderlust, unless roaming is the result of some deep-rooted psychological need.

10. It is true that an unspayed bitch is more predisposed to breast tumors and growths than a spayed bitch.

9

Mating, Pregnancy, and Whelping

Y our original reason for owning a dog will often determine whether you wish to mate your animal or not. And since it is the owner of the bitch who has the majority of the problems, most of the information in this chapter will concern the female. The owner of the male has few of the troubles and, unfortunately, few of the joys, unless he decides to help raise the litter. Even this is unlikely because the pups usually remain close to their mother until they are weaned at 3 or 4 weeks.

If you want a dog simply for companionship or sport, mating him or her is not for you. Or if you live in cramped quarters on a limited income or have a large family that needs constant attention, a litter of several pups might create more difficulty than pleasure. Unless you are a professional breeder, the deliberate decision to mate your bitch should be made for the sake of the enjoyment you will have in raising the puppies. When the litter does come, it will make work for you, but it will be rewarding work. Of course, if you look ahead to the puppies with fear and trembling, your delight in their arrival will be clouded by your own anxieties. But if you are enthusiastic about the idea, even while you recognize the possible trouble you will be put to, then by all means go ahead.

Bringing up a litter of puppies is one of the most satisfying experiences you can have. You can literally watch them grow before your eyes, with some of the larger breeds (Great Dane, Mastiff, Newfoundland) gaining fantastic amounts of weight in short periods of time—perhaps 10 pounds in a month. *In 90 percent or so of the litters, there are no special problems involved.* The dam (the mother of the litter) will do most of the work as well as the nursing. You may have to give the young puppies supplementary bottle feedings (see Chapter 3 for these details), but, unless there is an emergency, your chief job is to hover nearby.

If you read this chapter carefully and follow the instructions and advice, you should be well prepared when the event occurs. I will tell you what every dog owner should know about mating, the pregnancy of the bitch, and the whelping of the litter.

Every dog owner should know what he is getting into when he mates his bitch. Mating itself may take some time because many males—especially shy apartment types—are surprisingly awkward with a bitch. The only exception is a professional stud. Once the mating does take place, the bitch needs special treatment and feeding throughout her pregnancy. Then, once the puppies are born, they may need special care if there are more than the bitch can handle. Also, your children must be kept at a distance lest they unintentionally injure the pups, and because the nursing dam becomes very jealous and snappish when she sees anyone, no matter how familiar and dear, touching her pups. The dam may nip the person or even injure the pups. This is part of her instinct to protect her young.

MATING

Mating your bitch can be a lot of fun and a lot of work. If you have a purebred bitch and you wish to have her mated with a professional stud, then all the work is taken out of your hands. The owner of the stud will take care of the details. More on this later. If, on the other hand, you see a friendly, healthy dog in your neighborhood who you think would make a good sire, then you might ask his owner if he is willing to mate him with your bitch. In this case, all the work is yours; and most of the fun, if you keep your sense of humor and remain patient. If your bitch is purebred and your neighbor's dog is a purebred of the same type, then of course you know what the puppies will look like—exactly like the parents. If your neighbor's dog is of another breed, the puppies will be crossbreeds, with some characteristics of each parent—perhaps the head of a Scottie on the body of a Boston Terrier. If your neighbor's dog is a mongrel, or if yours is, you cannot tell what the pups will look like—they will be a mixture of the parents' characteristics.

Before you mate your bitch, think about what you will do with the puppies. Unless you are mating her for the sake of selling the pups, you may have four to six, or even more, to dispose of. Let us assume that you want one for yourself and another for the owner of the sire. How about the rest? Do your friends want them? Unless both parents are purebred, the puppies will have little sale value. If you feel any attachment to the pups, you may not want a commercial establishment to handle them, for they may not get the care and attention you think they deserve. You may of course give them to a humane society, which will try to find a home for them. Once you have made up your mind how you are going to dispose of them, you are ready to think about the mating itself.

As an owner of a female, you know or should know that she can usually become pregnant only twice a year, during a period that lasts about a week or less. It is best not to mate her at her first season or heat period (estrus) when she is 6 to 10 months old, but to wait for her second heat. This means that the bitch may be 14 to 16 months old before she is mated. Since she can produce a litter or two every year, there is no point in rushing her. If she is very young, she may be immature psychologically and insufficiently developed physically to cope with the sudden burden of all those puppies. Give her a chance to attain maturity before subjecting her to motherhood and all its burdens. The chances of her having a stronger, hardier litter are much greater at this time.

The signs of a bitch's seasonal heat or period are a swollen vulva (the lips of the vagina), an increased appetite—or poor appetite—and perhaps a general restlessness. She may urinate more than usual and even ignore her house-training. Bitches vary, of course, but this swelling may continue without any other sign for several days, possibly 5. Then a slight bleeding or discharge begins, which may not increase in intensity, depending on your particular bitch. Some bleed a great deal, others hardly at all. Either type of bleeding is normal for the particular bitch.

The bleeding may last a week or more, on the average. If your bitch bleeds for only 4 days before the discharge tapers off to a pinkish color, do not worry. Or if your bitch bleeds heavily for 10 or more days, do not think you have a problem. The period is governed by all kinds of complicated factors determined by the dog's metabolic system. What is normal for one is abnormal for another. Only if your bitch has more than two seasons a year, or if her season seems to be unnaturally severe (excessive bleeding), is there any reason for concern.

Incidentally, a bitch who bleeds a good deal at this time may stain rugs and furniture. You might consider keeping her quartered where she can do a minimum of damage. Also, there are sanitary napkins on the market, made especially for dogs, which will absorb the discharge. You may feel a little ridiculous in attaching one of these to your bitch, but it is an effective device. If you have children in the house who ask about the bleeding, tell them that it is entirely natural and not something to worry about.

When the bleeding tapers off, your bitch normally will be receptive to males. She will become playful and allow them to mate with her—this is the only time when she will accept them. So now, perhaps 10 to 12 days after the heat started, your bitch is ready to mate. It is the first day of possible conception and the best time for impregnation. The bitch will remain receptive for about 3 to 5 days, sometimes fewer, and the best time for mating is somewhere at the start of this period in which she accepts the male. The whole cycle may be charted something like this, allowing, of course, for differences among individual bitches and breeds:

1. A bitch will have her first season from the time she is about 6

to 10 months old, some bitches later, some sooner. You mate her at her second season, 6 months later.

2. Signs of season: swollen vulva, increased appetite or poor appetite because of nerves, restlessness, perhaps increased urination, breaking of house-training.

3. Swollen vulva lasts approximately 5 to 7 days.

4. Vaginal discharge begins after this 5-to-7 -day interval, and itself lasts for 4 to 7 days, after which it begins to taper off to a pinkish or cream-colored fluid. The discharge may be light or heavy.

5. As the discharge tapers off, the bitch becomes receptive to males. This period of receptivity lasts for 3 to 5 days. This will be sometime during the second week *since heat started.*

6. If you wish to mate your bitch, this is the time, in the 3-to-5-day period of receptivity. The best time is the early part of her receptivity, say the 12th to 14th day from the onset of heat. All this is approximate. *When the bitch accepts the male, then you know she is ready.*

7. After the period of receptivity, which begins at about 9 to 14 days from the beginning of the season, the bitch will suddenly reject males, sometimes viciously. At this time, her ovulation is ending.

8. During the final 2 or 3 days—about 3 weeks from the beginning— her season is over, and no impregnation is physically possible.

The time that has elapsed from the onset of the season, if you include the 5 to 7 days when the bitch has a swollen vulva, is less than a month. If you plan to mate your bitch, observe the indications of her first season carefully, and then by the second you will know what to expect. You must determine accurately your bitch's best days for conception if you wish to have her impregnated by a professional stud. Your veterinarian can make an examination of the bitch to tell the day she will be receptive to the male.

The Stud

Mating your bitch to a stud works something like this. If you have a purebred bitch and wish purebred puppies, you will yourself have to find a purebred male of this breed or use a stud. The chances are that you will use a stud. The American Kennel Club (51 Madison Avenue, New York, New York 10010) will supply you with information about breeders in your area. You will, then, far in advance of your bitch's season, get in touch with the breeder. He will probably want to approve your bitch before he allows his stud to mate with her. A breeder is interested in getting the best possible pups, and if he has doubts about your bitch he will not accept her. Keep in mind that the breeder makes and maintains his reputation by the quality of the dogs he breeds. A poor litter, or one with imperfections, is simply bad publicity for his stud.

Most breeders require a copy of the bitch's registration papers (which certify that she is purebred), a photograph of the bitch, and a certification of health from a veterinarian. Some want an x-ray, since certain large breeds are subject to hip problems (hip dysplasia—poorly formed joints), and should not be bred. If he thinks your dog is below standard, he will answer with a polite no. Do not be offended. Your bitch is still everything you thought she was. If your son or daughter had been turned down by Harvard, you wouldn't love him or her any the less. If the breeder accepts your bitch, of course he will indicate the terms of the contract.

In exchange for providing the stud, some breeders charge a flat fee—anywhere from $50 to $200, depending on the breeder, the breed, the quality of his stud, and the stud's record as a show winner. If you are interested in mating for quality, a high price is well worth paying. You can be sure that the breeder is giving you what you pay for. Some breeders request instead a choice of the best pup in the litter (a choice made at 6 to 8 weeks). Others ask both a fee and a puppy. Each breeder sets his own terms. The breeder will draw up the contract, and once you sign it, it is legally binding.

Most breeders permit a repeated mating if the first doesn't "take." Since the sire is known to be fertile, the failure to conceive may be the fault of the bitch. If you pay a flat fee and the second try doesn't succeed either, you have lost your money. If you have contracted to give the breeder the pick of the litter and the second try fails, then it is the breeder who has lost. Be sure you know what you are giving away or paying before you enter into the formal agreement. If, by chance, the bitch whelps only one pup, you may not be allowed to keep it if the breeder has been promised the pick.

When a professional takes care of the mating, all the details are up to him. If the breeder lives a good distance from you, you may have to ship your dog by train or air, but he will give you precise instructions on how to do that. *Also, be sure to ask about artificial insemination.* Often this method can replace a long trip for your bitch. The breeder may ship the semen, and your veterinarian can use it to impregnate your bitch.

If artificial insemination is impossible, you must be accurate about the time of your bitch's season when you ship her to the stud. If you sent her prematurely, you will have to pay a boarding fee to the breeder until she can be mated. And if you send her too late, you will have missed her season altogether and your bitch will be returned until her next season, six months later. If you have any doubts about making the calculations yourself, see your veterinarian. Remember that arrangements with the breeder must be made months in advance.

Less Formal Mating

If you decide to mate your bitch with a dog in the neighborhood, the arrangements are much simpler, although you must handle all the details of mating yourself. If your arrangement is with a neighbor, friend, or relative, be sure that you both understand the agreement. Usually, no money passes hands in such an arrangement; the most the owner of the male usually asks for is a puppy. Frequently, the two owners are so eager to see what kind of pups will result from a mating of their dogs that there are no other details to settle. You may, for example, see a healthy, happy male in your neighborhood and decide that your bitch should mate with him, whether for purebred pups or not. Or the owner of a male may take a liking to your bitch and want to mate the two animals, perhaps offering to take half the puppies off your hands. In any event, whatever arrangements for the disposal of the puppies need to be made, be sure they are agreed upon before the two dogs are brought together.

Before the actual mating occurs, be sure that your bitch is perfectly healthy. She should be examined for worms; her rabies and distemper immunity should be checked. Her coat and skin should be examined for mites, fleas, and other parasites. (Demodectic mange, for example, may be transferable to the pups.) These should be eliminated before breeding. Similarly, the male should be in first-rate shape—lithe, healthy, and free of all parasites. When you breed your bitch with a professional stud, you can of course take his perfect physical condition for granted. In an informal arrangement, however, you cannot. Although you may find it embarrassing to ask if the male is perfectly healthy, you have a right to do so, and you should for the protection of the litter. Healthy, immune, parasite-free parents give you the best chance for a successful, healthy litter of fine puppies.

The best time for worming the bitch, if it is necessary, is a couple of weeks before her season. If it is done too close to the season, her cycle may be upset. If you discover the need for worming after she is pregnant, it should be done immediately. After that, worming can be a shock at a time when she is least able to withstand it. If you plan to mate your bitch, take a sample of her stool to the veterinarian for a microscopic examination that will determine whether or not she needs worming.

Let us assume, then, that you have decided on mating your bitch with a neighborhood Romeo. You have found to your satisfaction that he is perfectly healthy, old enough (over a year) to fertilize the bitch's eggs, and the type of dog you wish to sire her litter of puppies. You are now ready to begin.

The Arena

The mating area itself is usually the home ground of the male. Moving him might upset him and make the mating more difficult than it should be. It may surprise you to discover that some males are not Don Juans but bashful creatures whose mating technique is touch-and-go. A male dog who has not been roaming at large really knows very little about mating. The chances are, in fact, that his opportunities have been few; perhaps he has had none at all if he is an apartment dog.

In such circumstances, you must usually help with the mating and not let the male become discouraged. The old-fashioned way of handling the mating was simply to bring the male and bitch together for a few hours and expect a litter to follow in 9 weeks. Sometimes it did, but often it didn't because the male frequently did not succeed in impregnating the bitch. Either she frightened him away or he simply didn't know what to do.

If you wish to eliminate the element of chance—and also the possibility of injury to the male (discussed later)—it is best that you be present. Also ask the owner of the male to be on hand, perhaps as a witness in case something goes wrong. After all, you are on his ground. The very best procedure would be to invite someone experienced at breeding to stand by in the event of difficulty, but there is unlikely to be any such person in the neighborhood. If no expert is present, then follow the instructions below and let the dogs' instincts carry them the rest of the way.

First, agree on a quiet place for the mating, to insure privacy. Try to select an area that can be closed off—a garage, a cellar, a large empty room, or a shed. You do not want any outside disturbances to upset the dogs. I assume that the dog you picked out for mating with your bitch is approximately the same size. If there is a difference—it should never be great, because a large male may injure a small bitch—you can ease the male's difficulty by providing a platform for whichever animal is smaller. (Some of this advice may sound foolish, and you probably feel that you will look ridiculous, but breeders do this all the time.)

So, the second thing is to select a wooden box—or newspapers or large books—to serve as a platform. Next, do not feed either the male or bitch on the day of the mating. A full stomach tends to discourage sexual activity, and may make a dog vomit. Also, you may wish to muzzle the bitch if she is a problem and becomes hysterical. She may even snap and nip at the male and thoroughly discourage him unless he is very aggressive and assertive, and might even injure him. Such behavior, however, is rare.

You now have the two dogs in an enclosed place. The male will usually be interested as soon as he smells the bitch in heat, and she of course will be very much interested if she is ready. If necessary, prop the male up so that he can reach the bitch's vagina with his penis; if the bitch is shorter, prop up her hindquarters on a level with his penis.

If everything goes right, they will begin to mate. Now, a male is so constituted that his penis becomes locked in once it has entered the bitch. At the root of the penis are two glands, and each has a bulbous end which enlarges considerably once the penis has entered the bitch. The bitch herself has a powerful sphincter, or muscular ring, at the rim of her vagina which squeezes behind the bulblike portion of the penis. This pressure holds the blood-filled penis in the vagina. Until the ejaculation takes place, the two dogs are tied or locked together. The dog cannot withdraw until he ejaculates and returns to normal size. This "lock" or "tie" may last for 15 or 20 minutes or longer.

Once the dogs are locked like this, you must take precautions that the bitch or dog does not try to break away. Either or both might be injured. The long tie or lock between the dogs is a natural device to make propagation certain, because the bitch is receptive for such short periods of time every year. If they should snap at each other as they wait for the break to become possible, speak calmly and reassuringly to both dogs. And don't let the bitch try to lie down in such a way that the male's genitals will be stretched or injured. In unusual cases, whenever any propping of either is necessary, you should support the animal. Of course, many dogs mate without any help at all.

Once the lock or tie is broken, the event is over. The owner of the male should take away his dog, while you remove the bitch. Unmuzzle her, if you have provided a muzzle, and let her have water and food. Both dogs are probably ready to eat, and certainly thirsty.

If you wish to make sure that your bitch is pregnant, mate the dogs a second time while the bitch is still in heat, preferably the very next day. You will probably find the second mating proceeds more easily. Of course if the bitch rejects the male entirely the second time, it means that she has passed her period of receptivity.

Difficulties in Mating

Now, throughout this discussion I have assumed that the two dogs mate with a minimum of trouble. But owners are not always that lucky. Often they must work hard to bring the dogs together. And when they do, the dogs may not want to mate. They may be afraid, or the conditions may not be perfectly favorable, or the male may simply not know how. Whatever the reason, if you are intent on mating them you will have to persist.

Some of these directions may seem ridiculous to you, but they are an old story to breeders and farmers. A farmer will guide the male until he penetrates the female, and you may have to do the same. If the male is having great difficulty, direct the bitch until she is in the most advantageous position. Do this with your hands firmly on her abdomen and back. She will cooperate, for she is receptive at this time. The chances are the male is eager also. Speak reassuringly to them so as to allay any fear or nervousness.

If after an hour of trying and retrying nothing happens, give the dogs a rest. Do not prolong the attempted mating until they are exhausted and your patience has been tried to the breaking point. You will probably be grateful for a rest yourself. Do not become grim about the matter. Do not blame the dogs. Remember that man partially muted the dog's know-how when he domesticated him. Unless a dog is accustomed to roaming free, the sudden call to mate is a new experience, and he may not be prepared to meet the challenge immediately. With time and your patience, he will respond to his natural sexual instincts, but he cannot be hurried.

During the rest period before you attempt another mating, do not give the male anything to eat. He is probably nervous and excited and not likely to retain his food. If he seems thirsty, as will usually be the case, give him some water, but not too much. Keep the dogs separated during the rest period so that a fresh attempt is really fresh. After an hour or two, bring them together again. Guide the bitch if both seem anxious to mate. No matter how trying the second attempt is, do not try to guide the male; you might unnerve him.

Give the affair two or three more tries—perhaps an afternoon of steady, patient work with several rest periods for you and the dogs. If after three or four tries there is still no success, give up gracefully and try again the next day. *Most matings are not difficult, and you should by no means expect all this trouble.* If there is still no success on the second day, you should perhaps abandon the project for this season. The two dogs, whatever the reason may be, are probably incompatible. If two dogs do not mate on successive days, you should look around for another sire when your bitch enters her next season.

But the chances are that things have gone well, and you can look forward to a litter in approximately 63 days from the time of fertilization. Fertilization itself occurs when the sperm enters the egg in the uterus or Fallopian tubes. This make take place any time up to 2 days after mating.

False Pregnancy

There is always a possibility that an unbred bitch may enter a condition called false pregnancy. In false pregnancy the bitch shows all the symptoms, physical as well as psychological, of being pregnant although there is no chance of her whelping a litter. This condition may occur in either a previously mated or an unmated bitch, *although it is not so common in the mated one.* Her teats will swell, her appetite will increase, she will develop a paunch, she will even make a nest for the coming event, possibly out of an upholstered chair. She might become aggressive and snappish—keep your children away at this time.

The false pregnancy lasts about two months, at the end of which time it is evident that there are no puppies. The "pregnancy" was purely psychological, due to a hormonal imbalance. At the first occurrence, you should discuss the matter with a veterinarian, even though he may tell you it is not uncommon. Repeated false pregnancies not responding to medication can only be prevented by having your bitch spayed, something that your veterinarian may recommend. In many cases, this is the only way to eliminate the condition.

PREGNANCY

We now assume that your bitch is pregnant. If you have not mated your bitch, but find her pregnant from a street experience, the following information on how to treat her will of course apply as well. I have mentioned before something that I should repeat here: As long as your bitch is in heat and receptive to males, she will mate whenever she has the opportunity, and more than one male can fertilize her eggs. If you wish pups from only a particular male, keep her away from all other males until her season is over; otherwise you may have a mixed litter from several sires.

The pregnant bitch should have her stool examined for worms before her third week if this was not done before she was mated. After two weeks of pregnancy, her condition may be too delicate for worming. Also, she should have already received any necessary inoculations. If you failed to see to that, however, it can be done after she is pregnant. The immune bitch passes on her own immunity to the newborn pups.

Incidentally, you can halt the pregnancy because of mismating (or any other reason) by a series of hormone injections. These are usually effective within 2 to 5 days after mating. The longer you wait, of course, the less chance you have of success.

The usual period of pregnancy lasts 63 days from the time of fertilization. The period of gestation for certain bitches and certain breeds may differ slightly from the 63 days, and this is no cause for alarm. Some first pregnancies may last only 60 or 61 days, while bitches who have had litters may not deliver their puppies before 65 days.

Pregnancy does not begin to show in the bitch for several weeks. After a month or so, her appetite may increase. At this time let her eat more food, perhaps broken into 2 or 3 feedings—she might be eating for 10 or 12 puppies! Increase the protein content of her diet. Be sure to give her a vitamin-mineral supplement, which contains all the vitamins and minerals she will need. The amounts to administer are indicated on the bottle. If she likes milk and it agrees with her, give her some every day.

Unless the bitch receives ample calcium and phosphorus (more than her usual requirement), she may suffer from eclampsia either during pregnancy or while nursing, for the puppies draw on her supply of minerals whether she can spare them or not. At a certain point she may become extremely nervous, pant heavily, suffer from a high fever, and even go into convulsions. Her symptoms are similar to those of an epileptic fit. If this condition does appear, get in touch with your veterinarian immediately. Eclampsia seems to be more prevalent in small breeds, possibly due to poor eating habits.

After the fourth or fifth week, the bitch's breasts may begin to swell, become firmer, and even in some cases begin to leak milk. If the breasts become inflamed, soothe them with baby oil.

At a later time—the end of the 6th or 7th week—you may by *gentle* examination of the dog's abdomen feel the formation of the lumps that will later be puppies. Do not poke or thrust—you may damage both the bitch and the puppies. But very carefully run your fingers over the abdomen—the method is called palpation. If you feel nothing, do not press inward, but ask your veterinarian to make this examination. He knows precisely where and how to feel.

By the end of the 6th week, or the beginning of the 7th, there should be a perceptible enlargement of the abdomen. By the 7th week, an x-ray of the bitch will show the foetal skeletons and you can determine once and for all that the pregnancy is real and not false—also, how many puppies there are. As the bitch's abdomen enlarges, so will her appetite increase. Feed her twice a day. Not only should her digestive system not be burdened with the sudden increase in food at one time, but there is pressure on her other organs—including the stomach—as the horns of her uterus expand.

Constipation may result from pregnancy, depending of course upon the individual bitch. Since constipation means an accumulation of waste material, and its toxins, it should be treated *immediately, but mildly. Avoid violent purgatives* as they may cause a miscarriage. You might give her small dosages of milk of magnesia (a teaspoonful or a tablet for each 10 pounds of her body weight) or a lubricant like mineral oil mixed with her food. Infant suppositories inserted in her rectum are especially recommended, for they usually work without creating any stomach or intestinal upset. Check with your veterinarian to see what he recommends, especially if the condition lasts for 2 or 3 days.

By the 50th day, the breasts may be enlarged, full of milk and about ready for the nursing puppies. The bitch will be becoming ungainly— enlarged teats, swollen abdomen, perhaps an overall gain in weight. Do not permit the bitch to gain excessive weight; if she is too fat, cut down on her food while making sure she is getting sufficient protein, vitamins and minerals. I would consider excessive more than a 10-pound gain for a 30-pound dog. A very fat dog, like a very fat person, has a harder time delivering. The bitch's appetite should be satisfied without being overindulged.

While it is perfectly natural that you should be concerned, you should not coddle the pregnant bitch. Give her the love that you honestly feel for her. But too much attention and coddling when she is in this condition can spoil her, and she may expect such treatment long after she has whelped. If you don't want a spoiled dog, don't hover over her day and night. But do show your affection, let her know your concern, speak to her gently, do not make any great demands upon her, let her feel your presence, assure her of your concern through your tone and manner. Unless a bitch is an experienced mother, she will be somewhat nervous and anxious at this time, and your affection and concern, in the right amounts, will help her considerably.

Don't break her daily routine—but be somewhat cautious when you exercise her. Do not by any means stop her exercise, but as she gets larger and more ungainly cut down on her running around and always allow her to rest when she wants to. If there are small children in the house, warn them that their pet is temporarily slowing down and must not be pushed. Very small children may not understand, and you must protect the bitch from them. They mean well, but they assume that their pet is the same as ever, ready to run and romp and roughhouse with them. Insist that they show due consideration, and since they love their pet they will learn to be gentle with her.

Many owners tend to halt all activity of the pregnant bitch. This can be as harmful as too much activity. Everything in moderation at this time. To maintain her health and to insure good digestion, she needs exercise. Constant sleep and rest will make her sluggish, lead to constipation, increase the chance of excessive flabbiness. Walk her several times a day. With the increased pressure on her bladder and her bowels, she will need more opportunities to eliminate. Rather than disappoint you, she may retain the waste products. If your bitch ordinarily requires several walkings a day, you may still have to double the opportunities. If she is outdoors a great deal, there is no problem. If it is an apartment dog, however, you may have to ask your neighbors to walk her when you are not at home. This is one of the small considerations that your pregnant bitch can rightfully demand, so you should not fail her.

Preparations for the Whelping

After about 8 weeks, with one week left before the actual whelping, you might do some preliminary work so that all details are not left for the zero hour. All long hair around the bitch's nipples and breasts should be clipped, if necessary, as well as the hair around her vulva and rectum. If the bitch is unusually hairy—like an English Sheepdog—it would be best for a veterinarian to do the clipping. The cleared area around the nipples and teats will make it easier for the pups to get at her milk, and the cleared space around her hindquarters will allow for a more sanitary delivery. If her breasts seem very sensitive to the touch or if she appears to be worrying them with her teeth and tongue, wash them gently with warm water and a mild soap, and then apply some mineral or baby oil to soften them. If they appear to be giving her persistent trouble, you should call your veterinarian.

The end of the 8th week is a good time to prepare a whelping box. If the bitch has been sleeping outdoors, it is better to bring her in for the delivery, particularly if the weather is cool. Make a *draft-free* wooden box for her, one large enough to enable her to move around freely. Make it from material that you can keep clean. Sanitation for the newborn puppies is absolutely necessary, as it is for a newborn baby. Make three walls of the box sufficiently high so that the dam and her puppies are protected against drafts while she is lying down, with the fourth wall somewhat lower for her to leave and enter by. Cushion the floor of the box with plenty of soft material like newspaper or shavings, which can be changed frequently. Also make sure that the boards are insulated with canvas or blankets or something of the sort. This insulation will keep out cold.

When you put a layer of canvas or blankets over the boards, tack it down so that a puppy cannot accidentally get crushed or lost under the material. Also be sure that the box is long enough for the bitch to stretch out on her side—this is the way she nurses. A good rule of thumb is to figure on a box 1½ to 2 times the length of the bitch. This will give her plenty of room in which to stretch and turn without crowding her or the puppies. Too small an enclosure might lead to her accidentally crushing a puppy by lying on it. For large breeds, make a small shelf around the inside of the box. The pups can get under it, and then the bitch can't hurt them by lying on them.

There is also some basic equipment that you should have on hand. In Chapter 3 I listed these articles, but I repeat them here in case the need arises after the whelping. Such equipment might prove completely unnecessary if the bitch nurses the puppies without difficulty, but on the other hand she may have trouble. If she does, you will have to stand by to give supplementary feedings to the puppies.

You will need a measuring cup with ounce gradations, a mixing bowl and spoons—all standard household equipment. *In addition, have handy, if the pups are of a small or average-size breed, several doll's baby bottles and doll's baby-bottle nipples.* If the puppies are of a larger breed, you may possibly use regular baby bottles and nipples, which would be too big for the smaller pups. Milk should not run rapidly from the nipple; you might try an anti-colic nipple, usually used for premature babies. This type runs very slowly and prevents any fluid from entering the lungs, where it can do serious damage. Particularly small puppies—Chihuahuas and the other toy breeds—may have to be fed with an eye dropper, and it is a good idea to have a couple of those on hand. As I've said, none of this equipment will be necessary if the bitch nurses correctly.

For the actual feeding of the puppies, turn to Chapter 3, where feeding, formulas, and schedules are presented in detail.

It is also a good idea to alert your veterinarian to the whelping date. You may not need him, but you should know where to get in touch with him—at both his home and his office—if you should wish to. The actual whelping may go easily, but it may require the presence of a veterinarian, particularly if all the puppies are not born. A Caesarean section may have to be performed. A bitch of one of the large-headed breeds— the Boxer, Bulldog, Pekingese, Toy Poodle, and Chihuahua—may require a Caesarean, for the head of the puppy occasionally may not be able to pass the cervix or uterine tunnel or pelvic opening—the bitch's labor will be unable to work it out.

You may also wish to have a receiving basket handy. If the litter is particularly large (more than 6 or 7), the bitch might not be able to nurse all the puppies at one time and you will have to remove a few at intervals to make sure all are fed. A well-padded, warm receiving basket is a good place to keep them while the bitch nurses the others.

Last Days of Pregnancy

You are now ready for the big event. As the time approaches, the bitch will become increasingly nervous and anxious. She may refuse to stay near the nest you have provided and head for her regular sleeping place. Show her that the nest is hers by placing her in it several times. She will pace back and forth and worry herself and you. She may whine and cry. Be patient—whelping time is very close. Generally, she will have no interest in eating. Do not force food on her—it's much better if her intestines are not overburdened. Otherwise, when she enters labor, the pressure might cause her to vomit.

A few hours before the actual time of delivery, the bitch's temperature may drop 2 degrees or more, and her vulva will begin to enlarge. Her anxiety will become intense, her pacing back and forth more pronounced. She is about ready. Try to assure her, although her own instinctive drives will carry her through. Speak to her in a gentle tone and pat her on the head. Do not, however, overdo it, as that may increase her natural nervousness.

She may wander around the house or apartment trying to make her own nest. When she does this, you should guide her firmly but gently back to the one you provided. As she becomes frantic, her labor is almost upon her. She will pant and strain.

At this time, the puppies are arranged in the horns of the uterus. Think of a straight road which leads to a fork, which itself comes to a dead end. The two horns of the fork, or Y, contain the puppies, which in labor will be expelled first from one horn and then from the other until they are all whelped. While being expelled, they come down the horns of the uterus to the juncture point, then through the cervix, where they enter the vagina for the final journey outward through the lips of the now-dilated vulva.

WHELPING

When labor begins, increased pressure in the form of waves (contractions) forces the first puppy from one fork past the juncture point. The puppy will emerge in a foetal envelope or amniotic sac. Attached to him at the navel will be the umbilical cord, through which he has received nourishment while he was in the uterus. While the foetus was lying in the uterus, the umbilical cord was attached to the placenta. Then under the pressure of the labor, the cord pulled the placenta free of the uterine wall. Thus, when the puppy is born, he will be in the sac or envelope, with the cord attached, followed by the placenta. *For every pup that emerges, there must be a placenta—if it remains in the uterus, the bitch may incur an infection.*

Before describing the whelping further, I want to warn you about some possible dangers you should watch out for. If you see any of these, call your veterinarian; the problem is no longer a home matter. First, if the bitch is in labor too long without giving birth, there may be an obstruction, and she may require help or a Caesarean operation to have the puppies removed. Such an operation—cutting directly through the abdominal wall into the uterus—is sometimes necessary to save the bitch and the puppies. Veterinarians perform Caesareans every day, almost always with complete success. By a long labor, I mean 5 or 6 hours of sustained labor (with straining and contractions), not simply the preliminaries. You can tell the difference between the preliminaries and the real thing by the severity of the contractions: The bitch may be straining with all her might, to no avail. Long labor is the first danger signal.

Such work with no results causes excessive fatigue and possibly great pain. The bitch may whine and yelp much more than the process of whelping ordinarily calls for. With the strain and fatigue, there may be vomiting, another sign that everything is not going as it should. The bitch may also have many of the symptoms of shock: chills, trembling or shivering, a state like collapse.

Any or all of these signs point to one thing: The whelping is not going well, and there is nothing you personally can do to make it right. Your kind words and gentle reassurances may calm the bitch, but only a veterinarian can give the medical help that is obviously needed. Get in touch with him as soon as you recognize these trouble signs.

Let me now return to the whelping. Under normal conditions, the first puppy will appear in his sac, trailing the cord, which is attached to the placenta. Count the placentas as they emerge; there should be one for each puppy although they may not follow each pup directly.

The bitch will usually do all the cleaning work herself. She will, if necessary, bite off the sac and lick the pup vigorously, and this starts the puppy's breathing. Sometimes the sac is already broken when the puppy emerges, in which case he is already breathing. The bitch will also bite the umbilical cord under normal conditions. These acts—the opening up of the sac (with the licking of the pup) and the biting of the cord—stimulate the breathing of the puppy. By the way, expect the puppy to become active once he is out of the sac—he may even crawl around.

Do not interfere unless you see that the bitch is not doing her work. Later I will tell you what to do if she fails to bite into the sac or fails to detach the umbilical cord.

Normally the bitch bends her body around so that her mouth is very close to her vulva. By twisting her body in this way, she also helps force out the puppies. As the first puppy emerges, and sometimes just before you see him, a fluid—the chorionic fluid—appears, which the bitch usually licks away. She may eat the placenta as soon as it comes out with the umbilical cord, or may lick the puppy clean before she eats the placenta. If the bitch chooses not to eat it at all, that too is her decision. Let her natural instincts dictate her action. *Your only concern is to be sure that the number of placentas equals the number of puppies.*

The whelping bitch will usually clean the puppy off before moving him toward a nipple. These are natural reactions; she senses that the puppy must be clean, dry, and warm, and then must be fed. Do not interfere with this phase unless you see something going wrong. I will tell you later what to do if the bitch seems indifferent to the welfare of her puppies. Then, and only then, is your help needed.

Some time will pass before the bitch whelps another puppy. Usually—but not always—the second puppy will not be born until she has had time to attend to the first one. These intervals also give her an opportunity to rest. Do not feed her or give her water during these periods, even though she may be panting and seemingly thirsty. Of course the length of the intervals depends on many factors: the number of pups she will have, the breed, the individual bitch herself. Small breeds tend to whelp the complete litter in 3 to 5 hours, while larger breeds may continue for 8 hours, perhaps longer. Some individual bitches may take an entire day, although when this happens it is best to have a veterinarian in attendance should the bitch need his help.

Difficulties in Delivery

Let us assume that your help is really needed at whelping time. The reasons for difficulty are numerous: The bitch may be too busy taking care of the first pups to give proper attention to succeeding ones; she may be indifferent to the pups; she may forget about some as she works over others; there may be a breech birth—in which the rear end of the pup instead of the head emerges first—which forces the bitch to strain; she may fail to cut through the sac enclosing the puppy and therefore not lick the pup to start him breathing; the pup may have too much fluid in his respiratory system; the placenta may remain in the bitch; the pup may not find or reach a nipple; the breasts might not be full enough to feed a large litter.

Whenever you think that the delivery is not going right, the best thing to do is call a veterinarian. This is why you have let him know the whelping date. Unless you are experienced in delivering puppies, you will feel more secure with a veterinarian in attendance. However, I will give you information to carry you through in an emergency if a veterinarian is not available.

The first real sign of difficulty comes when the bitch strains for a long time with no results—an abnormal occurrence. Even if she delivers a pup after a long, severe labor, the effort may have exhausted her. Under these circumstances, she may be unable to take care of the newborn pups, especially if the litter should be large. When you see her straining for a long time, try to calm her, for the effort may make her frantic. If she is frantic or frightened, she becomes tense and delivery is even more difficult. With a reassuring tone, you may be able to make her relax. This kind of condition, however, is very rare.

You can recognize another difficulty when the bitch, for reasons of exhaustion or indifference or lack of normal instinct, does not clear the sac from the puppy. This you must do or the pup will suffocate. The sac may entirely enclose the puppy or be partially ruptured. In any event, it must be removed. You do this by breaking the sac near the puppy's head. Lift the sac and stretch it very gently, being particularly careful not to drop the pup in your anxiety to free him. You may also poke a finger through the sac, again taking care that you do not injure the puppy or drop him. Remember that the sac and the puppy will be covered with fluid and therefore slippery. Your chief precaution must be to avoid injuring the puppy while freeing him from the sac.

The umbilical cord will also still be attached to the pup's navel if the bitch does not bite it off. With a pair of blunt scissors sterilized in alcohol, cut the cord about an inch and a half from the pup's navel. That part will eventually dry up and drop off. There is usually no need to tie the end unless there is bleeding. It should bleed very little; however, if it does continue to bleed, you must tie it. Simply loop a piece of thread or string around the hanging cord near the bleeding end. Pull it tight and knot it. That should stop the bleeding in a short time, but expect the bitch eventually to pull off the thread or string.

When you have cleared the sac, place the puppy near the bitch, who should clean him. The bitch usually licks off any mucus that may be impairing the pup's breathing. Many times, of course, the pup starts breathing as soon as the sac is broken, and there is no need to worry about mucus. If, however, the bitch ignores the pup and you see no signs of breathing, you must induce respiration. The pup may not be breathing because mucus is clogging his nose, throat, or lungs. You can wipe it away with a clean handkerchief, and then, if necessary, draw out any mucus from the mouth and throat with a medicine dropper. By now the pup should be breathing or perhaps gasping for air. If he is not, you must try what might seem to be harsh measures. Hold the pup firmly, with his head down, and swing him gently in an arc, stopping suddenly so that centrifugal force may push out any mucus present. Do not swing him violently, or you may injure his neck. To make sure you have a firm grip, wrap the pup in a fresh, clean dish towel or other cloth.

If none of this works at once, be persistent. A puppy does not die in seconds, and you may be able to save him. Rub his ribs vigorously with a towel. Do not push inward because the puppy's bones are very tender, and a jab can easily force a rib into a vital organ. If this treatment is not successful, use artificial respiration: Place a tube or a straw in his mouth and breathe into it, pressing gently on the area near his lungs. Breathe gently so that you do not burst his rib cage. If he still fails to breathe, try pulling gently on his umbilical cord while rubbing him with a towel over his rib area, alternately pressing gently on his chest. Keep this up for as long as 3 to 5 minutes.

Most puppies are breathing long before you must try any or all of these methods. In fact, the bitch usually does all the work, and you can stand by to watch a marvelous natural event. But if one puppy does have trouble in this way, your efforts may well save him. There is tremendous satisfaction in saving the life of a young animal. If despite all your work you cannot save the puppy, you know that he would have died anyway and you at least gave him a chance.

Sometimes the umbilical cord is already detached from the sac when the puppy is born. In this case, expect the other end of the cord to be attached to the placenta. Often the placenta is forced out by the pressure of the next pup. But whatever happens, make sure that it does come out. When you see a thick mass of tissue that is not being expelled, wrap your hand in a clean cloth and remove it.

In the event of a posterior presentation or delivery (the hind feet first), you may have to help the bitch. As the feet emerge, grasp them with a clean cloth and pull down toward the hind legs of the bitch. Pull *very gently* in rhythm with the bitch's straining. Do not pull against her labor contractions or you will do her no good and possibly injure the pup. Do not continue pulling if your efforts are not successful. The situation is surely beyond your control, and only a veterinarian can help.

If the whelping seems to be going well, but a puppy emerging head-first fails to be expelled, you can help the bitch in the same way by pulling ever so gently on the head. Hold the pup close to the neck and try to ease him out in rhythm with the bitch's labor contractions. Do not really pull and never turn the head, or you may injure the pup's neck. If the pup emerges farther, grasp the body with a clean cloth and gently ease it out.

If you think something is going wrong in part of the whelping, do not investigate by putting your finger into the bitch's vagina. You may injure her and the pups, making a bad situation worse. A veterinarian may have to use forceps to extract the remaining pups.

As the pups are whelped, make sure they are warm and dry. If you must do the work yourself because the bitch is unable to, clean off the fluid from each pup by rubbing him vigorously with a towel. This is good for his circulation, and it also warms him up. Then place him at one of the bitch's nipples so that he can get the colostrum or first milk. *For further details on the pup in every aspect, see Chapter 3.* If the litter is very large, the bitch may not have enough nipples (she has only 8) or milk to go around. In this case, remove some of the now warm and dry pups to a litter basket, where they can wait their turn at the nipple. Make sure they do have a turn, for with the first milk they get their initial immunity. With such a large litter, you will also have to supplement the puppies' feeding. All this information is in Chapter 3.

The End of Whelping

If you think the bitch has finished whelping, wait for some time and watch what she does. If she is resting, she may be finished. Feel very gently around her abdominal area, checking for lumps that may indicate other puppies. If you have any doubt, or if you feel a lump, call a veterinarian. If x-rays have been taken before whelping, you know the number of pups to expect.

It will be unusual if you have any of the above problems during whelping. My remarks have not been intended to frighten you, but are offered for an emergency—for the unusual case. Most bitches whelp easily and are fully able to care for themselves and their young. If you are present, you will witness a memorable event. Thousands of years of domestication have not destroyed the instinctive drive the mother has to protect and care for her young. She goes through all the motions that her ancestors did millions of years ago. Once you know that her instincts are stronger than her environment, you can be certain she is capable. And should she miss a point or two or should something happen beyond her physical control, then you will be ready to help her in one of the most important moments of her life.

POSTNATAL CARE

In Chapter 3, I describe the care of puppies from the moment of their birth. Here I continue with the bitch. After labor and whelping, she will probably want to relieve herself, if she has not done so while in labor (when she strains to expel the puppies, urine and feces may also be expelled). Give her a chance to go outside. If you are in an apartment, lead her on the leash, and if in the suburbs or country, stay close to her. She may be a bit groggy. Watch out for automobiles—in her condition she may forget all about them. The best thing is to keep her leashed.

Many bitches will not forget their house-training even during labor, unless the situation is beyond their control. I know of several cases in which the bitch has raced outdoors to relieve herself during labor, and then raced back to continue whelping, without missing a pup. Such incidents are not rare.

Avoid as much as you can any excitement around the bitch and the puppies. She is very sensitive about her litter. Do not allow small children to run into the room where she is caring for the pups. Noise and flurry may bother her and make her anxious. Remember that her milk flow is responsive to anxiety and nervousness. It flows best when she is at ease, calm, ready to devote all her energies to her young. Too much excitement can change the milk consistency and cause feeding problems for the puppies.

Not only children but adults outside the household should also be kept out of the room. If they must look in, they should enter on tiptoe and not move too close to the litter. *At the beginning, do not allow anyone to pick up the pups.* There are several dangers. The pups may accidentally be injured. And the person picking them up might suddenly find the bitch's sharp teeth wrapped around his leg or hand. The need to protect is so strong that the bitch may even snarl at her owner and on occasion bite. She has a right to do so. She has no way of knowing her owner's intentions.

One other reminder: Do not bring the father of the pups into the room. The bitch will not recognize him as the father, and in her excitement from the whelping she may attack him viciously. From her point of view, he is a potential enemy. But don't feel sorry for him. He won't remember the bitch, and the puppies will be meaningless to him. Dogs do not recognize their features in their progeny. Recognition comes to them by smell, and these puppies will have an unfamiliar odor.

As soon as labor is over, offer the bitch a snack of mild, easily digestible food. A bowl of milk with an egg yolk might encourage her to eat, or a bowl of chopped meat in its gravy. Keep the foot light for 24 hours, and then put her back on her regular diet. If she refuses to eat, do not worry. All her labor, plus the licking of the fluids and the eating of the placenta and sacs, might have made her indifferent to food for this first meal, but most bitches will eat at once. Make sure that she goes out to eliminate. You may have to force her if she doesn't want to leave the pups.

Continue to give her a balanced diet of proteins and fats—*plus supplementary minerals and vitamins.* As long as she nurses, you must provide these "extras," particularly if the litter is large. Even with a small litter of 3 or 4, she needs them. Feed her up to 3 times a day while she is nursing; even give her a snack at retiring if she requires it.

The bitch will know how soon she should return to her normal way of life. She will show you by her own actions if she wants more exercise. At the beginning, do not make any excessive demands upon her. Even after she has become accustomed to the puppies, keep down the excitement. If there are children in the house, let them look, let them touch, but keep them from roughhousing with her unless she wants to play. When she is outdoors, do not encourage her to run until she seems ready. General laziness for a few days is not unusual; she is simply enjoying one of the great moments of her life. But if she is listless for several weeks after whelping, then there might be some deficiency and you should have her checked.

A vaginal discharge that continues for 5 days or so may be perfectly natural. The discharge contains the lining of the uterus to which the placentas were once attached, and it should be eliminated. If it continues for longer than 5 days or if it seems particularly heavy, check with your veterinarian. If you see no discharge, the bitch may be licking it as it appears.

Watch for any possible infection of the breasts, a condition that can prove serious to both the dam and the puppies if it goes unnoticed and unattended. Do not confuse this with simple swollen breasts, which is a quite common occurrence after weaning. An infected breast is inflamed, very tender to the touch, and does not secrete milk. If you touch an infected breast, the bitch will jump, for the pain is intense. If you suspect such a condition, call a veterinarian. Infected breasts can give the bitch much trouble and lead to the early death of any puppies suckling them. The puppy contracts the infection as well as failing to get his required nourishment.

After 4 or 5 weeks, the milk will probably be exhausted, and the breasts will dry up. The puppies will cry with hunger. They should have been weaned by now in any event (see Chapter 3). Some bitches, however, may never run out of milk, and these need the care of a veterinarian.

10
Old Age

W HEN YOUR dog grows older, there is no reason to think that your
pleasure in him will diminish. These years can be among the best
for you and your dog. By this time he has become your constant companion and a part of the family. He knows that he counts in everything
you do and that you will not make any plans without considering his
welfare. He has accustomed himself to your way of life, knows your
likes and dislikes, follows your habits, and treats you as if you were
the only person on earth.

Such loyalty and devotion do not come easily. They are the result
of a long relationship, one that began perhaps in puppyhood and continued for ten or more years. But now your dog is getting old. While you
have always shown him love, consideration, and respect, this is the time
when you must pay special attention to him. From about 8 or 9, your
dog has started to slow down, as some people do from late middle age
on. Of course, certain breeds tend to age more rapidly than others—for
example, the Great Dane, Mastiff, Irish Wolfhound, and several kinds
of working dogs—and there are also variations among individual dogs.
Nevertheless, the dog of 8 or 9 generally begins to lose his sharpness.
His body is aging; his organs are functioning less efficiently; his sight
and hearing are losing their keenness. His slower metabolism necessitates
a somewhat different kind of life.

Although your dog is the same wonderful friend that he was several
years ago, do not expect him to behave the way he did in his early and
middle years. If, of course, you have an old dog who shows no signs of
aging, do not change his normal life simply because I happen to mention
that many dogs do slow up. But if you do see certain signs, such as
those discussed below, then regulate his activities accordingly. In this
way, both you and he can make the most of his late years.

You may ask what the characteristics of old age are in a dog. Are
they the same as in a human being? What are the equivalent ages of

dogs and people? What evidence does the owner have that age is affecting his dog? Does the dog himself become aware of any changes? What precautions should you take with an aging dog? How long can you expect your dog to live? And can special treatment prolong the life of your dog? These are some of the questions that owners ask me all the time. In this chapter I will try to answer them as well as many others.

We all feel it a kind of cruelty that a dog lives only about a fifth as long as a human being. Even with the small breeds, whose life span generally is greater than that of the large breeds, the expectation can be only about 12 to 14 years, with a top limit of about 20 years. With most dogs, the expectation is less: The Great Dane lives to 9 or 10 and the Beagle to 12, on the average. Terriers, however, are tough and seem to live the full 12 to 14 years; and some toys live up to 15 or 16. Sporting dogs and hounds, on the other hand, have somewhat shorter lie spans than toys, especially when their natural instincts for an active life in the field are frustrated by urban and suburban living. There is, incidentally, no difference in life span between males and females. One bit of good news is that the life span of dogs—like that of humans—is increasing with new discoveries in veterinary medicine. For example, the dog who lived only 10 years in 1940–50 now has a life expectancy of perhaps 12 years. A dog of 17 years or over is not the rarity that he once was.

The first year of a dog's life is roughly equivalent to the first 15 of a person's. In twelve months a dog becomes an adolescent. Thereafter, you can figure 5 or 6 years of human life as equaling 1 year of a dog's. A dog of 7 is broadly equivalent in age to a person of 45 to 51. A dog who lives 17 years is like a person living to 100 or more. The dog of 20, very rare, is longer-lived than any Civil War veteran.

There is little question that the average dog can enjoy a longer life if he is happy, secure, and looked after properly from puppyhood. By average dog, I mean a dog that suffers from no outstanding illness, whether acquired or inherited; the dog unfortunate enough to have been seriously sick may have his life span cut short no matter what you do. Correct nutrition for the puppy will extend into his later years, giving him sound bones, good teeth, and excellent muscle tone. A pleasant stable home and an affectionate owner will keep the dog's morale high, and morale, we now know, makes for a longer and better life. Not that any dog consciously wants to die—but if an old dog feels unwanted and unloved, he may simply give up.

Further, if he receives his necessary inoculations, he will not suffer illnesses that tend to undermine his health and shorten his life. He should be given a draft-free living area. Cold, damp, and drafts may lead to arthritis and rheumatism—to which the older dog is prone—at an earlier age than the dog would ordinarily develop them. Love and forbearance will also contribute to a dog's sense of security and stability, factors that prolong life by reducing anxiety and worry, however minimal they may be in an animal.

We know that a dog reacts strongly to the personality of his owner. A tense, nervous owner may make a dog feel insecure. Without a sense of security he may suffer from high blood pressure, a heart ailment, faulty digestion. Such a dog may either overeat or lose his appetite altogether. Like a child, a dog likes to know what to expect. He is a creature of habit. Apartment dogs are particularly sensitive to their owners' nervousness because they live in such close quarters with them. And since apartment life is already somewhat artificial for many hunting, sporting, and working breeds, such dogs tend to become supersensitive. Mongrels are as susceptible as purebreds to tenseness and anxiety in tense and anxious homes.

In the puppy, poor treatment and an unrelaxed atmosphere may not immediately bring about any clear psychological reaction. Like the young child, the puppy is concentrating on mere survival. But once he reaches 2 or 3 years, the reaction begins. By this time, he has become a full member of the family; his psychological—as well as physical—condition will now determine to some extent how long your dog will live.

For all the higher animals there is a process called homeostasis, a tendency to regulate the internal equilibrium of the body. Body temperature, pulse rate (heartbeat), composition of the blood, metabolism, and blood pressure are all kept in balance. As the individual person or animal ages, the precious balance which we take for granted in youth is upset or at least impaired. The living organism no longer responds in the same way to heat, cold, exercise, and other stimuli. Certain compensations are necessary to restore the equilibrium that the body once possessed. It is to provide such compensation that we give the older dog special attention.

Very often the aging process takes place over a period of several years, so gradually that it is almost imperceptible. And usually its effects do not all appear at precisely the same time or in the same degree of intensity. While one change is noticeable, another may not occur at all.

What, then, are the changes that begin to take place in the aging dog? As you read through this list, formidable though it may seem, *remember that most older dogs remain hardy.* Many of these ailments are minor matters that your veterinarian can clear up quickly. And most are ailments that will never afflict your pet. They are merely possibilities of which you as an owner should be aware. Later on in this chapter I discuss the ways in which you can help your dog if he suffers from one or more of these disabilities.

SOME SIGNS OF OLD AGE

The aging dog tends toward heaviness or leanness, depending on the amount of exercise he has been getting and, most of all, on the individual dog, either purebred or mongrel. As the dog's metabolism slows down, an unchanged calorie intake can well lead to excess weight. A dog of 40 pounds can go to 60, and then he is in trouble. On the other hand, the aging process can lead to digestive upsets—vomiting, diarrhea, constipation—that result in loss of weight. A dog of 40 pounds can go to 30 pounds. This does not mean that all dogs will go through either phase; some appear sparkling at 12, while others begin to lose their snap at 8.

The skin glands in the older dog become less active, resulting in drier hair, sparse hair growth on the abdomen, even a certain scaliness of the skin. The sheen and smoothness of the young dog's coat begin to disappear, and the hair around the muzzle turns white. The dog usually does not become bald unless from skin parasites, which are a separate problem. The skin will tend to thicken in places: Calluses will form on the hocks (the bone on the hind leg forming the joint that is the dog's true heel), on the elbows (the joint above the forearm on the front legs), and on other bony areas. Even the pads of the feet may thicken, forming a kind of horny spur that must be cut away.

Constipation is another condition the older dog may suffer from, due partially to inactivity. Sometimes accumulated secretions in the anal sacs will make elimination difficult and lead to constipation. Whatever the cause, be on the lookout for chronic constipation.

Digestive upsets, if they exist, are part of the systematic slowing down that takes place over a period of time. Corresponding disabilities occur in the cardiovascular (heart), respiratory, and genito-urinary (kidneys, bladder, uterus, ovaries, testicles) systems. These are evident in the dog's shortness of breath after exertion, in his lessened resistance to disease and stress, in dribbling in females, in the dog's decreased ability to stand extremes of cold and heat, in loss of muscle tone, sometimes in increased thirst, and in slowness of recovery and repair after illness.

The bitch's teats may begin to sag, with the nipples becoming enlarged and wrinkled. The unspayed bitch, particularly one who has never been bred, may develop tumors, cysts, and cancer of the mammary glands. Skin tumors become more prevalent in both males and females. With the loss of skin tone and the resultant dryness, the skin becomes less supple, more subject to diseases and to parasites.

There is also the possibility that your dog may become deaf. Blindness is another possibility, through cataracts or other afflictions. Further, the bulge-eyed or popeyed dogs are more subject to other eye ailments and injuries: If you have a Pekingese, Boston Terrier, French Bulldog, or Japanese Spaniel, you have probably become aware of eye injuries long before your dog has grown old.

Even the teeth may give the older dog trouble. While cavities are rare, they do occur. More common, however, is a general erosion, a loss of enamel, perhaps sensitivity, or gum recession leading to possible infection and loss of teeth. If a dog has gnawed on hard bones—or, in his younger years, on stones—his teeth may be worn down more than those of a dog who was accustomed to relatively soft foods and few bones. The teeth should be scaled (the tartar removed) to avoid gum recession.

Hernias may also appear. In the male, what is called perineal hernia is not uncommon, where the muscle weakens and ruptures, allowing the bladder or prostate to come through. Many times the hernia is caused by chronic constipation. This condition can be surgically repaired.

In addition to these possible afflictions, there may be growths, prostatitis (inflammation of the prostate gland), pyometra (pus in the uterus), ascites (fluid in the abdominal cavity), anemia, otitis (ear infection), increase in body and mouth odor, lameness, nephritis (kidney inflammation).

I will discuss in detail most of these ailments, but before that I want to assure you that veterinary medicine can now treat with success virtually every affliction your aging dog may suffer from. Whereas once surgery was not even attempted on the old dog, new techniques, new anesthetics, and new knowledge in the field of postoperative care make surgery a procedure that you need not fear. If your dog does suffer from any serious ailments in his old age, you can be sure that modern hospitals are ready to take care of him, that veterinarians are fully aware of the recent advances in their profession, and that the life of your dog is held precious by all who care for him.

As your dog grows older and certain physical activities become harder for him, or he suffers from aches and pains that are entirely new to him, he may begin to behave in a different way. He will be less adaptable to change, and he will expect the house routine to continue as he has always known it. Even the shifting of his dinnertime for an hour or so may upset him. He may not eat or he may cover up his food or carry it out of sight. While standing in front of his food dish, he may bark persistently. As he slows down, he will need more reassurance that he belongs in the family. Once he had his strength and youth to give him self-esteem, but now those sources of confidence are gone. He needs from you special reassurance that you love him and that the changes he senses in himself will not alter your relationship.

Do not be surprised if the aging dog becomes more jealous and possessive. As his physical vitality declines, he tries to hold on fiercely to his familiar world. In this way, like most people, he retains his stability and mental health. He will want to monopolize your time even if he is physically unable to enter into many of your more energetic activities. He may resent your attention to other members of the family and to pursuits in which he is not included. Usually, such resentments are not strong, but you should be aware of their existence so that you can treat him kindly and provide the compensations he requires. Whenever he comes to you for affection, be lavish in your attention and speak in a warm and kind tone.

If you should bring a puppy into the house against the day when your old dog will no longer be with you, do not concentrate all your affection on the new dog. While his cute ways will charm the entire family, do not slight your old pet, whose feelings will be shattered by the new center of attention. Assure him constantly that he stands first in your affection. Do this by plenty of play and patting. Spend time with him, perhaps even more time than when he was your only dog. Make sure the rest of the family are kind to him also. Do everything possible to make his last years as rewarding to him as the early ones when he gave unsparingly of himself. Do it because you love him and because he loves and needs you. Sometimes the arrival of a puppy, if handled correctly, gives the old dog a second lease on life: He will teach him tricks and run around with him, getting him used to the new environment.

If your old dog becomes snappish or irritable, do not think any worse of him. He may be suffering from twinges of rheumatism or arthritis, or from one of a hundred other ailments, all of which can make him feel antisocial. He has no way of telling you that he is suffering, and his periods of fretfulness may be your only clue. Be tolerant; he means well, and he loves you as much as ever.

Even if it entails some inconvenience on your part, try to keep his surroundings as much the same as possible. Familiar sounds and smells and sights offer him assurance, even when his sight and hearing become less keen. His sense of smell becomes his way of *knowing,* and compensates for the loss of other senses, when his eyes cloud over and his ears lose their sharpness. If his nose tells him that everything is pretty much the same, he will be satisfied. But a change in routine or environment will confuse and worry him at a time when he simply wants his daily life to continue as it has always been. Even in a matter as minor as the frequency of his meals, if you have accustomed him to one meal a day, do not change to two unless medical reasons call for it. Or if he is accustomed to one meal with a late snack, continue that.

Similarly, if he has received his exercise by walking with you at certain times of day to specific places, let him continue unless it is clear that he is overexercising. The old dog needs exercise if he is to keep healthy, but overexertion is bad. A walk to the store, or to school, or in the woods on the weekend is first-rate exercise for the aging dog as well as for the young one. If the outdoor temperature is extremely high or low, of course you must take the same precautions that you took when he was a young puppy. In most of these considerations, common sense is all the conscientious owner needs. By this time you know your dog so well that you almost instinctively know what you should and should not do.

You can really give your dog a psychological blow if you suddenly kennel him or board him out. The dog accustomed to being kenneled while you go on vacation will accept the annual event. But the old dog who has never been kenneled, or kenneled only infrequently, will sense, however dimly, that he has outlived his purpose and will never see you again. He may go on a hunger strike or simply lose interest in living. Any such reaction is caused by his attachment to you, not by a sudden desire to make life difficult for you. What was once evident in him as loyalty and affection now becomes despair as you appear to be deserting him.

Most kennels do not like to take an older dog, as he creates several problems. If you must leave him, either temporarily or permanently, make sure that you give the kennel owner a list of instructions, which he will try to follow as far as possible. This may cost you a little more than the kennel's minimum daily charge, but it is surely worth it. Leave with your dog a favorite toy or pillow or blanket whose smell will remind him of home. Try to maintain his same diet, with the same number of feedings; this too will provide continuity. If your dog does become anxious and depressed after he has been boarded out, do not blame the kennel owner; he has probably done all he could, but the aging dog will almost always react adversely to sudden changes in his routine.

The best thing is to keep your old dog at home. But if circumstances make it absolutely necessary—if your dog is so infirm that you cannot give him the care he needs—ask your veterinarian for the names of kennels that handle such dogs, or contact the humane society in your locality. The owner pays for the kind of treatment he wishes, he has visiting privileges, and his dog lives out his remaining time in a dignified, happy way. Unless he is suffering, these "old dogs' homes" are a fine alternative to euthanasia. Many old dogs thrive in the atmosphere once they accustom themselves to the change. If they are not ill, they can live out their lives in comfort and peace even if their original owners can no longer accommodate them.

GENERAL CARE

This section is devoted to the general care of the dog who does not suffer from any specific ailments resulting from old age; I discuss the ailments later on.

1. Keep in touch with your veterinarian when your dog passes 6 or 7 years of age, even if there is no history of illness. A six-month checkup is a good way of making sure that nothing serious is developing. Also, your veterinarian can give you advice.

2. Do not tire the aging dog. Set a more leisurely pace, even when he is willing to run. As a matter of pride, he will not admit to getting old. But do not let him fool you. Continue to exercise him, of course, but do not let him become exhausted. If the weather is very hot, keep him indoors, in a cool place. Make sure he has plenty of water, changed regularly. Also, be sure he is getting some salt; his body loses salt during

very hot spells. In cold weather, take care that he is warmly dressed when he goes out, especially if he will be out for a long time without much exercise to keep him warm. A coat that protects his chest is best. And indoors, keep him protected against drafts and sudden chills. The older dog's heating mechanism is less efficient than it used to be—he feels extremes of weather much more intensely. Allow him to rest after exertion.

3. Cut down on your dog's calorie intake as his exercise decreases. Reduce the fat content of his diet from its present rate (perhaps 10 to 15 percent) to about 5 percent, depending on how active he remains. If he continues as a work or field dog past the age of 7, do not cut the fat as much as you would for an apartment or suburban dog who sleeps most of the time. A dog's caloric needs, incidentally, are not based on his weight, but on his body surface. Since the surface of a small dog is proportionately greater for his weight than the surface of a large dog, the small dog requires more calories per pound. A reasonably active 20-pound dog may need 700 to 800 calories daily, while a reasonably active 100-pounder would not require 5 times as many calories, but perhaps 2½ to 3 times as many. Watch your dog, particularly in the abdominal and shoulder areas, to see if he is thickening. If he is, cut down—gradually, not drastically; you will not starve him. If he seems to be ravenous, give him his reduced amount of food in two meals instead of one. That should keep him contented. As long as your dog has plenty of flesh, he can live off it, and you do him more of a disservice by letting him stay fat than by gradually cutting his rations.

4. Take a stool specimen to your veterinarian about every 6 months to be checked for worms, even when there is no evidence of worms. The older as well as younger dog, and particularly the working and field breeds, are sometimes infected by heartworms, which can be diagnosed only by a blood test. (For full discussion of this, see the section on heartworms in Chapter 6.) If your dog tires easily. you may blame it on old age when actually the dog's strength may be impaired by heartworms. These worms are so called because the adult worms lodge in the right ventricle and the pulmonary artery, although they may also lodge elsewhere. The dog who roams the countryside is particularly subject to infection because mosquitoes transmit heartworm microfilarias, which are present in the blood. A house dog is usually adequately protected. Other symptoms of heartworms, in either the young or old dog, are listlessness, nervousness, convulsions, abdominal swelling, and a general rundown state of health. Only the veterinarian should attempt treatment, for the condition in an older dog, whose energy is already naturally decreasing, is serious. Sometimes an operation is required.

5. Whether your dog is longhaired or shorthaired, groom his coat more often. Frequent grooming stimulates the skin, keeps it fresh, and gives the hair a more vital look. Since age affects the skin texture and

quality, the older dog picks up parasites, fleas, and ticks more readily, and careful grooming will help eliminate them. Grooming is a matter not only of appearance but of health as well. Parasites can deplete the older dog's strength and lower his resistance, whereas as a young fellow he might have shrugged them off as a minor nuisance. For skin tone, your veterinarian may recommend supplementary vitamins and minerals as well as food additives.

6. Keep the nails trimmed. You can either have them trimmed or do it yourself according to my directions in Chapter 5. Since friction keeps the nails ground down, your dog's nails will grow more quickly because he is exercising less. This is especially true of the apartment dog, who walks on soft surfaces. What appears to be lameness or an awkward gait might be due to the dog's inability to walk properly on long nails. Also, when he has long nails and tries to walk on slick surfaces, he will slip and lose his balance, an embarrassing situation for an animal accustomed to preserving his dignity.

7. Certain breeds, like the Boxer, French Bull, English Bull, Boston Terrier, Pug, Japanese Spaniel, Pekingese, and English Toy Spaniel are more apt to suffer from heat prostration in very warm weather. As a result of selective breeding, these dogs have one or more of the characteristics—short noses, large, soft palates, and heavily muscled throats—that create respiratory difficulties under the best of conditions. With heat the difficulties increase. In very hot and humid weather, *any old dog should be watched carefully,* but keep an eye on these breeds in particular (as well as crossbreeds and mongrels with these characteristics). Keep them where air is circulating gently, give them plenty of liquids, add a small amount of salt to their food, and be sure they avoid exercise and excitement. An air-conditioned, draft-free room is the best place to keep them.

If your dog begins to vomit or breathe rapidly and heavily, seems to wobble on his legs or cannot stand at all, suspect heat prostration and call your veterinarian. (These symptoms also appear with rabies, but heat cannot make a dog rabid!) In the meantime, spray the dog with cool water, or place him in a shallow bath of cold water, or put him in an air-conditioned room or in front of a fan; even give him a cold-water enema to provide temporary relief.

I repeat that heat prostration may occur in a dog of any age, but older dogs—and particularly those breeds mentioned above—are especially susceptible.

8. For the dog whose teeth are troubling him, avoid hard foods. The cause is rarely cavities, but usually worn-down teeth. Do not give him bones of any kind, and if you give him biscuits, make sure that they are first well soaked in milk, water, or meat gravy. His food should be generally soft. Dogs who have eaten soft food all their lives get along very well. Many people think that dogs must always be gnawing at a bone to keep teeth sound and jaws strong, but if the dog is given a

balanced diet, bones can be eliminated.

9. If your dog's eyes run, and if the veterinarian has assured you there is no ailment, periodically wash his eyes out with a good eye wash. Your veterinarian may also recommend other treatment.

10. Any general listlessness or exhaustion in your dog beyond the natural decrease in energy that age brings might be caused by anemia. If you notice a drastic reduction in his physical activity, you might suspect that he is anemic—his red corpuscles are either reduced in number or deficient in hemoglobin. A veterinarian can easily tell by means of a blood test, and give your dog medicine that will bring his blood back to normal.

11. Avoid bathing an old dog unless the conditions are perfect—warm indoors or outdoors and no drafts. Even then, I don't recommend excessive bathing because he may become chilled and sick. Wash off your dog, instead, with a washcloth or sponge, deodorize him with a spray, and afterward be sure he is thoroughly dried. If he should be caught outside in the rain or snow, dry him thoroughly, right down to the skin. If you use soap to wash him, buy one of the nonirritant varieties—a Castile soap.

12. Certain kidney malfunctions, discussed later in this chapter in the section on ailments of the old dog, will increase his thirst. Your dog should always have a plentiful supply of fresh water available. *If you see a marked increase in urination, or a marked decrease in urination* (either extreme is a sign that something is wrong), *you can suspect a kidney or other ailment.* It may be very minor, or it may require treatment, but your veterinarian in any event should be alerted. He can determine precisely what it is.

13. If your dog shakes his head as though he wants to rid himself of something, suspect ear trouble. Floppy-eared dogs in particular are subject to ear ailments, most of which your veterinarian can treat and cure successfully.

14. Watch for any rise in temperature—check the eyes for discoloration (reddish) and the tongue for whiteness. There may be a general appearance of unhealthiness. If you suspect a fever, take your dog's temperature. Grease the thermometer lightly with vaseline and insert it gently in the dog's rectum; wait two minutes. Normal for most dogs is 101.5° F., somewhat higher for small breeds and somewhat lower for larger ones. By this time, you know what is normal for your dog. Anything significantly different from normal may mean that your dog is in the early or intermediate stages of some illness. Fever in an older dog, as in an older person, is more dangerous than in a younger animal.

If you discover a fever, alert your veterinarian. If your dog has an unchecked fever for several days, he may be incubating an illness or an infection that can have serious consequences.

15. Constipation is quite frequent in an older dog. In this respect too he is like an aging person. Constipation can result from many causes:

insufficient exercise, lack of coarse food in the diet, decreased peristalsis (movement of intestines), sluggish digestion, or hardened feces in the intestinal tract. You may think your dog is constipated when he suffers from an anal irritation and simply chooses not to evacuate, in order to avoid pain.

Unless there is an organic breakdown, some bulk added to the diet usually clears up constipation. A few tablespoonfuls of Shredded Wheat or All-Bran, or even vegetables, may relieve the condition. Or try milk of magnesia (about a teaspoonful or one tablet for every 10 pounds of the dog's body weight). Also, mineral oil as a lubricant may help.

Often an increase in the number of meals (the daily ration divided up) with roughage will aid in the cure of constipation. The dog's digestive organs have less to work on at one time and may therefore be more efficient. If none of these methods is effective and your dog's constipation continues, call in your veterinarian. Temporary constipation is of course not at all serious. But chronic constipation may be cause for alarm.

16. If your dog dribbles—a condition common in the older dog as his sphincter muscle weakens—perhaps your veterinarian will recommend treatment.

17. Expect a frequency in urination in the aging dog. You may have to walk him more often each day, sometimes up to five or six times. If this is impossible, leave plenty of newspaper for him, especially at night, for he might not be able to hold his urine. Besides the weakening in bladder control, the older dog drinks more water and exercises less. You must bear with him. Try to give him as many opportunities to urinate as you possibly can.

The problem of course is considerable with the large dog, whose bladder capacity is of corresponding size. In that case, an extra walk or walks will be absolutely necessary. Remember that a dog once house-trained takes pride in his good behavior and will urinate in the house only when he can no longer control himself. Do not be angry if he does this—he is as ashamed as you are.

18. Ask your veterinarian if vitamin-mineral supplements are necessary. Often they are, but do not give them on your own. They are used for the aging dog, the young dog, and for dogs with skin problems.

19. Watch out for warts. They are easily removed—but do not confuse them with other tumors, which create different problems. A wart is usually a small hard protuberance on the skin, frequently rough and raw from the dog's scratching. It is probably caused by a virus and can be removed surgically or even eliminated by a vaccine. Do not yourself attempt to remove a wart; your dog may hemorrhage.

20. See your veterinarian whenever you feel any growth on your dog's skin. Most growths if caught early can be removed without any harmful effects. If unchecked, such growths might develop into large tumors, which are more difficult to remove.

21. If your dog seems to be always blinking, look at the eyelids. Occasionally, tiny growths will form on the edge of the lids, and these are of course troublesome. A veterinarian can remove them or recognize any other eye disorder that may be developing.

22. General digestive upsets may occur in the older dog when his intestinal action is slowed down. The symptoms are discomfort, diarrhea, vomiting, and inability to absorb food, resulting in loss of weight, perpetual hunger, and general ill health.

To combat this condition, dietary changes may be necessary. If so, keep your dog off all gas-producing foods: vegetables, liver, kidneys. Instead, give him foods that are easily digestible—for example, chopped meat, chicken, lamb. Your veterinarian may recommend a dietary program for him. *There are prescription diets for old dogs,* and the veterinarian can tell you about them.

These twenty-two points cover all but the most unusual conditions which you will find in the older dog. In my discussion of ailments which follows, I describe those internal disorders that cause the changes you notice in your dog. Many of these ailments require immediate attention. Others are simply symptomatic of the aging process and are not responsive to treatment.

AILMENTS OF THE OLD DOG

A veterinarian must treat all serious ailments in the aging dog. As soon as you notice a symptom, consult with your veterinarian. By acting quickly, especially if the ailment is serious, you may add years to your dog's life. Surgery, if necessary, is now performed on older dogs with a high degree of success due to improvements in anesthesia. Certain kidney malfunctions, tumors, growths, inflammations, heart disorders, and abscesses need immediate treatment if you want your dog to survive.

Kidney Disorders

Kidney ailments (see Ailments, Chapter 6) are rather common, running from one kind in which the dog urinates frequently to another kind in which he retains his urine. The most common kidney ailment is nephritis, which is an inflammation of the kidneys. Some veterinarians report that nephritis occurs in 75 percent of older dogs (those over 8 or 9) in lesser or greater degrees. There are two types of nephritis, acute and chronic.

If your dog is very thirsty and empties his water dish more often than you are accustomed to filling it, you should suspect that something is wrong and take him to a veterinarian for diagnosis.

Once diagnosed, acute nephritis calls for several precautions and immediate treatment. Provide water in small amounts, but frequently, and do not let your dog exert himself too much. Avoid all foods that will increase his thirst—ham, bacon, and other salty foods (not recommended even for the healthy dog) or highly spiced foods that you might ordinarily give him as table scraps. Restrict him to his canine rations or put him on a special diet. What the young dog once ate and thrived on, the older dog may find difficult to digest.

If your dog suffers from chronic nephritis, some of the symptoms may be sharp increase in urinating, general unhealthy look, indifference, loss of weight, perhaps vomiting, bad breath, difficulty in walking, dull coat. He may well survive with this ailment, but he needs immediate treatment by a veterinarian. If you neglect the condition, your dog may develop uremia.

In the meantime, at frequent intervals provide plenty of liquids in small amounts: water, broth, fruit juice, skimmed milk if it agrees with him. Always take the chill off liquids, although you should not heat them. Room temperature is best.

For both chronic and acute nephritis, a prescription diet for kidney disorders may be necessary. If none is available, then a non-meat high-carbohydrate diet is recommended: *cooked* oatmeal, corn syrup, toast, rice, noodles, and pasta.

Such kidney ailments may well throw your dog off his house-training. If you possibly walk him more often or arrange for walks, do so. If that is impossible, then leave newspaper near his sleeping area. Check every so often and pick up all soiled papers. As I mentioned before, a dog takes great pride in keeping his living area clean, and if he does wet it, do everything you can to reassure him. Let him know by your tone and manner that you understand. Your dog knows your sympathetic attitude by the tone of your voice.

Dribbling

If dribbling is the problem, your veterinarian may recommend treatment; it may be a symptom of some specific disease. However, unless it is connected with some other disorder, dribbling is simply part of the aging process in which the dog's sphincter muscle loses its tone, and nothing can be done about it.

Tumors and Growths

Tumors and growths are common in older dogs. They are seen most often in unspayed females who have never been bred, and occur chiefly in the mammary glands. If you see a lump forming or even a persistent swelling or inflammation of the breasts, alert your veterinarian to the condition. The two breasts in the inguinal (or groin) region seem to be more subject to tumors or growths, for they are usually the most active and therefore the ones most easily irritated. A veterinarian might be able to control a tumor, if it is inoperable, through hormone injections. When he operates to remove the tumor, he might suggest that the bitch be spayed to prevent further female trouble.

If the growth turns out to be malignant, then, of course, recurrence is possible. After surgery, your dog may live to a ripe old age, provided that the growth has been completely removed. With modern methods of surgery and recently developed techniques in anesthesia, you should feel no qualms about surgery for your dog.

For the male dog, tumors are most common in the genital area, specifically in the testicles. If you notice an enlargement or inflammation of one or both testicles, or even of the tissue surrounding them, see your veterinarian. He will decide if surgery is necessary. At this age, your dog is probably past breeding, and the loss of even both testicles will not in any way interfere with his regular life and will make him more comfortable.

Tumors are of course possible in other parts of a dog's body, both male and female. When you brush or comb your dog, you may notice small growths on his skin. If these persist—a pimple will go away in time—take your dog to the veterinarian for an examination. Removed early, tumors, malignant or not, can be controlled, and your dog can life happily for many years.

Deafness

Deafness in the older dog is common, although certain precautions can be taken to postpone it. The floppy-eared breeds are especially subject to ear ailments because their ears tend to retain dirt and may become infected or irritated. Also, their ears retain water, which cannot be shaken out. The ears of straight-eared dogs, like the Boxer, allow the air to circulate, and have less surface to become infected.

If your dog begins to cock his head in a strange manner or paws at his ears persistently, you should suspect an infection or the beginning of one. Probably by the time you notice that something is wrong, the canal leading to the inner ear needs cleaning. Or the ear may simply be irritated, in which case the wax or collected dirt may easily be wiped out. As long as you don't try to dig into the ear yourself, you cannot do any damage. For a surface irritation or accumulation, use a piece of cotton dipped in baby oil. If the difficulty seems deep-seated, consult with your veterinarian immediately.

Often your dog will further irritate his ear if you allow the condition to run its course. It is part of a dog's nature to worry a wound. He will try to relieve his discomfort by clawing at what is bothering him. A spot already infected will worsen, for the dog's claws carry infection into the wound.

If your dog has an infection in which the lining of the ear is involved, it must be treated by your veterinarian.

Warts, also, may grow within the ear, and minor surgery under anesthesia may remove the trouble.

Despite all your care, however, the aging dog may gradually be growing deaf. If you notice that he is, be careful not to disturb him suddenly. He does not realize that he is growing deaf—he simply believes that the world has grown quieter. If you approach him from behind, and he cannot hear you, he will be startled when he suddenly finds you beside him. And if he is awakened from a sound sleep by a noise at his bedside, he will have an equally unpleasant reaction. In either case he may instinctively snap or bite. If there are small children in the house, be sure to warn them that he is not to be startled. If you have an infant crawling or just walking, you must keep him away unless the dog clearly sees the child coming.

Also, if you have usually let your dog run without a leash, remember that his deafness will prevent him from hearing the sounds of automobiles. From his point of view, if he hears no cars, there are no cars. He may be struck and severely injured, if not killed. It is best to keep an old dog (or any dog!) on a leash unless his running area is so distant from automobile traffic that he is perfectly safe.

Arthritis

Arthritis is another ailment the older dog may suffer from. One way to help him is to keep him in a warm, dry spot, away from drafts. Also, your veterinarian may recommend newer medication or injections that give long-term relief from the pain of arthritis. If your dog seems irritable and snappish as a result of arthritis, bear with him and let the veterinarian help him whenever he can. As temporary relief give half an aspirin.

Prostatitis

In the older male dog, there is the recurring problem of an enlarged prostate, known as prostatitis. The enlargement of the prostate gland may lead to difficulty in urinating. If he cannot pass his urine, the bloodstream will retain toxic products that will poison the animal. If you notice that your dog is having difficulty in passing urine and that he is constantly trying, you should suspect a prostate disorder. Of course, another kind of ailment may be present.

An enlarged prostate may also affect the dog's bowel movements because the gland presses on the large colon and makes elimination painful. This can lead to a toxic condition and also to troubles like irritation around the anus. Any kind of straining in the dog's eliminatory processes is a trouble sign. He may be suffering from stones in the kidney, which can block the passage of urine to the bladder. In the male, the stone may also pass from the bladder into the urethra, making it impossible for him to pass any urine. Surgery may be required before your dog regains his ability to urinate properly.

Female Ailments

The female may suffer from some specific ailments, such as metritis (an acute inflammation of the uterus) and pyometra (an accumulation of pus in the uterus). Pyometra is a condition often seen in unbred and even bred bitches as they pass their 5th or 6th year. Its symptoms are similar to those of many other ailments: greatly increased thirst and urination, vomiting, loss of appetite, abdominal swelling, perhaps pain in the abdominal area, as well as fever. The bitch will often give off a sickly sweet odor from the vagina. Metritis, if not treated, can lead to pyometra. Its symptoms may be vomiting, excessive thirst, little appetite, rise in temperature and swollen abdomen. There may or may not be a bloody discharge from the vagina. Both pyometra and metritis need diagnosis and treatment by a veterinarian and, most times, require surgery.

Abdominal Swelling

Any abdominal swelling that is more than a collection of fat or the temporary accumulation of excessive food should be brought to the attention of a veterinarian. Such a swelling may indicate ascites, and it may be the result of a heart, liver, or kidney ailment. The swelling may result from an accumulation of tumors, or from retention of fluids that the body would ordinarily assimilate. Although it may be temporary, it is rarely a condition that will clear up by itself. Delay in treatment may jeopardize your dog's chances of recovery.

Your dog, incidentally, will not keep an unhappy condition from you. His general responsiveness will decrease, his energy and appetite will wane, and his appearance will become unhealthy. Although these are general characteristics of old age, they will be intensified in the dog suffering from a particular ailment.

If the swelling is caused by a heart ailment, then of course your dog will need special care. Be sure to watch his weight and his exercise. The overweight dog loses months and years of his life even if nothing else is the matter with him. A heart disorder will shorten his life span even more. And don't demand much in the way of exercise from a dog with a heart ailment, no matter what his weight. He can exercise, but not overexert himself. There are, incidentally, special prescription diets for overweight dogs and dogs with heart disease. Consult your veterinarian about these, and see Chapter 4 for further information.

Eye Disorders

One of the common eye ailments of the older dog is conjunctivitis, although, of course, it appears in younger dogs as well.

Conjunctivitis is sometimes accompanied by a redness in the white part of the eye, as well as by watering of the eye and sensitivity to light. It may be caused by a number of things, from foreign objects in the air to a toxic, feverish condition in the dog. To give relief, wash out the eye with warm (not hot!) water. Use an eye dropper to deposit the water in the corner of the eye. When the dog blinks, the water will wash over the surface. You may also use an ointment or an eye wash. If the condition persists, it needs professional care.

Your dog may hesitate to jump on the sofa or on his favorite chair as he once did, or refuse to enter a darkened room. If you notice these symptoms, examine your dog's eyes. If there is a deep-seated bluish discoloration, he may have a cataract. This blue-white discoloration means that the eye probably has been developing a cataract for some time. Professional treatment, including surgery, may postpone loss of sight.

No matter what precautions you take and no matter how devoted your veterinarian is, however, a dog with cataracts may still lose his sight. Such a loss, while understandably painful for you to watch, is not as much a disaster for your dog as you may think. A dog's sense of smell will take him along all his old routes and to all his favorite places, while his other senses will tend to compensate for the loss of sight. Unless you suddenly put him in new surroundings, he can live a perfectly normal life. If he is suddenly moved—a difficult experience for any old dog, but especially for a blind one—he may feel lost. If you must place a blind dog in different surroundings, be aware of the upset it will cause him. Give him extra consideration, comfort him, let him get accumstomed to new smells. Always bring along several of his favorite objects—toys, blankets, dishes—so that he doesn't lose his connection with his previous life. In time he will of course adapt—his senses of smell and hearing will do that for him—but at the beginning he deserves your care and attention.

Some Minor Troubles

In addition to these major ailments, there are several minor ones that cause discomfort, although in themselves they are not dangerous. They will, nevertheless, make your dog unhappy.

Abscesses are more common in the older dog, particularly abscesses of the anal glands, between the toes, in the teeth, or on any part of the skin from an insect bite or a dog bite. Abscesses must be treated by a veterinarian.

For a full discussion of abscesses, as well as of flatulence and edema—two other ailments common in the older dog—see Chapter 6, on ailments.

Lameness is common in the old dog, or if not lameness then a tendency to favor one paw over another. The reason may be an infection between the toes. An older dog—particularly a heavy one—is subject to infections of the feet because of generally lowered resistance, less vitality, less active circulation. The dog will lick, gnaw, and rub the infected area. Soak it in warm water and Epsom salts or boric acid. If the condition does not clear up, take the dog to a veterinarian.

FINAL REMARKS

These are the major and minor ailments that an older dog may suffer from. The chances are good, however, that your dog will go through his later years with a minimum of trouble and that he will give you continued pleasure. If your veterinarian gives him a checkup every six months, you are reasonably sure of protecting him against any serious ailment. And if you take him in for an examination as soon as you suspect something wrong, you will control most ailments in time. These years with your dog may well be your finest, because he is an old friend, loyal and devoted. You want your dog to be at his best, for then your relationship will be at its happiest.

11

The Problem Dog

I F YOU can give your dog a natural life, the chances are slim that you will ever have a "problem dog." And even if you can't, *a problem dog is rare!* By a natural life, I mean one in which your dog is given plenty of exercise, handled kindly but firmly, and fed at regular hours on a balanced diet. Of course, even with such care, some dogs act strangely. After all, even under the best of conditions, most of them cannot roam freely and consequently have almost nothing to do. Such inactivity and lack of purpose are very different from what the primitive dog was accustomed to. But so great is the adaptability of the dog that even under the worst of conditions he reacts with kindness, love, and loyalty. *I repeat: A real problem dog is rare.*

Unless a dog feels unwanted, unloved, and threatened in some way, most of the problems he presents to his owner will be relatively minor, but annoying all the same. Perhaps the dog chases cars, or he jumps on people indiscriminately, or he barks uncontrollably and incessantly, or he nips people playfully as they enter the house, or he wanders away for days at a time. All these matters can usually be handled in such a way that the dog is rehabilitated into a good citizen. Occasionally, a dog simply will not change, but most of the time he can be trained successfully. Later on in this chapter, I will take up these problems one by one and advise you what to do. Of course your veterinarian may have his own ideas on the subject, and if so, by all means follow what he tells you to do.

To move for one moment from these relatively simple problems into the more difficult ones, we find that some dogs just do not want to give up their strange ways. Either because of something in his environment or because of some abnormal way in which he sees and feels things around him, your pet seems to resist whatever you attempt to do. Such a dog may be labeled a problem dog in the full sense of the term. I do not have in mind the dog whose abnormal behavior results from an illness,

417

such as distemper or some other shattering ailment. Such behavior is part of the disease and cannot be altered until the dog has recovered. I am talking about strange and bizarre behavior in the otherwise healthy dog.

Some dogs have a built-in nervous disorder, a genetic weakness or susceptibility that makes their behavior strange. Such dogs may bite, rip up property, or constantly fight. You should, in all fairness, try to find some solution, but since this behavior is due to some inherent abnormality, there is little you can do to change it. You naturally feel loyalty to your dog, particularly if he begins to do strange and disturbing things only in his later life and you have already shared many good times together. But if you cannot control him or keep him under constant surveillance and restraint, you should think twice about keeping him.

Some real problems can be caused by overexcitement or overstimulation, by the dog's inability to adapt to changes, and by his failure to come to terms with a given situation. In the first, overstimulation, the dog may be driven into a frenzy by certain phenomena in his home or neighborhood or by certain mannerisms of his owner. For example, the dog may react to certain sounds—car horns, traffic, loud radio or TV, telephone, doorbell, coughing—and become overexcited to the point that he is uncontrollable. Further, if he has to accept these annoying sounds without being able to escape them, he will, as a result of this *total* situation, act abnormally. In brief, he may become wild.

It is well established that a dog's temperament reflects the general temperament of his owner. A nervous owner sets the standard of anxiety, and the dog follows suit. Similarly, the calm, patient owner creates an atmosphere of calm, and the dog reacts accordingly, unless he is suffering from some congenital nervous disorder. You can be assured, then, that when a normal dog becomes an abnormal, strange one, there is a good reason for it. Perhaps his home life is full of tension and strain. Or perhaps he has been transferred from one owner to another and simply can't adapt to all the changes in his life. Dogs in this situation are very much like orphaned children who have been shifted from one home to another. Such dogs may be disorganized and confused for the rest of their lives.

The latest research strongly suggests that the problem dog generally gets to be the way he is in the first six months of his life. A dog that receives excessive attention or gives excessive attention is in danger of becoming a problem dog. He may not allow you to leave your house, or punish you by wrecking it before you get back; or he may make it uncomfortable for guests by jumping on them, barking, monopolizing your attention, even insisting on being taken out when he doesn't have to be. Don't send out double signals. Don't be permissive one minute and authoritarian the next. Don't try to get results by constant punishment and never by constant harassment or brute force; and don't insist on absolute obedience by shouting or raving. You may begin with a warm, stable, affectionate puppy, but you will end up with a real problem dog, one who digs to get out of the yard or kennel, jumps over fences and out of windows, runs away, who doesn't come when called, who scratches the furniture and doors, picks fights with every dog he sees when taken out, bites without reason, dashes out into the street or highway, mounts children, chews up clothing, urinates and defecates when left alone, destroys objects when not fed on time, or barks and howls constantly when no one is home. In other words, you have a dog who needs professional care (obedience training).

The best way to avoid problems with a dog is to give him a good home. Expect certain behavior from him, but do not make unusual demands. Allow him to be a dog; don't expect him to be a person. Give him a natural life. Show him love, consideration, and respect. Keep his activities regulated and constant so that he knows what to expect. Surprises may be fun for children, spouses, and friends, but dogs are creatures of habit. They react best when they know what to do. Their food should not change much, they should be fed at about the same time each day, walked at the same time, exercised at about the same pace every day. A dog who knows what he may expect and what is expected of him is generally a happy dog. And what can be more rewarding than to have a happy, healthy dog around the house, someone anxious to see you and showing his affection and loyalty!

Let us now look at the isolated minor problems that you can usually eliminate with a little planning and a lot of determination.

Food Difficulties

I hear of many cases in which a dog simply refuses to eat. The owner becomes extremely worried, especially if he owns a dog of a small breed who doesn't look as if he can afford to miss a meal. The first thing is to check for any definite symptoms of illness: fever, discharge from nose or eyes, a cough, diarrhea (with or without blood), vomiting (with or without blood), general listlessness and unhealthiness. If you do not see any of these symptoms and your dog seems otherwise healthy, then his refusal to eat is an emotional reaction.

Such a reaction may have various causes. You may have suddenly changed the dog's food from one prepared brand to another, or from fresh meat to dry meal, or from dry to wet food. Or the reason may be even simpler: You have changed his dish or moved it from its regular place. Or perhaps you changed the hour of feeding, or decided to feed him twice a day instead of once, or vice versa. Or there may be a lot of noise or too many people around, or even another dog. Some dogs become accustomed to eating with their owner and cannot adjust to eating alone. Or the dog may have changed owners or come from a kennel or pet shop to you, and his different environment has affected his appetite.

He may simply need time to adapt to his new surroundings and new diet.

You should be sympathetic and kind to a dog in his new environment, if that is the particular problem, but you should not coddle him. If your dog goes on a hunger strike, offer him his food every day at the same time, but offer him the same food. Leave it down for about twenty to thirty minutes, and then remove it. Offer him nothing else for the rest of the day. If you have children, make sure they are not secretly feeding him. On the following day, do the same thing. Give your dog the same opportunity to eat, and remove his dish if he is indifferent. (Do not leave food around, as it may spoil, especially in warm weather.)

No dog, I can assure you, will starve himself to death. Eventually your dog will consent to eat what you offer him. If you are changing his diet and that is the reason for his hunger strike, you might as a concession change his food gradually. You can do this by mixing his old and new foods in differing proportions each day, gradually increasing the amount of the food you want him to eat. If you try to tempt him into eating, he may remain a problem eater. Of course, if you have the time and the inclination to tempt him by varying his diet and cooking him tidbits, go ahead. Many dogs thrive on such treatment, and the owner himself is made happy. But if you simply want your dog to accept the diet you have chosen, follow my directions and your dog will eventually attack his food with relish.

Car Chasing

The best way to avoid car chasing is to keep your dog leashed at all times. Most city owners are forced by law to do just this, but in many suburban communities either there is no leash law or it is less strictly enforced, and there is a great temptation to let your dog run for just as long as he doesn't damage your neighbor's property.

Car chasing is a dangerous business, both for the dog himself and for pedestrians or children playing in the area, because the first reaction of a driver is to swerve, especially if the dog is foolhardy and plays it close. In addition, there is the added danger for the driver and for other cars. Discourage car chasing.

From the dog's point of view, the moving car may be a challenge of some kind, or it may be attractive simply because it is moving; perhaps the dog wants to try out his speed against the car's. It may even be that the sound of the motor has excited him. Whatever the exact reason, some dogs are inveterate car chasers.

If it is impossible for you to keep your dog on a leash or restrained within his kennel or on a long chain, you will have to take other measures. And remember that while the measures may seem harsh, the car-chasing habit is one of the worst. In this country, cars are the biggest killers of dogs. One way to break your dog of car chasing is to tie a rope around his body *(not neck)* with plenty of length—20 or 30 feet—and then let him race after a car. When the rope runs out, he will come to a startling halt. The shock will probably throw him off his feet, and you too if you don't brace yourself. Of course if you have a Great Dane or Mastiff who does this, you'd better tie the other end of the rope around a sturdy tree or else you will be pulled along by the dog.

Try this method a few times. Most dogs should be discouraged. If not, tie a length of pipe to the dog's harness so that the pipe dangles over his front legs when he tries to run. He may have bruised shins, but that is surely better than having him severely injured or even killed.

There are other methods to try, but all of them involve some danger. What is the worst your dog can do if you keep him tied or chained (on a long enough tether so that he can run around)? He will bark, and then you will have a barking problem. Let's see what you can do about that.

Barking and Howling (Yapping and Baying)

Let us start with the apartment dog who barks, and work our way to the suburban or country dog who barks and howls when he is chained to his kennel.

Unless you have a Caspar Milquetoast, an apartment dog obviously will bark when he is cooped up alone. If you want a nonbarker, then buy a Basenji. If you want a snappy, barking dog, then get a Terrier. If you have a Hound, expect him to bay—it's an instinct. Other dogs will bark some of the time and may be depended on to do so when they are confined.

When a dog is confined, every outside noise means potential thrills or excitement to relieve his boredom. Remember that if you are away a good part of the day, he has nothing to do but sleep or be bored. And while a dog normally sleeps for many hours, he also stores up energy that he has to get rid of. When he hears the telephone or the doorbell (yours or somebody else's), he is ready for action. His bark tells the world he is there and that he is prepared for a good walk or run.

Also, many dogs have a protective instinct toward their owners. When they hear a noise, any noise, they react instinctively as watchdogs. This is a habit you do not want to discourage. If you have children or old people in the house, such a dog is an asset for many reasons.

The problem exists only when your dog barks uncontrollably at noises, or if he howls or bays indiscriminately, whether stimulated by a noise or not. If you live in an apartment or a row house, this racket can make you very unpopular indeed. And justifiably. While you love and admire your dog, don't expect everyone else to feel the same way, especially if he barks incessantly when you are away during the day and howls at night when you step out. Perhaps man has no greater love than for his dog, but such love rarely extends to one's neighbor's dog.

As I mentioned before, certain breeds—mostly terriers and crossbred terriers—are howlers and yappers. They are nervous as well as energetic, and they react to sounds with their primitive instinct. Terriers were originally developed to kill vermin and badgers. They have the kind of temperament and physique that needs exercise; when they are inactive for a while they become edgy and snappish. This irritation is shown in their frequent barking. Beagles may bay, some more than others. Small breeds as a whole tend to be barkers, although the small toys can bark without disturbing an entire block. The larger breeds are subdued, provided you do not have an individual who requires special attention.

What, then, can you do? You should certainly give your city dog a chance to work off his energy. Frequent exercise—as much as you can give—will allow him to get rid of his frustration from long confinement. If possible, have a neighbor walk your dog or give him a good run in the park or elsewhere in your neighborhood (depending on the laws of your community). Do not neglect your dog when you are at home, or he will take out his peevishness in barking. From his point of view, it is a way of gaining attention. From your point of view, it is the wrong way.

Suppose that none of this works. Your dog continues to bark at the slightest provocation: doorbells, telephones, noises in the hallway or alley, passing automobiles, fire engines. If he is a puppy, you can still train him to restrain himself. In fact, a good deal of your dog's barking problem can be the result of too little training when he was younger. A puppy is impressionable, and you can usually curb excessive barking by being very firm with him. Whenever he barks or howls, you must be right there to reprimand him. Do it sternly and forcefully, with a loud "No!"

To get him accustomed to being alone, stay out for longer periods of time. One method goes something like this: On a weekend, leave the puppy for a short time. Give him his toys and other familiar objects. If he barks or howls, be close by so that you can return immediately to reprimand him. Then leave again. If he barks, repeat the reprimand. If he is quiet, stay away for a still longer time, but then return, so that he can learn that you will always come back. Go away again, extend the length of time, then return. In this way you may be able to accustom your young dog to your absence. If he is assured that you will always return, he may well be willing to stay alone without barking.

While this method is more effective with a young, impressionable puppy, the older dog may also be trained in the same way. The older dog is, of course, shrewder. If you go away for a short time, you must be sure that he doesn't hear or smell your presence. If you put him in a room to isolate him, make sure you really go away. If you close the door and go into another room to watch television or to read, he will know you are only fooling. Be certain that he can hear you leave. Then be prepared to return at a moment's notice. Be very stern. Even though the entire situation may strike you as absurd (it is, of course, just that, but not to your neighbors), don't let your dog see you laugh.

Most dogs will become reconciled to the idea of staying alone. If yours is the exception, then you have a problem dog, and you must arrange for him to be walked and quieted or else your neighbors may take their complaints to the police. Another possibility—a remote one for you—is to provide some kind of company for your dog. Another animal—not a dog!—is one such possibility, although you may view it as an additional source of trouble. Another dog might prove to be the answer, but then you would have to take the chance that both dogs could become howlers.

The dog who barks and howls while you are at home is much easier to train, unless you have lost all control over him. The chief thing to let him know is that he can't bark and get away with it. As soon as he howls for any reason, be there with a stern reprimand. A dog is usually responsive to the tone of his owner.

The suburban dog who howls and barks whenever a car passes, or whenever someone walks up the drive, is a nuisance for everyone except perhaps the owner. If he runs free, there is a chance that he may try to nip someone, possibly more from excitement than the desire to hurt. Whatever he does, he is a problem if he gets out of hand. It is fine if he barks at unfamiliar faces, just as it is a good idea for the apartment dog to stand watch over his owner's property. But when he barks at familiar faces and continues the barking despite your warnings, you must take action. Once again, this bad habit is best controlled when your dog is young, and then by stern reprimand or by clapping a folded newspaper against your hand or a nearby object while issuing a sharp warning. If, however, you have not trained your dog young, you may be forced to introduce to him every delivery boy, newspaper boy, and milkman who comes to your house. If the dog bristles as though to bark or nip, be on him immediately with a stern warning.

If your dog reacts well, let him sense your pleasure at his actions. Stroke him and address him in a reassuring tone. This should teach him that he must not bark at anyone whose smell he recognizes. It may be embarrassing to ask the cooperation of so many people in helping to train your dog, but you will find that most of them will be willing to help, especially if it means they will not have to face a barking, snapping animal when they make deliveries to your house.

If the chained dog howls at passing cars, or greets the delivery boy with snarling, rasping barks, you must really frighten him into silence. Once again, this type of training is most effective when your pet is young. After months or years of neglect, the dog believes he can get away with anything. When you suddenly crack down on him, he thinks you are playing or that you'll give up soon. You must show him that you are in earnest. Do not be afraid to make him conscious of your wishes on this score. He must be controlled, or your life will be miserable. As soon as he barks at a passing sound or starts howling at the moon, you must be on him. Once again, reprimand him sharply, strike a rolled-up newspaper near him so that he is frightened of being hit, grab his collar and, without hurting him, jerk his head around. All these moves will indicate your extreme displeasure. You cannot let up or he will simply return to his bad habits as soon as you go away.

If your dog begins to howl whenever you take out your car, try to do what the city fellow did. That is, go only a short way and then return. Give your dog a stern warning. Then leave again, repeating this until he becomes accustomed to seeing you go. Also, try to include your dog in as many activities as possible. Take him along whenever you can. And remember, if you leave him in the car, do not park in the sun or close the windows all the way. Give him air through the windows— leave them open just enough so that he cannot jump out. But expect him to bark as soon as you disappear from sight, unless you have trained him not to.

If your dog does not respond to your training efforts, he is a problem. You might seek out professional advise from a veterinarian, but if he or a professional trainer cannot help you, the sad conclusion may be that your dog cannot be trained. The best protection is early training. Start your dog young, and you can develop him to fit your needs.

Coprophagy (Eating of feces or stool)

Frequently, a puppy or even an older dog left alone with his bowel movement will eat it, something that understandably causes the owner considerable worry and annoyance. Some dogs will also eat dirt, a practice called geophagy.

The usual reason is boredom, but in some cases a dietary deficiency or extreme hunger. Another reason may be that the dog has worms, and he satisfies some abnormal need by eating whatever is at hand. Or he may be nervous or sick. Occasionally, the overconscientious dog who feels that perfection is required of him will eat his feces if he has evacuated inadvertently on the floor, because he wants to avoid a reprimand. Still another theory is that dogs carry over the primitive instinct of eating everything that is available against the time of famine.

If your dog is worm-free and has been receiving a well-balanced diet, with sufficient vitamins and minerals, you can be reasonably certain that he is "misbehaving" simply because the feces are available. Make sure that all stool is removed as soon as the dog has a bowel movement; this is the one sure way of breaking this unattractive habit.

Do not punish your dog when he eats his feces, because he will not understand what he has done wrong. And if you suspect that a dietary deficiency is responsible, take him to the veterinarian for a checkup. He may suggest some treatment.

Street Manners

It is essential to make your dog learn self-control when he is still a puppy. If you leave him to his own devices, the chances are excellent that he will jump on people, bark in their faces, nip at their ankles, and perhaps put a tooth or two through their dresses or trousers. Such behavior, while perhaps cute to the owner, is downright annoying and sometimes costly to your friends. Many people who are not owners like dogs but prefer that they keep their distance. As far as is possible, your dog's behavior should reflect your own manners and standards of courteous behavior.

It is also somewhat embarrassing for the owner if his dog barks violently at every moving object, whether person or vehicle. When you walk your dog, he should at all times be leashed, and if he suddenly barks, you should just as suddenly give a good wrench to the leash. Accompany the wrench with a stern reprimand, so that he knows that you won't stand for any nonsense. Such actions and words will be enough to keep most dogs in line. Repeat your warning at the slightest provocation, or else your dog—especially the older dog—will revert to his former behavior.

Some dogs will also try to fight with other dogs on the street. Once again, the only real preventive is to keep your dog on his leash and muzzled. This will save you a lot of worry, and it will as well save your pet from possible injury if the other dog is larger and tougher. Of course if the other dog is himself not leashed, you might be in for trouble. In that event, see my remarks below for how to handle your dog in a fight.

Two dogs may simply want to sniff each other; there is nothing wrong with that, provided their owners have no objections. Dogs receive such obvious pleasure from this bit of socializing that it is a good idea to let them play. If your dog is very young and has not yet received his vaccination, you have good reason for keeping him away from mature dogs. But very young puppies should not even be walked, and certainly not before they are immunized.

Incidentally, keeping your dog on a leash is not only an act of courtesy toward pedestrians and other dog owners; it is also an invaluable protection for your dog. As I have repeated throughout this book, more dogs are killed by automobiles than in any other way.

Biting

A dog will frequently have very good reasons for biting. Nevertheless, whatever his reasons, you must curb this trait, even if it ruins him as a watchdog. Many communities have laws that demand the destruction of a dog who bites. But even if your community has no such law, you might be sued for damages, and in any event you certainly do not wish to have a pet who bites.

The dog who nips is a nuisance. If you have children in the house, certainly you must train your dog not to nip even when the children provoke him and he nips in self-defense. The best time for this training is during puppyhood. At that time, you must teach him basic obedience. (For details of obedience, see Chapter 5.) But even obedience training is no guarantee against biting unless you take certain precautions.

If you see that your dog tends to be a biter—that is, he seems aggressive and snappish—you must keep him leashed when he is outdoors and contained within a given area when he is indoors. You cannot let him roam free in the neighborhood, to become the terror of mailmen and delivery boys; nor can you allow him the freedom of the house if every visitor must be exposed to the hazard of his teeth.

Some dogs are more disposed to biting than others. There is the dog who has problems, and biting or nipping helps him work off his aggression. There is the fearful dog, in whom biting becomes a temporary act of bravery. There is the out-and-out vicious dog—there are such individuals who should not be permitted to associate with people and other dogs. There is the dog who has been so spoiled as a puppy that he believes he can do anything he wants; the dog who has been overprotected fits into this category. There is, further, the dog who is confined so much that when he is freed, he breaks out with a vengeance. In brief, the reasons for a dog's antisocial behavior are much the same as a man's.

There are also certain situations that might cause an otherwise gentle dog to snap and bite. Objects suddenly coming into view might make him react instinctively with his teeth. Remember that a dog's teeth are his sole weapon, and they are made for tearing and clamping. A child may come upon a sleeping dog and fall on him with all the good will in the world, but the dog reacts as though attacked by an enemy. Or the child may roughhouse with the dog past the point of his endurance. He reacts with his teeth, perhaps as an act of self-defense. Possibly the dog has become enraged by being kept for a long time on a short chain. When a person approaches, he springs to nip him. Some large dogs go berserk and try to bite if kept muzzled.

If your dog is predisposed to biting, the very least you can do is to be aware of all the factors involved. Once a dog has developed to this stage of aggressiveness, it is difficult to change him. Then the only course of action involves precautions, so that he has no chance to carry through his threats.

The apartment dog is relatively under control. When someone unfamiliar comes, you can move the dog into a room and close the door. In the suburbs and the country, the problem is more difficult, for the dog usually roams a good deal. Fence in your property if possible, and then he has freedom of movement without being a menace to the public. Without a fence, you may have to control him with a chain, and that is the very thing that makes him worse if he is a problem dog.

Whatever the nature of the problem, you must be sufficiently aware of it so as to compensate for it—if you can. If the dog is cowardly, avoid sudden confrontations that will make him react with false courage. If he is tense and nervous, do not provoke him and warn others not to annoy him. If he is shy and therefore tends to break out uncontrollably to assert himself, tell your children and friends not to bother him. If he is confined too much, try to arrange for him to be walked whenever you cannot do it. Whatever the reason may be, if he is really vicious, it is best to get rid of him, harsh as this solution might seem once you have become attached to him.

House-Training Problems

While I handle house-training in Chapter 5, I take up special house-breaking problems here. Some dogs are more difficult to train than others, just as some children take longer to be toilet-trained than others. This is perfectly normal. However, if a dog continues to give trouble, something might be physically wrong with him, or he might have an emotional problem.

A tense or shy dog might wet on the floor if you reprimand him severely for some wrongdoing. He is not out to get revenge; he is simply frightened and loses control. You make matters worse in this case if you scold him for wetting. The best thing to do is to cultivate a softer, more patient tone with him. The wetting should stop if there is no physical ailment. Sometimes a male dog will urinate all over his room and possessions when another male dog enters the house. This is a primitive carry-over in which the dog "marks" precisely what is his and therefore out of bounds for the other animal. Or else a male puppy may urinate when an older male tries to exert authority. His wetting is a sign of his submission. All of these are nervous or emotional problems that can be easily solved once you become aware of them.

Occasionally, a nervous, insecure dog will urinate or defecate in the house whenever you leave him alone. What is worse, he may choose your bed or best furniture for his activities; in fact, he often seems to seek them out. Even if you wash out the spot, he will smell it and probably go there again. Your best protection is prevention. Whenever you go out, be sure to isolate him—lock him with his water dish and toys in the bathroom or kitchen if necessary. You may not stop the habit, but you can cut down on the annoyance. Make sure you lock him in a place that has plenty of air and light and is draft-free.

If there is uncontrolled wetting or defecating and no apparent emotional reason, your dog probably needs medical care. Wetting or piddling is more common in the older bitch than in other dogs and there are some treatments that may help the problem. Wetting is also a factor in kidney and bladder ailments—which, of course, may occur in the young as well as in the older dog. Also, some bitches in heat or with irritations urinate uncontrollably.

Unknown to you, your dog may have had an accident or been kicked so that his bladder or kidneys are affected. When wetting comes from such a cause, the most you can do is to tolerate his behavior with sympathy until healing occurs. He is as ashamed as you think he should be, but there is nothing he can do about it. Let him know that you still feel affection and are not angry with him. If he piddles or wets, try to keep him in an enclosed area with materials that can be either cleaned or replaced. If possible, keep him outdoors a good deal.

Some Random Problems

There are several nuisance problems you might encounter with your dog. The country or suburban dog who gets into garbage cans is annoying for your neighbors, who must clean up after him, and more than annoying for you if your dog gets sick. The only "cure" is prevention—keep your dog muzzled and leashed.

In many instances, a dog will destroy your property when you leave him alone in the house. Some of the favorite acts of vandalism of the lonely dog are committed on shoes, clothes, blankets, books, and furniture. Sometimes a bathroom or living room rug proves irresistible, and I have known dogs who go wild over drapes and curtains. While you expect this kind of behavior in the young puppy, you do not wish to tolerate it when he is older. If he doesn't improve, keep all such objects out of his reach or isolate him in the bathroom when you leave the house. Incidentally, a dog who has no regard for property may give your possessions a working over even when you are at home.

In this connection, you had better watch your guests' property when you give a party. An attractive hat or coat might catch your dog's eye and end up in his mouth. You will find yourself in an embarrassing situation, even a lawsuit, depending on the forbearance and sense of humor of your guest. And watch the dinner itself. Do not leave it on the kitchen table while you mix the drinks. Your dog probably appreciates your cooking and will want to sample everything.

A New Child in the House

If you own a dog before you bring a baby into the house, you may expect him to be jealous of your new acquisition. *This will not be true if you have a puppy,* but the older dog, used to your attention, will resent anyone who interferes. Most dogs will eventually accept the baby if you continue to give them the usual attention. If, however, you neglect your dog, he may react by growling at the child and even attempting to bite. You must prevent any such situation by watching your dog's behavior carefully. In the great majority of cases, your child will be safe. Dogs seem to love children of all ages. But in the odd instance when the dog turns nasty, you want to be there. And if the dog remains nasty, you may have a problem.

Your best protection here is to give the dog plenty of affection and not to curtail his usual activities. He is a creature of habit. Difficult as it will be to find time for him, you should do so. He deserves his place in the family, and his resentment is a natural response to a situation he cannot understand.

The Strange Dog and What to Expect

Most people, whether owners or not, are suspicious of strange, stray dogs. And they should be. Until you know whether a dog is friendly, you should give him a wide berth. How, then, can you be sure the dog is friendly? You can never be perfectly certain at first sight, but if the dog comes toward you frankly, tail wagging and held up, his nose working away to smell you, you are seeing the most obvious signs of friendliness. On the other hand, if a dog approaches you suspiciously, his tail held low, his body rigid and tense, his teeth snapping, his nose hugging the ground, perhaps snarling or barking or growling, you should suspect he is hostile. Such a dog may also try to get behind you.

The best thing to do when a strange dog comes near you is to wait for him to make the first move. Do not reach out to stroke him; he may attack you. For your gesture may startle him, and even a basically friendly dog might turn on you in fear or self-defense. Remain still, speak quietly if you speak at all, and be sure to keep him in front of you at all times. It is important for you to keep your eyes on the dog. Probably he will be cowed by your look, unless he is so vicious that nothing can intimidate him.

Even if you think you can make a getaway from an unfriendly dog, do not break into a run. No matter how fast you are, the dog is faster. If you become a moving object, he may decide to attack, for motion always seems to attract a dog. If you want to move away, do so without turning. If the dog moves with you, then stop; or else he will gain courage. Of course your first reaction is to run, but you must resist this natural impulse. Try to edge away slowly until you can put a fence or door between you and the dog.

Another warning: In this situation, do not try to frighten the dog away by hitting or kicking. Your aggressive act might be the very thing to make him attack.

Your chances of meeting with such a dog are slight. Most unfriendly dogs are leashed, and most strays are simply looking for a handout and are not in the least vicious. But you can never be sure, and precautions are necessary to protect you in the exceptional case. Of course, you should avoid any dog that is frothing or running around in circles or behaving in an unusual manner—*and you should report him immediately to the police, the health department, or the SPCA.* If you are bitten, you should immediately report the case to a doctor or to the police so that you may be treated and the stray dog can be caught and quarantined.

Suppose, for the moment, that none of these precautions works, and the dog attacks you. If it is a small dog, by lifting your knee straight up you can block the dog and probably knock him off balance. Always keep the dog in front of you; as he turns, you turn. *Keep your hands away from his mouth or you'll be bitten.* Call out for help, but do not turn and run, because the dog will run after you and bite your legs. If he pauses in his attack, stand still. Your initial block may have discouraged him, and he'll move off. When he does, report him immediately to the police department or the SPCA.

If a large dog attacks you, you must protect your face with your folded arms. When the dog leaps at you, twist your body to face him so that your shoulder or arm receives the weight and knocks him off balance. Do not let him get behind you, and do not move when he stands still. Do not run or you might suffer severe injury. Call for help and report the dog at the first opportunity.

Dogfights

The measures above are recommended for protection in the event you are attacked. What do you do if your dog is attacked, or if he attacks another dog? If you think you can break up the fight with harsh words, forget it. By this time, the dogs are so antagonistic that no verbal assault will work. If you think you can grab their collars and pull them apart, also forget that. In their desire to get at each other, they may bite you severely around the hands and wrists.

If you are alone, grab the tail of one of the dogs and heave him as far as he will go. Unless he is a toy, the fall will not hurt him, and usually this is enough to give him second thoughts about attacking. If you must do this, do it to your own dog. Once they are parted, try to control your dog with sharp commands; you have less chance of controlling the other dog, of course. If neither dog has a tail, you may be able to separate them by pulling on their hind legs and heaving, or by banging on anything available in an effort to frighten them. As a last resort, swat them with a board, stick, or tree branch, or, if possible, douse them with a bucket of water.

If the other dog is accompanied by his owner, each person should grab his own dog by the tail or hind legs and follow the above procedure. If your dog is bitten, follow the procedure for bites as outlined in Chapter 7, on first aid. Of course, your chance of stopping a fight is much greater with your dog on a leash.

The Dog and Livestock

If your dog lives on a farm or if he lives in the suburbs where you keep a few chickens, he must be taught not to molest them. The dog who molests livestock is a threat to the entire neighborhood unless you lock him up. Once your dog has killed a neighbor's chicken or mauled a sheep, you will be in for a great deal of trouble. You may be faced with a lawsuit, or the dog may be shot as a trespasser. The best protection is precaution, preferably while the dog is still a puppy.

The only way to prevent trouble is to accustom your dog—at whatever age—to the livestock. Hold a chicken near him, and watch him carefully so that he doesn't lunge or grab. He will be naturally curious to smell and you want to encourage that. But you must keep him away from the chicken run until he becomes accustomed to the odor. If you have larger animals—cows, sheep, or horses—do the same thing. Once your dog has become used to the smell, he is less aggressive, unless of course you have a pet who is more wolf than dog.

When you introduce the animals, be sure you have firm control of the dog. If he barks or pulls hard to get away, reprimand him sternly in a sharp tone of voice. If you have any doubts about his intentions, keep him on a leash until you feel he is a safe risk. Poultry and sheep, in particular, must be protected against the dog. He can mangle them in short order or cause them to panic and trample each other.

This training, if you have a lively and playful puppy, will take some time. Remember that he is feeling his youthful powers, and scaring a chicken or a lamb is for him great sport. Do not let the puppy run free until he has proved himself. When he can let a farm animal walk past him without growling or nipping, he is ready to roam freely.

The Wanderer

The male dog in particular may disappear for days at a time if he is allowed to roam free in the country or suburbs. Most of the time he is in search of a bitch in heat, although some dogs will wander off for no apparent reason. Occasionally, a dog who is mistreated will go off by himself to seek affection elsewhere. Some dogs who are treated well are simply seeking more companionship, which they hope to find elsewhere. And some dogs are too energetic to resist the call of the wild. A long journey suits their needs when they feel tied down.

Of course, all this is speculation. No one can tell exactly why one dog wanders away for long periods of time and another doesn't. A dog with the happiest of homes may become a wanderer, although you reduce the chances by giving him a good home. If you suspect that your dog is unhappy, try to make him feel wanted. Shower affection upon him, whenever possible take him with you on your daily rounds, play with him so that he senses your love. Unless he is a real problem, he should lose his wanderlust.

The "Oversexed" Dog

Many owners feel that their dogs are oversexed if they show any sexual interest. The male may rub against table and chair legs or try to mount the leg of a child or adult. He will often pump furiously. The bitch during her semiannual season may demonstrate similar behavior. She will rub her rear end against your leg or hand, or become coy and flirtatious.

Most of this behavior is perfectly normal, particularly for the apartment dog who is often frustrated. When dogs formerly ran free in packs, they could satisfy themselves as necessary. Now, an apartment dog is cooped up most of the day and has little or no contact with other dogs. Consequently, he works off his sexual feelings through rubbing and mounting. Only if your dog becomes aggressive in his behavior and refuses to listen to your commands do you have a problem.

For the bitch, this period lasts for 7 to 10 days twice a year; for the male, there is a persistent sexual desire, which can be satisfied through mating. If that cannot be done, you should exercise him a great deal to let him work off his energy. If the problem persists, professional treatment might work. There are injections for bitches that neutralize their heat periods without any aftereffects.

One warning: If you do have a sexually aggressive male, it is a good idea to watch your children with him. He may mount the child's leg, or a very large dog might push over a small child and frighten him.

The Problem Dog Who Remains a Problem

There are professional dog handlers who will work with a problem dog until they think he has returned to normal. Then you can take your dog back. He will in many cases be much improved, but there is always the possibility that he will revert to former habits even when you continue the training. This is a chance that you take, and since such training is expensive, you should think about it before putting your dog in the hands of a professional trainer.

Surely the best place for rehabilitation is at home; that is, if you love your dog enough to spend the time and energy required for rehabilitation. In this way, your dog recovers in his usual environment, and there is little danger of regression. The handler may be skillful and the training first-rate, but if you enjoy having your dog around, you will not want him away for long periods of time. Moreover, the sense of achievement you will feel in rehabilitating your dog will more than make up for the time devoted to him. Such training as is necessary will cement the relationship and offer the dog encouragement in his progress. Whatever the particular problem may be—whether one of the above or another one—discuss it with your veterinarian. His experience may provide the correct solution, or he may suggest the name of a professional handler who can advise you what to do.

A problem dog is a rarity unless conditions are such that the dog is forced into abnormal behavior. You should not expect any great difficulty with your pet if you use common sense in handling him. If you are too stern, he will act fearfully, and if you are too permissive, he will try to get away with everything. Somewhere in between you will strike the balance to make your dog happy and secure.

12

How to Protect Your Dog

A s ONE dog lover to another, I want to tell you about some precautions you should take to reduce the daily hazards for your pet. In many cases, you must take the same precautions with a dog that you would with a child, especially if you have a happy-go-lucky puppy.

The Automobile

The biggest killer of dogs in the United States is the automobile. By far. Yet there is a simple precaution that all owners can follow. *Do not unleash your dog when he is in the street.* This advice is especially important for the city owner, for two reasons: to insure the safety of his dog and to stay within the law that forbids him to unleash his dog. Here we are concerned with safety. Your dog may be steady and dependable, but one day he might suddenly dash into the street after a tantalizing odor or a delightful bitch. All dogs should be leashed when they are on the street.

For the suburban owner, the situation is still more dangerous. Here the temptation is even greater to let a dog roam free. Many people, in fact, move to the suburbs for just this freedom—for themselves, their children, and their pets. When the suburban owner allows his dog to run free, he is relying upon a nonrational creature to watch out for his own safety. The best protection is a fenced-in run or a fenced-in piece of back lawn. Lacking that, the suburbanite should keep his dog on a long chain. Another advantage in giving the dog a fenced-in concrete run is that he doesn't evacuate all over the neighbors' lawns, but is restrained to an area that can be easily cleaned.

The country owner has less of a problem if he lives far from highways and thoroughfares. But even here there are side roads. The chances of an accident are fewer, of course, because side roads do not permit much speed, but there are twists and turns that may hide the dog from the motorist. My advice to the country owner is to keep his dog restrained to his kennel area or on a long chain, unless the dog is being worked and therefore is under someone's eye. Most owners will reject this idea, but it does insure safety.

Outdoor Problems

Outdoor safety involves other factors besides precautions against automobile accidents. You must take care that your dog does not lick plants and leaves sprayed with insecticides, for these contain poisons that may be fatal to him. Also, if you keep paints in the garage, keep them on high shelves, so that your dog does not get into them. They contain lead that can damage his gastrointestinal system or even kill him. All corrosives, alkalies, and acids should also be put on high shelves in the garage or storage area. (This is advice for the apartment owner as well as for the suburban and country owner. Detergents and verminicides, as well as sleeping and reducing pills, are equally dangerous.) Remember that a puppy will try anything at least once, and many older dogs have still not learned caution. *Your best protection is prevention.*

If you plan to go into the country with your dog, find out what kinds of snakes are around, if any. Dogs and poisonous snakes do not go well together, and usually the dog loses. You will probably be wearing boots as protection, but the dog wears nothing, and he may boldly attack any snake he sees. You will probably not be able to treat a snake bite; for you the best method is prevention: Stay away from poisonous snake country. If you cannot do so, be sure you can reach a veterinarian in the area in the event of an emergency. I discuss temporary first-aid measures in the event of snake bite on page 362.

Another danger is porcupines. Few dogs die from porcupine quills (in contrast to the many who die of snake bites) but the porcupine can make your dog very miserable indeed. If there are porcupines in your area, you should be on the alert for them and restrain your dog when they come near. See also my discussion on page 363.

There is the additional possibility that your dog may be bitten by an animal carrying rabies—a fox, squirrel, or rat, or even a bat. If ever your dog is bitten, do not attempt treatment yourself. Find out ahead of time what veterinarians are in the area, and then in the event of an emergency, there will be little delay. See page 361 for first-aid treatment.

As your dog grows older, you should take some caution in exercising him. The older dog slows down in all his capacities, much like an older person. But unlike a person, the older dog throws caution to the winds and overextends himself. He may drop dead from exhaustion. In the heat of the summer, particularly, the older dog should not be overexercised, or he may become a victim of heat prostration or heat exhaustion. Remember that an old dog doesn't like to admit that he is old. He will carry on as long as his strength holds up, and then he will collapse if too much is expected of him.

Overexercise is also bad for a puppy, especially when the weather is hot and humid. The puppy, too, will carry on as long as he is able, and then fall unconscious or suffer heat exhaustion. The same is true for the overweight dog. Extra weight is bad enough for any dog, but for the dog exercising violently in the hot weather it can be fatal. When the weather is very hot, keep the old dog, the puppy, and the overweight dog off the streets. Let them rest until the cool of the day arrives and then walk or exercise them. Even then, take it easy.

While on the subject of extra weight, let me point out that you shorten the life of your dog if you allow him to become overweight. The natural appearance of a dog, from his first year through old age, should be lean and sleek. As long as his bones are covered with flesh and his health is good, he needs no extra weight. A good rule of thumb is this: Keep your dog at the *minimal* weight needed for maximum health. If you see him broadening through the shoulders or bulging around the abdomen, cut down on his food or increase his exercise until he loses the surplus poundage. If he remains lean, you will have a healthy dog growing well into old age.

A few other country matters: A dog left to himself will often swallow stones, rocks, pebbles, which cause serious trouble. When he is bored or curious, he will take nearly anything into his mouth, and it will probably end up in his stomach. He will also grind down his teeth on stones, wear away the enamel, and end up with stumps. The only preventive is to clear his run of stones, if this is possible, or else lay cement around his kennel. Not all dogs eat stones, of course, but you may wish to take normal precautions against the eventuality. If your dog is a chronic stone eater, there probably isn't much you can do about it short of locking him up.

There are two other possible dangers. Make sure that your dog does not have access to outside electric wires that are alive. The curious puppy, as well as the mature dog, may bite through the insulation and suffer severe shock and burns. If there are lines on your property that extend to outside appliances, raise them so that they are beyond the dog's reach. The second danger—drowning—can be prevented if you do not assume that all dogs can naturally swim. Most can, but not all. Unless you know surely by experience that your dog is a natural swimmer, do not put him in a situation in which he has to sink or swim. Most dogs learn to swim very quickly, and so if you want to be sure, lead your dog to water and let him try a few strokes on his own.

Dogs can get used to nearly anything, but they should not be shifted suddenly from warmth to cold, from a hot, steam-heated room to the cold, windy outdoors. If you plan to have your dog sleep outside in a kennel, he should always sleep outdoors from the time he is 6 months old. In order to protect him, his coat will grow more dense and thick. The same dog kept inside will have a lighter coat. This is nature's way of providing protection. But you upset the balance if you condition your dog to indoor living and then move him outdoors. The kennel itself should be dry and insulated, although it needs no direct heat. The warmth of the dog's own body will be enough if the kennel is draft-free.

The Dog Indoors

The dog kept indoors is relatively safe if you take normal precautions. Do not, for example, leave sleeping and reducing pills, medicines, liquids, or capsules where your dog can reach them. What may be harmless medication for you can be fatal to the dog. Small quantities of strychnine, for instance, are found in tonics, which are helpful to you but possibly may make a dog very sick.

If you have children, be careful that they do not get into medicines and leave them around—for their own protection and for the dog's. Children's aspirin is a particularly fine treat, flavored as it is with sugar and orange. The dog that gets hold of an open bottle might eat all the tablets and be in serious trouble. So many medicines are now syrupy or sweet-flavored that dogs are as attracted to them as are children. All of these items should be kept on a high shelf, tightly closed.

The same advice applies to soaps, detergents, powders, bleaches, corrosives, drain cleaners, and so on. Just as the suburban owner should keep dangerous articles out of reach in his garage or storage area, so should the apartment owner take similar care. If there are children in the house, your care obviously serves a double purpose. Remember that a puppy or young dog is devilish. The same vitality and curiosity that make him so much fun as a pet also drive him to put his nose into things that might harm him.

Your sewing equipment should also be kept where the dog can't reach it. Puppies seem to love needles, and a needle in the puppy's throat or intestines can do untold damage. If you are a fisherman, keep your fishhooks in a box, and be careful to gather them all up if you drop any. A dog who picks up a hook in his mouth may find the hook through his lip, a very painful situation. Watch out for nails, thumbtacks, and screws—many a dog has ended in the hospital because he thought these objects were edible. Splinters, too, may injure your dog—they can lodge in the throat, stick in the pads of the feet or between the toes, or pierce the eyes.

Children's toys, especially small objects like jacks, dice, and marbles, may find their way into your dog's stomach, where they are indigestible. Even larger objects may disappear, only to turn up in an x-ray of the dog's stomach or intestine. The mature dog may have sense enough to leave such objects alone, but the puppy is incorrigible. You must keep him away from these objects.

Electric cords may seem like spaghetti to some puppies, but if they are connected to an outlet, they will provide a kick that can prove fatal. Certainly shock and burns will result if a dog eats through the insulation into the wire itself. If you have a network of cords from lamps, radios, television sets, and other equipment, keep your dog away from them. When you go out and leave him alone, close the doors to rooms containing electric cords so that in his loneliness and boredom he doesn't investigate them and do himself harm.

Just as you are careful to keep a dog from pills and medicines, as well as splinters, needles, and children's toys, so also keep your eye out for broken glass. Your dog may be attracted by the shiny pieces, begin to play with them, even put them in his mouth, and cut himself rather badly. A playful dog will push bottles off shelves that he can reach. He may also be attracted by any slivers he discovers. A sliver can pierce the dog's skin, and is even more dangerous if it is swallowed.

If you have children who are particularly wild and energetic, you may have to protect your dog against them. The children may mean no harm, but in their play they can injure the dog, especially a small breed or a toy, who is somewhat delicate to begin with. If you have rough children who want to enjoy the dog, your pet should be sturdy and able to roughhouse. If he is frail and small, roughhousing may tire him easily and make him snappish or irritable.

A puppy, in particular, should be protected from your children, no matter how well-meaning they are. The pup does not have full strength, although he has the desire to frolic. In overextending himself, he may have an accident or suffer some other ailment. Also, the very small dog should not be picked up by children unless adequate precautions are first taken. The child should be taught how to lift a puppy (see Chapter 3), or he may injure the dog by dropping him. The puppy will squirm and try to get away, and can quite easily slip out of a child's arms.

If your dog is sick or is convalescing after an operation, he should be kept in a quiet, confined place. Certainly let your children see their pet; in some instances, their affection will help him recover. I know of many occasions on which a sick dog would eat only if a child fed him. But take normal precautions. The ailing or convalescing dog does not know his own weakness. Provoked by the child, he may exhaust his energy and suffer a setback. If the veterinarian advises quiet and rest, you should try to provide them, for only in this way will your dog fully recover and become once again a happy, functioning member of the family.

Other Considerations

There are certain health precautions that you and every other dog owner should take. One is to be sure that your dog is fully protected against distemper, rabies, canine hepatitis, and both types of leptospirosis. After his initial inoculations against these, your dog should receive annual booster injections to make sure he is immunized. No vaccination is 100 percent certain, but the odds are good that the dog receiving his annual inoculations is protected. Since these illnesses are so fearful—rabies is always fatal, and distemper often is—you owe this kind of protection to your dog.

Periodic health examinations are also a good idea—about every six to twelve months. A veterinarian may be able to catch in the early stages any conditions that need treating. Tumors, for example, if discovered early, may be removed before they become a threat to the dog's life.

You might have your dog's stool examined regularly—about every six months—to see if worms are present. While the fully grown dog tends not to have worms—the incidence is much higher among puppies— many mature dogs nevertheless do suffer from worms that go undetected for a long time. Let your veterinarian be your guide in advising examinations and the form they should take. He may want to do a urinalysis, blood test, and so on. By the way, don't get the impression that you must make a trip to the veterinarian every day—one visit every six months or so should be ample to keep your dog in good health, unless he needs special treatment because of an accident or illness.

For those owners interested in showing their dogs at exhibitions, there is always the danger that a disease will be spread. Whenever a large group of dogs is assembled, there is danger if one dog is incubating an illness. He may seem perfectly well; otherwise the owner would not be showing him. But shortly after the show, the dog may become ill. During the incubation period he can have infected several other dogs.

There isn't much you can do about this situation. At virtually every show, a veterinarian checks the dogs and rejects those who show any signs of illness. But he cannot reject those who show no signs. The most you can do is to have your own dog fully protected with inoculations and hope for the best. If you are aware of the danger involved (not a very great one), you will watch your dog carefully for symptoms in the days after a show. If you see anything suspicious—running nose, squinting eyes, diarrhea, vomiting, fever, listlessness—have the dog examined immediately.

You take the same chance if your dog attends an obedience school. In an obedience school (see Chapter 5), your dog learns the basic commands that are necessary if he is to be shown. Many people who are uninterested in showing also take their dogs to such schools. Certainly every owner acts in good faith when he brings in his dog—he assumes he is healthy. Still, your only sure protection is to keep up your dog's inoculations and to be suspicious of any signs of illness. Certainly you cannot keep your pet in isolation, any more than a parent can isolate a child to make sure he remains well.

Those owners who board out their dogs in kennels while they go on vacation also take a risk, slight though it is. Most kennel owners are perfectly honest and will not knowingly take a sick dog. But they, too, cannot tell that a dog is sick if he shows no signs when he is brought in. Let us say that your perfectly well dog becomes ill after he has been at the kennel for two days. Did your dog catch something at the kennel, or was he incubating an illness for a few days before he entered? Consider that distemper symptoms sometimes take 5 to 7 or more days to appear.

No kennel can guarantee that your dog will not become sick while he is boarded. For no kennel knows the exact condition of every dog brought in. Kennel life involves certain hazards, the same hazards involved in dog shows and obedience schools. After all, most parents continue to send their children to summer camp even though some become sick through contact with the other children. The only thing you can do is to be sure that the kennel is clean and responsibly run. In Chapter 13, I tell you what to look for in a kennel. But no matter how fine the kennel looks or really is, you have no control once you leave your dog. A simple precaution is one I have suggested several times before: Make sure your dog's inoculations are up to date.

Whenever in doubt about what to do with your dog, fall back upon common sense. The dog is a living organism, like you and your children, and therefore he is subject to the same hazards as all living organisms. The only difference is that a dog has no discretion. He won't deliberately fall from a cliff or attack a lion, but in most situations, the dog will give all of himself regardless of the consequences. His all-or-nothing attitude makes a dog refreshing and lovable; yet it is this very trait that makes him a danger to himself. Your role is to protect him, so that you can enjoy his love as long as his natural life lasts.

13

Services and Travel

W E ARE a nation of services. If there is a chore that we cannot or do not wish to do, no matter how trivial, we can always find someone to do it for us. Travel agents plan our vacations, nutritionists plan our meals, baby-sitters look after our children, decorators design our homes, telephone-answering services take messages for us. In short, there are thousands of services available to us that we know about because they concern us. There are also countless services available for our dogs, many of them concerning travel, that you may not know about and perhaps will want to use.

BOARDING KENNELS

Should you go on vacation and not wish to take your dog, or should you suddenly be called away, you may want to board him at a kennel. There are thousands of boarding kennels in the country, and many in your vicinity. How do you choose the best one for your dog?

Knowledge and experience should be your guide. Ask your veterinarian to recommend one (after all, he is in charge of your dog's health), or ask a friend who has used one. Once a kennel has been recommended to you, by all means inspect it. Be sure it is clean and sweet-smelling, because that will tell you the owner is interested in the health of his dogs as well as his own and his workers' health. Watch out for fleas and flies, especially flies in the summer. No food should be left uncovered. There should be no dog droppings. Make sure that brushes, pails, and brooms are absolutely clean. No old rubbish should be in evidence. Check also how the dogs behave. They should have a healthy, thrifty, alert look; they should be well groomed, clear-eyed, and seem well-fed.

There should be long outside runs and an exercise yard. Check for proper ventilation as well as heat and cold control. Some kennels are air-conditioned and heated and have germicide lights burning twenty-four hours a day to guard against airborne diseases.

Make sure that your dog will receive a balanced diet of high quality. Ask about the personal attention your dog will get and the kind of discipline used. Also, if your dog has special needs, whether medical or nutritional, be certain the kennel will provide them. You will, of course, have to pay extra for special services.

SHIPPING SERVICES AND TRAVEL

It is always best to take your dog with you if at all possible. If, however, you must ship your dog, the airlines and the railroads have the facilities to do the job.

Airlines

If you want to transport your dog to any part of the United States, or to any country abroad, for that matter, you can be certain that every major airline will handle him. Before you make any arrangements to ship your dog, write or call the cargo traffic manager of the airline you intend to use and ask the following questions:

1. Does your airline transport dogs throughout the United States or abroad? (For the large airlines, this question is unnecessary.)

2. What health certificate or legal papers must my dog have to enter the state or country of his destination?

3. If the state or country demands a health certificate, to whom should it be presented?

4. May I take my dog into the cabin of the airplane?

5. If I may take my dog into the cabin, what preparations must I make?

6. If I cannot take my dog into the cabin, how can I ship him?

7. Are there any restrictions on the size of a dog that may be shipped as air freight or excess baggage?

8. Will a dog shipped as (a) excess baggage or (b) air freight always be on my plane?

9. How far in advance before flight time should I reserve space for my dog as (a) excess baggage or (b) air freight?

10. Where and when must my dog be delivered?

11. Must I deliver my dog in a carrier? If so, what should the carrier be like and what information should appear on the outside?

12. What arrangements does your airline make for dog food, water, blankets, and first aid?

13. Can I take out insurance on my dog?

14. What is the cost for transporting my dog?

A word of caution. Most people have told me that airlines have done a good job in looking after their dogs. But there are owners who contend that airline personnel neglected their dogs, handling them like ordinary pieces of freight; some have even charged that their dogs arrived at their destinations completely dehydrated.

Railroads

Every important railroad will transport dogs throughout the United States. Before making any arrangements, write or call the baggage agent of the railroad you intend to use. Ask the following questions:

1. May I take my dog with me (a) on a coach train or (b) in a private room of a Pullman car?

2. Must I have my dog in a carrier if he is in a compartment?

3. If my dog cannot ride with me, how do I ship him?

4. Does the train provide carriers or must the owner supply his own?

5. What information should appear on the outside of the carrier?

6. How much does it cost to ship a dog on your railroad?

7. How far in advance must I make a baggage car reservation and where and when must I deliver my dog?

8. Can I insure my dog with your railroad?

9. What facilities does your railroad provide for my dog, particularly on a long trip and during the summer and winter months?

Once you've settled on where you want to be and how you want to ship your dog, take the following precautions before you begin your trip.

1. Get a certificate of health from your veterinarian stating that your dog is in good health, free of all infectious and communicable diseases, that he comes from an area free of rabies, and that he has been vaccinated against rabies within six months. This certificate is not only required by all states, but it may well save you a good deal of bother, worry, and heartache should your dog be bitten by another animal, particularly a wild one, or should your dog accidentally bite a person.

2. If you plan to settle in one place for more than a week, find out the name, address, and phone number of the nearest veterinarian as well as the address and phone number of the nearest humane society and SPCA. You never know when you may need them in an emergency.

3. If you plan to ship your dog by air, consult the airlines about flight conditions and then ask your veterinarian if you should expect any difficulty.

4. If you transport your dog by train in warm weather, make sure that the railroad has someone aboard who can give your dog

water. The cars get very hot during the summer months. Also make sure that your dog will not be traveling in a sealed compartment. If you ship your dog in the winter, cover the carrier with burlap or other material as insulation against the cold and drafts.

5. Don't ship your dog by air or by rail if he has been recently ill, if he is old and infirm, or if he is very nervous. The dog should be in excellent health before you ship him.

6. Many dogs are generally nervous during travel; obviously, they don't know what to expect. Further, they are surrounded by new sounds, new smells, etc. Put an article of your clothing in the kennel, and the dog will be comforted. Also, ask your veterinarian about the suitability of a tranquilizer.

Traveling Abroad

For most people, the prospect of taking a dog abroad seems like an overwhelming burden and a risky adventure into the unknown. To begin with, how do you get a dog into a foreign country? What about import laws, quarantine restrictions, travel hazards? And once you've brought your dog into a foreign country, will you be able to keep him with you most of the time? Will you be able to take him into hotels and restaurants, streetcars, buses, and trains? Will you be able to get in touch with a veterinarian quickly, and will there be clinics or hospitals available for your dog should he need them? The whole business of taking a dog abroad seems hopelessly complicated and frightening, and most of us give up at the start.

But should we give up? My answer is a definite *no,* if you know the laws that the country of your destination has made for dogs and you follow them *to the letter. For information on laws about entry and living, phone, write, or, if you can, go to the consulate of the country you intend to visit.* For example, if you plan to go to Ireland, Scotland, England, or the Scandinavian nations, you must check the quarantine regulations for these countries.

This takes considerable time and trouble, but is worth the effort required if you plan to remain abroad for a year or more. Europeans and many others have a much more enlightened attitude toward dogs than we have. Generally, you will be able to take your dog into most restaurants and keep him at most hotels. In the majority of European countries, canned dog food is available.

When you arrive abroad, you can obtain the names of veterinarians from the local phone book or from the American Consulate or Embassy, or even by asking a policeman. In the same way, you can find out where emergency treatment is available. If you take the trouble, your dog can be as happy and healthy abroad as he is here.

As a service for tourists heading abroad, the American Society for the Prevention of Cruelty to Animals (441 East 92 Street, New York, New York 10028) has prepared a pamphlet called *Traveling Abroad with Your Pet,* which contains the latest information about requirements for taking cats and dogs into 62 foreign countries.

Returning to the United States

If you obtain a dog abroad, a vaccination against rabies is required for a dog unless:

(a) The dog comes directly from Australia, New Zealand, Bahama Islands, Denmark, Ireland (Eire), Iceland, Jamaica, Norway, Sweden, Great Britain or Northern Ireland.

(b) The dog is less than 3 months old at the time of arrival. If so, the dog upon arrival must be placed in confinement and remain in confinement for at least 1 month following vaccination at 3 months. Any vaccination given to a dog under 3 months will not be recognized.

How shall a vaccination be done?: (a) with nervous tissue vaccine more than 1 month but not more than 12 months before the dog's arrival, or (b) with chicken-embryo vaccine more than 1 month but not more than 36 months before arrival.

What about a certificate of rabies vaccination? When the vaccination is required, the dog shall be accompanied by a validated certificate that identifies the dog, which is signed by a licensed veterinarian, and that specifies that the veterinarian vaccinated the dog with nervous tissue vaccine or with chicken-embryo vaccine within the time limits required.

For a dog you have taken abroad: (a) The owner needs a health certificate, issued by a licensed veterinarian, stating that the dog is in good health and free from all contagious diseases. (b) He also needs a certificate of vaccination against rabies within 6 months.

OTHER SERVICES

Insurance

Almost any comprehensive personal liability policy provides protection that all dog owners should have. These policies, sold by every insurance broker, will insure you against any damages your dog may cause.

But a few companies also issue life insurance policies for dogs. While they do not insure you against the dog's death from natural causes or disease, you are "protected" if he dies from a number of accidental causes: fire or lightning, flood accident to a conveyance while he is on it, being hit by a car not owned and driven by the owner or his family, collapse of building or bridge, attacks by dogs or wild animals, accidental shooting, and drowning. Ask your veterinarian for particulars.

Humane Societies

There are hundreds of humane societies throughout the United States. The general aim of these societies is to prevent cruelty to animals, to enforce all laws for the protection of animals, to provide adoption services, to maintain a shelter for lost or unwanted animals, and to dispense general information about the care of the dog, especially about laws and licensing. Some provide medical and surgical care.

Several humane societies give courses in training dogs in obedience, with specialists teaching you and your dog such basic obedience procedures as heeling, sitting, staying, etc. See your local phone book or ask your veterinarian or local kennel owner for the addresses of these societies.

Funeral Chapels and Dog Cemeteries

Canine funeral chapels offer a complete funeral for your dog, including all the rites presently existing for humans. They offer embalming, restoration, trim, removal from place of death, and provision for burial in a memorial park. They also have a complete selection of burial caskets—polystyrene, hardwood, and metal—with any interior the owner wishes. Your veterinarian or local humane society can be of help in supplying names and addresses.

Dogs for the Blind

The American Foundation for the Blind, Inc. (15 West 16 Street, New York, New York 10011, 212–924–0420), has the most up-to-date information on organizations throughout the country that provide trained guide dogs for blind people.

The American Kennel Club

Established on September 17, 1884, the American Kennel Club (51 Madison Avenue, New York, New York 10010, 212–481–9200) is a non-profit organization devoted to the protection and advancement of purebred dogs (the recognized breeds now number 121). It is made up of more than four hundred dog clubs in the United States. The American Kennel Club has the latest and most authoritative information on rules and regulations for dog shows, obedience trials, and field trials. It has all the information on purebred dogs and their ancestors registered since September 17, 1884. It maintains an extensive library on the dog, with several of the books dating back as far as the sixteenth century. Many others are rare out-of-print books or are in foreign languages. This is possibly the best library on dogs in the world. The American Kennel Club also has a Breeders' Information Service, which answers questions about breeds and gives the names and addresses of breeders and kennels throughout the country.

Hospitals and Clinics

There are dog hospitals—more than 5,000 of them—in just about every state in the Union, and most of them provide the newest and finest care available today. They have virtually every facility that a human hospital has, including boarding facilities for dogs who require prolonged hospitalization. Some are open twenty-four hours a day and provide ambulance service. You can get particulars from the classified section of your phone book or from your veterinarian as well as from kennels and the police.

Products and Services

The products and services for your dog are almost as varied and extensive as those for people. Today in many pet supply shops and large department stores, you can buy for your dog boots, pajamas, raincoats, mink coats, jeweled collars, berets, turtleneck sweaters, shampoos, hair tints, deodorants, portable comfort stations, tranquilizers, pep pills, pacifiers, TV dinners, chewing gum, and a thousand other items.

You can obtain baby-sitters, walking services, and, in some cities, psychological treatment for your dog. You can even send him to a gymnasium to keep him in shape. Dog shops offer stripping, trimming, plucking, shampooing, nail cutting, and ear cleaning. For information on these services, ask your veterinarian or local kennel owner.

Obedience Schools

As I mentioned in Chapter 5, there are many schools throughout the country that teach obedience and house-training. Experienced trainers teach your dog (accompanied by you) to sit, stay, heel, turn, etc. They also teach you how to handle and even house-train your dog. Some other obedience schools offer training for your unaccompanied dog, and still others offer training for the problem dog. Find out about obedience schools in your vicinity from your veterinarian, the SPCA, or from a local kennel or petshop owner.

Gaines Dog Research Center

The Gaines Dog Research Center (250 North Street, White Plains, New York 10625) will send you several pamphlets either free or at a very small cost:

1. *Touring with Towser* ($.50)—a key to hotels and motels in each state that will accept dogs, and the conditions under which they are accepted.

2. *Where to Buy, Board or Train a Dog*—a directory of kennels in each state, telling where to purchase, board, or train a dog.

3. *Planning a Kennel*—information on how to build a kennel for your dog.

4. *Standards of Judicial Practice and Field Trial Procedure* ($.25)—a handbook of rules for field trial procedures.

Licensing

When you pay for your dog's license, what do you receive in return? First, your dog can be easily identified from his tag—a very necessary safety precaution if he runs free. Second, part of the fee goes toward operating dog pounds, shelters, and other organizations, which try to make life easier for the dog. Third, in many rural areas, the fee goes toward an indemnity fund for livestock killed or injured by dogs. One final caution: If an unlicensed dog roams free, he may be picked up and used for medical purposes in those states that permit vivisection, while the licensed dog will ordinarily be returned to the owner.

Licensing differs in each locality, according to the age and sex of the dog. Most communities set 6 months as the legal age of a dog. In some areas, the license for a spayed bitch costs less than one for an unspayed bitch. Many communities, however, make no distinctions, and a license generally costs from $5 to $10.

For those owners living in New York City, the Veterinary Medical Association (9 Rockefeller Plaza, New York, New York 10019 212–246–0057), provides information on veterinarians, their hospital affiliation, hospitals and clinics, their hours, and the kinds of medical services they specialize in.

Glossary

ACTION: A dog's style of walking or running.

ALL AROUNDER: A judge licensed to pass on all the breeds recognized by the American Kennel Club.

ALMOND EYES: Eyes slanted at each end and oval-shaped like an almond; best example is the eyes of the Bull Terrier.

ALTER: To castrate (a male); to spay (a bitch).

ANGULATION: The angle made by two bones of the leg, shoulder, or upper arm.

ANTICIPATING: An obedience term, said of a dog who goes through an exercise before he gets his commands from a trainer.

APPLE-HEADED: Having a skull rounded on top; not desirable in most breeds. Many English Toy Spaniels and Chihuahuas have this fault.

APRON: The long hair on the throat and below the neck on long-coated dogs, seen on most Collies.

ASCOB: The standard abbreviation for "any solid color other than black."

B. or b.: Abbreviation for bitch, used in most announcements at dog shows.

BABBLING: Barking in the field when not trailing game.

BANDOG: Any dog tied during the day and released at night.

BANDY: Bow-legged.

BARRELED: Having a large, round chest.

BAT EARS: Large, stiff open ears pointing outward, like those of the French Bulldog.

BAY: The bark of a hound, usually made when trailing game.

BEARD: Profuse, broad, and bushy whiskers, as of the Brussels Griffon. They are not the same as terrier whiskers.

BEEFY: Having ham muscles that are overdeveloped.

BELTON: A finely mottled color combination, usually blue-and-white or orange-and-white, in the coat of a dog; most often seen in English Setters.

BENCH SHOW: A dog show at which all dogs are leashed on benches.

BEST IN SHOW: The dog judged to be the best of all the breeds accredited by the American Kennel Club in a show; prize awarded annually at the Westminster Dog Show and at other shows throughout the country.

BIRD DOG: Any breed of dog, usually Pointer or Setter, used for hunting birds.

BITCH: The female dog.

BITE: The position of the teeth when the mouth is shut.

BLANKET: Color of dog's coat between neck and tail.

BLAZE: A white marking running up the center of the face and between the eyes; often seen on Papillons and St. Bernards.

BLINKER: A bird dog who points at birds and then goes away before they are flushed; often he will go past the birds even when he knows they are there.

BLOCKY: Having a square or boxlike head, as in the Boston Terrier.

BLOODED: Pedigreed.

BLOOM: The glossiness of a coat in the very best condition.

BLUE MERLE: See MERLE.

BOBTAIL: Another name for the Old English Sheepdog.

BOLT: To drive an animal out of hiding.

BONE: The conformation and appearance of a dog's limbs, which should look strong and ready to spring.

BOSSY: Having shoulder muscles that are too thick and muscular.

BRACE: A pair of dogs of the same kind.

BREECHING: The tan hairs on the inside and the backs of the thighs, seen in Manchester Terriers and other breeds.

BREED: A distinctive type of purebred dog.

BRINDLE: A mixture of dark and light hairs in a dog's coat, gray and brown usually being the main colors; often seen in Scottish Terriers.

BRISKET: The part of the lower chest that includes the breastbone.

BROKEN COLOR: The color of a dog's coat whose main color is broken up by white or another color.

BROKEN-HAIRED: Having a tough, wiry coat.

BROKEN-UP FACE: A heavily wrinkled face with a pushed-out lower jaw and a receding nose; characteristic of the Bulldog, Pug, and Pekingese.

BROOD BITCH: A female kept for breeding.

BRUSH: A tail with thick, bushy hair, like that of the Alaskan Malamute.

BURR: The irregular inner part of the pinna of the ear.

BUTTERFLY NOSE: A nose of two colors, usually dark brown or black, spotted with flesh color.

BUTTOCKS: A dog's hips.

BUTTON EAR: Ear that folds over in front, with tip drooping forward, as in the Fox Terrier.

CARP BACK: Arched back.

CASTRATE: Remove a dog's testicles through surgery.

CAT FOOT: A short, round, compact foot, as in a Greyhound or a good English Foxhound.

CATCH DOG: Dog used by hunters to catch and hold an animal so that it can be captured alive.

CHARACTER: The essential, correct characteristics of a breed, such as posture, temperament, expression.

CHEEKY: Having a heavy, pronounced development of the cheek, as in Bulldogs.

CHEST: That part of the body in front of the abdomen and above the brisket.

CHINA EYE: A clear, light-blue eye.

CHISELED: Having a well-defined, clear-cut head, especially around and between the eyes.

CHOKE COLLAR: A chain or leather collar that can be tightened or loosened to control a dog.

CHOPS: The thick upper lips that hang below the lower jaw; seen in the Bloodhound and Bulldog.

CLIP: A kind of trim used on some breeds, especially the Poodle.

CLODDY: Having a low and very thick-set build.

CLOSE-COUPLED: Having a short back or a short body.

COAT: The hair on a dog's body.

COBBY: Strong, compact, neat, and muscular, like a cob horse.

CONFORMATION: Agreement of a dog's shape and structure with breed's standards.

CORKY: Well-built, spirited, and alert; term usually applied to terriers.

COUPLE: A pair of hounds.

COUPLING: (1) That part of the body between the shoulders and the hipbones. (2) A leash or collar ring for handling a pair of dogs.

COURSING: Hunting hares with Greyhounds.

COW-HOCKED: Having hind legs whose joints point inward; often very large breeds, like the Bernese Mountain Dog, have this structural defect.

CRANK TAIL: A short tail curving down and then away from the body.

CREST: The upper arched part of a dog's neck.

CROP: Clip off the tops of (the ears); illegal practice in some states and in Great Britain.

CROSSBRED: Born of purebred parents of different breeds.

CROUP: The rump, or the part of the back above the hind legs.

CROWN: The top part of the head.

CRY: The baying of hounds on the trail.

CRYPTORCHID: A male whose testicles have not descended into the scrotal sac; the dog has no testicles.

CULL: A puppy far below standard quality for the breed.

CULOTTE: Long, bunched-up hair on the back of the thighs, seen especially in Pomeranians and Schipperkes.

CUR: A mongrel.

CUSHION: Thick, very full upper lips and foreface, as in the Mastiff and Bulldog.

DAM: The mother dog; but usually applied to a bitch from the time she whelps to the time she weans her last pup.

DAPPLED: Having a mottled color—usually patches of silver with tan, black, or black and tan.

DEADGRASS: Color varying in shade from tan to dull straw.

DERBY: A bird dog under 30 months.

DEWCLAW: The useless fifth claw or toe on the inside part of the leg just above the foot.

DEWLAP: Loose hanging skin under the throat and chin, as in the Bloodhound.

DIEHARD: Commonly used name for the Scottish Terrier.

DISH-FACED: Having a nose that is tilted higher than the stop and appears to turn up slightly; can be seen in Pointers.

DISQUALIFICATION: A fault that makes a dog ineligible to enter bench-show competition.

DISTEMPER TEETH: Teeth marked, pitted, ringed, and often stained due to distemper or other severe infection.

DOCK: Shorten (a tail) by cutting.

DOG: A male dog.

DOME: A term used for the rounded part of the skull, as in Spaniels.

DOUBLE COAT: Undercoat of soft, thick hair to warm the body and an outer coat of coarse, strong hair to keep out dampness and cold, as in Retrievers.

DOWN-FACED: Having a face that goes downward from the stop to the nose, as in a Bull Terrier.

DOWN IN PASTERN: Weakness in ankle joint.

DROP EARS: Soft, flopping ears that hang close and flat to the head and cheeks.

DROPPER: A crossbred obtained by mating a Pointer to a Setter.

DRY NECK: A neck free of any unnecessary flesh; skin is tight and sleek.

DUAL CHAMPION: Dog who has won championships in both dog shows and field trials.

DUDLEY NOSE: A flesh-colored nose, often pink or yellowish, distinct from a Butterfly Nose, which is particolored.

ELBOWS OUT: Elbows pointing away from the body, as in the Bulldog.

EWE NECK: A neck with an inward curve from the skull to the withers.

EXPRESSION: Combination of color, size, and features of the head typical of a particular breed.

EYETEETH: The fangs, equivalent to the upper canines in people.

FALL: Long and loose hair hanging over the face, as in the Skye Terrier and the Yorkshire Terrier.

FALLOW: Pale yellow color.

FAWN: A rich, light golden-tan.

FEATHERING: Long, silky strands of hair on the ears, legs, chest, and abdomen; typical of Setters and Spaniels.

FEET EAST AND WEST: Toes turned out.

FEIST: A small mongrel of the terrier type.

FIDDLE FACE: An elongated, pinched-in foreface.

FIDDLE FRONT: The front of a dog with bandy or crooked forelegs.

FIELD TRIAL: Hounds and Sporting Breeds competing in finding and retrieving game and following a game trail.

FLAG: A long, bushy tail, usually found in Setters and some Retrievers.

FLANK: Loin and upper thighs.

FLAT-SIDED: Having too little roundness in the ribs.

FLECKED: Lightly ticked with small spots of a darker color; coat is usually white and the spots are brownish-orange or gray-black.

FLESH NOSE: Pink or tan nose.

FLEWS: Hanging upper lips, as those in the Bulldog; usually refers to the lateral parts of the lips.

FLY EARS: Semi-erect ears pointing in opposite directions and looking as if they were about to fly away; a fault in the Fox Terrier and the German Shepherd.

FOREFACE: The part of the head from the eyes to the tip of the nose.

FOULCOLOR: Any color not characteristic of the breed.

FRILL: Long hair under the neck and on the forechest.

FROG FACE: A face with an extended nose, a receding jaw, and undershot teeth; term is used with such short-faced breeds as Bulldog, Boxer, and Boston Terrier.

FRONT: The whole front part of the body.

FURROW: A groove running down the center of the skull, as in the Dalmatian and the Bulldog.

GAIT: A way of walking, running, or trotting.

GAY TAIL: A tail carried straight up.

GAZE HOUND: The obsolete name for a hound who tracks game with the eyes rather than the nose; term now used is SIGHT HOUND.

GIVING TONGUE: Baying on the trail of game.

GOOSE RUMP: A sharply sloping rump.

GRIZZLE: Steel-gray or iron-gray color.

GUN DOGS: Dogs trained to help the hunter in the field: Setters, Pointers, Retrievers, and Spaniels.

GUNS: Those who shoot at field trials.

GUN-SHY: Frightened by the sound of a gun being fired.

HACKLES: Raised hair on back and neck when a dog is frightened or angry.

HACKNEY GAIT: A vigorous, proud, high-stepping gait.

HAM: Well-developed hind-leg muscles just above the knee.

HANDLER: A person who handles a dog at dog shows, field trials, or obedience tests.

HARDMOUTHED: Given to biting down hard on retrieved game; a serious fault.

HAREFEET: Long, narrow, close-toed feet, as in the American Foxhound.

HARLEQUIN: A combination of colors in patches on a solid ground, as in the coat of a Great Dane; usually black on white.

HAUNCHES: Back part of the thighs, on which the dog sits.

HAW: The red membrane in the inside corner of the lower part of the eye, called the third eyelid; seen in dogs with heavy wrinkled faces, as the Bloodhound and St. Bernard.

HEEL: Command by handler or owner to keep the dog close with his head up to the handler's or owner's knee.

HEEL FREE: Command in which the dog must heel without a leash.

HEIGHT: Dog's height measured from the ground to the top of the shoulders.

HOCKS: The dog's ankles.

HOUND COLORS: White, tan, and black, in order of predominant color.

HUCKLEBONE: The very top of the hip joint.

INBREEDING: Mating in the same family—as a bitch to her sons or a male to his daughters.

IN SEASON: Ready to be mated (applied to the bitch).

IN WHELP: Pregnant.

ISABELLA: A brownish red-yellow or a light bay color.

KINK TAIL: A short, bent tail, characteristic of Bulldog and Boston Terrier.

KISSING SPOTS: Attractive spots or markings on the cheeks of some dogs, especially toys, like the King Charles Spaniel.

KNUCKLING OVER: Condition in which front legs bend forward at the wrist (carpus).

LANDSEER: A Newfoundland that is not all black, but white with black.

LAYBACK: A receding nose with an undershot jaw, characteristic of many short-faced breeds, especially the Bulldog.

LEATHER: The soft skin of the ear flap of hounds like Foxhound, Bloodhound, and Dachshund.

LEGGY: Having legs too long for the body.

LIAM: Leash.

LIGHT EYES: Yellowish eyes.

LINE BREEDING: Mating of dogs within the same family—like breeding a male to his granddaughter.

LIPPY: Having thick, hanging lips.

LITTER: All the offspring of a bitch at one birth.

LIVER: A dark reddish-brown color.

LOADED SHOULDERS: Shoulders that are much too thick and heavy.

LOIN: The part of the body between the last rib and the back legs.

LUMBER: Superfluous flesh.

LURCHER: A crossbred hound, usually a cross between a Greyhound and a Retriever, large Terrier, or Collie.

MANE: Abundance of long hair about the neck and throat.

MANTLE: Dark part of coat on shoulders, back, and sides (St. Bernard).

MASK: The dark part of the foreface and muzzle.

MERLE: Blue-gray color flecked or ticked with black.

MOLERA: Imperfect or abnormal coming together of bones of the skull.

MONGREL: A dog whose parents are a mixture of many breeds.

MONORCHID: A male, one of whose testicles has not descended into the scrotal sac.

MUZZLE: That part of the head containing the mouth and nose.

MUZZLE HEAD: A head that has white marking around the muzzle.

OCCIPUT: Bone at the top of the skull between the ears, prominent in hounds.

OPEN BITCH: Bitch that can be used for breeding.

OTTER TAIL: Tail thick at the root and slowly tapering.

OUT AT ELBOWS: Said of a dog whose elbow joints noticeably turn away from the body.

OUTBREEDING OR OUTCROSSING: Mating of two dogs of the same breed but of different families.

OVERHANG: A heavy or pronounced brow, as in the Pekingese.

OVERSHOT: Having the upper jaw project beyond the lower.

PADS: The tough, cushioned soles of the feet.

PAPER FOOT: Foot with thin pads.

PARTICOLOR: Having two distinct colors in equal proportions, generally red-and-white or black-and-white.

PASTERN: Lowest part of the leg, below the wrist on the foreleg or below the hock (ankle) on the hind leg.

PEAK: An unusually prominent occiput.

PEDIGREE: Written record of the names of a dog's ancestors, going back at least three generations.

PENCILING: Thin black lines on the tan of the toes, found in the Manchester Terrier.

PEPPER-AND-SALT: Coat color consisting of even mixture of gray and black hair.

PIED: Having two colors in unequal proportions, usually in irregular patches.

PILE: The thick undercoat of breeds having a double coat.

PILEY: Having a thick undercoat.

PINTO: Piebald or mottled, spotted.

PLUME: A tail with long, soft hair, like that of a Pomeranian or Pekingese.

POINT: Rigid stance a hunting dog adopts when he is showing the hunter the position of the game.

POMPON: Ball of hair left on the end of a Poodle's tail after he has been clipped.

PRICK EAR: An ear carried stiffly erect and pointed at the tip, as in the Scottish Terrier.

PUPPY: Any dog not over 12 months old.

PUREBRED: A dog whose parents are of the same breed and who themselves have an ancestry of the same breed.

PUT DOWN: To kill a very old or incurably ill dog.

RACY: Lean, long-legged, slightly built.

RAM'S NOSE: A nose that is a little arched, the muzzle appearing convex in profile.

RAT TAIL: Long pointed tail, with short thin hair.

RING TAIL: A tail that curls into a circle.

ROACH BACK: An arched back extending from the shoulders to the base of the tail, as in the Dandie Dinmont and the Whippet.

ROAN: Mixture of white with another color, usually blue or red, in equal proportions, as in the English Cocker Spaniel.

ROSE EAR: An ear that folds backward, exposing the inner ear, as in the Bulldog.

ROUNDING: Shortening and trimming (the ear) to a round edge by cutting; ears of Foxhounds are rounded to prevent injury by underbrush.

RUDDER: The tail.

RUFF: Thick, long hair on the neck and shoulders, as in the Chow Chow and Collie.

RUSSIAN WOLFHOUND: Borzoi.

SABLE: The color of a light coat shaded with black, as in the Collie.

SADDLE: A solid rectangular area of black extending over the shoulder and back.

SCISSORS BITE: A bite in which the upper front teeth slightly overlap the lower front teeth.

SCREW TAIL: A short, twisted tail tapering to a point.

SECOND THIGH: Muscular development of leg between the stifle and the hock.

SELF-COLORED: Of a single color, or of one color with lighter shadings of the same color.

SEMI-PRICK EARS: Ears that are straight and stiff with tips pointing forward.

SEPTUM: Very thin dividing wall between the nostrils.

SHELLY: Having a long and narrow body, like that of a Borzoi.

SICKLE TAIL: A fairly long tail curving into a semicircle.

SIGHT HOUND: A hound who tracks game with the eyes rather than the nose.

SIRE: The father of a litter of puppies.

SKULLY: Having a heavy, coarse skull.

SLOPING SHOULDERS: Shoulders laid well back on the body.

SMOOTH COAT: Short, sleek hair lying close to the skin.

SNIPY: Having a narrow, weak muzzle.

SOFTMOUTHED: Able to carry retrieved game in the mouth without damaging it.

SPAY: Remove by surgery the reproductive organs (of a bitch).

SPECTACLES: Dark markings around the eyes, as in the Keeshond.

SPLASHED: Having a colored coat with irregular patches of white, or a white coat with irregular patches of any color.

SPLAY FEET: Feet with toes spread wide apart.

SPREAD: Width of the chest between the forelegs.

SPRING OF RIBS: Degree to which a dog's ribs are well-rounded and elastic.

SQUIRREL TAIL: A tail curving forward and over the back.

STANDARD: The ideal dog in each breed.

STANDOFF COAT: Rough, coarse hair that stands away from the body, as in the Chow Chow and Samoyed.

STARING COAT: Coarse, hard hair, curling at the end.

STATION: Height of dog from the ground.

STERN: The tail, but used only in reference to hounds and sometimes to sporting dogs.

STIFLE: Thigh joint in the hind legs that is the same as a man's knee.

STILTED: Having a stiff, awkward way of walking.

STOP: Depression in front of the eyes, deep in Pugs and nonexistent in Borzois.

STRAIGHT HOCKS: Hocks that are absolutely straight vertically.

STRAIGHT SHOULDERS: Shoulder blades running almost straight up and down, without any angulation.

STUD: Male used for breeding.

SWAY BACK: A sagging back.

THROATY: Having far too much skin around the throat.

THUMB MARKS: Round black marks around the ankles.

TICKED: Condition of a dog's coat, having small dark specks on a white background.

TIMBER: Another name for bone; almost always refers to bones of the legs.

TONGUE: Noise made by hounds when on the trail of game.

TOPKNOT: A knot of long hair on the top of the head, as in the Bedlington Terrier, the Irish Water Spaniel, and the Dandie Dinmont.

TRACE: A dark line of hair running down the back of some dogs, as the Pug.

TRICOLOR: Having a coat of black, tan, and white, as in hounds.

TRIM: To groom by plucking or clipping.

TUCKED UP: Having a sharp rise in the underbody just behind the ribs, as in the Borzoi, Greyhound, and Whippet.

TULIP EARS: Ears carried stiff and straight, slightly open and leaning forward.

TYPE: Those unique characteristics that make a dog the ideal representative of a breed.

UNDERSHOT: The opposite of overshot; having the lower jaw projecting.

UPFACE: A foreface slanting upward, as in the Bulldog.

UPPER ARM: That part of the front leg between the wrist and the shoulder blade.

VARMINTY: Having a bright, searching, very alert expression; usually said of terriers.

VENT: Both the rectum and the small area of light hair directly beneath the tail.

WALLEYED: Having eyes particolored white and blue.

WEEDY: Having a slight, rather scrawny build.

WHEATEN: Fawnlike pale-yellow color.

WHEEL BACK: Another term for the ROACH BACK: a back that is arched or convex.

WHELPING: Giving birth to puppies.

WHELPS: Newly born puppies.

WHIP TAIL: A tail that is stiff and straight, as in the Pointer when he is pointing.

WHISKERS: The beard of a dog, as in terriers, such as Miniature Schnauzers.

WHITELIES: White body color with red or dark markings (Pembroke Welsh Corgi).

WIREHAIRED: Having a tough, dense, harsh coat.

WITHERS: Highest point in the shoulders, where the neck joins the body.

WOLF COLOR: Black, brown, and gray distributed in equal amounts.

WRINKLES: Loose folds of skin on the cheeks and the forehead, as in the Bloodhound and the St. Bernard.

WRY MOUTH: Upper and lower teeth not lined up properly; bite is off.

Bibliography

GENERAL AND HISTORY AND DEVELOPMENT OF THE BREEDS

American Kennel Club. *The Complete Dog Book.* 730 Fifth Avenue, New York, New York 10019: Howell Book House, 1975, 672 pp., illus.

Amberson, Rosanne. *Raising Your Dog.* 419 Park Avenue South, New York, New York 10016: Crown, 1975, 282 pp., illus.

Ames, Felicia. *The Dog You Care For.* 1301 Avenue of the Americas, New York, New York 10019: New American Library, 1968, 128 pp., illus., color.

Ashworth, Lou Sawyer. *The Dell Encyclopedia of Dogs.* 1 Dag Hammarskjold Plaza, New York, New York 10017: Delacorte Press, 1974, 240 pp., illus., color.

Bailey, Kenneth. *The Beauty of Dogs.* Advance House, 101–109 Ladbroke Grove, London W11 1PG: Triune Books, Trewin Copplestone Publishing Limited, 1972, 144 pp., illus., color.

Bartos, Bob. *The Dog for You.* 1 Dag Hammarskjold Plaza, New York, New York 10017: Dell, 1974, 189 pp., illus., color.

Boorer, Wendy. *The World of Dogs.* 42 The Centre, Feltham, Middlesex, England: Hamlyn House, 1969, 141 pp., illus., color.

Boorer, Wendy. *Dogs: Selection; Care; Training.* 51 Madison Avenue, New York, New York 10003: Grosset and Dunlap, 1974, 160 pp., illus., color.

Braund, Kathryn. *The Uncommon Dog Breeds.* 219 Park Avenue South, New York, New York 10003: Arco, 1971, 76 pp., illus.

Fiorone, Fiorenzo. *The Encyclopedia of Dogs.* 665 Fifth Avenue, New York, New York 10022: Thomas Y. Crowell, 1970, 447 pp., illus., color.

Fox, Michael. *Understanding Your Dog.* 200 Madison Avenue, New York, New York: Coward, McCann and Geoghegan, 1972, 240 pp., illus.

Hamilton, Ferelith. *The World Encyclopedia of Dogs.* 2231 W. 110, Cleveland, Ohio: World, 1971, 672 pp., illus.

Hamlyn, Paul. *The Book of the Dog.* Feltham, Middlesex, England: Hamlyn House, 1970, 151 pp., illus., color.

Lampson, S. M. *Dogs.* 40 Bedford Square, London WC1B 3HE: Frederick Warne & Co., 1970, 192 pp., illus.

Liebers, Arthur. *Companion Dogs.* Forsgate Avenue, Cranbury, New Jersey 08512: A. S. Barnes, 1973, 319 pp., illus.

Miller, Frank. *Wonderful World of Dogs.* 870 Market Street, San Francisco 94102: Chronicle Books, 1972, 202 pp., illus.

Sefton, Frances. *Complete Dog Guide.* 600 South 4th, Harrison, New Jersey: The Pet Library LTD, 1969, 250 pp., illus., color.

Sidewater, Ab. *Dog Standards Illustrated.* 730 Fifth Avenue, New York, New York 10019: Howell Book House, 1975, 320 pp., illus.

Sprung, Dennis B. *Dog Lovers Complete Guide.* 219 Park Avenue South, New York,

New York 10003: Arco, 1975, 287 pp., illus., color.

Unkelbach, Kurt. *How to Bring up Your Pet Dog.* 79 Madison Avenue, New York, New York 10016: Dodd, Mead & Co., 1972, 119 pp., illus.

THE BREEDS

AFFENPINSCHER:

Jackson, Tobin, and D. V. Giggs. *How to Raise and Train an Affenpinscher.* 211 West Sylvania Avenue, P. O. Box 27, Neptune, New Jersey: T.F.H. Publications, 1969, 64 pp.

AFGHAN HOUND:

Miller, Constance O., and Edward M. Gilbert, Jr. *The Complete Afghan Hound.* 730 Fifth Avenue, New York, New York, 10019: Howell Book House, 1975, 304 pp.

AIRDALE TERRIER:

Edwards, Gladys Brown. *The Complete Airdale Terrier.* 730 Fifth Avenue, New York, New York 10019: Howell Book House, 1966, 128 pp.

AKITA:

Van der Lyn, Edita. *How to Raise and Train an Akita.* 211 W. Sylvania Avenue, P. O. Box 27, Neptune, New Jersey 07753: T.F.H. Publications, 1964, 64 pp.

ALASKAN MALAMUTE:

Berger, Charles J. *How to Raise and Train an Alaskan Malamute.* 211 W. Sylvania Avenue, P. O. Box 27, Neptune, New Jersey 07753: T.F.H. Publications, 1963, 64 pp.

AMERICAN STAFFORDSHIRE TERRIER:

Rosenblum, Edwin E. *How to Raise and Train an American Staffordshire Terrier.* 211 W. Sylvania Avenue, Neptune, New Jersey 07753: T.F.H. Publications, 1964, 64 pp.

AUSTRALIAN TERRIER:

Fox, Mrs. Milton. *How to Raise and Train an Australian Terrier.* 211 W. Sylvania Avenue, Neptune, New Jersey 07753: T.F.H. Publications, 1965, 64 pp.

BASENJI:

Shafer, Jack, and Bob Mankey. *How to Raise and Train a Basenji.* 211 W. Sylvania Avenue, Neptune, New Jersey 07753: T.F.H. Publications, 1966, 64 pp.

BASSET HOUND:

Johnston, George. *The Basset Hound.* 178–202 Great Portland Street, London W1: Popular Books LTD, 1969, 224 pp.

BEAGLE:

Nicholas, Anna Katherine, and Joan McDonald Brearley. *The Wonderful World of Beagles and Beagling.* 211 W. Sylvania Avenue, Neptune, New Jersey 07753: T.F.H. Publications, 1975, 735 pp.

BEDLINGTON TERRIER:

Young, Elinore W. *How to Raise and Train a Bedlington Terrier.* 211 W. Sylvania Avenue, Neptune, New Jersey 07753: T.F.H. Publications, 1966, 64 pp.

BELGIAN MALINOIS:

Dangerfield, Stanley, and Ellsworth Howell. *International Encyclopedia of Dogs,* 730 Fifth Avenue, New York, New York 10019: Howell Book House, 1971, 480 pp. Also, see book on BELGIAN SHEEPDOG, below.

BELGIAN SHEEPDOG:

Dykma, Frank E. *How to Raise and Train a Belgian Sheepdog.* 211 W. Sylvania Avenue,

Neptune, New Jersey 07753: T.F.H. Publications, 1964, 64 pp.

BELGIAN TERVUREN:
Laurin, Mrs. Edeltraud. *How to Raise and Train a Belgian Tervurin.* 211 W. Sylvania Avenue, Neptune, New Jersey 07753: T.F.H. Publications, 1965, 64 pp.

BERNESE MOUNTAIN DOG:
Dangerfield, Stanley, and Ellsworth Howell. *International Encyclopedia of Dogs,* 730 Fifth Avenue, New York, New York: Howell Book House, 1971, 480 pp.

BICHON FRISE:
Brearley, Joan McDonald, and Anna Katherine Nicholas. *This Is the Bichon Frise.* 211 W. Sylvania Avenue, Neptune, New Jersey 07753: T.F.H. Publications, 1973, 320 pp.

BLOODHOUND:
Owen, Hylda. *How to Raise and Train a Bloodhound.* 211 W. Sylvania Avenue, Neptune, New Jersey 07753: T.F.H. Publications, 1964, 64 pp.

BORDER TERRIER:
Weiss, Seymour N. *How to Raise and Train a Border Terrier.* 211 W. Sylvania Avenue, Neptune, New Jersey 07753: T.F.H. Publications, 1966, 64 pp.

BORZOI:
Gordon, John F. *The Borzoi.* 219 Park Avenue South, New York, New York 10003: Arco, 1974, 112 pp.

BOSTON TERRIER:
Miller, Evelyn. *How to Raise and Train a Boston Terrier.* 211 W. Sylvania Avenue, Neptune, New Jersey 07753: T.F.H. Publications, 1959, 64 pp.

BOUVIER DES FLANDRES:
McLean, Claire D. *The Complete Bouvier des Flandres.* Croton-On-Hudson, New York 10520: Dreenan Press, 1974, 253 pp.

BOXER:
Somerfield, Elizabeth. *The Boxer.* 219 Park Avenue South, New York, New York 10003: Arco, 1970, 178 pp.

BRIARD:
Tingley, Mary Lou. *How to Raise and Train a Briard.* 211 W. Sylvania Avenue, Neptune, New Jersey 07753: T.F.H. Publications, 1965, 64 pp.

BRUSSELS GRIFFON:
Weiss, Seymour N. *How to Raise and Train a Brussels Griffon.* 211 W. Sylvania Avenue, Neptune, New Jersey 07753: T.F.H. Publications, 1969, 64 pp.

BULLDOG, ENGLISH:
Goudy, Jean S. *Pet English Bulldog.* Fond du Lac, Wisconsin: All Pet Books, 1960, 80 pp.

BULLDOG, FRENCH:
Pronek, Neal. *How to Raise and Train a French Bulldog.* 211 W. Sylvania Avenue, Neptune, New Jersey 07753: T.F.H. Publications, 1965, 64 pp.

BULLMASTIFF:
Prescott, Mary A. *How to Raise and Train a Bullmastiff.* 211 W. Sylvania Avenue, Neptune, New Jersey 07753: T.F.H. Publications, 1964, 64 pp.

BULL TERRIER:
Rosenblum, Edwin E. *How to Raise and Train a Bull Terrier.* 211 W. Sylvania Avenue, Neptune, New Jersey 07753: T.F.H. Publications, 1965, 64 pp.

CAIRN TERRIER:
Marvin, John T. *The Complete Cairn Terrier.* 730 Fifth Avenue, New York, New York 10019: Howell Book House, 1975, 255 pp.

CHIHUAHUA:
Harmar, Hillary. *The Complete Chihuahua.* Duncan Street, Edinburgh, Scotland: John Bartholomew and Son, 1972, 373 pp.

CHOW CHOW:
Shryock, Clifford. *How to Raise and Train a Chow Chow.* 211 W. Sylvania Avenue,

Neptune, New Jersey 07753: T.F.H. Publications, 1965, 64 pp.

COLLIE:

Young, Anne. *Collie Guide.* 600 South 4th, Harrison, New Jersey: The Pet Library LTD, 1969, 250 pp.

COONHOUND, BLACK AND TAN:

Henschel, Stan. *How to Raise and Train a Coonhound.* 211 W. Sylvania Avenue, Neptune, New Jersey 07753: T.F.H. Publications, 1964, 64 pp.

DACHSHUND:

Brunotte, Hans. *Dachshund Guide.* 600 South 4th, Harrison, New Jersey: The Pet Library LTD., 1969, 250 pp.

DALMATIAN:

Frankling, Eleanor. *The Dalmatian.* 730 Fifth Avenue, New York, New York 10019: Howell Book House, 1969, 214 pp.

DANDIE DINMONT TERRIER:

Kirby, Mrs. William M. *How to Raise and Train a Dandie Dinmont Terrier.* 211 W. Sylvania Avenue, Neptune, New Jersey 07753: T.F.H. Publications, 1964, 64 pp.

DOBERMAN PINSCHER:

Curnow, Fred, and Jean Faulks. *The Doberman.* 730 Fifth Avenue, New York, New York 10019: Howell Book House, 1973, 197 pp.

FOXHOUND, AMERICAN:

Hart, Ernest H. *How to Raise and Train an American Foxhound.* 211 W. Sylvania Avenue, Neptune, New Jersey 07753: T.F.H. Publications, 1967, 64 pp.

FOXHOUND, ENGLISH:

Hart, Ernest H. *How to Raise and Train an English Foxhound.* 211 W. Sylvania Avenue, Neptune, New Jersey 07753: T.F.H. Publications, 1968, 64 pp.

FOX TERRIER:

Williams, Elsie. *The Fox Terrier.* 219 Park Avenue South, New York, New York 10003: Arco, 1970, 198 pp.

GERMAN SHEPHERD DOG:

Pickup, Madeleine. *German Shepherd Guide.* 600 South 4th, Harrison, New Jersey: The Pet Library LTD., 1969, 250 pp.

GIANT SCHNAUZER:

Lockley, Arthur S. *How to Raise and Train a Giant Schnauzer.* 211 W. Sylvania Avenue, Neptune, New Jersey 07753: T.F.H. Publications, 1964, 64 pp.

GREAT DANE:

Johnston, Mary K. *Great Danes.* 211 W. Sylvania Avenue, Neptune, New Jersey 07753: T.F.H. Publications, 1973, 125 pp.

GREAT PYRENEES:

Trois-Fontaines, Mme. J. Harper. *My Travelling and My Dogs.* London: Stone and Cox, 1948, 251 pp.

GREYHOUND:

Mueller, Georgiana. *How to Raise and Train a Greyhound.* 211 W. Sylvania Avenue, Neptune, New Jersey 07753: T.F.H. Publications, 1965, 64 pp.

HARRIER:

Jones, William J. *How to Raise and Train a Harrier.* 211 W. Sylvania Avenue, Neptune, New Jersey 07753: T.F.H. Publications, 1965, 64 pp.

IRISH TERRIER:

Kidd, Drusilla and George. *How to Raise and Train an Irish Terrier.* 211 W. Sylvania Avenue, Neptune, New Jersey 07753: T.F.H. Publications, 1965, 64 pp.

IRISH WOLFHOUND:

Westover, Frederic and Margaret. *How to Raise and Train an Irish Wolfhound.* 211 W. Sylvania Avenue, Neptune, New Jersey 07753: T.F.H. Publications, 1964, 64 pp.

ITALIAN GREYHOUND:
Russo, Louis F. *How to Raise and Train an Italian Greyhound.* 211 W. Sylvania Avenue, Neptune, New Jersey 07753: T.F.H. Publications, 1964, 64 pp.

KEESHOND:
Peterson, Clementine. *The Complete Keeshond.* 730 Fifth Avenue, New York, New York 10019: Howell Book House, 1971, 255 pp.

KERRY BLUE TERRIER:
Montgomery, E. S. *The New Complete Kerry Blue Terrier.* 730 Fifth Avenue, New York, New York 10019: Howell Book House, 1965, 294 pp.

KOMONDOR:
Beregi, Oscar, and Leslie Benis. *How to Raise and Train a Komondor.* 211 W. Sylvania Avenue, Neptune, New Jersey 07753: T.F.H. Publications, 1966, 64 pp.

KUVASZ:
Alvi, Dana I., and Leslie Benis. *How to Raise and Train a Kuvasz.* 211 W. Sylvania Avenue, Neptune, New Jersey 07753: T.F.H. Publications, 1969, 64 pp.

LAKELAND TERRIER:
Weiss, Seymour N. *How to Raise and Train a Lakeland Terrier.* 211 W. Sylvania Avenue, Neptune, New Jersey 07753: T.F.H. Publications, 1966, 64 pp.

LHASA APSO:
Berndt, Robert J. *Your Lhasa Apso.* Box 189, Fairfax, Virginia: Denlinger, 1974, 160 pp.

MALTESE:
Berndt, Robert J. *Your Maltese.* Box 189, Fairfax, Virginia: Denlinger, 1975, 128 pp.

MANCHESTER TERRIER:
Mack, Janet. *Pet Manchester.* Fond du Lac, Wisconsin: All Pet Books, 1956, 64 pp.

MASTIFF:
Moore, Marie A. *How to Raise and Train a Mastiff.* 211 W. Sylvania Avenue, Neptune, New Jersey 07753: T.F.H. Publications, 1964, 64 pp.

NEWFOUNDLAND:
Drury, Mrs. Maynard K. *This Is the Newfoundland.* 211 W. Sylvania Avenue, Neptune, New Jersey 07753: T.F.H. Publications, 1971, 335 pp.

NORWEGIAN ELKHOUND:
Crafts, Glenna Clark. *How to Raise and Train a Norwegian Elkhound.* 211 W. Sylvania Avenue, Neptune, New Jersey 07753: T.F.H. Publications, 1964, 64 pp.

NORWICH TERRIER:
Fournier, Barbara S. *How to Raise and Train a Norwich Terrier.* 211 W. Sylvania Avenue, Neptune, New Jersey 07753: T.F.H. Publications, 1967, 64 pp.

OTTER HOUND:
Mouat, Hugh R. *How to Raise and Train an Otter Hound.* 211 W. Sylvania Avenue, Neptune, New Jersey 07753: T.F.H. Publications, 1965, 64 pp.

PAPILLON:
Gauss, D. Christian. *How to Raise and Train a Papillon.* 211 W. Sylvania Avenue, Neptune, New Jersey 07753: T.F.H. Publications, 1964, 64 pp.

PEKINGESE:
Nicholas, Anna Katherine, and Joan McDonald Brearley. *The Book of the Pekingese.* 211 W. Sylvania Avenue, Neptune, New Jersey 07753: T.F.H. Publications, 1975, 336 pp.

PINSCHER, MINIATURE:
Boshell, Buris R. *Your Miniature Pinscher.* Box 189, Fairfax, Virginia: Denlinger, 1969, 160 pp.

POINTER:
Hart, Ernest H. *How to Raise and Train a Pointer.* 211 W. Sylvania Avenue, Neptune,

New Jersey 07753: T.F.H. Publications, 1966, 64 pp.

POINTER, GERMAN SHORTHAIRED:

Dapper, Gertrude. *Your German Shorthaired Pointer.* Box 189, Fairfax, Virginia: Denlinger, 1975, 160 pp.

POINTER, GERMAN WIREHAIRED:

Compere, Newton I. *How to Raise and Train a German Wirehaired Pointer.* 211 W. Sylvania Avenue, Neptune, New Jersey 07753: T.F.H. Publications, 1967, 64 pp.

POMERANIAN:

Hughes, Pauline B. *Your Pomeranian.* Box 189, Fairfax, Virginia: Denlinger, 1969, 128 pp.

POODLE (MINIATURE, TOY, STANDARD):

Hopkins, Lydia, as revised by Mackey J. Irick, Jr. *The New Complete Poodle.* 730 Fifth Avenue, New York, New York 10019: Howell Book House, 1969, 384 pp.

PUG:

Spirer, Louise Ziegler, and Herbert F. Spirer. *This Is the Pug.* 211 W. Sylvania Avenue, Neptune, New Jersey 07753: T.F.H. Publications, 1968, 223 pp.

PULI:

Anderson, Ellanor H. *How to Raise and Train a Puli.* 211 W. Sylvania Avenue, Neptune, New Jersey 07753: T.F.H. Publications, 1964, 64 pp.

RETRIEVER, CHESAPEAKE BAY:

Henschel, Stan. *How to Raise and Train a Chesapeake Bay Retriever.* 211 W. Sylvania Avenue, Neptune, New Jersey 07753: T.F.H. Publications, 1965, 64 pp.

RETRIEVER, CURLY-COATED:

Clarke, Eileen. *How to Raise and Train a Curley-Coated Retriever.* 211 W. Sylvania Avenue, Neptune, New Jersey 07753: T.F.H. Publications, 1966, 64 pp.

RETRIEVER, FLAT-COATED:

Terroux, Sally J. *How to Raise and Train a Flat-Coated Retriever.* 211 W. Sylvania Avenue, Neptune, New Jersey 07753: T.F.H. Publications, 1968, 64 pp.

RETRIEVER, GOLDEN:

Fischer, Gertrude. *The Complete Golden Retriever.* 730 Fifth Avenue, New York, New York 10019: Howell Book House, 1974, 288 pp.

RETRIEVER, LABRADOR:

Howe, Dorothy. *This Is the Labrador Retriever.* 211 W. Sylvania Avenue, Neptune, New Jersey 07753: T.F.H. Publications, 1972, 336 pp.

RHODESIAN RIDGEBACK:

Lutman, Frank C. *How to Raise and Train a Rhodesian Ridgeback.* 211 W. Sylvania Avenue, Neptune, New Jersey 07753: T.F.H. Publications, 1966, 64 pp.

ROTTWEILER:

Klem, Joan R., and P. G. Rademacher. *How to Raise and Train a Rottweiler.* 211 W. Sylvania Avenue, Neptune, New Jersey 07753: T.F.H. Publications, 1964, 64 pp.

SAINT BERNARD:

Anderson, Marlene J., and Joan McDonald Brearley. *This Is the Saint Bernard.* 211 W. Sylvania Avenue, Neptune, New Jersey 07753: T.F.H. Publications, 1973, 384 pp.

SALUKI:

Watkins, U. H. *Saluki: Companion of Kings.* 21 Mount Ephraim Road, Tunbridge Wells, Kent, England: Fenrose, 1974, 95 pp.

SAMOYED:

Brearley, Joan McDonald. *This Is the Samoyed.* 211 W. Sylvania Avenue, Neptune, New Jersey 07753: T.F.H. Publications, 1975, 384 pp.

SCHIPPERKE:

Martin, Mrs. Darwin J. *How to Raise and Train a Schipperke.* 211 W. Sylvania Avenue, Neptune, New Jersey 07753: T.F.H. Publications, 1964, 64 pp.

SCHNAUZER, MINIATURE:

Gordon, John F. *Miniature Schnauzer Guide.* 600 South 4th, Harrison, New Jersey: The Pet Library LTD., 1969, 250 pp.

SCHNAUZER, STANDARD:

Hertz, Hamilton and Joan. *How to Raise and Train a Standard Schnauzer.* 211 W. Sylvania Avenue, Neptune, New Jersey 07753: T.F.H. Publications, 1965, 64 pp.

SCOTTISH DEERHOUND:

Benbow, Audrey M. *How to Raise and Train a Scottish Deerhound.* 211 W. Sylvania Avenue, Neptune, New Jersey 07753: T.F.H. Publications, 1965, 64 pp.

SCOTTISH TERRIER:

Ruggiero, Len and Debra. *Scottish Terriers.* 211 W. Sylvania Avenue, Neptune, New Jersey 07753: T.F.H. Publications, 1973, 126 pp.

SEALYHAM TERRIER:

Weiss, Seymour N. *How to Raise and Train a Sealyham Terrier.* 211 W. Sylvania Avenue, Neptune, New Jersey 07753: T.F.H. Publications, 1965, 64 pp.

SETTER, ENGLISH:

Tuck, Davis H., and Elsworth S Howell. *The New Complete English Setter.* 3rd. Ed. Revised., 730 Fifth Avenue, New York, New York 10019: Howell Book House, 1972, 368 pp.

SETTER, GORDON:

King, Bart. *How to Raise and Train a Gordon Setter.* 211 W. Sylvania Avenue, Neptune, New Jersey 07753: T.F.H. Publications, 1965, 64 pp.

SETTER, IRISH:

Brearley, Joan McDonald. *This Is the Irish Setter.* 211 W. Sylvania Avenue, Neptune, New Jersey 07753: T.F.H. Publications, 1975, 480 pp.

SHEEPDOG, OLD ENGLISH:

Brearley, Joan McDonald, and Marlene J. Anderson. *This Is the Old English Sheepdog.* 211 W. Sylvania Avenue, Neptune, New Jersey 07753: T.F.H. Publications, 1974, 320 pp.

SHEEPDOG, SHETLAND:

Riddle, Maxwell. *The New Shetland Sheepdog.* 730 Fifth Avenue, New York, New York 10019: Howell Book House, 1974, 224 pp.

SHIH TZU:

Dadds, Audrey. *The Shih Tzu.* 730 Fifth Avenue, New York, New York 10019: Howell Book House, 1975, 208 pp.

SIBERIAN HUSKY:

Brearley, Joan McDonald. *This Is the Siberian Husky.* 211 W. Sylvania Avenue, Neptune, New Jersey 07753: T.F.H. Publications, 1974, 543 pp.

SILKY TERRIER:

Lehnig, Beverly. *Your Silky Terrier.* Box 189, Fairfax, Virginia: Denlinger, 1972, 128 pp.

SKYE TERRIER:

Brearley, Joan McDonald, and Anna Katherine Nicholas. *This Is the Skye Terrier.* 211 W. Sylvania Avenue, Neptune, New Jersey 07753: T.F.H. Publications, 1975, 560 pp.

SOFT-COATED WHEATEN TERRIER:

O'Connor, Margaret A. *How to Raise and Train a Soft-coated Wheaten Terrier.* 211 W. Sylvania Avenue, Neptune, New Jersey 07753: T.F.H. Publications, 1966, 64 pp.

SPANIEL, AMERICAN WATER:
Rutherford, Constance. *How to Raise and Train an American Water Spaniel.* 211 W. Sylvania Avenue, Neptune, New Jersey 07753: T.F.H. Publications, 1968, 64 pp.

SPANIEL, BRITTANY:
Riddle, Maxwell. *The Complete Brittany Spaniel.* 730 Fifth Avenue, New York, New York 10019: Howell Book House, 1974, 288 pp.

SPANIEL, CLUMBER:
Meyer, Mr. and Mrs. R. Wilton. *How to Raise and Train a Clumber Spaniel.* 211 W. Sylvania Avenue, Neptune, New Jersey 07753: T.F.H. Publications, 1965, 64 pp.

SPANIEL, COCKER:
Miller, Evelyn. *How to Raise and Train a Cocker Spaniel.* 211 W. Sylvania Avenue, Neptune, New Jersey 07753: T.F.H. Publications, 1972, 64 pp.

SPANIEL, ENGLISH COCKER:
Gannon, Robert. *How to Raise and Train and English Cocker Spaniel.* 211 W. Sylvania Avenue, Neptune, New Jersey 07753: T.F.H. Publications, 1962, 64 pp.

SPANIEL, ENGLISH SPRINGER:
Goodall, Charles S., and Julia Gasow. *The New English Springer Spaniel.* 730 Fifth Avenue, New York, New York 10019: Howell Book House, 1974, 287 pp.

SPANIEL, ENGLISH TOY:
Paine, Mrs. Milton J., *How to Raise and Train an English Toy Spaniel.* 211 W. Sylvania Avenue, Neptune, New Jersey 07753: T.F.H. Publications, 1964, 64 pp.

SPANIEL, FIELD:
Gordon, John F. *The Spaniel Owner's Encyclopaedia.* 26 Bloomsbury Street, London, W.C. 1: Pelham Books, 1967, 183 pp.

SPANIEL, IRISH WATER:
Hutzman, Erwin. *How to Raise and Train an Irish Water Spaniel.* 211 W. Sylvania Avenue, Neptune, New Jersey 07753: T.F.H. Publications, 1966, 64 pp.

SPANIEL, JAPANESE:
Alexander, Mrs. Claude V. *How to Raise and Train a Japanese Spaniel.* 211 W. Sylvania Avenue, Neptune, New Jersey: T.F.H. Publications, 1968, 64 pp.

SPANIEL, SUSSEX:
Gordon, John F. *The Spaniel Owner's Encyclopaedia.* 26 Bloomsbury Street, London, W.C. 1: Pelham Books, 1967, 183 pp.

SPANIEL, WELSH SPRINGER:
Gordon, John F. *The Spaniel Owner's Encyclopaedia.* 26 Bloomsbury Street, London, W.C. 1: Pelham Books, 1967, 183 pp.

STAFFORDSHIRE BULL TERRIER:
Gordon, John F. *The Staffordshire Bull Terrier.* 178–202 Great Portland Street, London, W. 1: Popular Dogs, 1971, 192 pp.

TIBETAN TERRIER:
Murphy, Alice W. *How to Raise and Train a Tibetan Terrier.* 211 W. Sylvania Avenue, Neptune, New Jersey 07753: T.F.H. Publications, 1964, 64 pp.

VIZSLA:
Strauz, John X., and Joseph Cunningham. *Your Vizsla.* Box 189, Fairfax, Virginia: Denlinger, 1973, 128 pp.

WEIMARANER:
Hart, Ernest H. *This Is the Weimaraner.* 211 W. Sylvania Avenue, Neptune, New Jersey 07753: T.F.H. Publications, 1965, 256 pp.

WELSH CORGI, CARDIGAN:
Pym, Mrs. Michael, and Mrs. Henning Welms. *How to Raise and Train a Cardigan Welsh Corgi.* 211 W. Sylvania Avenue, Neptune, New Jersey 07753: T.F.H. Publications, 1965, 64 pp.

WELSH CORGI, PEMBROKE:
Niccoli, Ria. *How to Raise and Train a Pembroke Welsh Corgi.* 211 W. Sylvania Avenue, Neptune, New Jersey 07753: T.F.H. Publications, 1964, 64 pp.

WELSH TERRIER:
Thomas, I. Morlais. *The Welsh Terrier Handbook.* London: Nicholson and Watson, 1959, 164 pp.

WEST HIGHLAND WHITE TERRIER:
Marvin, John T. *The Complete West Highland White Terrier.* 211 W. Sylvania Avenue, Neptune, New Jersey 07753: T.F.H. Publications, 2nd Ed., 1965, 128 pp.

WHIPPET:
Cormany, Christine. *How to Raise and Train a Whippet.* 211 W. Sylvania Avenue, Neptune, New Jersey 07753: T.F.H. Publications, 1964, 64 pp.

WIREHAIRED POINTING GRIFFON:
Extracts from the History of the Wire-Haired Pointing Griffon. Translated from the French by Percivall Rousseau, 14 pp.

YORKSHIRE TERRIER:
Migliorini, Mario. *Yorkshire Terrier.* 219 Park Avenue South, New York, New York 10013: Arco, 1971, 76 pp.

TRAINING, MANAGEMENT, AND HOUSEBREAKING

Brander, Michael. *The Roughshooter's Dog.* 175 Fifth Avenue, New York, New York 10010: St. Martin's Press, 1971, 198 pp., illus.

Brown, Marsha Hall, and Bethny Hall Mason. *The Junior Showmanship Handbook.* 730 Fifth Avenue, New York, New York 10019: Howell Book House, 1971, 127 pp., illus.

Daglish, E. Fitch. *Care and Training of Your Puppy.* 219 Park Avenue South, New York, New York 10003: Arco, 1971, 80 pp., illus.

Davis, L. Wilson. *Go Find: Training Your Dog to Track.* 730 Fifth Avenue, New York, New York 10019: Howell Book House, 1974, 159 pp., illus.

English, Margaret. *A Basic Guide to Dog Training and Obedience.* 51 Madison Avenue, New York, New York 10003: Grosset and Dunlap, 1975, 160 pp., illus.

Forsyth, Jane, and Robert Forsyth. *Successful Dog Showing.* 730 Fifth Avenue, New York, New York 10019: Howell Book House, 1975, 194 pp., illus.

Kenworthy, Jack. *Dog Training Guide.* 600 South 4th, Harrison, New Jersey: The Pet Library LTD., 1969, 250 pp., illus., color.

Kessopulos, Gust. *Dog Obedience Training.* Cranbury, New Jersey: A. S. Barnes and Co., 1974, 214 pp., illus.

Koehler, William. *Guard Dog Training.* 730 Fifth Avenue, New York, New York 10019: Howell Book House, 1967, 399 pp., illus.

Pearsall, Margaret E. *The Pearsall Guide to Successful Dog Training.* 730 Fifth Avenue, New York, New York 10019: Howell Book House, 1973, 351 pp., illus.

Robert, Martin J., and Napoleon A. Chagon. *Toward the Ph.D. for Dogs.* 757 Third Avenue, New York, New York: Harcourt Brace Jovanovich, 1975, 382 pp., illus.

Saunders, Blanche. *The Complete Book of Dog Obedience.* Englewood Cliffs, New Jersey 07632: Prentice-Hall, 1954, 241 pp.

Schneider, Earl, Ed. *Know How to Train Your Dog.* 600 South 4th, Harrison, New Jersey: The Pet Library LTD., 1969, 64 pp., illus., color.

Siegal, Mordecai, and Matthew Margolis. *Underdog: Training the Mutt, Mongrel and*

Mixed Breed at Home. Scarborough House Briarcliff Manor, New York 10510: Stein and Day, 1974, 249 pp., illus.

Strickland, Winifred Gibson. *Obedience Class Instruction for Dogs.* 866 Third Avenue, New York, New York: Macmillan, 1971, 299 pp., illus.

Whitney, Leon F. *Dog Psychology.* 730 Fifth Avenue, New York, New York 10019: Howell Book House, 1964, 327 pp., illus.

Wolters, Richard A. *City Dog: Revolutionary Rapid Training Method.* 201 Park Avenue South, New York, New York: E. P. Dutton and Co., 1975, 184 pp., illus.

GROOMING

Harmar, Hilary. *Modern Grooming Techniques.* 219 Park Avenue South, New York, New York 10013: Arco, 1970, 306 pp., illus.

Kohl, Sam, and Catherine Goldstein. *The All Breed Dog Grooming Guide.* 219 Park Avenue South, New York, New York 10003: Arco, 1973, 249 pp., illus.

Schneider, Earl, Ed. *Know How to Groom Your Dog.* 600 4th., Harrison, New Jersey: The Pet Library LTD., 1969, 63 pp., illus., color.

Sheldon, Margaret Rothery, and Barbara Lockwood. *Dogs and How to Groom Them.* 26 Bloomsbury Street, London, W.C. 1: Pelham Books, 1968, 139 pp., illus.

BREEDING

Asdell, S. A. *Dog Breeding.* 747 Third Avenue, New York, New York: Little Brown and Co., 1966, 194 pp., illus.

Harman, Hilary. *Dogs and How to Breed Them.* 211 W. Sylvania Avenue, Neptune, New Jersey 07753: T.F.H. Publications, 1968, 299 pp., illus.

Meisenzahl, Hilda. *Meisen Breeding Manual.* Box 189, Fairfax, Virginia: Denlinger, 1975, 128 pp., illus.

Smythe, R. H. *The Breeding and Rearing of Dogs.* 219 Park Avenue South, New York, New York 10003: Arco, 1969, 160 pp., illus.

HEALTH, NUTRITION, FIRST AID

Hart, Allan H. *Dog Owner's Encyclopedia of Veterinary Medicine.* 211 W. Sylvania Avenue, Neptune, New Jersey 07753: T.F.H. Publications, 1971, 186 pp., illus.

Scott, Jack Denton, Ed. *Your Dog's Health Book.* 866 Third Avenue, New York, New York: Macmillan, 1956, 289 pp.

Whitney, Leon F. *The Health and Happiness of Your Dog.* 105 Madison Avenue, New York, New York: William Morrow and Co., 1975, 272 pp.

LAW AND DOGS

Greene, Edward H. *The Law and Your Dog*. Cranbury, New Jersey: A. S. Barnes and Co., 1969, 145 pp.

LEADING DOG MAGAZINES IN THE UNITED STATES

GENERAL

American Kennel Gazette. $8.00 a year, $1.00 a copy. Monthly. 51 Madison Avenue, New York, New York 10010. Lists dates and places of shows throughout the country. Articles on dogs, some advertisements by kennels, and names and addresses of breeders of all breeds. Also lists clubs devoted to each breed and name and address of secretary of each club.

Dogs. $7.50 a year, $1.25 a copy. Monthly. 257 Park Avenue South, New York, New York 10010. Excellent articles, often in depth, on every aspect of dog life. Breeds covered. Book review section.

Dog World. $10.00 a year, $1.00 a copy. Monthly. 469 East Ohio Street, Chicago, Illinois. Lists of coming shows, general articles on dogs, news about dog clubs, kennel advertisements for all breeds.

Kennel Review. $17.00 a year. Monthly. 828 North La Brea Avenue, Hollywood, California 90038. Special features on breeds, shows, canine diseases. Advertisements for all breeds, information about dog shows.

Showdogs. $18.00 a year, $1.50 a copy. Monthly. 257 Park Avenue South, New York, New York 10010. Special features on shows, kennel clubs, breeds. Articles on canine diseases.

SPECIFIC BREEDS

The American Brittany. $12.00 a year, $1.50 a copy. Monthly. 4124 Birchman, Fort Worth, Texas 76107. News of field trials, general articles on the Brittany Spaniel, show news, and lists of kennels.

The American Cocker Review. $8.00 a year. Monthly. 202 South Clovis Avenue, Fresno, California 93727. General articles, show news, advertisements for Cocker Spaniels and news from around the country.

The American Cooner. $3.00 a year, $.25 a copy. Monthly. Seeser, Illinois. Magazine devoted to information on field trials, hunts, shows, and kennel advertisements.

The American Dachshund. $8.00 a year, $.50 a copy. Monthly. 1501 Oak Creek Road, El Cason, California 92021. General information, articles on winners of shows, information on shows.

American Field. $10.00 a year, $.50 a copy. Weekly newspaper. 222 West Adams Street, Chicago, Illinois 60606. Complete information on all field trials and hunting events for sporting breeds.

The Basenji. $5.00 a year. Monthly. 935 42nd Avenue North, St. Petersburg, Florida 33703. Publishes general information, show reports, advertisements by breeders.

The Boxer Review. $7.00 a year. Monthly. 8760 Appian Way, Los Angeles, California 90046. General articles, kennel advertisements, information on Boxer doings throughout the United States.

The Chase. $5.00 a year, $.50 a copy. Monthly. 1140 Industry Road, Lexington, Kentucky 40505. Magazine of the Foxhound. Publishes reports on field trials, shows, advertisements by breeders.

The Gazehound. $10.00 a year, $2.50 a copy. Bimonthly. 16258 Lovett Place, Encino, California 91436. Publishes general articles, show news, advertisements by breeders. Each issue covers the Afghan, the Borzoi, the Greyhound, the Irish Wolfhound, the Italian Greyhound, the Saluki, the Scottish Deerhound, the Whippet.

The German Shepherd Review. $8.50 a year, $1.25 a copy. Monthly. P.O. Box 1221, Lancaster, Pennsylvania 17604. For owners and breeders of German Shepherds. General information, articles, stories about winners of shows.

German Shorthaired Pointer News. $9.00 a year, $1.00 a copy. Monthly. Publishes articles on dog health, shows, field trials. Advertisements by breeders.

The Greyhound Review. $10.00 a year, $1.00 a copy. Monthly. Box 543, Abilene, Kansas 67410. General articles on breed, show news, advertisements by kennels.

Harp and Hound. $8.00 a year. Biannual. 11 Rutland Lane, Melville, New York 11746. Devoted to Irish Wolfhound. Show news, general information, advertisements by kennels.

Hounds and Hunting. $6.00 a year, $.75 a copy. Monthly. Box 372, Bradford, Pennsylvania 16701. Devoted to the Beagle. Information on shows, field trials, articles on Beagles, advertisements by breeders.

Irish Setter Club of America. $6.00 a year. Bimonthly. 25 East Magnolia Avenue, Maywood, New Jersey 07607. Book reviews, news about shows and field trials, advertisements by kennels.

Pekingese News. $9.00 a year. Monthly. P.O. Box 5195 Terre Haute, Indiana 47805. Publishes news about the breed, articles on dog health, advertisements by kennels.

The Poodle Review. $9.00 a year. Monthly. 26 Commerce Street, New York, New York 10014. Lists dates and places of shows, winners of shows, and carries advertisements by breeders.

Retriever News. $15.00 a year, $1.55 a copy. Monthly. 4213 South Howell Avenue, Milwaukee, Wisconsin 53207. Devoted to field trials for all retrievers, especially Labradors. Advertisements by breeders.

Rottweiler. $6.00 a year. Monthly. 3320 Wonderview Plaza, Hollywood, California 90068. Articles on general health, book reviews, show news, advertisement by breeders.

Saluki World. $9.50 a year, $4.50 a copy. Biannual. R.D. 1, Box 12, Neshanic, New Jersey 08853. Articles on shows, book reviews, names of regional champions, advertisement by breeders.

Schnauzer Shorts. $10.00 a year, $1.50 a copy. Monthly. Post Office Drawer A, La Honda, California 94020. News about shows, clubs, advertisements by breeders.

Shih Tzu News. $9.00 a year. Monthly. P.O. Box 5195 Terre Haute, Indiana 47805. Publishes general articles, show winners, advertisement by breeders.

Siberian Husky News. $7.00 a year. Bimonthly. P.O. Box 5195 Terre Haute, Indiana 47805. Consists mostly of articles on all aspects of Husky life.

Springer Bark. $7.50 a year, $2.50 a copy. Quarterly. P.O. Box 2115, San Leandro, California 94577. Articles on health care, shows, field trials, advertisements by kennels, news about coming events.

Terrier Type. $10.00 a year, $1.50 a copy. Monthly. Post Office Drawer A, La Honda, California 94020. Devoted to all Terriers. Publishes show news, advertisements by kennels.

Top Dobe. $12.00 a year. Bimonthly. P.O. Box 205, Spring Valley, New York 10977. Devoted to Doberman Pinscher. Publishes general articles, show news, advertisements by breeders.

The Vizsla News. $12.00 a year, $1.00 a copy. Monthly. 11031 Aqua Vista Street, North Hollywood, California 91602. General articles on Vizsla, show news, advertisements by breeders.

The Weimaraner Magazine. $10.00 a year, $1.00 a copy. Monthly. P.O. Box 6086, Weimaraner Club of America, Heathdowns Station, Toledo, Ohio 43614. News of field trials, general news about owners, results of shows, and a stud directory.

Index

Norman H. Johnson, D.V.M.

Senior staff clinician of the American Society for the Prevention of Cruelty to Animals, Dr. Norman H. Johnson has been associated with that organization for thirty-two years. He belongs to the American Veterinary Medical Association, the New York State Veterinary Medical Society and the Veterinary Medical Association of New York City, Inc. Dr. Johnson was educated at the New York State Veterinary College at Cornell University. He practiced privately for some years, and during World War II served in the Veterinary Corps of the U.S. Army Air Force. He is Chief of Staff at the Henry Berg Memorial Hospital of the SPCA.